Monotheism, Intolerance, and the Path to Pluralistic Politics

CHRISTOPHER A. HAW

University of Scranton

CAMBRIDGE
UNIVERSITY PRESS

CAMBRIDGE
UNIVERSITY PRESS

University Printing House, Cambridge CB2 8BS, United Kingdom

One Liberty Plaza, 20th Floor, New York, NY 10006, USA

477 Williamstown Road, Port Melbourne, VIC 3207, Australia

314-321, 3rd Floor, Plot 3, Splendor Forum, Jasola District Centre, New Delhi - 110025, India

103 Penang Road, #05-06/07, Visioncrest Commercial, Singapore 238467

Cambridge University Press is part of the University of Cambridge.

It furthers the University's mission by disseminating knowledge in the pursuit of education, learning and research at the highest international levels of excellence.

www.cambridge.org
Information on this title: www.cambridge.org/9781108810296
DOI: 10.1017/9781108888912

First published 2021
First paperback edition 2022

A catalogue record for this publication is available from the British Library

Library of Congress Cataloging in Publication data
NAMES: Haw, Christopher A., author.
TITLE: Monotheism, intolerance, and the path to pluralistic politics / Christopher A. Haw, University of Scranton.
DESCRIPTION: Cambridge, United Kingdom ; New York, NY, USA : Cambridge University Press, 2021. | Includes bibliographical references and index.
IDENTIFIERS: LCCN 2020041355 (print) | LCCN 2020041356 (ebook) |
ISBN 9781108841306 (hardback) | ISBN 9781108810296 (paperback) |
ISBN 9781108888912 (epub)
SUBJECTS: LCSH: Monotheism. | Religious tolerance. | Religion and politics.
CLASSIFICATION: LCC BL221 .H39 2021 (print) | LCC BL221 (ebook) |
DDC 201/.723–dc23
LC record available at https://lccn.loc.gov/2020041355
LC ebook record available at https://lccn.loc.gov/2020041356

ISBN 978-1-108-84130-6 Hardback
ISBN 978-1-108-81029-6 Paperback

Monotheism, Intolerance, and the Path to Pluralistic Politics

Discussions of monotheism often consider its bigotry toward other gods as a source of conflict, or emphasize its universality as a source of peaceful tolerance. Both approaches, however, ignore the combined danger and liberation in monotheism's "intolerance." In this volume, Christopher A. Haw reframes this important argument. He demonstrates the value of rejecting paradigms of inclusivity in favor of an agonistic pluralism and intolerance of absolutism. Haw proposes a model that retains liberal, pluralistic principles while acknowledging their limitations, and he relates them to theologies latent in political ideas. His volume offers a nuanced, evolutionary, and historical understanding of the biblical tradition's emergence and its political consequences with respect to violence. It suggests how we can mediate impasses between liberal and conservative views in culture wars; between liberal inclusivity and conservative decisionism; and, on the religious front, between apologetics for exclusive monotheism and critiques of its intolerance.

Christopher A. Haw is Assistant Professor of Theology at the University of Scranton.

Contents

Preface

I wrote this book for a few reasons. First, I have grown to approach "faith" in a way that might be considered, in Paul Ricoeur's terms, a "second naivety." This involves an initial religious faith that eventually dies under the pressures of study, reflection, and experience. But, through patience and charity, one returns to the ashes of a destroyed faith and creatively retrieves the "rationality of the symbol," excavating the truths that had been obscured or buried in one's original naivety. My first naivety included a mild Catholic upbringing, then a deep dive into evangelicalism. But you could say my faith, in pointing me to pursue truth, paradoxically destroyed itself. This entailed rejecting numerous literalistic fundamentalisms and the harsh Christian supremacy that seems to come along with the tasteless, monotheistic idea of "the One True God." But my pursuit of truth constrained me to dig for any profundity that may still glow from under the rubble. One of the many figures who aided such a patient retrieval for me was René Girard and his naturalistic theory of human evolution and religion.

But, second, while Girard provoked fresh rereadings of religious faith, it became apparent that his mimetic theory is best treated not as a new fundamentalism but as having its own limitations. This led me to initially conceive, in my doctoral work, that one task of a dissertation could be to comprehensively catalogue and weigh the critiques of Girard's work. While my study of them was informative, such analysis remained passive. Further, the critiques of mimetic theory cover a dizzying array of disciplines: Girard was a raging generalist. I instead wanted to drill down into a specific topic within his oeuvre that provoked in me deep interest, but about which I had heard nothing: that "monotheism is a refusal to divinize victims." He similarly claims monotheism is at the root of an epochal change in our sensitivity to victims. Is this accurate and, if so, what does this mean? There are few topics of study that promise such perilous historical complexity as monotheism, and few as absolutely relevant to today as its relationship to violence, intolerance, diversity, and victimization.

I name that central trunk – of a theological second naivety and sifting Girard's program – because, even while "Girard and monotheism" seems a sufficiently delimited topic, readers may find I've spared little temporal expense in exploring the many branches attached to it. Besides Girard, I draw upon political theory of liberal democracy; I give Freud a generous hearing; the thickest weeds of the study grow around historical monotheistic scholarship and Axial Age theory; and I conclude with a theological bricolage that attempts to point toward a faith that eludes my linguistic description. This is the price of touching a generalist's theory. In that fray, the reader might be oriented by my brief *why I wrote this* up front, naming the simplest germs that spawned the whole. Further, that forecasts how my method will consciously violate conventional siloization between a religious studies, naturalistic analysis on the one hand, and – after deconstruction – a desire to constructively retrieve and theologically manage doctrines I have inherited.

While this book extends from my dissertation research at the University of Notre Dame, it has been restructured and enriched in content. I have treated Chantal Mouffe's social theory more as a starting point for rethinking tolerance, which frames my exploration of monotheism. And besides renovating the entire work in light of later research, I reconfigured my chapters on categorizing religion, violence, translatability, and Jan Assmann's political theory of polytheism.

Despite the changes, I still owe a debt of gratitude to those who helped shape this work in its earlier doctoral stage. I would like to thank Dr. Catherine Hilkert for her patient and generous guidance as my study evolved, and Dr. Cyril O'Regan, who kindly joined in the effort once my study took on a philosophy of religion dimension. I am indebted to Dr. Ann Astell for her Girardian guidance, Dr. Jason Springs for scholarly wisdom and introducing me to Mouffe, and Drs. Ebrahim Moosa and Ernesto Verdeja for their interdisciplinary, peace studies acuity.

I humbly thank Jimmy Haring for his specialist leads on monotheistic scholarship and his review of much of my work when it looked in even worse shape than you see here, offering insights that helped me find my center and burn the chaff. My affectionate gratitude extends to my wife,

Cassie, for her suffering through and editing multiple drafts. Garret FitzGerald was generous to review my accuracy and lucidity with respect to Mouffe and help me hone my thesis. I thank Scott Cowdell, James Alison, and Terrence Moran for their guidance, edits, and suggestions on the project overall. And I extend my warm appreciation to Michael Yankowski for his being a vibrant intellectual sounding board, gracious spiritual support, and conversation partner throughout.

Finally, I would like to acknowledge my daughter, Amelia, whose accident and miraculous recovery in the middle of this study shed more grace and perspective on me than lifetimes of contemplation ever could. May we never cease our compassion until all children enjoy such transfiguration. And I join in giving thanks with Cassie and Simon, who also enjoyed with me the waves of gratitude as our family – along with all our friends and community – persevered in the face of death.

Abbreviations

JAN ASSMANN

ATM	*Akhenaten to Moses*
CMA	"Cultural Memory and the Myth of the Axial Age"
GG	*Of God and Gods*
IR	*The Invention of Religion*
ME	*Moses the Egyptian*
MPC	"Monotheism and Its Political Consequences"
PM	*The Price of Monotheism*

SIGMUND FREUD

MM	*Moses and Monotheism*

RENÉ GIRARD

EC	*Evolution and Conversion*
ISS	*I See Satan Fall Like Lightning*
TH	*Things Hidden since the Foundation of the World*
TOB	*The One by Whom Scandal Comes*
VS	*Violence and the Sacred*

ROBERT GNUSE

NOG	*No Other Gods*

CHANTAL MOUFFE

AG   *Agonistics*
DP   *The Democratic Paradox*

WOLFGANG PALAVER

RGMT *René Girard's Mimetic Theory*

REGINA SCHWARTZ

CC   *The Curse of Cain*

MARK SMITH

EHG   *The Early History of God*
GIT   *God in Translation*
TOBM *The Origins of Biblical Monotheism*

ERIC VOEGELIN

OH   *Order and History*, vol. 1: *Israel and Revelation*
SPG   *Science, Politics, and Gnosticism*

Footnotes reserve publication information and subtitles for the Bibliography, which follows the Cambridge University Press convention of excising publisher names. After a first citation, footnotes resort to last name and shortened title.

Introduction

Monotheism and Pluralism

"Everything that destroys social unity is useless."

Jean-Jacques Rousseau

"I came not to bring peace but division."

Jesus Christ

Few phrases feel so pretentious and belligerent as *"the One True God."* This monotheistic expression seems to capture the spirit of religious violence, if not the heart of intolerance and conflict itself. For pregnant in it we find belief not merely in one God, but "the belief in *only* one God," who just happens to be my god, while the other gods are false, wrong, or maybe to be persecuted. And, with such an all-encompassing creed, we face what seems an intractable anti-pluralism, dangerously prone to turn a sense of religious supremacy into political violence and suppression of difference. Thus, monotheistic religion often seems to us, as Egyptologist and ancient historian Jan Assmann writes, less the opiate of the people and more "the *dynamite* of the people."[1] That is, monotheism can appear as a uniquely absolutist "political theology" – how we imagine and represent political power's relation to divinity[2] – that

---

[1] Jan Assmann, *Of God and Gods* (hereafter *GG*), 5.

[2] I refer to the species of political theology, as debated between Carl Schmitt and Erik Peterson, that attends to the imaginary of sovereignty, making this partly a subject of political science (Giorgio Agamben, *The Kingdom and the Glory*, 9). In this sense, the term includes analysis of how divinity and cosmic power relate (or not) and a sociology of how political and religious concepts interpenetrate one another. Such a mode of political theology can overlap with, but differs from, an alternate mode: confessional expressions of how faith calls believers to act politically.

conflates the religious Other with political enemies to be killed, repelled, or repressed into orthodoxy. Monotheistic political theology seems to evoke a monolithic, patriarchal imaginary that leads to imperial homo- geneity and even the sterility of monocropping.[3]

Apologists of monotheism may refuse this line of thinking and instead remind us of how violent polytheistic religions were and construe mono- theism as a bastion of universal tolerance, inspiring a benevolence that transcends partisanship, a loving erasure of the lines drawn up between enemies. In this view, a true monotheism stands above all "othering" and us vs. them thinking. But, the more this pacific universal benevolence is emphasized, the more biblical stories of violence and intolerance clang with dissonance. What are we to make of the immense violence flowing from the supposed historic font of monotheism itself – the Bible? We find there God's command to Moses to murder idolaters, the Joshuanic con- quests, Elijah's slaughter of Ba'al priests, the Maccabean mercilessness, Revelation's fantasies of a bloodbath, and so on.[4] Even if some of these scenes may never have happened, as many historians suggest, Assmann nonetheless urges that, compared to the ancient religions, it seems highly significant that monotheism "attaches so much importance to violence in its narrative self-presentation. Violence belongs to what could be called the 'core-semantics' of monotheism. I do not state that monotheism is violent; merely that it dwells on scenes of violence in narrating its path to general realization."[5] Why this dwelling, where does it come from, and is it unique to monotheism? "Does the idea of monotheism, the exclusive worship of one god instead of a divine world, or the distinction between true and false in religion, in which there is one true god and the rest are false gods, imply or entail violence?"[6] Simply, is monotheism bad for us? Given the great anxieties about violence in a shrinking world, and the need for at least a modicum of pluralistic coexistence, it is not unreason- able that many conclude monotheism only makes things worse.

The suspicion that monotheism presents a unique threat to coexistence has deep roots – a history we will sketch at the beginning of Chapter 3. For now, we can simply note some modern objections. David Hume was

---

[3] An ecological analysis of the malignant imaginary of monotheistic homogeneity can be found in Solomon Victus, "Monotheism, Monarchy, Monoculture."

[4] Ex 32–34; Deut 13:6–10; Num 25; 1 Kgs 18; 2 Kgs 23:1–27; Ezra 9–10; 1 and 2 Macc; Revelation *passim*. GG 116; Jan Assmann, *From Akhenaten to Moses* (hereafter *ATM*), 50.

[5] Jan Assmann, "Monotheism and Its Political Consequences" (hereafter *MPC*), 142.

[6] GG 109.

among those who suggested, in *The Natural History of Religion* (1757), that monotheism harbors a special violence in contrast with polytheism's tolerance. Edward Gibbon regarded biblical monotheism's triumph in the West as producing an intolerant and totalizing ethos, giving rise to fanaticism and violence (*c.*1780), echoed in Comte's lamenting its irreconcilability with benevolence (*c.*1891). More recently, Regina Schwarz's *The Curse of Cain: The Violent Legacy of Monotheism* (1998) and Jonathan Kirsch's *God against the Gods: The History of the War between Monotheism and Polytheism* (2004) have presented monotheism's intolerance and exclusivism (its sense of the "scarcity" of truth) as incompatible with pluralistic coexistence.[7] Monotheism "reduces all other gods to idols" and "all other worshippers to abominations," salted for destruction.[8] Others have identified in monotheistic religion the "vivisectionist impulse" – a fervor for finality, certitude, and the possession of ultimate truth, resulting in the urge to "other" and execute wrath on the supposed heathen.[9] Steven Pinker's *The Better Angels of Our Nature: Why Violence Has Declined* (2011), used by the United Nations to structure its Human Security Report (2013), opens and frames his book by emphasizing how the Bible is "one long celebration of violence."[10] And in proportion to our shedding of its murderous superstitions, the world becomes more pacific in adopting "modern principles" like "nonviolence and toleration," and "Enlightenment rationality and cosmopolitanism."[11]

How are we to think about monotheism's ostensible threat to pluralism, tolerance, and diversity today? In a world in which the liberal ship of tolerance seems to be overwhelmed by storms of backlash, where myopic stubbornness is a constant fuel on the world's fires, wouldn't we do well to finally throw monotheism overboard? The words of Gandhi come to mind, "How can he who thinks he possesses absolute truth be fraternal?" Or Symmachus: "such a great secret is not attainable by a

---

[7] See also Robert Gnuse, "Intellectual Breakthrough or Tyranny?," 87. For other "monotheism and violence" literature, see Renée van Riessen, "A Violent God?"; Daniel Timmer, "Is Monotheism Particularly Prone to Violence?"; Stephen G. Nichols, "Doomed Discourse"; Peter Sloterdijk, *God's Zeal*.

[8] Regina Schwartz, *The Curse of Cain* (hereafter CC), 33.

[9] E.g., Christopher Hitchens, *God Is Not Great*; Arjun Appadurai, "Dead Certainty." Or, "Surely there is no point more redolent of potential violence than this kind of spiritual certitude itself" (Douglas John Hall, "Against Religion," 30).

[10] Steven Pinker, *The Better Angels of Our Nature*, 6.

[11] Ibid., 11f, 17.

single path."[12] Or, the famous bumper sticker that aligns the symbols of major world religions to form the word, "Coexist." Should not our coming to peaceful terms with a plural world necessitate the tolerance of many gods or a reduction to none?

But the critique of intolerance has grown more complex and spread beyond monotheism: a deepening critique of liberalism and secularism as harboring intolerance has gone mainstream. By "liberalism," we can consider the Belgian political theorist Chantal Mouffe's broad definition: the political traditions emphasizing the rule of law, tolerance, inclusion, universal human rights, and respect of individual liberty.[13] Among liberalism's many layers, I share with Mouffe a particular interest in the widespread emphasis on a tolerant inclusivity aimed at overcoming exclusion and forming a "common belonging beyond all differences."[14] And by secularism I mean a species of liberalism, which, in seeking to diminish exclusivity, aims to construct a religiously "neutral" and open public space. But liberalism and secularism, so the critique goes, far from diminishing oppressive authoritarianism, are in fact the new intolerant regime. The cases of lodging this critique range widely. Consider France's controversial headscarf and burkini bans and the critique that this enforced "neutrality" is intolerant of religious and cultural differences. Or, in the United States, the political-cultural left has been increasingly critiqued as a despotic "regime of tolerance" that silences any opponents in violent mobs – whether in political correctness discourse, the #metoo movement, or cancel culture.[15] Furthermore, we have seen recent considerable waves of right-wing populist backlash against liberalism, in widespread resurgent nationalism, anti-globalist revolts, and rising authoritarianism. The ubiquity of the latter has evoked a wave of scholarship suggesting the "liberal world order" may be headed toward global failure.[16] If liberalism, a chief framework for thinking about "tolerance" is so profoundly

---

[12] Symmachus, *Relatio*, 3.10.
[13] Chantal Mouffe, "Religion, Liberal Democracy, and Citizenship," 319.
[14] Chantal Mouffe, *Agonistics* (hereafter *AG*), 22; 20.
[15] E.g., Jonathan Chait, "The 'Shut It Down' Left and the War on the Liberal Mind"; Greg Lukianoff and Jonathan Haidt, "Better Watch What You Say"; N. D. B. Connolly, "Charlottesville Showed that Liberalism Can't Defeat White Supremacy. Only Direct Action Can."
[16] E.g., Patrick Deneen, *Why Liberalism Failed*. For one exploration of this as a "theologico-political predicament," see Paul E. Nahme, "God Is the Reason."

fraying, we will need, in turn, to deeply reconceive and rebuild a contested root symbol of intolerance, monotheism.[17]

It is common-enough sense to see monotheism as antagonistic to pluralism and that, instead, polytheism is the fitting analog to plural coexistence. H. Richard Niebuhr, for example, made such a connection, saying "pluralism of the gods has its counterpart in the pluralism of self and society."[18] In a different manner, William Connelly promoted a pluralism whose necessary religious implication is the dictum "there is not only one god."[19] But I will argue in this book that this simple equation between monotheism and anti-pluralism is mistaken and fails to grasp the paradox of intolerance. I aim to describe here a deeper connectivity between monotheism and intolerance that is deeply relevant to our fragile, critical concerns of pluralism and democracy today.

Central to the pluralistic theory one finds in Chantal Mouffe is the refusal to lay claim to any monopoly on the Absolute, on the foundations of society. This refusal deeply resembles what I find in monotheism as "apophatic intolerance": a refusal to worship God as immanentized in any political representation. This crucial renunciation, that I argue monotheism and pluralism share, is increasingly important now that we have begun to take seriously the limits and dangers of liberal tolerance. Both monotheism and liberalism entail the potentials of universalist absolutism and intolerance; but both are of immense value, if only we can integrate their intolerance into civic practice and disposition. Central to that integration is the apophatic refusal of laying claim to a monopoly on the Absolute. My answer to the intolerance embedded in both monotheism and liberalism is not to simply get rid of it and double down on "tolerance." Instead, we need to grasp the radical ambivalence – both dangerous and liberating – at the heart of monotheistic intolerance and its relevance to pluralistic coexistence today.

---

[17] My frequent use of the word "symbol" connotes how multiple meanings (story lines, references, implications, allusions, critiques, reception history) are "thrown together" and subsist within a word, story, text, creed, or image – oversaturating that sign. My use does not imply anti-realist referentiality, but rather the Ricoeurian sense that "symbols give rise to thought." I take the early references to the Christian creed as a "symbol" as exemplary: the meaning and experience of what is signified exceeds the ingredients of the thrown-together sign.

[18] H. Richard Niebuhr, *Radical Monotheism and Western Culture*, 30.

[19] William Connelly, *Why I Am Not a Secularist*, 154.

INTRODUCING RENÉ GIRARD, JAN ASSMANN, AND CHANTAL MOUFFE

I make the above argument through interacting with a range of scholars in different disciplines, predominantly René Girard, Jan Assmann, and Chantal Mouffe. Let me briefly introduce them here.

Girard and Assmann both analyze monotheism within the larger time line of human civilization and evolution, maintaining its epochal importance while not downplaying its dangers or its messy origins in polytheism. Jan Assmann (b. 1938) is a German Egyptologist who analyzes the epochal transformations in politics, culture, and religions of the ancient near east. He argues that the most consequential breakthrough from that time and place is biblical monotheism and its "Mosaic distinction." This distinction originally concerns loyalty to or betrayal of Yahweh amidst the other gods, while it accrued in time a universal distinction between "true" and "false" religion. It is "Mosaic" in that it flows from the legend of Moses and his exodus from idolatrous injustice in Egypt. Ultimately, the Mosaic distinction concerns "the idea of an exclusive and emphatic Truth that sets God apart from everything that is not God and therefore must not be worshipped, and that sets religion apart from what comes to be shunned as superstition, paganism, or heresy."[20] This distinction is foreign to any previous religions and did not exist before Israel's construction of it (with a not-exactly-relevant exception in Akhenaten's Egyptian revolution around 1350 BCE).

Assmann insists the historic impact of the Mosaic distinction cannot be overstated. More profoundly than *any political upheaval*, it has radically reshaped our world and cognition, marking "a civilizational achievement of the highest order."[21] Among its most consequential effects, he argues, is the novel separation of religion from politics, which had previously been almost indistinguishably intertwined. This Mosaic distinction, Assmann argues, has penetrated the Western psyche and is epistemologically impossible to escape, such that "we cannot live in a spiritual space uncloven" by it.[22] In this sense, it has been at least as consequential as the "scientific intolerance" that originated with Parmenides in Greece, with its principle of noncontradiction in logic (that knowledge of truth also includes knowledge of what is not true).[23] But this Mosaic distinction

[20] *GG* 3; Jan Assmann, *The Invention of Religion* (hereafter *IR*), 79.
[21] Jan Assmann, *The Price of Monotheism* (hereafter *PM*), 13.
[22] *PM* 1, 42.
[23] Ibid., 12–3.

harbors a unique intolerance that has saturated our civilization and has thus come at great cost: it is "possible or even probable that the radical polarization of the world is connected with the Mosaic distinction between true and false religion."[24]

And yet, crucially, Assmann's emphasis on monotheistic intolerance is not a siding *against* it or an assertion that monotheism is essentially violent. While he avoids simplistic declarations on monotheism's pure "essence" – as if that were possible – he explores the potentialities that it has unleashed. What new ways of being, thinking, worshipping, imagining, and organizing society does this religious concept open up and close off? On the whole, for him, the Mosaic distinction has made possible a liberating counter-power to the political sphere, and it is in fact worth its dangerous cost. This nuanced position has been almost entirely misunderstood by a wave of critics as eminent as Mark S. Smith and Joseph Ratzinger. The attempt to abolish the Mosaic distinction through emphasizing the "unity of all religions," praising polytheistic tolerance, or downplaying the intolerance of monotheism, Assmann rejects as misguided.[25] Rather, we must sublimate this intolerance, through ongoing negotiation and reflection.

When one situates his work amidst other axial theorists and biblical scholars, as I do in Chapters 4–6, one finds that his *historical* points largely harmonize with adjacent scholarship. Where his work has been controversial on matters of monotheistic intolerance, my research agrees with the few who have found it as in fact setting a new standard of analysis.[26] His method avoids the noted extremes of rendering monotheism pacific or simplistically condemning it for its antagonism; he also interprets Jewish monotheism, for all its uniqueness, as more *unintentionally* developed than many other theorists give it credit. These nuances are useful not only for correcting imbalanced appraisals of monotheism but for carefully reconceptualizing intolerance today. In drawing on him, I do not ignore crucial thinkers like Eric Voegelin and others who have contextualized biblical monotheism for its political consequences. Yet Assmann gets focal attention not only for his being more up to date; he has centered intolerance and violence in a way that has attracted not only

---

[24] *MPC* 154f.
[25] Assmann adds, it "has never occurred to me to demand that [the Mosaic distinction] be abandoned. I am advocating a return neither to myth nor to primary religion. Indeed, I am not advocating anything; my aim is rather to describe and understand" (*PM* 13).
[26] Jens-André P. Herbener, "On the Term 'Monotheism,'" 641.

my interest but also a widespread misunderstanding that warrants corrective. Although largely affirmative of Assmann's conclusions, I critically part ways with him in Chapter 7, finding his interaction with Christianity insufficient.

If Assmann suggests that monotheism draws a distinction between right and wrong religion, René Girard's mimetic theory argues for what exactly makes monotheism "right": monotheism means an exodus from the myths that surround our scapegoating. Girard (1923–2015) treats monotheism's strict anti-idolatry as the *refusal to divinize victims* and a *devicitimization of God*. Such an enigmatic claim spawned this study, as it invites serious investigation. To unpack the claim, in sum, he argues that polytheistic archaic religions safeguarded societies by "containing" violence in the double sense of the word: expressing and restraining violence.[27] Religion emerged not from credulous attempts at explaining mysteries of the universe, nor as a cognitive invention of priests, but in early humanity's experience and management of violence: gods were divinized scapegoats of group violence, misremembered in myths, creating a sacred pole against which groups fear, unite, expel, and respect.[28] But monotheism, Girard argues, involves an exit from and critique of archaic religion; it emphatically places God on the side of scapegoats, robbing society of its ability to effectively unite around the sacred. As such, Girard accords with Assmann that monotheism endangers the world. While for Assmann the danger (and liberation) is in the Mosaic distinction, for Girard monotheism endangers us by its slowly dissolving sacred social hierarchies, taboos, and sacrificial safeguards. Monotheism has changed our perception of myths, revealing the truth of the victims under them, secularizing the world. But it has also destabilized society, courting chaos in its dissolving of archaic religion's containment of violence.[29]

Leveraging Girard's theory on the question of monotheistic intolerance is touchy, even radioactive. For among his most controversial claims is that, regarding anthropological insight on violence, "the superiority of the Bible and the Gospels can be demonstrated scientifically."[30] George Heyman retorts that this claim to the "defeat of violence is itself a form of

---

[27] René Girard, *The One by Whom Scandal Comes* (hereafter *TOB*), 83.
[28] Ibid., 39.
[29] "The more Christianity made its influence felt, I believe, the more widespread rivalry and internal mediation became" (Ibid., 125).
[30] René Girard, *Evolution and Conversion: Dialogues on the Origins of Culture* (hereafter *EC*), 210. He clarifies that this superiority applies only to the *insight*, while *in practice*

violence."[31] That is, Girard's mimetic theory would seem subject to the critique of absolutist monotheism and its incompatibility with pluralistic coexistence. Edward Schillebeeckx's caution about religious violence comes to mind: the sense of the superiority of one's religion is a root of violence. For Schillebeeckx, any "intolerance toward other religions and rejection of interreligious dialogue on an equal footing" is not liberating but betrays the true character of Christianity. Schillebeeckx urges that we must focus on whether our "professed relationship with the ultimate, the transcendent – the 'mystery' – liberates or endangers humanity."[32]

Against such a claim, the paradox in mimetic theory is pronounced: for Girard argues that the biblical inheritance both liberates *and* endangers humanity. Liberation endangers. Furthermore, he excavates where exactly we got this anti-ethnocentric conviction that the sense of superiority is wrong. It is not a universal idea, but it comes from historical contingencies that stem back to Judaism bequeathing us certain sensitivities – namely, directing our attention to the innocence of victims and, in my gloss, the monotheistic intolerance of representing the Absolute. We remain ethnocentric if we fail to see what a unique achievement anti-ethnocentrism is – and for Girard it is indeed a child of biblical revelation.[33] A proper genealogy of intolerance, then, will ask about how and why we have come to think it is morally superior to oppose any sense of superiority. This paradox runs parallel to a chief political dilemma today, of how to rid ourselves of intolerance without becoming intolerant in turn.

Whether or not one finds the accusation of Girard's "biblical supremacy" resolved by his emphasizing the above paradox, my problem with his theory is more substantive. His weakness on the monotheism question is not in his failure to soften its tones of superiority but simply his under-demonstrated argument for it.[34] That is, he seems to engage in what Robert Gnuse calls an outdated presumption of biblical monotheism's radical difference from its polytheistic world. Eric Gans likewise questions Girard's sui generis account of divine monotheistic revelation: "nowhere, to my knowledge, does René reflect on what peculiarities in the ethical

---

only "recalcitrant minorities" in Judaism and Christianity successfully resisted contagious violence (*TOB* 37).

[31] George Heyman, *The Power of Sacrifice*, 154.

[32] Edward Schillebeeckx, "Culture, Religion, and Violence," 179.

[33] René Girard, *I See Satan Fall Like Lightning* (hereafter *ISS*), 165, 169.

[34] Bruce Chilton argues that Girard declares the breakthrough of biblical revelation "with remarkably little argumentation" (Bruce Chilton, *The Temple of Jesus*, 18).

organization of the Hebrews made them, among all the peoples of the ancient world, the 'chosen' discoverers/inventors of monotheism."[35] Exploring those peculiarities requires turning to monotheism's emergence in the ancient context. In so doing I build a more intricate, historical account of monotheistic intolerance, finding common cause with Girard's wishes later in life that he could rectify and rewrite his project within a larger time frame and global, interreligious context – or, as Raymund Schwager hoped, in relation to axial age theory.[36]

My effort to draw up an account of monotheistic intolerance that is sensitive to its dangers, but detects its liberative potentials, offers a more nuanced approach than one might find in "religion in public life" scholarship. I refer to methods that emphasize a simple "ambivalence" or "dual potential of religion." In such approaches, "religion" at its best is good for society, as an ahistorical, universal vector of moral good; and it is only the corruption of otherwise good religion that courts violence.[37] But if polytheistic religions "contained violence," as my research shows, the problem is much more radical. If monotheism, even in its "best" forms, robs us of some of the polytheism's containment of violence, does it thereby "unleash" violence? We must be able to imagine how truth and goodness – even if in a religious form – can be socially deleterious. Meanwhile, we need to be able to conceptualize how the seemingly evil falsehoods of archaic religion – that is, restrictive taboos, prohibitions, hierarchies, and sacrificial violence, etc. – served as social safeguards that biblical religion is dissolving. Again, enlightenment may endanger us.

This more radically ambivalent hermeneutic of religion helps us read the deep history of violence differently than the critics of monotheism mentioned previously. For example, contrast Steven Pinker's *Better Angels* and its modernist optimism toward violence's Enlightenment-inspired decline, with Girard's ambivalence-laden apocalypticism that both the good and bad are escalating. Where Pinker sees in the Bible merely "one long celebration of violence," Girard reads a slow exodus from violence; for Pinker, the cross of Christ is a cliché mythological sanction of divine violence, while for Girard it is a myth in reverse that dissolves the sacrificial impulse. Where Pinker sees modern, secular

---

[35] Eric Gans, "René et moi," 23.

[36] *EC* 43. That aim was only partially fulfilled in Girard's brief work on Hinduism: René Girard, *Sacrifice*. See also Michael Kirwan, *Girard and Theology*, 40.

[37] Atalia Omer, "Religious Peacebuilding"; Atalia Omer, "Can a Critic Be a Caretaker?," 482.

values, Girard sees a by-product of Christianity. Indeed, theology is unavoidable even for secular accounts of violence, as it greatly affects one's reading of the empirical "facts" of violence, its diminishments, and where to look for them.

In sum, claiming that monotheism has *de*stabilized civilization by doing away with the deep connections between divinity and politics reframes the intolerance problem in a fresh paradigm. Attending to the radical ambivalence of monotheism's political consequences moves us beyond the tired, simplistic questions of "does monotheism cause violence" or "is it intolerant," and turns instead to a more nuanced analysis and interpretation, less laden with pro- or anti-religious prejudice. We need an account of monotheism that avoids unfounded emphases on biblical monotheism as a triumphant, discontinuous break from the ancient near east; and yet we must also grasp monotheism's radical implications for politics, social theory, and tolerance today. All of the above requires grappling with both political and theological paradoxes.

Finding paradox crucial for interpreting monotheism, this study takes great interest in the paradoxes of liberal democracy, emphasized in Chantal Mouffe (b. 1943). Mouffe is a Belgian social theorist known for combining a "leftist populism" with, among other ingredients, the kernels of truth in Carl Schmitt's infamous political theory. While partly sympathizing with various global waves of anti-liberal backlash – often rooted in the critique of neoliberal capitalism – Mouffe does not join in the call to abandon liberalism. Rather, she sees in liberalism great dangers amidst liberating potentials. This ambivalence stems precisely from liberalism being "incompatible" with the political sphere. For Mouffe, liberalism's ideals cannot be perfectly instituted in this world without paradoxically turning into illiberal oppression. For liberalism to not turn into yet another intolerant regime, it requires, in my theological glossing of her political idiom, an *intolerant anti-idolatry*, an apophatic intolerance. That is, the Absolute must remain uninstantiatable; no one can lay claim to a monopoly on the foundation of society. This means that liberalism's "intolerant" ideals of inclusivity must live in constant, unresolved tension with democracy's unavoidable exclusions. This is the heart of her pluralistic theory, and its subtleties distinguish her from other more straightforwardly liberal theorists – like Rawls or Habermas – who have largely conceived of liberalism and democracy as compatible; in so doing they have promoted paradigms of inclusion and tolerance without sufficiently considering the exclusions, dangers, and intolerance latent within liberalism. And yet, Mouffe steers us away from those who would have us abandon liberalism on account of its dangers. Her reading of liberalism is so remarkably akin to Assmann's notion of monotheism that the resonances must be explored: namely, it is possible for a tradition to be born amidst expressions of intolerance and violence, to have a dangerous penchant for universalizing ideals, to be incompatible with every governing structure – and yet it can still be liberating and worth it.

Throughout my chapters, I will argue that monotheism's intolerance toward politically representing the Absolute – and in Christianity's worshipping the innocent Victim as that Absolute – helps birth an enlightened critique of any absolutist politics. This denied ancient royalty of its divine aura, first in Israel, and slowly the rest of the world. In other words, the "intolerant" aspect of monotheism is indeed potentially dangerous, abetting chauvinistic universalism and underwriting religious violence. But an intolerance for "representing the Absolute" is also precisely what helps us critique and relativize all Absolutes and divinized political powers. In turn, a mature pluralism for today, I will argue, means refusing to imagine all society under a totalized non-hegemonic unity; it sees the inclusive question "can't we just get along" as expressive of a mythic concord that hides divisions under a naturalized status quo. Rather, a mature monotheism and pluralism disavow representing such an Absolute, answering with a more agonistic "can't we just argue?"

And so this book does indeed offer something of an apologia for monotheism, that monotheism has deep consequences in the way we perceive political division and tolerance, but not at all on the usual grounds of emphasizing its pacific universalism and tolerance. Rather, in exploring the complex origins of monotheism's intolerance amidst the ancient world's political theology, we see the increased potential dangers *and* liberations that came with its emergence. This comparative work is particularly important in light of recent archaeological and biblical scholarship that has been dissolving the common treatment of monotheism as a sui generis historical breakthrough of incomparable uniqueness, which seems to fuel the monotheistic superiority-complex. Instead, a tidal shift in historical-critical scholarship over the last half century has shown biblical monotheism, far from being a sharp and simplistic break from ancient polytheism, to be far more pagan and polytheistic in its genetic origins.[38] To speak honestly today of biblical monotheism's "unique

---

[38] Robert Gnuse, *No Other Gods* (hereafter *NOG*), 15, 23, 270, 275ff, *et passim*. He describes ancient Israel's *novel reconstrual* of preexisting ideas (like divine intervention, a divine plan for people, social deities, social justice, exclusive veneration), while adding,

breakthrough" amongst any more than a choir of co-religionists requires more detailed comparative analysis of the ancient world than many theologians seem willing or prepared to do.[39] The simplistic common narrative of monotheism's singular revelation to Abraham or Moses, unlike any God known, which thereafter either improved the world with truth or destroys it with intolerance, needs to be reframed in light of a far more complex array of historical data. Overall, my approach attempts to move beyond simplistic attacks on monotheism's intolerance, defending its tolerance, or repeating such dichotomies with respect to liberalism's potentially hubristic universalism.

CHAPTER OUTLINE

In Chapter 1, I lay out the paradox of "intolerance" as analyzed in the work of Chantal Mouffe. Her understanding of the incompatibility between liberalism and democracy illuminates the complex relationship between pluralism and intolerance. Of crucial concern is how Mouffe's pluralism requires what I describe as apophatic intolerance, a refusal to lay hold of the Absolute and a refusal of political closure and pure tolerance.

In Chapter 2, I introduce Girard's mimetic theory with emphasis on his understanding of gods, "the victim mechanism," and monotheism. What does it mean that monotheism interrupts archaic polytheistic religion by dividing God from the victim? This invites us to venture out into other monotheistic scholarship, like Assmann's and its Freudian roots.

Chapter 3 begins the introduction to Jan Assmann through material that is shared between him and Girard: Sigmund Freud's *Moses and Monotheism*. This text stepped into a multi-century discourse that tried to abolish the monotheistic distinction between "Israel" vs. "Egypt." But, contrary to simplistic readings of Freud as the enemy of religion, he

---

"Contemporary authors need to relinquish the use of the word 'unique' when describing biblical thought ... [but rather] how old ideas were transformed" (266, 271). My argument largely concurs but will use "unique" as a shorthand for "novel reconstrual and transformation." Others see the diminution of monotheistic-discontinuity as a welcome return to the best of nineteenth-century biblical scholarship, counteracting a "Barthian century" (Rainer Albertz, "Monotheism and Violence," 375).

[39] One can extend the critique to Christian theological method: "The obsession with discerning the uniqueness of the biblical text has served ... to segregate these texts from the ancient literary domain(s) of which they were indeed a part" (Richard C. Miller, *Resurrection and Reception in Early Christianity*, 98f).

ultimately argues (with mixed veracity) that monotheistic intolerance is a beneficial "progress in intellectuality." This introduces much of Assmann's topics: that is, comparing monotheism between Akhenaten and Egypt, Moses and Israel, and theorizing monotheism's relationship to violence and politics.

Chapter 4 begins an in-depth exploration of Assmann's advances on Freud, by distilling key terms from Assmann and his cognate "axial age" scholarship: different kinds of "religions," their "translatability" with other religions, and different kinds of violence.

Chapter 5 uses those terms to describe, through Assmann, a case study of polytheistic political theology in Egypt. This will help illustrate how polytheism (or better, "cosmotheism") may be understood as rooted in the "victim mechanism," in Girard's terms. This puts to rest naïve notions of polytheism's putative "tolerance," seeing it more subtly as a socio-political force that "contains" violence and an invitation to examine biblical monotheism.

Chapter 6 outlines a political theology of monotheism using Assmann's concepts of the Mosaic distinction, supplemented by other scholars like Mark S. Smith, Robert Gnuse, Rainer Albertz, et al. We dwell closely here on Israel's political conditions of sovereignty, subjugation, and exile that all help illuminate – as we saw in Gans' critique – what historical peculiarities constitute the Hebrew discovery of monotheism. I explore how monotheism could be composed of polytheistic building blocks – first in state-based religion and political symbols, like monolatry and despotic vassal treaties – but transform among an exiled people into a division of God from political representation.

Chapter 7 pivots to conceptualize how, if monotheism "separates" God from the political sphere, rendering them incompatible, this does not result in what Mouffe denounced as depoliticization. For this, I turn to examining Christ as carrying forward the monotheistic "separation" from the political sphere while yet agonistically engaging the mechanisms of scapegoating. That is, if monotheism involves the refusal to divinize victims, Christ the scapegoat-God offers an odd but creative model for contemplation. In Christ the victimized-divinity we do not have a regression into polytheism; nor yet do we find an "escape" from the sacrifice and exclusion that polytheism contained. Rejecting both as insufficient, I consider Girard's paradox that Christianity is an "exit from religion in the form of a demythified religion." Drawing cues from Mouffe's critiques of liberalism, I see in monotheism not an escape from intolerance into an exclusion-free utopia but something more like exclusion-in-reverse in which intolerance is a photographic negative. I thus illustrate Christ as embodying a monotheism that – precisely *through*, not despite, his intolerance – points us toward the marginalized other and pluralistic concerns today.

In sum, we must learn to sublimate the power of monotheistic intolerance, just as we must sublimate the intolerance of liberalism – the emphatic, inclusivist push for human rights against despotism – without turning it into a "regime of tolerance." Monotheism is a dangerous but liberative symbol. It can evoke an agonistic forbearance that rejects the catharsis of monopolizing the foundation of society. For, the heavenly city, founded as it is on a slain lamb, cannot be politically instantiated without contradicting itself. And yet, we inescapably live and act within the earthly city of exclusions, law, and the containment of violence. My hope is this vision of monotheism and pluralism's "intolerance" provides a mutually beneficial conversation relevant to citizens of any city, theologically inclined or not.

I

Pluralism's Requisite Intolerance

One of the more influential books written in recent decades on the dangerous intolerance of monotheism is Regina Schwartz's *The Curse of Cain* (1997). There, Schwartz rightly concedes that monotheism, having complex historical roots, need not "necessarily" produce a "violent notion of identity."[1] But, beyond this caution against essentialism, she argues, monotheism is uniquely responsible for the poison of collective identity formation in our world.[2] For the font of violence, she urges, is in an identity formed negatively against the other. "Violence is the very construction of the Other … defining ourselves against the Other sets in motion a cycle of violence that no legislation can hold."[3] Monotheism, with its antagonistic theology of being the true religion against the pagans, and "not-Egypt," constructs the other with a vengeance. As such, it is a core ideological root of violence. Try as one may to bend monotheistic ideology toward a generous, plural coexistence, this is working against its very nature: "in the myth of monotheism, pluralism is betrayal."[4]

Schwartz's antidote is that we must "embrace multiplicity instead of monotheism," preferring "not one, but many gods."[5] We must shed monotheism's intolerance, its us/them identity formations, and imagine sociality in tolerant, open, and limitless forms, embracing ethics, peace,

[1] CC 31.
[2] Schwartz treats the prohibition of kinship allegiances and exogamy as unique to monotheistic violent identity-constructs (ibid., 79).
[3] Ibid., 5, 37.
[4] Ibid., 46.
[5] Ibid., 38, 176.

and the promise of universalism. The problem, she notes, is not particularism per se – and she briefly pauses to consider that universalism may have some imperial dangers – but the heart of the monotheistic problem is its tapping into the very heart of violence itself, which is again "any conception of identity forged negatively, against the Other, an invention of identity that parasitically depends upon the invention of some Other to be reviled."[6] In light of this danger, her overarching conviction is that we must envision divinity as "not confining or totalizing but opening and proliferating: as a principle that does not circumscribe limits, but endlessly transgresses all possible limits."[7] And, in contrast with the violent biblical legends, apparently stemming from its monotheistic othering-identity, she summarizes that the biblical themes more consonant with pluralistic coexistence are, naturally, the more polytheistic ones: "When the biblical text moves more explicitly toward polytheism, it also endorses a more attractive toleration, even appreciation of difference."[8]

Schwartz's *Curse of Cain* speaks for a widespread frustration with the epoch of malignant monotheism – and the hope for its end. As both a scholarly and humanistic endeavor, one can appreciate her analysis of monotheism's complex political history and pagan roots, as well as her exposing its violent reception history in Christendom. Her work echoes out in analogous theological attempts to construct a spirituality beyond us versus them, as one finds in works like David E. Fitch's *The Church of Us vs. Them* or Sauls and Lyons' *Jesus Outside the Lines* or Rempel's *Life at the End of Us versus Them*. Jan Assmann also identifies a theological movement intent on deactivating monotheism's intolerance through emphasizing its inclusivity. In such efforts, polytheism is characterized by each deity representing "a distinction," some delimiting exclusion; whereas a generous monotheism "cancels and revokes all such distinctions." In such a view, "before the One God, all people are equal. Far from erecting barriers between people, monotheism tears them down," making deity accessible to all.[9]

But, while much of this scholarship can be affirmed for its sensitivity to the Other, such approaches not only fail to account for the intense intolerance within monotheism but also speak from within a liberal framework that is rightly undergoing critical revaluation. We need a more

[6] Ibid., 88; 33.
[7] Ibid., 33; x, 4.
[8] Ibid., 31.
[9] PM 16.

nuanced exploration of tolerance, plurality, and monotheism. While eschewing a theology that "depends upon the invention of some Other to be reviled," I will propose to not abandon this intolerance but radically retain and reverse it. We must conceive of "identity" not as the post-political transcending of us/them constructs but as haunted and destabil-ized by our own unrecognized scapegoating of the Other – how our identities are tragically forged negatively against the Other. Monotheism is a key to such an "intolerance in reverse."

Defending such a thesis first requires reconceptualizing conventional notions of "tolerance" while not merely reacting against them. Belgian political theorist Chantal Mouffe offers resources for such a rethinking in her wide-ranging combination of Marxist economic analyses, liberal democratic convictions, and even the notorious right-wing analyses of Third Reich jurist Carl Schmitt. Her critique of reigning social theories of tolerance, and her proposed alternatives, make possible, in turn, a more incisive appraisal of monotheism's promise and danger than what we find in works like Schwartz.

Mouffe's political theory entails four themes relevant to this endeavor: (1) Tolerance contains intolerance. (2) Reason does not provide an escape from exclusion or hegemony. (3) There is a beneficent incompatibility between liberalism and democracy; we should maintain that incompati-bility by refusing unity-myths that conceive of a society beyond hegem-ony. (4) Lastly, one must provisionally work with identity constructs, using "us and them" relations in the agonism of politics. In all, Mouffe reconceptualizes tolerance in a manner that paves the way for a deeper analysis, in the following chapters, of the dangers and benefits of mono-theistic intolerance and its meaning for us today.

A. HOW TOLERANCE CONTAINS INTOLERANCE

Mouffe defines "liberalism" as the diverse sociopolitical traditions that have championed individual liberty, universal rights, the rule of law, tolerance, inclusion, and pluralism.[10] Some of the numerous historical layers and traditions to liberalism are quite contradictory – ranging from libertarian anthropologies to socialist statecraft. But amidst the varieties of liberalism, Mouffe is most concerned with a prevalent mode – which I find particularly relevant to monotheistic exclusivity and intolerance –

---

[10] *AG* 29.

that advocates a primary allegiance to the "worldwide community of human beings." Mouffe identifies this as an internationally shared predominant ethos of liberalism today: This allegiance aims to form a "common belonging beyond all differences";[11] it is a rationalism hoping to construct a totally consensual political order without division, breaking down barriers, excluding no one. "Tolerance" in such a framework means aiming to overcome political divisions through inclusive rational procedures, making a politics without adversaries, attaining a society beyond hegemony.[12] And by "hegemony" here, Mouffe means a delimited, enforced political order that aims at winning consent through practices that both create and fix the meaning of its social institutions.[13] As we will see, she refuses to see hegemony as an escapable feature of human life: There is no getting "beyond" hegemony. The question is rather what sorts of hegemonies we construct.

We can trace the roots of this inclusive aspect of liberalism to the social contract tradition of John Locke and Jean-Jacques Rosseau.[14] In Rousseau, for example, we find the aspiration to create what political theorist Paul Dumouchel describes as "a form of association such that power would never be able to exercise its violence against those who were subject to it because, owing to their agreement, the strength that power uses against citizens is, by definition, not violence."[15] Here, a chief aim is inclusion – but without exclusion, violence, or hegemony. Thus, while there are many ways to define liberalism and tolerance, it is this political aspiration for inclusion beyond exclusion, politics beyond hegemony, that Mouffe sees as a key characteristic of liberalism today – and a deeply problematic one in need of intervention.

Markedly distinct from liberalism, Mouffe defines "democracy" as a tradition that emphasizes "equality, identity between governing and

---

[11] AG 22; 20.
[12] Mouffe sees this exemplified especially in John Rawls, *A Theory of Justice*.
[13] She thus speaks of seeking not to escape hegemony but to "establish a more democratic hegemonic formation" (Chantal Mouffe, *For a Left Populism*, 36, 44, 88). Her definition includes Antonio Gramsci's notion of the way by which a ruling class "wins the consent" of society – including groups outside its own immediate interests – constructing a "collective will" through manipulating cultural symbols and values. See Ernesto Laclau and Chantal Mouffe, *Hegemony and Socialist Strategy*.
[14] See John Locke's *Letters concerning Toleration* (*c.*1690) and his anonymous *Two Treatises of Government* (1689), and Roger Williams, *The Bloudy Tenent of Persecution for Cause of Conscience* (1644).
[15] Paul Dumouchel, *The Barren Sacrifice*, 32.

governed, and popular sovereignty."[16] While we in the West might generally consider ourselves as living in "liberal democracies," she insists there is no *necessary* relation between the liberal and democratic traditions. They in fact emphasize different, even incompatible, principles.[17] For example, liberalism as she defines it speaks of "humanity" in abstract, universal, and unconditional ideals. The democratic tradition, by contrast, concerns not "humanity," but a particular *demos*, a specific people. Democracy concerns less "universals" and more the application of laws for specific people and circumstances. Lacking liberalism's universal, individual, and moral emphases, democracy is specifically *political*, legal, and statist in scope. In the democratic tradition, "equality" is a political concept and means *citizenship*, a legal equality. By contrast, liberalism's idea of equality is our *shared humanity*, more like a substantive or metaphysical equality.[18]

The friction of these idioms is evident, for example, in the popular protestor's maxim, "no human is illegal." This conviction stems from a liberal idiom that seeks to transcend the exclusive and dehumanizing boundaries of immigration politics to embrace the migrant in our shared humanity. But how does this universal sentiment intersect with particular laws? Does it only imply a rhetorical shift – that, while laws and crimes remain in place, we should speak not of "criminals" but only "humans"? Or, is it to be taken politically, suggesting open borders or the abolition of certain immigration enforcement? Even the most inclusive of answers to this question would *inescapably* entail exclusions, new definitions of crimes, implementation of laws in structuring citizenship, taxation, and so on. The moral, transcendent idiom of liberalism can attempt to reshape the boundaries of law, but it cannot abolish them without engendering new ones. Edmund Fawcett summarizes the friction between our two idioms: Liberalism's universality is about restraining authority and improving the moral and material conditions of life – promising nonexclusive, civic respect to anyone and everyone. Democracy, however, is "about who belongs in that happy circle of voice, protection, and progress." They are not the same topics; they are a matter of *how* and *who*. Liberalism's promise of nonexclusivity is its "single highest bid"; and delivering it is its biggest challenge.[19] The challenge of liberal democracy

---

[16] Chantal Mouffe, *The Democratic Paradox* (hereafter *DP*), 3; *AG* 29.
[17] *AG* xiii.
[18] *DP* 40–1.
[19] Edmund Fawcett, *Liberalism*, 20.

requires negotiating this evident incompatibility, of the universal clashing with the particular.

This point of incompatibility concerns "the political." "The political" is the aspect of human association that inescapably involves divisions, boundaries, and decisions between conflicting alternatives.[20] Mouffe calls our reigning liberal ethos a "depoliticized" view of politics – you might even call it a "counter-political" ethos, in its desire to transcend the political and create inclusion without exclusion. But all societies necessarily embody the political in excluding certain behavior through taboo or punishing crimes. Even if, for example, a society's social divisions and conflicts were well managed through very inclusive and tolerant governing strategies of deliberation and committees, these would still be expressions of a new power relation, a new division, a new exclusion. Even Rousseau admits that his ideal form of human association contains some violence and exclusion; but he hoped that, through our "consent," this violence is cleansed of arbitrary despotism. In practice, there is no such thing as a purely tolerant society, nor would we want one. For *all* associations, even supposedly inclusive ones, involve an us/them configuration, a hegemonic dimension. Intolerance and exclusion are in fact *constitutive* of association and disassociation, of law and order. "The political," in this sense of the inescapability of decision, is an encompassing dimension of human association. It is often expressed through, but different from "politics," by which Mouffe simply means the various practices and institutions that aim to organize human coexistence.[21] I will at times refer to "the political realm" or "the political sphere," by which I mean the interface between politics and the political. The inescapability of the political clarifies how the dichotomous choice between inclusion or exclusion, tolerance or intolerance, is a false one. Even inclusivity and tolerance eventually run into the paradox of not tolerating what is outside their range of acceptable difference.

Critiques of liberalism have often seized upon this contradiction, of universal rhetoric clashing with the particular. In its earlier roots, the critique is evident in Johann Hamann, who argued Immanuel Kant's

---

[20] "'The political' refers to this dimension of antagonism which can take many forms and can emerge in diverse social relations. It is a dimension that can never be eradicated" (*AG* 2–3). She is borrowing partly from Carl Schmitt, for whom the political concerns "the ever-present possibility of the friend-and-enemy grouping" and who determines and decides upon such groupings (Carl Schmitt, *The Concept of the Political*, 43, emphasis added; 25, 32, 35, 37).

[21] *AG* 130f.

universally hued reason is not so much universal as it is a concomitant of his language and culture.[22] But the critiques concern not only epistemology but the way by which liberalism can become, in practice, the purveyor of great intolerance and violence. Ideologies that characterize themselves as champions of inclusion, humanitarianism, openness, and peace can be distorted by pretending to have escaped – by rhetorical evasion – exclusivity. Critics of "democratic peace," "liberal peace," or "universal human rights" have argued that these seemingly pacific concepts paper over the West's neoliberal hegemony.[23] Such ideologies of "tolerance" often avoid saying what they do *not* tolerate, what they exclude, and thus scandalize those excluded by this "regime of tolerance." Such critiques point out liberalism's hypocrisy, its "failure to perform according to its own self-image,"[24] including its imposed "common sense," anti-religious bias, or the attempt to forge a religiously "neutral" space. In such a critique, liberalism is exposed as the ideology of Western hegemony, parading as if it were neutral and universal, while "human rights" serve as a pretext for imperialistic invasions.[25] Other critiques note how the liberal policing of a particular version of "open-mindedness" can make for a violent, silencing "regime of toleration," as is now often cited in US culture wars about political correctness. An infamous twentieth-century critic of liberalism was the Third Reich jurist Carl Schmitt who spoke of the violence hidden in "universal brotherhood."[26] Such rhetoric, he insisted, paints opponents as inhuman and thus worthy of annihilation, using the liberal prohibition on violence as a new justification for violence.[27] (He found this in post–World War I Germany, wherein the "humanitarian" League of Nations hid their retribution in pulverizing economic sanctions.)[28] Walter Benjamin also critiqued how all societies, especially liberally inclined ones, are prone to lose consciousness of their own founding violence. Rather, they decay through perceiving their own legal institutions as pacific and others as violent, failing to see how even nonviolent

---

[22] See Robert Alan Sparling, *Johann Georg Hamann and the Enlightenment Project*, 57–75.

[23] E.g., Oliver Richmond, "A Post-Liberal Peace."

[24] Jason Springs, "On Giving Religious Intolerance Its Due," 2. Springs identifies Stephen Carter, Thomas Nagel, Kent Greenawalt, Robert Audi, Amy Gutmann, Dennis Thompson, and Michael Perry as representative of this discourse.

[25] E.g., Martti Kokenniemi, *The Gentle Civilizer of Nations*, 500.

[26] Hans Joas and Wolfgang Knöbl, *War in Social Thought*, 166.

[27] Ibid., 167; Schmitt, *The Concept of the Political*, 69.

[28] Schmitt, *The Concept of the Political*, 60–61, 70–71.

diplomacy and legal contracts contain violence.[29] Or, on the matter of universal rights, the United Nations' *Universal Declaration of Human Rights* appears less inclusively "universal" once we consider how Islamic councils found the declaration insufficient and penned their own Universal Islamic Declaration of Human Rights.[30] Would it not be better to admit, critics ask, that liberalism makes a space that is not universal but delimited and exclusive?[31]

The critique of liberal hubris would seem to invite, for some, the abandonment of liberal democracy. Theologians like Stanley Hauerwas or John Milbank, or philosopher Alasdair MacIntyre have, each in their own way, become famous for their varieties of abandonment. MacIntyre retorts that "human rights are as mythical as witches and unicorns,"[32] while Hauerwas writes that justice, liberally conceived, "is an unchristian idea" – as incompatible as retribution and forgiveness.[33] Far from religious identities being the source of intolerance today, they argue, it is the state and its universalist rights discourse serving as cover that are the greatest purveyors of violence. Hauerwas – for whom Christian particularism necessitates, with respect to governmental power, a pacifist, anarchist, or "theocratic" identity of being resident aliens – rejects accusations that he is being violently sectarian. No, he insists, the true sectarian is the liberal state and its *libido dominandi*.[34] The contrastive rhetoric in such theologians has aggravated some liberal pragmatists, like Jeffrey Stout, to urge Hauerwas – a potential ally in democratic politics – not to see liberalism in terms of a black–white rivalry, or at least admit that "justice might not be a bad idea."[35]

We can pause to notice how these critiques reframe the entire monotheism–intolerance discourse. They help expose, in the words of David Martin, "the potential violence inherent in all forms of human solidarity, not merely the solidarity conferred by religion."[36] The critique of liberal violence and intolerance suggests we add to our lexicon that

---

[29] Walter Benjamin, *Reflections*, 288. See also Brad Evans, "Liberal Violence."
[30] E.g., Slavoj Žižek, "Against Human Rights."
[31] E.g., David Scott and Charles Hirschkind, eds., *Powers of the Secular Modern.*
[32] Alasdair MacIntyre, *After Virtue.*
[33] Stanley Hauerwas, *War and the American Difference*, 100. Also, Stanley Hauerwas, "Rights Language and the Justice of God."
[34] Stanley Hauerwas and William Willimon, *Resident Aliens.*
[35] E.g., Jeffrey Stout, *Democracy and Tradition.* See Scott MacDougall, "Scapegoating the Secular." Stephen L. Carter, "Must Liberalism Be Violent?"
[36] David Martin, "Axial Religions and the Problem of Violence."

includes "religious violence" another category of "liberal violence."[37] Liberal violence, in light of these critiques, is distinct on account of its justification: It may not necessarily sanction itself with respect to a legal order or polity – and certainly not a god – but instead universal "humanity" or human rights, executed in a posture of neutrality, or possessing the natural and universal position. Such violence is exhibited, in varying degrees, in the Glorious Revolution, the French Revolution, the Reign of Terror, and the American Revolution – not to mention contemporary wars wherein humanitarian concerns serve as *casus belli*. We will later discuss the dangers of the Mosaic distinction between true and false religion; but we can see in liberalism too its own intolerant distinction between true and false societies. The "liberal distinction," for better and worse, judges illiberal societies as wrong, false, or at least less than true. The point of these critiques, overall, is that liberalism too, for all its potential benefits, also harbors a dangerous intolerance.

But Mouffe carefully argues that liberalism, though dangerous and incompatible with democracy, should *not* lead us to abandon it. Rather, she urges that we must consider how to orient its inclusivity in relation to the exclusions of the political realm. Liberalism, Mouffe insists, has opened up beneficent modes of law and human organization in its vision of a society not founded on exclusion. But such zeal inevitably runs into the paradox of becoming "intolerant" and exclusive in practice. Liberalism may entail radical distinctions that endanger and polarize our world, but its benefits may be worth the price. Maintaining this tension distinguishes Mouffe from the simplifications of anti-liberal and pro-liberal discourse. For her, the question is not "whether or not to be intolerant," which would be impossible, but *how* to be intolerant – what to exclude and include, and how.

B. REASON IS NO ESCAPE FROM EXCLUSION

Mouffe argues that liberal theorists, instead of acknowledging the inescapable tension between the exclusions of democracy and the universality of liberalism, have aimed to "resolve" it through an appeal to "reason," achieving consensus, and inclusive procedures. In so doing they

---

[37] See also Brad Evans, *Liberal Terror*; Michael Dillon and Julian Reid, *The Liberal Way of War*; Brad Evans and Julian Reid, *Resilient Life*; Richard Brian Miller, *Terror, Religion, and Liberal Thought*; Slavoj Žižek, "The Violence of the Liberal Utopia."

fail to grasp the political. She notes for example a key liberal theorist, John Rawls, among whose most important ideas is the pursuit of an "overlapping consensus." Rawls' ideal is to create a society that is founded not on any exclusion but on the consent of all governed. Such a consensus would be sufficiently encompassing and neutral, and thereby more stable and pacific, not an imposed tyranny. This would lay the foundation on which we can safely tolerate objectionable differences amidst our pluralities. Rawls thus imagines a well-ordered society as one in which the political "has been eliminated."[38] Rawls' ideal aims to close "the gap between justice and law," as if they are ultimately compatible and could fully and definitively coincide.

Mouffe reads a similar ideal in Jürgen Habermas, whose "deliberative democracy" promotes the exchange of reason and deliberation as an alternative to the exclusion of opponents. This preference for procedure and norms is supposed to lend "credibility and legitimacy to the democratic process, guaranteeing that such a consensus was obtained by reasoned assent and not mere agreement or subjugation."[39] In debates over the European Union, Mouffe identifies a similar ideal, that "through informed participation and discussion, citizens should be able to reach an agreement about the best policies."[40]

Mouffe sees these liberal conceptualizations of pluralism, while well intentioned, as ultimately evading the political. They fail to "acknowledge the hegemonic nature of every form of consensus" and indeed "every kind of social order."[41] For, once this consensus is supposedly reached, she insists, it simply becomes the new exclusion, the new order of which there is no right to question.[42] Even inclusion is exclusive. Once we ask whose legitimacy and whose rationality would enforce consensus procedures, we see that these would not only restrain political hegemony but would also be an *expression of it*. Tolerance contains intolerance; and consensus contains hegemony. "Consensus in a liberal-democratic society is – and

---

[38] *DP* 91; 29; *AG* 55.

[39] *DP* 87. Similarly, Seyla Benhabib promotes a kind of "legitimacy" that is an "impartial standpoint which is equally in the interests of all" (ibid., 47), and Hannah Arendt advocated the replacement of parties with councils, so as to obtain inter-subjective agreement (*AG* 10).

[40] *AG* 54.

[41] Ibid., 11–2.

[42] "Once the very idea of an alternative to the existing configuration of power disappears, what disappears also is the very possibility of a legitimate form of expression of the resistances against the dominant power relations" (*DP* 5; 43, 45).

will always be – the expression of a hegemony and the crystallization of power relations."[43]

Mouffe is not being pessimistic about human nature – or rejecting the use of reason in public discourse – so much as naming the paradox of inclusion. The paradox can be described in the observation that if liberalism's ideals were ever to become fully realized in a politico-juridical form – that is, in a certain plural cosmopolitanism – it would *paradoxically no longer be liberalism*, at least in any objective sense of inclusivity, pluralism, and openness. That is, "the very condition of the creation of consensus is the elimination of pluralism from the public sphere."[44] In light of this, we ought not imagine that "pluralist democracy could ever be perfectly instantiated, since the condition of possibility of a pluralist democracy is at the same time the condition of impossibility of its perfect implementation."[45] To lay a foundation in consensus is still to exclude.

The above paradox clarifies how much "unity" political strategies can actually achieve. Mouffe thus argues that theorists like Rawls and Habermas have envisioned not a genuine pluralism but a privatized pluralism "whose legitimacy is only recognized in the private sphere and that it has no constitutive place in the public one."[46] Their attempts to ground legitimacy on reason erroneously treat political disagreements and divisions as merely *incidental*, as if they could be definitively overcome by some kind of rational procedure. But division is not merely an incidental breakdown of political order; division is inescapably constitutive of political order.[47] Politics cannot preempt hegemony by using reason and common sense, because politics *is* "the terrain where competing interpretations of shared principles struggle in order to *define* the 'common sense' and establish their hegemony."[48]

Given this ineradicability of division, the political sphere can channel and modify divisions; but it cannot referee, much less abolish, them

---

[43] *DP* 48f; 42.
[44] Ibid., 49.
[45] Ibid., 16.
[46] *AG* 55.
[47] *DP* 139; *AG* 3, 89. The etymology of law aids us: *nomos* (law) stems from *nemo*, "to divide and attribute in parts." See the German cognate of *nomos* in *nehmen* (to take): the grabbing and partitioning of land (*landnahme*) is the primordial origin of law. Wolfgang Palaver, "A Girardian Reading of Schmitt's Political Theology," 54.
[48] Chantal Mouffe, "Religion, Liberal Democracy and Citizenship," 323, emphasis added; Mouffe, *For a Left Populism*, 44.

without, in turn, reproducing a new division. Even the most inclusive of politics inescapably involves "the creation of an 'us' by the determination of a 'them.'"[49] For expunging or escaping this us/them reality only creates a new one. (Marxism, too, succumbs to this evasion of the political, in its attempt to abolish all divisions and construct a final unity.)[50] Mouffe thus concludes it is impossible to constitute a "form of social objectivity which would not be grounded on an originary exclusion."[51]

The blind spot and liability of certain liberal social theorists, then, is their *depoliticization*, their habitual inability to conceptualize the political.[52] Such thought fixates on the "norm," where the rules of consensus and inclusion pacifically work, while evading the "exception," where decisions are made without any legal foundation, outside the law. For example, when Habermas emphasizes procedures of deliberation, so as to guarantee the moral impartiality of democracy, Mouffe notices a conspicuous lack of thinking the exception, of placing any "limits on the scope and content of such deliberation."[53] And yet the limits surely remain, hidden in whoever referees the deliberation. What will not be allowed in the deliberation? Who will decide that, and how will it be excluded? In painting an optimistic picture of deliberation, Habermas evades the "negative aspect of sociability" and avoids "the recognition that violence is ineradicable."[54] Instead, he wrongly imagines that once we engage the other's difference "violence and exclusion could disappear ... as if politics and ethics could perfectly coincide."[55] Such an idealized view of social relations presumes that pacific-sounding words like "reciprocity" or "cooperation" solely make for the peaceful realization of the good. But, as Girard's mimetic theory will emphasize (and Mouffe cites him on this point), reciprocity involves not only the norms of peaceful exchange but the exceptions of violent solidarity and cooperative antagonism.[56] In other words, Mouffe draws upon Carl Schmitt's insistence that mature political theory must "think the exception with

---

[49] *DP* 101.
[50] Thomas Decreus and Matthias Lievens, "Hegemony and the Radicalization of Democracy," 682f.
[51] *DP* 11.
[52] *DP* 43.
[53] Ibid., 86.
[54] Ibid., 132.
[55] Ibid., 134.
[56] Ibid., 130–1. She makes implicit connections with Girard at ibid. 11, 32.

a passion." "The paradigm that defines the proper functioning and structure of the law is not the norm but the exception."[57]

Mouffe thus asserts that reason is not the opposite of violence, not an escape from exclusion. Rather, reason contains violence: it is not only a restraint on violence – per social contract theory – but is an expression of it. What we so often view as "common sense" or universal reason must be recognized as a contingent "result of sedimented hegemonic practices" – the cultural norms, decisions, and practices which are repeated to such an extent that "the political origin of those contingent practices" becomes erased and thus naturalized. This sedimentation results in our intuition of "common sense"[58] and emanates an illusory, "fictive coherence and objectivity to social identity."[59] Reason does not supply absolute, objective access to universals. As Dumouchel argues, reason is not an escape from the monopoly on legitimate violence but stems from it. This monopoly supplies the context and basis for what constitutes "reason" as contrasted with unreason/violence. "*The difference between reason and violence, on which we would like to base the unanimous agreement of members of society, does not precede the action that establishes the political order, but flows from it.*"[60]

For example, the "common sense" of much Western anthropology centers on individualism and liberty as the defining characteristics of what counts as "reasonable." Such a view of reason tends to treat any communal identities (any "we" that has more claim on me than my "I") as irrational, divisive, and violent, belonging to "a bygone age when reason had not yet managed to control the supposedly archaic passions."[61] But this appears less like universal reason once we see how many other societies have viewed humans as innately interdividual, where *harmony*, not liberty, is society's orienting principle. In this light, our rationalist individualism is by no means universal or objective common sense. Western individualism is more a result of particular Enlightenment inheritances, histories of anti-monarchical revolutions, and so on. Even more, Mouffe critiques our rationalism as deficient because it fails to come to

---

[57] Giorgio Agamben, *The Time That Remains*, 104. "The exception is more interesting than the rule. The rule proves nothing; the exception proves everything: it confirms not only the rule but also its existence, which derives only from the exception" (Schmitt, *Political Theology*, 15).

[58] AG 89.

[59] James Martin, *Chantal Mouffe*, 3.

[60] Dumouchel, *The Barren Sacrifice*, xvii.

[61] AG 4; 137.

terms with the political: it fails to see how *every* identity is relational. However much we want to disarm "us vs. them" thinking, the very "creation of an identity always implies the establishment of a difference."[62] The modern self-impression of rationality, as *cogito ergo sum*, fails to see how every "I" is first and primordially a "we."

This account of reason leads Mouffe to insist that we cannot escape the "struggle between conflicting views of the common good," in which each contends for their place as "the 'true' incarnation of the universal." "No rational resolution of that conflict will ever be available."[63] To identify this inextricable link between reason and hegemony is not at all to abandon reason or give into relativism but to insist on the contingency and contestability of every social order. "Every social order is a contingent articulation of power relations that lacks an ultimate rational ground."[64] The supposed natural order of society "is never the manifestation of a deeper objectivity that is exterior to the practices that brought it into being."[65] This idea, that common sense is not so common, enables us to denaturalize every supposedly natural power and conceive how, if needs be, they "can be transformed through counter-hegemonic interventions."[66] So Mouffe has no illusions of reason offering a depoliticized "escape" from identity-constructs or the divisions of politics. She is likewise suspicious of full "revolutionary ruptures" that seek to overthrow or relinquish the liberal democratic principles of legitimacy. We must pursue hegemonic transformation, "revolutionary reformism," from within.

Trying to attain "consensus" or enrich decision-making through deliberation may helpfully *reconfigure* exclusion by making it more flexible or generous. But it does not abolish exclusion. Any consensus, at best, she urges will always be a *conflictual consensus* – a continued process of dispute where conflicting interests are battled out, in what Mouffe calls "agonism." Such a conflictual consensus still excludes certain positions as falling outside the ever-contested boundaries and terms of engagement and dispute.[67] At the same time, an agonistic public space can never arrive

---

[62] Ibid., 5.
[63] Ibid., 79.
[64] Ibid., 131; Mouffe, *For a Left Populism* 88.
[65] AG 2.
[66] Ibid., 90. She also speaks of "disarticulating the sedimented practices of an existing formation" and seeking a "new hegemonic social formation" – but *not* a revolutionary rupture (Mouffe, *For a Left Populism*, 44–5).
[67] DP 103; 13; AG 139.

at a balanced, definitive, pure agonism, stabilized in law. For whoever regulates and referees that agonism would again be a contestable hegemony. Once we grasp the inescapability of the political, we see a certain inevitable *circularity* to agonistic engagement. For Mouffe, a stabilized, "pure agonism is impossible …. Or maybe it is possible, but you cannot call it political anymore."[68] In the common liberal view, "the public space is the terrain where one aims at creating consensus." But Mouffe's idea of politics is bolder, in emphasizing the inescapability of division; and yet it is also more modest, in that finalized unity, she admits, is simply not possible. We must admit that politics involves "necessarily unstable forms" that rationality, procedures, and tolerance simply cannot eliminate.[69] Agonism means the public space is where "conflicting points of view are confronted without any possibility of a final reconciliation."[70] Politics cannot eliminate hostility; rather, it "consists in domesticating hostility and in trying to defuse the potential antagonism that exists in human relations … there can only be contingent hegemonic forms of stabilization of their conflict."[71] Politics, we could say in anticipation of Girard, is about as lasting as archaic sacrifices; it dissipates conflicts into a provisional unity around certain exclusions.

C. MAINTAINING THE INCOMPATIBILITY THROUGH REFUSING ILLUSIONS OF UNITY

Despite the dangers of liberalism – its potential for hubris and pretentious universality, its incompatibility with democracy, that reason cannot ultimately render it inclusive in political practice – Mouffe insists we should not abandon it. In fact, we must, first of all, appreciate the beneficent intolerance of the liberal tradition: its constantly exerted pressure for the extension of rights and inclusivity, its intolerance of tyranny, its representation of minority voices.[72] These are liberalism's *cataphatic* intolerances – to use the theological term of positive representation and affirmation, through concepts, imagery, and metaphor. That is, liberalism

---

[68] Decreus and Lievens, "Hegemony and the Radicalization of Democracy," 684. One of Mouffe's critics misses this nuance, while asking fair questions about international agonism: Mathias Thaler, "The Illusion of Purity."

[69] DP 11.

[70] AG 92.

[71] Mouffe, "Religion, Liberal Democracy, and Citizenship," 323.

[72] DP 45.

can exert beneficent intolerance in its active, critical traditions. "By constantly challenging the relations of inclusion-exclusion implied by the political constitution of 'the people' – required by the exercise of democracy – the liberal discourse of universal human rights plays an important role in keeping the democratic contestation alive."[73] Much of the liberal tradition, too, has been catalytic in making more visible "what the dominant consensus tends to obscure and obliterate, in giving a voice to all those who are silenced within the framework of the existing hegemony."[74] Given these strengths, Mouffe is akin to those who insist liberalism's keystone concept of human rights should not be rejected as an idolatrous credo of a global secular religion, or as an imperialistic, totalizing "conversation stopper."[75] Universal human rights and the liberal discourse, one must admit, are indeed very dangerous, in that they draw up a distinction between societies that do well at observing such rights – while those who do not are seen as somehow deficient, unjust, or wrong. But, we must appreciate, as scholar of religion Atalia Omer argues, how human rights, despite their potential dangers, can be used as "a starting point and diagnostic lens for illuminating the underlying root causes of conflict …. It is important to safeguard against a wholesale rejection of everything 'liberal.'"[76]

Instead of seeking to abolish liberalism on account of its intolerance, it is critical to consider how these intolerances inescapably intersect with the political – particularly, our democratic context. Besides giving liberalism's intolerance its due, we must recognize how it is "only thanks to the democratic logics of equivalence that frontiers can be created and a *demos* established, without which no real exercise of rights could be possible."[77] In other words, the rubber of universal rights hits the political road in democracy's specifically political, thus hegemonic, exclusive, and contestable, forms. To maintain liberalism and democracy in a productive tension thus requires acknowledging that these logics inconclusively confront each other; we are faced with "two logics which are incompatible in the last instance and that there is no way in which they could be perfectly

---

[73] Ibid., 5.

[74] *AG* 93.

[75] Amy Gutmann, ed., *Human Rights As Politics and Idolatry*; John Corrigan and Lynn S. Neal, eds., *Religious Intolerance in America*. For a critical retrieval of liberalism, see Atalia Omer, "Modernists Despite Themselves."

[76] Atalia Omer, "Can a Critic Be a Caretaker?," 478. See also *AG* 30; Raimundo Panikkar, "Is the Notion of Human Rights a Western Concept?," 81–2.

[77] *DP* 9.

reconciled."[78] This negation of any perfect, final incompatibility is what I call *apophatic intolerance*, a crucial counterweight to liberalism's cataphatic intolerance. Apophasis in theological discourse is the requisite negation of cataphatic affirmations, recognizing their insufficiency of all language and representations of the Absolute.[79] What I am calling an apophatic intolerance in Mouffe is a refusal of unity illusions; it is a negation of any presumption to political completion; it is an awareness that liberalism cannot be institutionalized without ironically becoming illiberal. This is an awareness of a certain inescapability of exclusion, a deep awareness of the exception, of that which law cannot contain or institutionalize. Such apophatic intolerance, for Mouffe, means repudiating the illusion that we could ever attain a non-hegemonic social unity. We ought to "abandon the very idea of a complete reabsorption of alterity into oneness and harmony."[80] Engaging in liberal democracy means abandoning "the ideal of a democratic society as the realization of a perfect harmony in transparency."[81] As reason itself stems from originary, founding divisions, we must abandon "the very idea that there could be such a thing as a 'rational consensus'; namely, one that would not be based on any form of exclusion."[82] Mouffe is not here valorizing conflict or irascible divisiveness. Rather, she is insisting upon viewing politics from the position of the exception, the viewpoint from which we see how all manifestations of law, reason, and power relations are not "natural," with respect to some eternal fixed essence, but are in fact contingent and contestable.[83] One must think these exceptions with a passion. Mouffe sees this apophatic intolerance as a requisite counterweight in pursuing a more just social order amidst plural, contending interpretations. Without such apophasis, liberalism's cataphatic intolerance ironically becomes totalitarian anti-pluralism.

---

[78] Ibid., 5.
[79] The Fourth Lateran Council combined the cataphatic and apophatic in the formula that "between Creator and creature no similitude can be expressed without implying a greater dissimilitude." The cataphatic mode concerns expressions of similarity whereas the dissimilarity of infinite difference is the apophatic.
[80] Ibid., 33; *AG* 22, 49.
[81] *DP* 100.
[82] Ibid., 32.
[83] She resembles, at least on this point, William Connelly's pluralism, which emphasizes the "profound contestability of our practices" (William Connelly, *Why I am Not a Secularist*, 36).

For example, a chief myth of oneness today is especially visible for Mouffe in "neo-liberal hegemony."[84] This myth's version of "unity" entails enforced deregulation, austerity, and privatization, at the cost of justice and planetary sustainability. Political moderates and "third way" proponents have been especially prone to capitulate to neoliberalism, ignore its divisions, paint it as natural and reasonable, and mythologize it as fate. For example, Margaret Thatcher's continued refrain that "there is no alternative" to neoliberal globalization painted it as our natural, unquestionable destiny.[85] Or, Mouffe also noted Tony Blair's rhetorical appeals that "'we are all middle class,' so we should all be able to agree with one another." In this we have little more than rhetorical attempts to make conflict disappear before a false state of tolerance strewn with divisions.[86] One also sees gestures in the United States to transcend racial-power conflicts – between "black lives matter" and "blue lives matter" – with appeals that "all lives matter," and that we should "set aside our differences" and just get along. In the more legislative register, William Cavanaugh similarly observes how national "unity" is often invoked in the United States in the context of defending tax cuts for the ultra-rich, saying its critics are "sowing divisiveness."[87] In such cases, the originary divisions are mythologized as nonexistent, while any critical identifications of them is ironically painted as discordant. As Dorothy Day observed, the rich mysteriously turn from just war theorists into universalist pacifists once "class war" is broached; they even pretend that the conflict is not there.[88]

In such cases of mythic unity, Mouffe sees contingent, human constructs conflated with "nature" – a naturalization of particularities into universal "common sense." Such a sedimentation then serves as a "foundation," an illusion of objective reason, ossified beyond contestation, immune to dispute or conflicting interpretations. In such forgetfulness, it confuses its particular reality with the norm, failing to think the exception with a passion. A chief danger in this misapprehension, of course, is that what has often counted as "natural" in human society – slavery, racism, sexism, etc. – has been so *unnatural* or merely convention. What I am calling Mouffe's apophatic intolerance involves vigilant awareness of this

[84] *DP* 5; Mouffe, *For a Left Populism*, 12.
[85] *AG* 131.
[86] Decreus and Lievens, "Hegemony and the Radicalization of Democracy," 698.
[87] William Cavanaugh, "Killing for the Telephone Company," 264.
[88] Dorothy Day, "Why Do the Members of Christ Tear One Another," 1.

contingency and contestability. This, again, results in refusing to represent the "the totality" of a society, refusing to lay hold of a final political "foundation." Given the unavailability of absolute knowledge, "no agent should be able to claim any mastery of the *foundation* of society," or a monopoly of the foundation.[89] Such a refusal is crucial for keeping political strategies from hardening into totalitarian and fascist regimes, many of which throughout the twentieth century laid claim to their "foundation" by laying claim to their righteous victimhood as the national unity-myth.[90]

In sum, the incompatibility between liberalism and democracy should not lead us to choose between the two. Nor ought the dangers of liberalism's intolerance lead us to soften it. Liberalism's power is found precisely in its universalist, "intolerant," ideals – even if they cannot be instantiated without becoming hegemonic. Liberalism has helped exert constant pressure toward increased inclusion and justice, in tension with the constitutive exclusions, decisions, and boundaries of the political. Maintaining liberalism's intolerance and accepting this ongoing incompatibility is Mouffe's path toward sane social theory. Mouffe thus writes, "even while we must admit to the constitutively divisive nature of the political," we should not abandon liberal democracy.[91] Instead of seeking to resolve the incompatibility, we must appreciate how agonistic tensions within democracy – conflicts perhaps *intensified* by the pressures of liberalism – can be productive and liberative. Maintaining this tension requires a negative, apophatic intolerance, a refusal to lay hold of the society's foundation.

---

[89] *DP* 21. See also Connelly, *Why I am Not a Secularist*, 83, 155. One hears similarity with Niebuhr, in a point that will emerge throughout: "The democratic process may be carried on within the context of monotheistic faith. Then no relative power, be it that of the nation or its people as well as that of tyrants, can claim absolute sovereignty or total loyalty" (Richard H. Niebuhr, *Radical Monotheism*, 77).

This refusal for Mouffe stems from her understanding of the democratic tradition as involving a symbolically "empty" place of power, even if, in practice, a constraining power is always exercised. In regard to this emptiness, "totalitarianism is the attempt, after the democratic revolution, to reoccupy the empty place of power. Totalitarianism can only come after democracy. It is democracy that opens up the danger of totalitarianism" (Decreus and Lievens, "Hegemony and the Radicalization of Democracy," 680). Parallels will be evident in Assmann: monotheism's distance from the political makes possible a new kind of violence to fill that distance.

[90] For Hitler's victim rhetoric see Wolfgang Palaver, "The Ambiguous Cachet," 76.

[91] *DP* 45.

D. US VERSUS THEM

Mouffe is careful to point out how this "refusal of closure" can be abused in yet another evasion of the political through a depoliticized pluralism. She identifies this in William Connelly, for example, whose pluralistic vision partially aligns with Mouffe in his suspicion of consensus, questioning the political imaginary of wholeness, and abrogating claims to an authoritative center. And yet in his draining away of epistemic certainty Mouffe detects a mere "valorization of multiplicity" that avoids "any attempt to construct a *we*."[92] This evasion of the political makes Connelly "unable to grasp the nature of the hegemonic struggle" – that even pluralism "will necessarily imply some form of closure"[93] in various exclusions and identity constructs. Any pluralism today that attempts to abolish us/them alliances leaves neoliberal hegemony insufficiently critiqued – per a "can't we just get along" motif.[94] Again, "it is only when division and antagonism are recognized as being ineradicable that it is possible to think in a properly political way."[95]

"Identity" for Mouffe thus involves not the abrogation of having adversaries (i.e., abolishing us/them constructs) but respectful engagement with them. This stands in contrast with those who might interpret the command to love one's enemies as implying that "no one is an enemy." But a mature pluralism for Mouffe does not abolish the notion of enemies or any sense of "us/them" from our vocabulary. Democracy's institutions do not (and cannot) abolish antagonism; they must instead reduce it into agonism, subduing potential enemy relations into adversary relations.[96] This clarification means that the central feature of politics is not the enemy to be expelled, as Schmitt argued, but the *adversary* to be engaged in the political realm. An adversary is, for Mouffe, an opponent in interpreting shared, founding, constitutional principles. "Adversaries

---

[92] Ibid., 20.

[93] *AG* 14–5; William E. Connelly, *Pluralism*. Mouffe's critique is largely accurate, in that Connelly often speaks in a depoliticized idiom of "deferrals and diversities" and "engagements" and less of decisions, exclusions, limits, and restraints – although one finds some exceptions (Connelly, *Why I am Not a Secularist*, 5, 8, 154).

[94] Niebuhr sees a similar pattern in the "religion of humanism," which starts in "protest against the doubtful assurance and the partial loyalties of closed societies," but it then "ends with an enlarged but yet dubious and partial closed-society faith. It remains a kind of henotheism" (Niebuhr, *Radical Monotheism*, 35).

[95] *AG* 15.

[96] Ibid., xii. For a rich exploration of the social analyses necessary for this agonism, with special attention to prophetic voices like Cornell West et al., see Jason A. Springs, *Healthy Conflict in Contemporary American Society*.

fight against each other because they want their interpretation of the principles to become hegemonic, but they do not put into question the legitimacy of their opponent's right to fight for the victory of their position."[97] Such adversarial relations are as inescapable as interpretation.

In other words, a mature pluralism does not abolish conflict but treats adversaries with respect, even while opposing them. We might regard consensus-oriented liberalism as operating under a spirit of "can't we just get along?" By contrast, agonistic pluralism for Mouffe asks, "can't we just argue?" This agonism is a crucial element in what is also known as conflict transformation, wherein conflict is seen as a positive opportunity – it might even need to be provoked – so as to more deeply pursue just relations. One is here reminded of Martin Luther King Jr.'s response, in the "Letter from Birmingham Jail," to the accusation that the civil rights movement was causing division. His rejoinder was that the absence of tension is, in fact, a placid mirage hiding injustice; and the pursuit of justice may in fact require fostering tensions that force us to confront the issue. Importantly, however, those who create such a crisis, are *not* "the creators of tension. We merely bring to the surface the hidden tension that is already alive."[98] In a sensible irony, we find the ones truly devoted to "peace" may manifest as provocative agonists, seemingly bent on division and identity-politics; meanwhile those safeguarding the conditions of injustice ("the white moderate") may manifest as the cool-headed bastions of reason, gentility, and unity.

Mouffe argues we do not create a more just, inclusive world through eliminating collective identities of us/them through reason or privatizing our passions – which have been hallmarks of Rawlsian-styled liberalism. Rather, we must use and redirect "those passions by mobilizing them toward democratic designs, by creating collective forms of identification around democratic objectives."[99] Failure to recognize and name us/them political divisions is again to fall into the liberal evasion of the political.[100] Instead of evading any constructing of "us," identity formation ought to be oriented toward clarifying and transforming conflicts. Mouffe thus affirms, for example, how a social movement like Via Campesina – an international peasant's movement fighting for environmental justice,

---

97   *AG* 7.
98   Martin Luther King Jr., "Letter from a Birmingham Jail."
99   *AG* 9.
100 E.g., Waleed Shahid, "America in Populist Times."

water, land, and migrant rights – explicitly constructs a "them" in its rhetoric and action, opposing itself to "big multinational agribusiness corporations."[101] Is this not, in a sense, an "identity forged negatively against another"? Maybe so. But it is far more in touch with reality than white-washed unity. Mouffe, by contrast, is suspicious of "moralistic" approaches to global justice, often visible in charity events or mobilizing compassion, which avoid naming the structural, economic adversaries who abet and profit from global injustices.[102] We must risk constructing and using "us" terms, even while allowing that construct to be provisional, aware of its potential for ossification. But respectful adversarial relations do not mean the abolition of them.

E. MONOTHEISM AND INTOLERANCE

These themes extracted from Mouffe's oeuvre spur us to reconceptualize intolerance and monotheism today. Let us revisit, by way of contrast, Schwartz's *Curse of Cain*. While Mouffe's argument is primarily political and Schwartz's is theological, their ideas meet on the pitch of social theory – and Mouffe brings a weightier realism. Schwartz urged that monotheism's us/them construct is its deep, malignant root. But – while we will have much to say of monotheistic antagonism – Mouffe argues that us/them configurations are a fundamental, constitutive dimension of human association. In fact, the very attempt to construct a we without a they, to make a consensus without an exclusion, "is impossible because the very condition for the constitution of a 'we' is the demarcation of a 'they.'"[103] From Mouffe's perspective we can now see why it is misguided to use "intolerance" as a simple term of derision, accusation, and critique – either of monotheism or liberalism. Per Mouffe's critique of inclusivism and universality, it is no longer so obvious that a mature pluralism today means, as Schwartz put it, shedding of us/them identity formations and imagining sociality in tolerant, open, and limitless forms, embracing ethics, peace, and the promise of universalism. Mouffe affirms, but also radically qualifies, any rhetoric that "does not circumscribe limits, but endlessly transgresses all possible limits":[104] exclusions and limits must bear forcefully upon our minds.

---

[101] *AG* 63.
[102] Ibid., 64.
[103] Mouffe, *For a Left Populism*, 91.
[104] *CC* 33; *x*, 4. Schwartz rightly admits that, the Deuteronomist's "graphic depiction of violence against the Other" may in fact involve some sympathetic depictions of the outcast. Thereby the text "invites us not to reject the rejected Other" (31).

To suggest that "identity formation" must eschew any us/them config-uration in pursuit of "limitless openness" evinces a liberal evasion of the political. While we will in later chapters explore ways by which monothe-ism indeed involves an identity deeply charged by antagonism, we do well to acknowledge the inescapable dimension of the political, which, again, insists the very "creation of an identity always implies the establishment of a difference."[105] Schwartz's rhetoric of unconditionality too simplistic-ally regards inclusivity and limitlessness as good, and exclusivity/limits as bad. Such rhetoric does not see how consensus is an exclusion and tolerance contains intolerance. It fails to countenance the constitutive boundaries and limits of even inclusive democratic procedures.

As an exemplary other point, Schwartz laments the exclusivity involved in the canonical dimension of monotheism, with its sense of a fixed, exclusive truth. She is right to note how the biblical canonization process was not the result of an all-embracing, open deliberation, but that it entailed exclusion and even violence.[106] But her proposed solution to canonical exclusion through consensus is an evasion of the political: she proposes a "substantial archive" as opposed to a "closed corpus." This is, however, not the abrogation of exclusion but an invitation to another configuration of power, interpretation, and control of the archive. Even openness will guard its version of openness just as consensus is an exclu-sion. Likewise, the "embrace of difference," politically speaking, still takes place in the context not of unlimited openness but in an enforced range of acceptable difference. Recognizing the contingency and contest-ability of that range – refereed as it is by a reigning hegemony – is crucial to what I have called apophatic intolerance, the necessary counterbalance to the beneficial, cataphatic intolerance of liberalism's desire to create a society without exclusion.

Schwartz's critique of monotheism stems partly from her mistakenly grouping it together with particularist *monolatry* and universalist *henotheism*. These latter two are indeed supremely *political* theologies of the ancient world, which we will discuss in later chapters; and it is appropriate to see them all sharing some sense of "exclusive alle-giance."[107] But, failing to account for their complex historical differences

---

[105] AG 5.
[106] CC 146.
[107] She justifies the conflation based on the fact that there are so few strictly monotheistic utterances in the Bible, and "since everyone uses *monotheism* to mean monolatry ... I will stick to the customary usage" (ibid., 17).

amidst similarities, monotheism alone becomes for Schwartz the catchall word for violent, exclusivist ideology. Chapter 6 will identify how the ingredients of monotheism's intolerance are not novel but in fact derived *from* the common polytheistic, political symbols of the ancient world.

As for monotheism's "transcendence," in which God is seen as separate from the cosmos, Schwartz saw in this only the "inaccessibility" of God. And this is, for her, necessarily a bad thing for human sociality, linked with greedy attitudes of scarcity.[108] Taken without qualification, the separation of God from the cosmos indeed involves the potential for ecological exploitation and, in reaction, a theological backlash to see the cosmos as the body of God. But once we begin to see how God, in ancient states, was so often seen as homologous with the political body (Chapters 4–6), we can begin to see with Mouffe how the inaccessibility of divinity (prohibited from representation, as it were) is in fact a psychological *prerequisite* to a mature pluralism; the inaccessibility of the universal position is crucial in the resistance to absolutism. Despite the dangers, there are great advantages in seeing divinity as somehow separated from the cosmos and all representability – just as there is a beneficence to liberalism's being *incompatible* with the political order. The challenge, however, is how to conceive of that separation and incompatibility (taken up in Chapter 7 and the Conclusion).

A crucial theological implication of Mouffe's pluralism is how it offers resistance to idolatry. While idolatry is, roughly, the treating of a human construct as divine, this is a matter of "religious" as well as political representation. Idolatry involves the treating of contingent particularities as eternal, natural, or "just the way things are." Political idolatry involves the positing of a Unity where there is in fact none, of saying "peace, where there is no peace" (Jer 6:14). It is a failure to see how the "common good" is usually good for some, yet very bad for others. We may interpret Jesus, in this framework, as something of an agonistic prophet in critique of idolatry; "I came not to bring peace but division" (Lk 12:51; Mt 10:34). Compare this with Rousseau for whom "everything which destroys social unity is worthless."[109] What if a social "unity" is maintained through unjust divisions and needs to be critiqued and negated? Indeed, when has a social unity *not* been constructed through some dubious or violent means? A genuine pluralism requires attentiveness to the contingency of

---

[108] Ibid., 116.
[109] Jean-Jacques Rousseau, *Rousseau*, 147; Robert Erlewine, *Monotheism and Tolerance*, 26.

our sedimented notions of social unity, understanding that "there is no single entity called 'society,'" while rejecting "the reduction of such a diversity of publics to a single sovereign will."[110] It is absolutely crucial to see how monotheism can be precisely the *rejection* of a mythologized "single sovereign will" over a people. The description of such an intolerant rejection emerges in the subsequent chapters.

Idolatry may be seen as the malignant mirage of idealized consensus, the "dangerous utopia of reconciliation," an "illusion of rational consensus."[111] Such idolatry is dangerous in that – though it may construct a provisional unity in one sense – it can so repress our divisions that they eventually provoke, in Mouffe's analysis, "particularist and violent reactions" of antagonistic excess. These arise today in jingoistic populism, pogroms, and mobs – examples of which Mouffe sees in torching and looting in France.[112] There, she argues, the forced and false unity of neoliberalism robbed people of alternatives, distinctions, and channels for confrontation, which reduced the political vocabulary for voicing grievances. With grievances but no "words" (viable, lawful alternatives to neoliberalism), what could have been a manageable agonism of dispute and democratic contestation boiled over into raw antagonism. This is why idolatry is dangerous.

Healthy pluralism requires refusing idolatrous unity. For Mouffe, this requires negating deterministic fates, like the "material forces of production," or "the development of the spirit,"[113] or, I would add, "being on the right side of history" as a rhetorical manipulation. Such mythic unities are at best shorthand appeals to the crowd; but, worse, they tend not to make us more aware of oppression so as to remedy it, but excuse whatever is the necessary sacrifice. Suspicious of such idolatrous unity, Mouffe urges that any and every political order "should never be justified as dictated by a higher order and presented as the only legitimate one."[114] This strikes me as resonant with what we will find in monotheism's refusal to unite religious and political realities: this refusal is an apophatic intolerance, symbolized in the prohibition of representing God. This refusal to claim a monopoly on the foundation of society, Mouffe admits, is paradoxically its own kind of "foundation." To refuse to lay claim to

---

[110] Cavanaugh, "Killing for the Telephone Company," 260.
[111] *DP* 28f.
[112] *AG* 27–8, 122, 146.
[113] Ibid., 132.
[114] Ibid., 17.

this monopoly is like an ever-opened-up foundation, ever exposed to its contingency and its exclusions. This foreclosure of absolutism affects our notion of time and expectation, or we might say eschatology: "full objectivity can never be reached."[115] We must come to terms with our "lack of a final ground and the undecidability that pervades every order."[116]

Schwartz envisions, in contrast with monotheism's closed and exclusive identity, "what would happen if we were to base our ethics on a utopian condition, one presupposing an ideal of plentitude instead of the world of scarcity?"[117] If we take Mouffe as a guide, a proper response is that we must perpetually negotiate this laudable utopianism with the inescapable decisions and exclusions of democracy. Schwartz's formulation strikes Mouffian ears as asking, "What if we based our ethics not on the limits of democracy but on the unconditionality of liberalism?" This ideal of plentitude would, in practice, inescapably take on delimited and hegemonic forms. Schwartz comes close to acknowledging this when she admits that "the work of law," with its prohibitions, exclusions, and punishments, will have to "let ethics do *other* work."[118] In other words, she recognizes how law and ethics do not perfectly coincide. But Mouffe's attentiveness to the political gives no quarter on this front: she insists that ethics and values do *not* escape the political; for the very work of interpreting and naming ethics *is* political, as is the work of constructing a narrative and a "we." Mouffe insists, "the ethical and the political are intertwined and depend on each other. Normative theory denies this. It places ethics outside or above the realm of the political."[119] Thus, Mouffe doesn't treat "liberalism" as a cipher for ideals, morals, or norms – which then belong in some private or transcendent realm of values – while politics deals with hard, objective facts. No moral or norm is sheerly universal and non-contingent; rather, norms contain hegemony. Without this awareness, liberalism again evades the political. While one may affirm Schwartz's vision to "endlessly compose and recompose temporary and multiple identities,"[120] in practice, this inevitably entails boundaries, exclusions, and decisions. Openness in pursuit of a victimless politics is laudable, indeed it must be pursued with vigor. Liberalism may help agitate toward drawing our boundaries differently – perhaps for the

---

[115] Ibid., xi, 17.
[116] *AG* 2.
[117] *CC* 34.
[118] Ibid., 34.
[119] Decreus and Lievens, "Hegemony and the Radicalization of Democracy," 689.
[120] *CC* 37.

better and with greater generosity. But whatever its political expression, it will not move us "beyond hegemony" or escape exclusion. Ideally, liberalism's intolerance may provoke agonistic conflict in seeking to transform sociopolitical structures; at worse, it ironically collapses into antagonism, yet another regime of despotism with entrenched divisions that can only dress up as unity.

These observations suggest, by extension, that certain theological attempts to abolish monotheism of its intolerance and its identity constructs stem from an evasion of the political. Our context of depoliticized liberalism inhibits a clear-minded interpretation of monotheistic intolerance today. Instead of trying to burnish an unconditionally tolerant and open monotheism – as if our choice is whether to be intolerant or not – the more fundamental question is *how* one excludes, *how* one is intolerant. So, how would a mature monotheism teach us to be "intolerant"? To develop an answer, we move outward from Mouffe to Girard and other scholarship on religion, violence, and monotheism. Mouffe will be periodically revisited in the coming chapters, as her themes ultimately help us conceptualize a monotheistic intolerance that transforms identities forged negatively against the Other.

2

Girard's Mimetic Theory and Monotheism's Ambivalent Effects

No author more provocatively describes the relationship between biblical "intolerance" and violence than the late René Girard. His interdisciplinary mimetic theory has spawned numerous research agendas, ranging from neuroscience and archaeology to theology and political science.[1] Stemming from his psychology of desire, he argues that the perception of the divine stems from a long primordial history of humanity's misperceived violence. And he argues monotheism is a disruption of this deep legacy, as a "refusal to divinize victims" and a "devictimization of God." Monotheism as such has not only radically affected the way divinity is perceived and represented in "religion," but it affects even the political management of violence. This unconventional and opaque approach to monotheism can be elucidated only in reference to Girard's entire theory of religion and its role in human evolution.

His theory entails three modes of analysis: (1) mimetic desire, (2) the victimage-mechanism originating culture and religion, and (3) biblical revelation. In summation of all three, we could say: (1) the way humans desire and scapegoat others has (2) benefited our species' evolution since our origins, but (3) this misapprehension is slowly being unveiled through a different relationship to divinity and the political, for better and worse. Or, an even shorter attempt: scapegoating abetted human evolution, but with the revelation of the victim, we must now learn to live without scapegoats. Surely other formulations could work, but we have it there

---

[1] Chris Fleming, *Rene Girard*, 153. Von Balthasar deemed Girard's theological program "surely the most dramatic theological project on offer" (Hans Urs von Balthasar, *Theo-Drama*, 4:299).

in brief, ready for elaboration. This chapter will lay out this theory, drawing out his idea of monotheism and its relevance to the noted intolerance problem. Thereafter, it can serve as a base theory for further critique and exploration. I have organized his theory in a slight deviation from the tripartite form above:

(1) Mimesis ("misapprehension"):[2]
   (a) A synchronic analysis of mimetic desire and rivalry.
   (b) A diachronic analysis of the scapegoat mechanism as generative in evolution.
(2) Truth and Revelation ("apprehension"):
   (a) A synchronic analysis of biblical themes, in siding with the victim. Girard's idea of monotheism abides here.
   (b) A diachronic analysis of revelation as courting both chaos and development in a history without gods.

By dividing up what usually constitutes Girard's third idea of "revelation" into two parts, and noting the synchronic and diachronic dimensions of his work, the theory appears more elegant. We might say he had two main ideas, each thought in synchronic and diachronic ways. And, as I suggested in my Introduction, the second idea (revelation) is both what makes his theory famous and controversial while also being the very aspect that suffers from remarkably little argumentation. While I will offer in this chapter nothing more than an introduction to his sweeping history of Western Civilization and the Common Era (2b), this book's overall interest concerns the synchronic analysis of monotheism: its genealogy, its intolerance, its relation to the political sphere.

A. MIMESIS AND DIVINIZING OTHERS

Girard's first major idea concerns human desire and imitation, generally speaking. Developed initially through literary criticism, his core claim builds on Aristotle's observation: while humans have many instinctual desires, like hunger, we also have, compared to other species, an elevated level of *imitation* grafted onto our instincts.[3] We do not desire objects

---

[2] One should not place too much emphasis on my referring to mimesis here as a "misapprehension" – as Girard often discussed the *positive value* of mimesis, as I will discuss. I simply wish to emphasize an elegant problem/solution form in the theory.

[3] "Imitation is natural to man from childhood, one of his advantages over the lower animals being this, that he is the most imitative creature in the world and learns at first by

"directly" but we desire according to others, which he calls mimetic desire.[4] Such desire means wanting things because we anticipate or see others desiring them – suggesting that we do not so much want objects themselves but *others*. Our desire triangulates between our self, a model (who inspires our desire), and objects.[5] Our "I" is always pre-othered.

While mimesis can certainly lead to conflict with models, the pacific and beneficial mode of mimetic desire Girard terms external mediation. This involves desiring a model, what they have, what they are; but social hierarchy, distance, death, or taboo keep our desire at a relatively safe distance. As such, there is no envy of, or conflict with, the model, but simply a source of inspiration and intuitively imbued lessons.[6] Perhaps the model's "object" is some virtue or some helpful skill.

But this desiring to be the model is often felt as "lacking being"; others always seem to have *more being* than we do and we want to *acquire* what they are and have.[7] It is as if we intuitively say to ourselves: "if the model, who is apparently already endowed with superior being, desires some object, that object must surely be capable of conferring an even greater plentitude of being."[8] A chief temptation, then, especially when a model has what we cannot have, is to "make this distance evil and grasp toward its closure."[9] When social safeguards and taboos do not restrain such grasping, mimesis can intensify to interior mediation, a desire to close this distance from the model, who becomes a rival and obstacle to be overcome.[10] As such, any concern over a desired object begins to fade, and a direct obsession with the model dominates. This leads to a conflictual snowball effect: the imitator seeks to take over the being of the model, and

---

imitation" (Aristotle, *The Basic Works of Aristotle*, §1457 [1448b]; 1458 [1448b]; 1460 [1449b]; René Girard, *Things Hidden Since the Foundation of the World* [hereafter *TH*], 1).

4 René Girard, *Deceit, Desire, and the Novel* (Hereafter *DDN*), 4, 21; or Shakespeare's "suggested desire" in the *Rape of Lucrecia* and "love by another's eyes" (René Girard, *A Theatre of Envy*, 121f). Whereas "imitation" bears a connotation of cognitive awareness, Girard prefers the preconscious connotations of "mimesis," or "imitated desire." René Girard, *Violence and the* Sacred (hereafter *VS*), 146, 148.

5 *DDN* 2, 48; *TH* 16, 18.

6 *DDN* 9; *EC* 61.

7 This "lacking being" is akin to Sartre's analysis in *Being and Nothingness*; Wolfgang Palaver, *René Girard's Mimetic Theory* (hereafter *RGMT*), 74.

8 *VS* 146; *RGMT* 77.

9 *Skandalon* for Girard, as visible in the Gospels, means "that ridiculous reciprocal antagonism and resentment that everybody feels for each other, for the simple reason that our desires are sometimes frustrated" (*EC* 82).

10 *DDN* 9; *EC* 57.

when the model resists it only confirms the desirability of their being, causing a reciprocally escalating resistance.[11]

Mimesis' path to conflict thus involves not merely conflictive "differences" but *undifferentiation* between subject and model: "eventually the subject will become the model of his model, just as the imitator will become the imitator of his imitator. One is always moving toward more symmetry, and thus always toward more conflict."[12] Without any cultural taboos and safeguards, such acquisitive mimesis can infect an entire group: "if two persons are fighting over the same object, then this object seems more valuable to bystanders. Therefore, it tends to attract more and more people, and as it does so, its mimetic attractiveness keeps increasing."[13] While this pattern can snowball into a conflict of all against all, it can be redirected into a unifying or reconciling kind of imitation, where a group coheres through *sharing conflict* against a scapegoat, all against one.[14] One might see this, of course, in lynch mobs or any sort of group-jeering and polarization, as we will discuss more in Section B.

While this cycle of safe-, to dangerous-, to reconciling-mimesis is very common in human relations, Girard does not define conflict or aggression as "essential" to human nature.[15] Even if conflict might appear to arise "naturally," this does not make it something we cannot resist in ourselves. Girard, speaking normatively, urges readers to resist rivalrous mimesis while also not regarding mimesis itself as "bad" or inherently violent. Rather, Girard is located, in Wolfgang Palaver's assessment, between the two poles of Aristotle and Aquinas' optimistic *homo homini amicus*, on the one hand, and Hobbes' pessimistic *homo homini lupus* on the other. The emulsifier between the two is Augustine's nuance: humanity is "social by nature and quarrelsome by perversion."[16] We thus have here an emphasis on the "natural" human inclination toward peace and

---

[11] *DDN* 12, 16, 18; *EC* 57. Escalating in conflict, Girard calls this acquisitive mimesis, *VS* 187; *TH* 26. Note how this acquisitive mimesis inclines toward antagonism, whereas conflictual mimesis brings people together in a shared antagonism toward another.

Hobbes writes "if any two men desire the same thing, which nevertheless they cannot both enjoy, they become enemies; and in the way to their End ... [they] endeavor to destroy or subdue one another." René Girard, "Victims, Violence, and Christianity," 132. Thomas Hobbes, *The Elements of Law Natural and Politic*, 59.

[12] *EC* 70; 57.

[13] Ibid., 64.

[14] Ibid., 66.

[15] *TH* 197.

[16] *RGMT* 37, 96.

other-orientation that, in practice, easily distorts into conflict.[17] *Homo reciprocus*, for Girard, means not only pacific cooperation, but also the ability to escalate conflict reciprocally and cooperatively.[18] Girard thus is keen on emphasizing desire's pervasive penchant for rivalry. Anything like Rousseau's optimism is mislead.

Mimetic theory, then, is not only about desire. It is also a theory of unity and conflict, seeking to explain what leads to conflict between humans and groups, and, in turn, what can ameliorate it. Some conflict theories emphasize the roots of violence in *ideology* (e.g., Nazis were so violent because of their anti-Semitism),[19] or *instrumentality with respect to scarcity* (e.g., violence is done to get land or resources),[20] or *irreconcilable difference* (e.g., civilizations clash because of deep-seated differences).[21] Schwartz's opening analysis – on *us versus them constructs* as a root cause of violence, an identity formed parasitically through othering – is surely one of the more prominent explanations for conflict.[22] These explanations are not necessarily incompatible with the idea that mimetic desire leads us into conflict. Though, mimetic theory would qualify each above-mentioned explanation, arguing that mimetic desire precedes our cognitive ideologies; and our conflicts are exaggerated by, but not limited to, resource- or object scarcity; rather, conflict is about how desire, objects, taboos, and relationships are configured. Furthermore, it is not only our differences but our *convergence* toward each other, our attractions into a rivalrous-mirroring or sameness, that can court conflict.[23] In sum, mimetic theory places relatively stronger emphasis on how *inter-group relationships* and the contagiousness of *desires* – however arbitrary, fleeting, or illusory – can drive our conflicts.[24] In this generalization of conflict, mimetic theory parallels

---

[17] Girard regards the positive aspect of mimetic desire as a "divine grace" (Rebecca Adams, "Violence, Difference, Sacrifice," 25).

[18] *EC* 14.

[19] For ideological scapegoating, see Peter Glick, "When Neighbors Blame Neighbors." For anti-Semitism in genocide, see Daniel Jonah Goldhagen, *Hitler's Willing Executioners*.

[20] For land and resources as motivations, see Benjamin Valentino, *Final Solutions*, ch 3.

[21] For clashing differences, see Samuel P. Huntington, *Clash of Civilizations and the Remaking of World Order*.

[22] Jensen and Szejnmann's edited volume on *Ordinary People As Mass Murderers* convincingly describes the dangers of *us vs. them*, while my approach is framed by Mouffe's notion of the *inescapability* of this othering.

[23] *TOB* 15.

[24] "One must never exclude the possibility of violence that has nothing to do with mimetic desire but simply with scarcity ... [though it can always] become impregnated with mimesis" (*EC* 74).

Mouffe's rejection of the singular, Marxist diagnosis of class as driving all conflict; the human dimension of antagonism is variegated, fluid, and not attached to singular objects.

We can also see here resonances in Georg Simmel's and Sigmund Freud's notions that sharing a common enemy brings us together, even if the glue is to collectively oppose one's group to another by narcissistic "minor differences."[25] This has been explored in works like Hedges' *War Is a Force That Gives Us Meaning*, or Michael Ignatieff's observations that hatred of the enemy is the other side of self- and national-adulation.[26] Selengut employs Girard's theory to interpret the Israel/Palestine occupation, showing how the loss of a shared external enemy brought on paroxysms of internal violence in parties to the conflict.[27] We also see parallels in Waller's (*inter alia*) evolutionary reading of violence, in that cooperation and competition are not opposites but two sides of the same coin.[28] The interdisciplinary works employing mimetic theory toward conflict theory and peacebuilding are considerable.[29]

Girard regards desire in the modern era, amidst our dramatic social and cultural changes, as characterized by an increasing dissolution of differences, closing the distance between subjects and models. We can now *become one another* more than ever as traditional social taboos, hierarchies, and restraints are being dissolved; and the world is wagering, so to speak, that positive mimesis will win out over conflictual mimesis.[30] Girard's wariness on this modern wager is that modernity's increasing equality is a mixed blessing, in that it can in fact intensify social

---

[25] Sigmund Freud, *Civilization and Its Discontents*, 751; *RGMT* 65. Michael Ignatief, *The Warrior's Honor*, 61. "The communal feeling of groups requires, in order to complete it, hostility toward some minority" (Sigmund Freud, *The Standard Edition of the Complete Works of Sigmund Freud*, 23:90.

[26] E.g., "Emotions stirred up within commonality are more violent than those aroused by pure and radical difference; the closer, the more hostile" (Ignatieff, *The Warrior's Honor*, 47).

[27] Charles Selengut, *Sacred Fury*, 45–55.

[28] James E. Waller, "The Ordinariness of Extraordinary Evil," 154. Pierpaolo Antonello, "Maladaptation, Counterintuitiveness, and Symbolism," 52.

[29] E.g., Joel Hodge, "Terrorism's Answer to Modernity's Cultural Crisis"; Geneviève Souillac, "Violence, Mimesis, and War"; Jean Pierre Dupuy, *The Mark of the Sacred*; Scott Cowdell, Chris Fleming, and Joel Hodge, eds., *Violence Desire, and the Sacred*, vol 1; Scott M. Thomas, "Culture, Religion and Violence"; Vern Neufeld Redekop and Thomas Ryba, eds., *René Girard and Creative Reconciliation*; Phil Rose, "Divinizing Technology and Violence."

[30] *EC* 61f; *TOB* 15.

violence.[31] The modern shift from monarchy into democratic equality comes with a cost: "Idolatry of the tyrant as mediator 'is replaced by hatred of a hundred thousand rivals … democracy is one vast middle-class court where the courtiers are everywhere and the king is nowhere' – hence *'men will become Gods for each other.'"*[32]

And yet, Girard's proposed response to modernity's decaying hierarchies is neither conservative retrenchment nor progressive iconoclasm. In the former, one seeks to rebuild social stratifications or taboos on desire. Yet such opposition to our world's increasing equality is not only futile, but often immoral and can provoke more antagonism.[33] Equally implausible is the liberal aim to escape from imitation. Such "coolness" is partly admirable in its aversion to the crowd, eschewing conformity to group think. But the pretention to escaping imitation has its contradictions, as it remains locked in an antagonism and identity formed negatively against the others. Girard resonates with theological and ethical traditions that reject the prideful attempt to root one's self in one's self. Metaphysically, pride is the rejection of the Other as one's root source. Psychologically, pride is the inability to see one's self as always received, always pre-shaped by the other.[34] The assertion of the self-authenticated-self, evident in fashions of nonconformity, is as futile as it is arrogant.[35] Identity, we must admit, is always forged through the other. Imitation is psychically inescapable; we cannot simply "think" our way out of this; we must, paradoxically, choose our models wisely and imitate them.

So, while mimesis can be pacific, cooperative, and beneficial, it can also lead to a sort of grasping for the model, which can escalate into conflict. The answer – and this is a self-involving, normative theory – is that we must begin to see how our desires are not simply sincere and come "from our heart." Failing to admit this, human desire is characterized by a false, "romantic" misperception and "lying" character, seeing desire as autonomous and authentic. True maturation, instead, requires the "novelistic truth"[36] – realizing that others, in fact, suggest our desires to us. To recognize this distortion and one's self-opacity is to reject the desire to

---

[31] Palaver sees here the influence of Alexis de Tocqueville in *Democracy in America*, wherein the dissolution of a privileged class opens the door to universal competition (*DDN* 120; *RGMT* 61–2).

[32] Scott Cowdell, *René Girard and Secular Modernity*, 25, original emphasis; *DDN* 119.

[33] *VS* 88.

[34] *TH* 299–302, 307, 338, 389; Girard, *Theatre of Envy*, 333.

[35] *DDN* 100.

[36] *DDN* 17.

become the model, accept that the other is anterior to our self, and that there is no such thing as a self-made, self-complete person.[37] Rather, we are much more permeable and inter-dividual than our modern notions of the autonomous-self lead us to think. We must embrace our "lack of being" without anxiety – seeing it as a good that orients us toward others and the Ultimate beyond ourselves. Hence Augustine's famous embracing of his anxiety: our hearts are restless until they rest in God.

Idolatry, in psychological terms, is the impatient failure to accept our lack of being. To grasp at one another and their objects is to ultimately divinize others or ourselves as suppliers of being. Nationalism, we could say from Mouffe, is especially prone to this divinization in a collective idolatry – in positing a great unity over a society. Such metaphysical togetherness, as known in the state and its theo-political symbols, will remain an overarching theme in this book. National monotheism (what we will explore as "henotheism") is idolatrous in its reifying a unity that papers over divisions. As I will come to show, mature monotheism and pluralism refuse to take any consolation in this false unity construct, this idolatrous desire, even while us/them configurations remain inescapable, per Mouffe.

Girard's overall concept of mimesis and its connection with conflict stems from a long tradition, from Plato to Aquinas to Kant.[38] And while his concept of mimetic desire has many contemporary parallels and confirmations in the behavioral sciences, it also has some critics – which we will have to bypass here.[39] In summary, this first part of his theory concerns how we desire not just objects but *others*. Specifically, it is not that there is an "I" who desires the others; but my "I" is forged by the other's desire. Such mimesis inclines toward divinizing the other or the self, easily drawn into rivalry and conflict. All of this, however, remains on an abstract, synchronic level. The plot thickens as we consider how mimesis may have evolved over time, diachronically, in the human species to its current, very pronounced level.

---

[37] Ibid., 89, 101, 269, 272, 293, 305, 310; *EC* 148.

[38] For a review of Aeschylus, Plato, Aquinas, Hobbes, Spinoza, Rousseau, Kant, Max Scheler, Georg Simmel, Adam Smith, Walter Benjamin, and Auerbach on mimesis, see *RGMT* 66, 93, 101–2, 107, 109; *TH* 15; *EC* 42, 139–40.

[39] For psychological analysis, see Jean-Michel Oughourlian, *The Mimetic Brain*; Scott Garrels, ed, *Mimesis and Science*. For critique of the mimesis concept, see Bruce Chilton, *Jesus and His Context* and Philippe Lacoue-Labarthe, "Mimesis and Truth."

B. MIMESIS EVOLVED: THE VICTIMAGE MECHANISM
AS A GOD-MACHINE AND BASIS OF CULTURE

After Girard developed this concept of mimesis, he put it into conversation with evolutionary theory and anthropology, contributing to theories on the origin of culture and religion. He argues that mimesis, when understood as a genetic and cultural mutation that grew extravagantly among humans over millions of years, helps us understand how and why humans evolved with rituals, taboos, myths, and gods so intimately baked into our cultures. Mimesis helps us interpret not only conflict today, but it helps us understand numerous ethnographies of ancient cultures, blood sacrifices, and archaeologies of religion. This second part of his theory treats "the mimetic victimage mechanism" as the foundation of human culture, a generative mechanism by which proto-humanity crossed the threshold into humanity, distinguishing itself from the animals.[40]

While other animals have some minimal mimetic capacity, their pecking orders and dominance patterns generally keep them from imitating each other too much and escalating into mass violence that could extinguish their species.[41] But humans, on the other hand, are famously capable of imitating each other too much and escalating beyond dominance patterns into great violence and murder, both individually and on a group level. Where does this relative indifference to dominance patterns come from, and how is it that it hasn't yet extinguished our species?

A common answer – offered by social contract theorists and cognitive theorists of religion – is that *reason* has kept violence at bay: instead of going to war, early humans at some point started to make rational, cultural-linguistic agreements to give up violence in exchange for the group's role in monopolizing violence, thus enacting "the social contract." Being a rational animal is the foundation of our being a political animal. And later, once humanity's political organizing settled us down, granting us more time for speculation, "religion" was later invented as a first superstitious attempt at science, explaining natural phenomena and origins. Girard finds this all too cognition-driven, insufficiently accounting for how and why reason and language could manage violence before having experienced it. "In order to have language, an embryonic form of culture is needed, some kind of cultural sheltering from violence."[42] Such

---

[40] *EC* 144f.
[41] *TH* 90.
[42] *EC* 124; *TOB* 120.

a sheltering, he argues, came through the non-linguistic, pre-rational elements of religion, myth, and ritual – which are simultaneously the by-products and managers of violence. Human culture, at its root, is not the abrogation of violence but its channelization.

His evolutionary hypothesis is that wherever mimesis in the proto-human species was naturally selected (by genetic mutations and their fitness value) this began to overwhelm the older animal dominance patterns and pecking orders. Such mimetically increasing groups would have either destroyed themselves by imitating each other too much, or, stumbled upon a polarizing pattern: instead of an annihilating war of all against all, there mimetically formed a war of all against *one*. In cases where this pattern never consistently materialized, these groups probably died off.[43] Put differently, imagine a mob converging upon a single victim, bringing order to disorder; and then imagine how this could have also brought early humans together. In this framework, mimetic conflicts are resolved through (pre-cognitive, pre-rational) mimetic attention upon a scapegoat, and everyone else's joint attention on them. This directs all other potential rivalries onto one that is killed or expelled, ideally one from whom no vengeance can rebound.[44]

Girard argues that this pattern replaced dominance patterns and served as a generative, evolutionary mechanism whose mimetic problem is also its mimetic solution. This doubly useful feature made for a feedback loop[45] of natural selection over generations. Increasing mimetic capacity resulted in increasing intellectual fitness; but it also abetted mimetic conflict; and yet it could *also* – if the group stumbled upon such a pattern – abet increased mimetic attention upon a victim. This exercised and grew the mimetic faculty while bringing its violent by-product to a relatively pacific stability in a way the old dominance patterns never could. The very mimetic violence that seems a sign of chaos is precisely where mimetic scapegoating came to the rescue. The solution grew along with the problem. As such, the scapegoat mechanism is a group fitness machine.[46] This unconscious, serendipitous, evolving, and order-producing

---

[43] *EC* 67; *TOB* 86f, 90.

[44] *EC* 65.

[45] By feedback loop, the theory conceives of the long-term spiraling of group events that are "catastrophic but also generative in that they would trigger the foundation mechanism and at each step provide for more rigorous prohibitions within the group, and for a more effective ritual canalization toward the outside" (*TH* 96; 84, 88). The higher the level of crisis, the higher the intellectual level of human groups (*EC* 111; *TOB* 90).

[46] *EC* 99.

mechanism, over perhaps hundreds of thousands of years,[47] helped channel, protect, and thus catapult human mimetic-intelligence and brain size
into its current extreme disproportion compared with other species.[48] In
sum, as pre-humans slowly crossed a certain threshold of its naturally
selected mimetic capacity, this began to overwhelm the formerly effective
safeguards against violence (dominance patterns); this made possible
increased mimetic conflicts which, *simultaneously*, "produced its own
antidote by giving birth to the single victim mechanism, gods, and sacrificial rituals."[49]

We have here, in other words, a sociological or naturalist account of
religion – religion as not only about the cognitive quest for meaning or
spirituality[50] but an unconscious social mechanism in human evolution,
wherein genetic and cultural mutations are naturally selected in their
coevolving around a mimetic-victimage dynamic. Let us define the key
terms of this account: gods, myths, taboos, and sacrificial rituals.

i. Gods

"Gods," for Girard emerged as the misperceived victims (or scapegoats)
of group murder.[51] As is often the case with group killings, a victim of the
violence is often demonized – a projection of a group's problems, chaos,
or social crisis.[52] But a victim is also retrospectively worshipped, divinized
for how their death "solved" and calmed the crisis; and they continue to

---

[47] Ibid., 97, 105.
[48] He cites anthropologists and neuroscientists like Lewin, Foley, Tomasello, and Donald
concerning human brain growth tripling in the last three million years, wildly outpacing
other species' rates and brain/body ratios, begging for explanations of some irregular,
almost "artificial" or cultural nature (*TH* 84, 88, 100; *EC* 105).
[49] *ISS* 94; *EC* 65; *TH* 94.
[50] Cowdell, *René Girard and Secular Modernity*, 59; Girard, *Sacrifice*, 23; *TH* 13, 32.
[51] *TH* 81, 99. "When I say 'god,' I mean a sacred force that is believed to be outside the
community and is powerful enough to punish as well as to protect it ... the victim is
always seen as the god or replaces it, since this victim brings back peace with his or her
death" (*EC* 119; 66). On the resurrection of the victim of disorder: *TOB* 35. This
definition need not necessarily contradict more conventional etymologies of god – like,
"the luminous heaven of day" per De Lubac, or "to be first, to be powerful," or that gods
as ancestors/heroes (Henri De Lubac, *The Discovery of God*, 18; Mark Smith, *God in
Translation* [hereafter *GIT*], 15; Isa 8:19; 29:4; 1 Sam 28:13). In Hebrew, "gods" (*'lym*)
are akin in spelling to "chiefs, rams" (*'lym/'ylm*) (*GIT* 149), suggestive of sacrificial-
political genes per mimetic theory.
[52] *EC* 226; *GR* 219.

save in their "absence," as we attend to their memory. For Girard, the instinctual unity forged in group violence, and its resolution in expulsion, slowly birthed in the early human mind the capacity for a sort of transcendence: "even though the mechanism is totally endogenous, it is perceived as something *external*."[53] So, in the earliest stages of human evolution, "the sacred" or divinity is not "applied" to the victim, as if it already existed as a concept in the mind. Rather, the sacred is *born* in proto-human history through this traumatic, intensely contrastive experience between violence and peace, danger and tranquility, hinged upon the victim. Theologian James Alison has seen in this an anthropological description of "original sin": the birth of humanity's unique consciousness itself coincides with mis-remembering our transference upon victims.[54] The *sacred* as such "is the sum of human assumptions resulting from collective transferences focused on a reconciliatory victim at the conclusion of a mimetic crisis."[55] The sacred is early humanity externalizing its violence and learning to control it – "transforming it into a transcendent and ever-present danger to be kept in check by the appropriate rites."[56] This bequeaths to us the *mysterium tremendum et fascinans*, the sense of blessing and curse that surrounds the sacred, as well as the perceived "externality," transcendence, or perpetual absence of the god.[57]

Given this ambivalence, many of the gods have monstrous, hybridic forms, of being both similar and salutary to humans while different and evil: "The wrath exacted upon a double to expel them from the safety of the community imputes monstrous characteristics on this other."[58] From our perspective today – when seen through ethnocentric studies of tribal peoples – this transcendence seems "distorted," superstitious, or idolatrous cognition. But the sacred is not a distortion of or additive to otherwise previously clear cognition. Rather, the sacred helped *birth* cognition. This early sacred "can be defined as 'social transcendence' in

---

[53] *EC* 37, 81, 105f; *TH* 28.
[54] Alison, *The Joy of Being Wrong*, 35; 133; 224–5.
[55] *TH* 42.
[56] *VS* 134.
[57] Raymund Schwager, *Must There Be Scapegoats?*, 19. Or, the sacred is "violence seen as something exterior to man and henceforth as a part of all the other outside forces that threaten mankind. Violence is the heart and secret soul of the sacred. We have yet to learn how man succeeds in positing his own violence as an independent being" (*VS* 31).
[58] *EC* 115; 68.

Durkheim's terms, or idolatrous transcendence from the point of view of the Judeo-Christian perspective."[59]

Numerous creation myths entail gods who were killed and dismembered, perhaps cannibalized, to create the world through their body parts. Girard regards these as distorted memories of *real*, historical events. Their bodies are mythologized as the source of their tribe, nation, land, and culture because their lynching truly did cohere the group order. Hence the foundations of Rome are laid on the carcass of Remus;[60] the assassinated Krishna makes the world; Purusa is dismembered to create the universe;[61] the cliff-thrown Tikarau of the Solomon Islands gives birth to the entire cultural order;[62] from the ashes of Milomaki of the Yahuna (burned alive), the first paxiuba palm in the world grows; Ninhursag creates "mankind out of clay and animates it with the blood of a slain god"; an Ojibway god was thrown into the lake by his fellow thunder-gods, from whom come all the Great Lakes' animal totems; Omorka is cloven in half to make heaven and earth; the world is made of the body parts of P'an Ku, the Sumerian Lamga gods, or Kingu and Tiamat.[63] Barbara Sproul, independent of Girard, calls this type of creation-from-a-body "typical." Mircea Eliade points out several more examples in the Middle East and China.[64] Thus Girard concludes: "Every time the scapegoat mechanism works, a new god emerges ... all gods begin first by dying."[65]

ii. Myths

"Myths" are the distorted remembrance and retelling of real group-killings into a tolerable story, re-drawing the group together through imputing guilt to the killed victim and innocence to the lynching group.

---

[59] Ibid., 198. "An effective scapegoat is necessarily perceived as a divinity who came down incognito from heaven to visit the community. The mysterious visitor treats the people very harshly at first but ultimately rescues them from all harm" (Vattimo and Girard, *Christianity, Truth, and Weakening Faith*, 99).

[60] T. P. Wiseman, *Remus*, 9–11.

[61] *Rigveda* 10.90.

[62] Raymond Firth, *Tikopia Ritual and Belief*, 230. See also René Girard, "Origins," 29.

[63] Barbara Sproul, *Primal Myths*, 19, 114, 121. Tikva Frymer-Kensky, "The Atrahasis Epic and Its Significance for Our Understanding of Genesis 1–9," 155.

[64] Mircea Eliade, *A History of Religious Ideas*, 1:72. See also Eric Voegelin, *Order and History*, vol 1: *Israel and Revelation* (hereafter *OH*), 44.

[65] *EC* 199, 220; *ISS* 16; Friedrich Nietzsche, *The Gay Science*, §125. J. Z. Smith emphasizes the crucial feature in divinity: "immortality is not a prime characteristic of divinity: gods die" (Jonathan Z. Smith, "Dying and Rising Gods," 521f).

They express and galvanize the unanimity of a group's expulsion, keeping the process from being unveiled of its cognitive dissonance and thus rendered ineffective. "Myth is primarily the accusation of the victim presented as guilty."[66] Myths, then, are both about forgetting and remembering. Although – given that myths are a by-product of our interacting with something as old as violence – implicit, non-verbal "myths" would have emerged long before even language.

The components that Girard finds in explicit myths, as recorded in ethnographies and histories, are as follows: (1) the breakdown of social distinctions, rules, taboos, and castes, known as a crisis of undifferentiation. This breakdown "corresponds to the orgiastic elements in rituals," wherein conventional distinctions are transgressed so as to reproduce the crisis and its ritual resolution. (2) Some sign that singles out a villain; (3) an expulsion/killing of this villain, usually depicted as a hero "because he/she eventually saves the community" through their death. Myths then usually end in the imposition of taboos and the offering of sacrifices.[67]

The logical inconsistencies apparent in so many myths, in spite of their diversity, Girard writes, "point to the presence of a common cause of logical distortion at the threshold of human culture. I believe this cause is the original founding murder, and myths do their best – unconsciously at first, and then more consciously – to erase the traces of scapegoating."[68] Some myths have existed for so long and been cleaned up for so many generations, that the original violence may be entirely washed out and forgotten – leaving behind a story almost unrecognizable to the original event.[69]

When we can today see the clear scapegoating in an old story – like in witch hunts or Jews poisoning medieval wells – and we can see it is a "myth," this disrupts what would have been its original "fitness value" of maintaining group unanimity. But if a lynching could be misremembered in the palatable form of killers = innocent, killed = guilty, as myth does, this makes it no longer a "scapegoating" story but a necessary and good expulsion. Effective myths then will never show clear signs of a "scapegoating theme." Hiding this helps gain unanimous assent to the group's

---

[66] *EC* 146; 68, 85, 159, 196.

[67] Ibid., 162; *TH* 142.

[68] *EC* 163.

[69] "[In Greek philosophy] gods must be neither criminals nor victims and, because [the gods] are not recognized as scapegoats, their acts of violence and criminality – the signs that point to them as victims – including the crisis itself, must be gradually eliminated" (John Ranieri, *Disturbing Revelation*, 196).

"necessary" violence contained in the myth. As such, the memory and its repetition represent the community's unanimity, its "cleansing," its justice, its protection. "Archaic religions were based on a complete absence of criticism regarding this unanimity."[70] For Girard, mythical unity obscuring the marginalization of victims is the social function of "mythology" – *muthos* from the root *mu*, "to close" or "to keep secret."[71]

We can see deep resonance between this account of mythology, as the distorted mode of cultural consciousness, and Mouffe's notion of "common sense" and reason. It is not that reason and myth have no connection to reality. Reason and myth stem from real events and founding divisions that are subsequently enculturated (not through rational objectivity or intentional invention) into norms: they stem from primordial divisions and, "through a process of sedimentation, the political origin of those contingent practices has been erased; they have become naturalized."[72] In sum, myths safeguard cultural unity through distorted remembrance of its own violence, and they were naturally selected as a form of protective misapprehension. Myths of collective unity – and their relation to founding exclusions – are crucial to our discussion of monotheism and the refusal to divinize victims.

iii. Taboos and Rituals

Taboos and rituals are two sides of the same coin. Both were naturally selected in human culture as gestures that either avoid any escalation into mimetic crisis (taboo) or carefully reproduce such a crisis for the sake of its resolution (ritual). Taboos and prohibitions restrict the contagiousness of mimetic escalation by forbidding anything that catalyzes acquisitive gestures, antagonism, and thus disorder and violence – anything resembling the originary crisis. Taboos dissimulate this suppression "beneath the major symbols of the sacred, such as contamination, pollution, etc.,"[73] protecting the group from the dangers of undifferentiation. "Rituals" – and most conspicuously sacrificial ones – are attempts to repeat the

---

[70] René Girard, *Battling to the End* (hereafter *BTE*), 23.

[71] "*Muo* means to close one's eyes or mouth, to mute the voice, or to remain mute .... The literal meaning of Greek word for truth, *aletheia*, is 'to stop forgetting" (Gil Bailie, *Violence Unveiled*, 33) – or disclosure, unconcealed. "Myth is thus the lie that hides the founding lynching, which speaks to us about the gods, but never about the victims that the gods used to be" (*BTE* 22).

[72] AG 89.

[73] VS 13, 16, 19–21; TH 10, 13, 17.

cathartic effect of the originally spontaneous murder through a controlled re-sparking of a mini-crisis and resolution.[74] Rituals imitate the formerly dangerous but "miraculous event that put an end to the crisis," substituting new victims for the first.[75] Rituals and taboos are basically what one must do and not do to protect the community – and their instinctual necessity is even more basic to the sacred than symbols, words, myths, and gods. "Archaic religions have little to do with gods and a lot to do with two institutions: sacrifices and prohibitions ... their survival value justifies, *for a while*, their compromises with human violence."[76]

Taboos and rituals give boundary and form to the sacred, which is homologous with violence. "The sacred is violence, but if religious man worships violence it is only insofar as the worship of violence is supposed to bring peace."[77] If these archaic religious institutions contain violence, it is because they restrain violent disorder through a careful expression of violence. The most obvious examples of such containment are ritualized and mock warfare, contests and duels, sports, regularized raiding, or, simply, immolation of human- or animal victims. In each case, the point is to repeat, in a controlled way, the founding chaos and resolution that brought the group together. "Ritual is an effort to repeat the scapegoat mechanism."[78] There is ultimately no antinomy in human evolution between normal order and exceptional chaos, regularity and upheaval. For the exception – in group violence, both chaotic and ritualized – has been crucial to humanity's adaptive mechanisms.[79]

Blood sacrifice is the ritual repetition of an originally spontaneous murder, its conditions, and its resolution through immolating a replacement victim.[80] Girard argues that the fitness value of such sacrifice explains why virtually all primitive religions seem to have practiced some

---

[74] *EC* 169; *TH* 19f.

[75] *EC* 28, 103.

[76] René Girard, "The Bloody Skin of the Victim," 60.

[77] *VS* 32.

[78] *EC* 70, 169.

[79] Girard suggests this insight is not his but as old as the pre-Socratics. See, for example, Anaximander: "The source from which existing things derive their existence is also that to which they return at their destruction, according to necessity; for they give justice and make reparation to one another for their injustice, according to the arrangement of Time" (*TOB* 15; Kathleen Freeman, *Ancilla to the Pre-Socratic Philosophers*, 19).

[80] "This victim ... [is] a *symbol* of the proto-event; it is *the first symbolic sign* ever invented by these hominids. It is the first moment in which something *stands* for *something else* ... in order to deal with the cognitive complexity of this handling of an emerging symbolic sphere, a larger size of brain was then required, and the scapegoat mechanism acted as a form of evolutionary pressure, as an element of natural selection" (*EC* 107).

form of it.[81] We can see why the gods "required" sacrifices: the original victim continues to "exist" in their absence because they indeed continue to save as we obey their command to offer sacrifices in their memory. The acquiring of humans during raids or wars, to later be sacrificed, or the replacement of such sacrifices with animals, or the group taunting and killing of animals we see in Çatalhöyük's archaeological record, finds its explanation in the fitness benefits of this mechanism.[82] In sum, it is not that religion "causes" violence or scapegoating. Rather, "religion itself is produced by the scapegoat mechanism,"[83] which from the earliest stages in human evolution, contained violence, in the double sense of restrain and express.

iv. Politics and the Scapegoat Mechanism

The rudiments of political order derive from the decisions and distinctions stemming from the scapegoat process, and thus similarly contain violence. We will eventually talk about the "Mosaic" distinction, in its division of true and false religion; but mimetic theory identifies a primordial distinction crucial to all human order that would have preceded monotheism by perhaps hundreds of thousands of years. The scapegoat mechanism is this distinction, hinging upon the victim's death, giving birth to all cultural, social, and moral distinctions. Crisis is characterized by the undifferentiation of good and bad, wherein the distinction between true and false is undecided. But, as Palaver notes, "the scapegoat mechanism clarifies this uncertainty: the victim is guilty; the others are innocent." From this elementary differentiation, stem "all social distinctions such as ranks, hierarchy."[84] The tragic decisiveness around which culture and politics hinge is an echo of the fundamental decision on the victim. The victim and enemy both constitute the boundary and form of the political community.[85]

---

[81] On this point there is a lack of substantiation, as the hunter-gatherer record of sacrifice is unclear. Girard admitted that Walter Burkert's hunting hypothesis (that *hunting*, not group lynching of other humans, gave birth to sacrifice) to be somewhat consonant with his theory in light of evidence of animal-scapegoating in Çatalhöyük's artwork. See René Girard, "Animal Scapegoating at *Çatalhöyük*"; Ian Hodder, ed., *Violence and the Sacred in the Ancient Near East.*

[82] Ian Hodder, ed., *Religion in the Emergence of Civilization*, 344, 348.

[83] *EC* 108.

[84] Wolfgang Palaver, "A Girardian Reading of Schmitt's Political Theology," 49f.

[85] "De-cision," with its etymology in "cutting off," perhaps even slitting the throat of the victim, is intricately tied with the victim. Decision is not *based* on law but creates law from the state of exception (Giorgio Agamben, *The Time That Remains*, 105).

Political monarchy – a key topic in the coming chapters – is yet again a *by-product* of the victim mechanism, not a cognitive invention of the social contract. Examining the sacrificial rituals that surround enthrone-ment, Girard argues, monarchic power emerged from the tribal practices of obtaining prisoners, perhaps through ritual raiding, and consecrating them for eventual immolation. While held, they enjoyed the community's protection and taboo: they were not to be killed outside the confines of ritual.[86] Leading up to the day of their sacrifice, during their holding, they were treated like celebrities, enduring whatever combination of group ridicule, derision, or acclaim. As these practices became increasingly effective lightning rods for groups, the time between their consecration and immolation would have increased. The longer the wait, the more these human sacrifices morphed into monarchs.[87] Nature selected for the institution's coalescing mimetic attention, making the group safer from itself. This helps explain the apparently irrational rules and rituals sur-rounding coronations and enthronements, in which is a king is somehow linked with victimage. In some societies, a king is forced to eat taboo foods and commit incest – and thereafter covered in the blood of an animal slain next to him. In others, a king's enthronement entails the group threatening or hitting him as well as expressions of adoration.[88] The point of the rituals is to "channel mimetic antagonism" and make him responsible for "the transformation that moves the community from mimetic violence to the order of ritual."[89]

This again suggests sovereignty, monarchy, and political authority are not the intentional, rational creation of humans consenting to the social contract that founds legitimacy. Why would aggressively egalitarian hunter-gatherers – our earliest and oldest form of human order, among whom the dictum "those who exalt themselves will be humbled" seems to have been violently enforced[90] – ever have opted for a king? The answer is that the earliest political communities did not choose rulers; they mobbed

---

[86] This bears an intriguing resemblance to Giorgio Agamben's excavation of the *homo sacer*, though the pattern is inverted: the cursed and hallowed oath breaker can be killed with impunity but not sacrificed (Giorgio Agamben, *Homo Sacer*, 2, 72).

[87] Paul Dumouchel, "A Covenant Among Beasts," 17; *EC* 137.

[88] *TH*, 72. *VS* 274–80; *ISS* 92; *EC* 116–8; Cf. J. Z. Smith, "The Domestication of Sacrifice," 199. For ethnography on the oscillation between ritual warfare and a scapegoat king, see Simon Simonse, *Kings of Disaster*. "Both animal domestication and monarchy are 'by-products' of sacrificial rituals" (*EC* 169; *TH* 51–8.).

[89] *TH* 52.

[90] See Christopher Boehm, "Retaliatory Violence in Human Prehistory," 518–34; 522, 527f: "Well-armed egalitarians will not allow enough authority to develop for alpha-

scapegoats and ritually selected victims. Victims turned into kings. It is no surprise, then, that in the great ancient temple-religions "the king was the supreme priest"[91] – for he is still the mediator of the sacrificial regime, just redirected. The throne emerged from the altar.[92] This pattern eventually evolved so far from its roots that we eventually came to regard, as we tend to now, kings, presidents, or governments as "natural," rational, common-sense inventions of "leadership" in human culture. But these are not the result of reason. With Mouffe, we can see our political structures as resulting not from reason but "sedimented hegemonic practices," which – in slowly losing touch with their origins and founding violence – we confuse with nature and common sense.

Insofar as this is true, the Israelite notion of a "Messiah," rooted in the Davidic dynasty, should not be exempt here. The familiar etymology of "anointed one," should include in its deep genes the scapegoat-king pattern.[93] Anointed *to rule* was surely a root meaning, but this was inextricable from the anointing of the sacrificial animal at the Jerusalem temple – always accompanied by libations. The very notion of such an "anointing," to mimetic theory ears, echoes of a consecration to be sacrificed. James Williams, for example, notes how the "anointed" King Saul bears "obvious traces of a scapegoat king," being the target of violence but also enjoying sacred protection, in that he could not be killed without incurring great guilt.[94] In any case, Girard's overarching point is to penetrate how monarchy contains group violence: not merely by rational or strong "leadership" but more essentially the polarizing scapegoat.

As our coming chapters will dwell in Egypt, I briefly note how this scapegoat framework offers new ways to interpret the famous pharaonic monarchy. An intense cultural feedback loop, likely intensified by the Nile's bounty, appears to have accelerated ancient Egypt's transition from smaller, tribal structures organized around scapegoat-poles into imperial

---

style peacemakers to step in and stop hot conflicts." See also Ian Armit, "Violence and Society in the Deep Human Past," 502, 510, 512.

[91] Rodney Stark, *The Discovery of God*, 75.

[92] *TH* 52, 57; Brian Collins, *The Head Beneath the Altar*, 135, 189. For the ritual of bowing before kings as a reconfiguration of sacrifice (self-immolation), see Desiderio Parrilla Martínez, "Mimesis, Ritual Sacrifice, and Ceremony of *Proskynesis*."

[93] Raymond Brown, *Introduction to the New Testament*, appendix 1. Cf. Burton Mack, *The Christian Myth*, 114.

[94] 1 Sam 24, 26; 26:9; James G. Williams, *The Bible, Violence, and the Sacred*, 134–5. Wolfgang Palaver, *Politik und Religion bei Thomas Hobbes*, 1, 217–23.

monarchy. Commanding extravagant devotion and totalizing organizing powers, from the moment many pharaohs were born, people were preparing for their deaths. This transformation was evidently less severe in less bounteous lands; we see much more hybridic, less galvanized kinds of scapegoat-kings in Sudan even up into the twentieth century.[95] There, "kings" were targets of threats or death if they failed to stop blight or other problems; on the other hand, if warring with nearby tribes monopolized the group attention, then the king became an uninteresting marginal figure. The ancient pharaonic office was comparatively far more intensified and singular in form – with the staggering pyramids as just one testament to ancient Egypt's transformation of the victim into the sovereign. It is of great interest that some of the first imperial forms of "monotheism" emerge there.

v. Religion Domesticated Humanity

Girard argues that numerous anatomical and cultural features can be understood as by-products of the accelerated "artificial selection" that the above mimetic mechanisms wrought on human evolution. Our omnivorous digestive tract, our birth canal, our brain/cranium size, our recessed incisors are all clues for consideration. Animal sacrifice's growing importance gave birth to animal domestication,[96] which otherwise had no immediate fitness value in contrast with the economics of hunting and gathering.[97] And it was only the growing importance of sacrificial sites that would have catalyzed human settlement; we did not settle first and then invent religion, as Marx and the old Neolithic Revolution theory had it.[98]

---

[95] On the oscillation between passive victim and active king, see Simonse's study of scapegoat-kingship in Sudan. Simon Simonse, "Tragedy, Ritual and Power in Nilotic Regicide," 67–100; Simon Simonse, "Kings and Gods As Ecological Agents," 31–46.

[96] Girard observes how societies that never abandoned human sacrifice also never domesticated animals, like pre-Colombian Mexico (*EC 117*; *TOB* 88f; David Carrasco, *City of Sacrifice*).

[97] E.g., S. Angus Martin, "The Origins of Agriculture," 96; Marshall Sahlins, *Stone Age Economics*; *EC* 121.

[98] *EC* 117, 121, 124, 141. This branch of his theory enjoys considerable archaeological engagement in Çatalhöyük research: Ian Hodder, ed., *Religion in the Emergence of Civilization*. See also Joseph Watts, et al., "Ritual Human Sacrifice Promoted and Sustained the Evolution of Stratified Societies."

Cognition, language, symbols, and reason itself are also understood as not vaguely emergent faculties of human evolution but as contingently constructed through the mimetic, victim mechanism. Language emerged from a precognitive matrix, in which its first index is the dangerous experience of a collective violence, subsequent peace, and the victim's corpse as humanity's Ur-symbol.[99] Religion, contra cognitive theories of religion, was not the superstitious distortion of a previously clear cognition. Rather, our particular form of cognition *owes* its blurry birth to the leaven of an exogenous "sacred."

In summary, this second aspect of mimetic theory argues sacrifice domesticated humanity and the gods really did create humanity – not the other way around.[100] Religion "contained violence" at the generative core of human evolution.[101] Religion is not an additive to human nature. Primitive myths, religions, and taboos ought not be dismissed as mere superstitions, fables, or failed-science; rather, they are protective misapprehension. It would take us too far afield to contextualize the anthropological tradition into which Girard entered, as would detailing the recent archaeological, anthropological, and psychological corroborations.[102]

This quadrant of his theory most resembles a falsifiable scientific hypothesis, but it can be read in a strict or loose way. In the strict sense, this is indeed an archaeological hypothesis about what exactly facilitated human origins – from sacrifice preceding settlement to the exact functioning of our brain, etc. A considerable set of articles and monographs in

---

[99] *EC* 37, 105f: "In order to have a symbol, you must have totality . . .. One needs a *center of signification*, and the *scapegoated victim* provides this center."

[100] "Man makes religion; religion does not make man ... by dispelling the illusion, the divine substance is reincorporated in man, and man becomes superman" (Karl Marx, "Contribution to the Critique of Hegel's Philosophy of Right. Introduction," 43; Eric Voegelin, *Science, Politics, and Gnosticism* [hereafter *SPG*], 64, 96).

[101] *EC* 72; 125.

[102] The analysis of gods as products of immanent historical events emerges at least as early as Euhemerism, from the fourth century BCE philosopher, Euhemeris of Messene. The method is visible in Greek philosophers like Xenophanes, who spoke of projecting ourselves onto divinity. The Euhemeristic method became useful in early Christian apologetics. Tertullian, for example, argued that the gods were in fact misrepresented humans (Tertullian, *Apologeticus*, 10, frag 3, regarding Saturn as a man).

The Orphics saw murder as the veiled basis of cultic sacrifice, and thereby are among the few groups who did not offer sacrifice in the classical era, seeing meat as an estrangement from the gods, searching for a time before murderous sacrifice began (Daniel Ulucci, *The Christian Rejection of Animal Sacrifice*, 61 n163).

Besides the tradition of demystifying gods, a more modern anthropological tradition into which Girard entered contains, e.g., Robertson Smith, Durkheim, Frazer, Radcliffe-Brown, Malinowski, Banier, Fiske, Mauss, Hubert.

recent years have developed this, much of which can be corroborated in non-"Girardian" research.[103] Notably, Girard refused to give his hypothesis any specific dating and classifications, other than referencing the importance of the Paleolithic innovation of wielding stones with *Homo habilis* 1.8mya. By that time, nature must have selected at least some amount of fear and taboos regarding the increased dangers and excesses of internecine violence – and he leaves it vaguely at that.[104]

But, taken in a loose sense, his scapegoat-foundation idea simply serves to locate mimesis, desire, violence management, and religion as all *prior* to reason – aligning with Mouffe's notion of reason stemming from hegemony. Kant saw this as a fundamental question for the whole of human order: whether a rational social contract came first, and power followed, or whether power came first and laws and rationality followed.[105] Kant saw it as dangerous to unearth an answer, but Girard affirms the latter: that religion, taboo, and law all channeled and restrained an anterior violence – even while thereby abetting it. Reason didn't corrupt into religion; rather, reason grows *from* this originary matrix. In this view, civilization is not the problem, *pace* Rousseau; it is a symptom. Reason alone is not a terminal answer to violence, as reason itself is a symptom of the sacred's containing violence. Nor even is the problem "competition," against which one should champion rational "cooperation." Rather, both competition and cooperation are two sides of the same mimetic coin.

In the loosest possible sense, Girard's theory simply urges us to see how religion, as the fundamental cultural dimension, was generative of our biological and psychological structure from our origins – for better and worse. This means coming to grips with the fact that humanity, as the great anthropologist Roy Rappaport argues, evolved from our proto-human condition through the mediation of religion.[106] This offers all the more reason to take stock of the radical religious changes from poly- to monotheism in recent millennia, as matters of evolutionary significance. Crucial to the monotheism question, here, is how the political order is a by-product and expression of the victim mechanism. The violence of the political order is natively religious, sacred, even when it

---

[103] E.g., Pierpaolo Antonello and Paul Gifford, eds., *Can We Survive Our Origins?*; Pierpaolo Antonello and Paul Gifford, eds., *How We Became Human*; Chris Haw, "Human Evolution and the Single Victim Mechanism."

[104] *EC* 113.

[105] *RGMT* 275; Immanuel Kant, *Metaphysics of Morals*, 95.

[106] Roy Rappaport, *Ritual and Religion in the Making of Humanity*, 1.

is not employing "religious" language. For violence *is* the originary sacred. The polytheistic religions that grew among ancient empires and city-states contained this violence. This archaic sacred – in its gods, taboos, and rituals – constituted the ancient political context from which biblical monotheism grew and which it critiqued. Here we have something like a schematic "political theology of polytheism" from which Girard's understanding of biblical revelation and monotheism, we will see, breaks.

C. TRUTH AND BIBLICAL REVELATION

If human thought and culture are so thoroughly wrought with *misapprehension*, how could one ever step *outside* of it to have offered the above analyses? Girard's answer is that the biblical tradition has made this possible, even if in an "indirect and unperceived" way.[107] When compared and contrasted with other myths, tribal religions, and the entire polytheistic framework, the biblical tradition for Girard, starting with its monotheism, advances us beyond the misapprehension of early religion.

Girard argues that the biblical tradition not only birthed a unique sensitivity to victims but also *epistemologically made possible* anthropological knowledge of the founding principle of human culture, summarized above.[108] The Bible does not just offer some supernatural myth for those who assent; it demythologizes myth and offers knowledge about humanity, promising "to teach us the most about the origin and operation in human societies of what the Gospels call earthly powers."[109] So the above ability to analyze the victimary foundations of culture and see scapegoating more clearly, he insists, is not his insight, nor of the passive accruements of reason over time. He is simply representing in modern anthropological terms what the biblical tradition has called "revelation," which he defines as "the true *representation* of what had never been completely represented or what had been falsely represented,"[110] namely, the scapegoat mechanism. This revealing of the unconscious operations of

---

[107] *TH* 138, 161.
[108] Fleming, *René Girard*, 114.
[109] *TOB* 40.
[110] As such, the New Testament "spells out everything we need to reject our own mythic view of ourselves, our belief in our own innocence" (*ISS* 127; 137). Or, "revelation is the reproduction of the victimary mechanism by showing the truth, knowing that the victim is innocent and that everything is based on mimeticism" (*EC* 205).

human culture has, in his analysis, begun to subvert the protective sacred and has, perhaps more than any factor in history, dramatically shaped the world since.

Just like his first idea of mimesis, one can divide up this part of his theory into two parts: (1) his synchronic interpretation of the biblical symbols leads him to suggest (2) that the biblical tradition has had a diachronic sociological effect on society and the dissolution of the protective sacred over the last two millennia. This book concerns especially that first, synchronic concept: his reading of biblical symbols and monotheism and their revelatory value compared with other religions and mythologies. After reviewing that, I follow noting how he reads the Common Era as undergoing a destabilizing exorcism, as it were.

i. Biblical Monotheism and Siding with Victims

By "biblical revelation" Girard means that the Bible, in contradistinction to the mythology and polytheism of its context, uniquely takes the side of the victims, defending their innocence. In itself, this assertion is not entirely controversial; Max Weber famously noted the unique attention the Tanakh devotes to victims (e.g., in his comparison of Tammuz with Deutero-Isaiah and a "fundamental change of meaning" therein).[111] Simone Weil also wrote on the tendency for the Bible to side with victims.[112]

But unlike Girard's expansive walk through great literature or a meticulous survey of ethnography and human evolution, he argues for this biblical uniqueness through a fairly limited set of myths compared with biblical myths, as follows. Regular mythologies of a divinized scapegoat, he writes, might take a form like Oedipus, who would have originally been some historic lynchee who was demonized for his crimes (like incest and murder) and later divinized, resultant from his being victimized. But, compare Oedipus with its literary cousin, the story of Joseph in Genesis. In Oedipus, the "message is that the plague will be cured if and when the Thebans expel from their midst the right victim, the individual

---

[111] Max Weber, *Ancient Judaism*, 19–22, 86, 174, 475–7, 492–5; Fleming, *René Girard*, 124. Weber, for example, discusses Tammuz and a guiltless martyrdom vs. the dying and rising vegetation gods trope.

[112] Simone Weil, *Intimations of Christianity among the Ancient Greeks*, 60, 137, 161; Simone Weil, *Letter to a Priest*, 14, 18, 24, 64.

about whom they can all agree that he is the one who brought them the plague."[113] By contrast, Joseph is not divinized but humanized; the accusations against him turn out to be false; his being scapegoated was the effect of jealousy and resentment. The story does not make him a god-demon-scapegoat but insists on his innocence and exposes the mindless vengeance of his accusers – ultimately "rehabilitating the victim" and imbuing a "desacralizing effect."[114]

Girard sees this theme strewn throughout the Bible, where the point is not so much historical referentiality of its myths as its substantive contrast in meaning with other myths.[115] The Bible may entail a mythical form but with a reversal of the mythical relationship to the victim; as such, the Bible offers us myth in reverse, or a "founding murder in reverse."[116] He sees in the biblical tradition an "attempt to get back to origins and look once again at constitutive acts of transference so as to discredit and annul them – so as to contradict and demystify the myths."[117] The Bible teaches us to sympathize with Abel, laying blame on Cainite culture, "showing that this culture is completely based upon the unjust murder of Abel. The story of Romulus and Remus does not lay blame upon the city of Rome since the murder of Remus is presented to us as being justified."[118] And the Bible extends this violence-demystification as a running theme, exonerating victims from Abel onward.[119] The Psalms are the first major body of literature "written largely from the perspective of the victim," often of one being hemmed in by enemies.[120] Job defends the afflicted against group accusations. Isaiah's Suffering Servant centers on the one afflicted by a mob; the Prophets are always siding with the victims or the poor. The supposed antipathy toward sacrifice in many prophets bespeaks their

---

[113] *ISS* 132f. The Oedipus myth makes him indeed guilty of incest (René Girard, *The Scapegoat*, 103).

[114] *TH* 152.

[115] "The story doesn't have to be referential to be true. It is true in so far as it is *the denial of the myths*" (*EC* 200).

[116] *BTE* xv.

[117] *TH* 153; *EC* 141.

[118] René Girard, *Girard Reader* (hereafter *GR*), 153. In contrast with a similar myth, "The murder of Remus appears as an action that was perhaps to be regretted but was justified by the victim's transgression" (*TH* 146). And while Romulus became a High priest who incarnates Roman power, Cain is not divinized.

[119] *TH* 147, 149.

[120] E.g., "I hear the whispering of many – terror all around! – as they scheme together against me, as they plot to take my life" (Ps 31:13).

awareness of the faultiness of the whole system down to its foundation in the victim.[121]

The Gospels all hinge upon a founding murder, Christ's unjust lynching, crystallized in the observation "he was hated without reason."[122] The Passion is, in Girard's analysis, the first historic identification of the "unconscious" as woven into a social matrix of misapprehension (not the sense of the unconscious as an "individualistic depth" as one finds in Jung): forgive them, Father, for they know not what they do.[123] In each case, a chief theme is "God taking the side of the victim," or stories written from "the perspective of the victim," emphasizing the innocence of scapegoats in contradistinction with myth taking the side of the victimizer. Summarizing the substance of this revelation, one often finds the refrain in Girard that in myths victims are to be blamed while the group is always innocent, and the biblical texts reverse this valence: "In revealing their innocence, the Judeo-Christian tradition desacralizes scapegoats and brings the age of myth to a close."[124] The Passion, in particular, "fully *represents* the mimetic mechanism, and thus it can reveal its nature, by the sheer fact that it always sees the essential point: the innocence of the scapegoat victim."[125] By contrast, mythic cycles, since our origins, evaded clear representation of this mechanism. Or, if some did, this could have diminished their collective abilities to polarize violence and thereby court extinction.[126]

While the above might seem a mere bias for his native religion, Girard suggests he is simply developing upon the insights of the biblical tradition's self-proclaimed enemy, Friedrich Nietzsche. Nietzsche, by Girard's lights, is the first to clearly point out that, while the Christ-story appears in the *structure* of myth – for example, the story of a killed and resurrected god like "Dionysius," who Nietzsche treats as a metonymy for all mythology – it radically diverges on its internal *content*. This similarity,

---

[121] Girard may overemphasize the prophets' anti-sacrificial message. One can argue most prophets condemned the *misuse* of sacrifice, devoid of a context of justice, but did not condemn sacrifice itself. See Ulucci, *The Christian Rejection of Animal Sacrifice.*

[122] John 15:25; Ps 35:19; *TH* 238; Girard, *The Scapegoat*, 114.

[123] Girard, *The Scapegoat*, 110–1. "Father forgive them because they don't know what they are doing" (Lk 23:34) is taken to be the first exposition of the collective unconscious, echoed in Acts 3:17: "I know brothers, that you acted in ignorance, just as your leaders did."

[124] *TOB* 35.

[125] *EC* 208f; 83, 160. Also: "Some myths do, of course, downplay the guilt of victims; but not one of them incriminates the persecuting community" (*TOB* 37).

[126] *TOB* 39.

however, mediates their massive difference: the Gospels' emphasizing the innocence of the suffering victim corrupts the strength and stability of the sacred. Thus, Nietzsche understands the archaic and the biblical as similar only in the sense of, say, that of a photographic negative and its developed picture: the outer form is the same while the substance is diametrically inverted. Both involve a decisive killing, but their meaning differs radically. What matters is which one is the normal, life-affirming, normative one? Nietzsche calls this the essential "antithesis." For him, the "normal" one is summarized as *Dionysus*, in contrast with biblical one, summarized as *the Crucified*. In the former, life – in its "eternal fruitfulness" – just *is* destructive, wild, full of torment and "the will to annihilation." And a properly natural person will embrace and affirm that world for what it is. But in the case of the "Crucified as the innocent one," Nietzsche finds an unnatural objection to reality, a condemnation of life itself, a reversal of the principle of natural selection.[127]

Drawing upon Nietzsche's comparative mythology, Girard insists he is not merely plying a biblical bias, but, "I am just repeating here what Nietzsche said, although I am doing it *in reverse*."[128] Nietzsche, Girard insists, has read the biblical symbols rightly; he has uttered "the most important thing said in theology since the time of St. Paul" – that "in myth the victim is always expelled and killed justly … whereas the community bears no blame" and that the Bible inverts this.[129]

If Nietzsche is in error, it is rather on his seeing *ressentiment* as the *source* of this biblical disposition toward victims. That is, Nietzsche accused the biblical ethos as simply the vengeful jealousy of the weak toward strong winners – and so they valorized and sanctified their weakness as "holy," in revenge against the strong, inverting all reasonable standards of morality. Girard differs: the biblical siding with victims comes from a great courage to contradict the world's unjust persecutions; resentment is merely an illegitimate heir, not the father of the biblical tradition.[130] Nietzsche's praise of Dionysius, rather, gives into the mob mentality, taking sides with the persecutors.[131] Nietzsche wants to stand on the side of "strength," "life," and affirm that the sacrifices of society are not to be lamented – they are to be embraced for the sake of the whole,

---

[127] Nietzsche, *The Will to Power*, §246, §1052; René Girard, "Dionysus versus the Crucified," 816–35; *TOB* 35f.

[128] *EC* 197.

[129] Gianni Vattimo, *Christianity, Truth, and Weakening Faith*, 67.

[130] René Girard, *Job*, 108; *GR* 252.

[131] *EC* 197.

for the sake of life. For Nietzsche, Christianity so absolutely directed our attention to the individual such "that he could no longer be sacrificed." But Nietzsche, with the freshly printed pages of Darwin in his mind, concludes that "the species endures only through human sacrifice." We can hear in Nietzsche some of the logic of Caiaphas, that "it is better that one man be sacrificed than the whole town erupt in violence." As such, the aristocratic Nietzsche rejects as unnatural the notion that all "individuals are equals" – the Christian keystone – because this would ruin our species: "the species requires that the ill-constituted, weak, degenerate, perish: but it was precisely to them that Christianity turned as a conserving force."[132]

The ruin of the species, we could say, is another word for the biblical symbol of apocalypse. Biblical revelation has caused elevated levels of victim-sensitivity to seep into the drinking water of civilization, for better and worse.[133] With this epitomized in the Passion, and crucifixes now hanging all around the world, the mechanism that evolved and organized humanity since its origins can no longer successfully contain chaos. For the decisive element of human association, the victim, can no longer be imagined as guilty.[134] Whatever one makes of the theological claims of Christianity, its anthropological claims essentially amount to the unnerving *"cultural and moral acknowledgement of the sacrificial origins of our culture and our society."*[135]

ii. Polytheism and Monotheism

My summary started with the Bible's attention to victims in general, but quickly – through Nietzsche – turned to emphasize Christianity and the cross. Rightly so, as it is where Girard's biblical commentary most naturally centers, given the gospels' explicit representation of mimetic group violence. But if we drill deeper here, Girard's *logical* bedrock of the biblical tradition is not just a general siding with victims but *the epochal shift from polytheism to monotheism*. This shift means, for Girard, an

---

[132] Nietzsche, *The Will to Power*, §246; *The Antichrist*, § 2. One wonders how *Antichrist* might have been written differently had he been, say, black in the United States in 1895.

[133] Girard thus affirms Nietzsche's assessment that "the 'sword' that Jesus said he brought [is] the sword destructive of human culture" (*GR* 254).

[134] *EC* 261.

[135] Ibid., 12.

affirmation of the old dictum, "truth comes from the Jews."[136] In that shift, the gods of the victimage mechanism are critically engaged. If polytheism was a by-product of the victimary mechanism, monotheism means the "devictimizing" of God."[137] Monotheism means anthropological critique of mimetic contagion as much as metaphysical critique. Its refusal of idolatry means no longer turning victims into divinities or divinity into a victim but worshipping a God who is not a product of scapegoating:

> For the first time in human history the divine and collective violence are separated from one another. The refusal to deify victims is inseparable from another aspect of the biblical revelation, the most important of all: the deity is no longer victimized . . . . What characterizes the biblical tradition is above all the discovery of a divine reality that no longer belongs to the sphere of the collective idols of violence . . . . The [sacred] stems from the deceptive unanimity of persecution. In the Bible, by contrast, the confusion of the victimization process and the divine is dissolved and gives way to an absolute separation of the two . . . . Monotheism is both the cause and the consequence of this revolution.[138]

The movement from polytheism to monotheism involves not only a moral choice to side with the victim but a change in how divinity is perceived, enacted, and represented in relation to the political realm. Whereas divinity in a polytheistic framework had been formerly perceived as embedded within the sociopolitical order through the god-once-victim, divinity in monotheism is conceived as discontinuous with, transcending, or incompatible with the political order. We thus encounter in monotheism ultimately a desacralization of the traditional political order, an epochal shift in religiopolitical arrangements.[139] As we will find in the coming chapters, this monotheism does not simply coincide with an enlarged, political henotheism of the empire. Rather, we are encountering an entirely different *genus* of religion and divinity in the evolution of humanity.

This shift from gods to God – from archaic religion to biblical monotheism – is for Girard a movement from "the sacred to the holy." Unlike the old sacred, the new face of the divine is "holy,"[140] entirely unlike

---

[136] François Aubral, et al., "Discussion avec René Girard," 556.

[137] *EC* 199.

[138] *ISS* 106–7, 121; *EC* 199f, 204.

[139] "The sacred quality of social order becomes questionable where God is understood as transcending creation . . . Christianity continues the inheritance of Israel in radically de-divinizing social order" (Ranieri, *Disturbing Revelation*, 218).

[140] *EC*, 198, 218. Girard's perspective fends off accusations of Marcionism through his seeing the Hebrew Scriptures as the catalyst in developing the archaic sacred into the

anything we can imagine, for our imagination itself was forged in a distorted framework. This epochal shift is perhaps still only in its early, experimental stages. For, on the evolutionary scale, monotheism has only existed for a fraction of time compared to the longer "sacrificial safe-guards" of archaic religion. Given the longer evolutionary predominance of the latter, it may be impossible to imagine peace without some originary exclusion, some founding victim, or the containment of violence. And yet the biblical notion of God without the sacred, or a divinity without victimization, or a politics without a scapegoat, involves contemplating a peace that surpasses our current abilities in comprehension.

One rightly asks of such a grand theory the question of Eric Gans: Where does this supposed monotheistic break from polytheism come from, and how did it happen? Girard admits that monotheism did not establish itself in one fell swoop starting at Moses. While he calls the Bible one long "exodus from violence," this is a slow process with regressions and advances; and thus the Bible ought to be regarded as a mixed text, grown from polytheistic soil. Thus, the Bible is full of blurry overlaps in this transition – for example, polytheistic names for God, like *elohim*, and residues of the violent, archaic sacred, even if these are "vestiges without a future."[141] Thus the revelation unfolds in two stages: "First of all, there is a shift from myth to the Bible, where, as I said, God is devictimized and the victims are dedivinized; then you have the full evangelical revelation. God experiences the role of the victim, but this time deliberately, in order to free man from his violence."[142]

Thus, Girard's monotheism involves a complex dynamic of separation and unification. On the one hand, monotheism involves a dialectic breaking away of God from violence or scapegoating, a critique of all religion, a treating the false sacred as an idolatrous projection of human violence. But on the other hand, he sees in Christ a complex, if seemingly pagan notion of God as the divine victim. But this is again something like a *myth in reverse*, wherein Christ's divinity is not the by-product of scapegoating: "If Christ had in fact been divinized as the result of a violent act of sacralization, then the witnesses to the Resurrection would have been a

---

holy. Using photographic negative as a metaphor, as I will in Chapter 7, the form of the sacred is slowly changed, through Israel's religious transit, into that which may share superficial forms of the sacred but is increasingly *opposed* in *content*. Christianity is not a different picture from Judaism, but the resultant one: the representation of the unrepresentable God as the crucified scapegoat.

[141] *ISS* 119; *TH* 157; *EC* 226f.
[142] *ISS* 106–7, 121; *EC* 199f, 204.

mob howling for him to be put to death, and not the few individuals who proclaimed his innocence."[143] This subtlety, stemming from the minority community proclaiming Christ risen, is what keeps Girard from seeing Christianity's divine victim as reversion into pagan polytheism. At issue here is less metaphysical oneness and more a *division* from the falsehood of the victimage mechanism. We will return to this complex issue in Chapter 7, after having more closely analyzed Jewish monotheism.

Girard can admit that the Bible may even involve *more* representation of violence, compared to ancient near eastern literature. His explanation, quite thin, is that this violence is largely the pangs of exorcizing the archaic sacred, and we should not be tempted into polytheism's seeming tolerance.[144] We might see the world of polytheistic literature as somehow more harmonious or playful, contrasted with our own world now so shaped by an "overly serious monotheism." But he insists this is only because, in the ancient world, "ruptures in the harmony are generally resolved by triggering a single victim mechanism," while its victims – who spring forth as a new god – so rarely appear in texts *as* victims. Monotheism, however, "deprives" us of such resolution. In reality, the world of gods was more mournful and destructive than their myths advertise.[145]

In the following chapters, I will draw upon monotheistic scholarship to sift and supplement Girard's conceptualization of monotheism, seeing as it suffers from inadequate argumentation. His demonstration of the biblical breakthrough is mostly limited to a few cases of comparative mythology and is not conversant with ancient near east scholarship. This invites more detailed examination, in the coming chapters, on the birth, growth, and political meanings of monotheism in Egypt and the ancient near east.

D. HISTORY DEPRIVED OF GODS

Lastly, Girard interprets the biblical critique of archaic religions, which contained violence, as now *unleashing* powerful social forces, for good and bad, in the flow of world events. This unleashing is a consequence of the revelation of founding murder, centered upon the Crucified one. And

---

[143] *TOB* 39.
[144] Girard, "Violence in Biblical Narrative," 387–92. Palaver, "The Ambiguous Cachet of Victimhood," 71.
[145] *ISS* 106–7, 121; *EC* 199f, 204.

its chief result is the slow destruction of the "ignorance and superstition" – the protective misapprehension – that accompanies the collective perception of the sacred. While this liberation has rendered society more dynamically creative, it has simultaneously left it more fragile. For in the slow dissolution of sacred institutions, we no longer have the reliable "safety rails of archaic religion."[146]

The dramatic sociopolitical changes since the birth of biblical religion, the accelerations of the modern era, and even the growth of atheism, he regards as largely related to, if not by-products of biblical revelation.[147] Tribal religions and archaic religions as compacted with the state – with their taboos, rituals, and laws – helped to "contain" violence in the sense that St. Paul spoke of the *katéchon* (2 Thess 2:6–7): the powers that contain violence through their false transcendence. With the slow dissolving of their legitimacy, the secularized *katéchon* of today make up somewhat for this loss.[148] These are forces, as Cowdell observes, like democratic ideology and institutions, technology, mass media, or market society.[149] But even these restraints, which corral our mimetic energies, cannot hold indefinitely. Everything is accelerating and increasing. The evils of antagonistic violence and the race to rechannel and manage mimetic rivalry are not only on the increase; but increasing in tandem also are the goods of victim-awareness and the resolve to care for the marginalized.[150]

---

[146] *BTE* xiii, 15, 47; *EC* 219. Fleming sees "the eclipse of the sacred" as linked with "the constantly eroded salvific power of ritual, the generalized crisis of authority ('legitimation crisis'), and the loosening of legal constraints characteristic of modernity and late modernity" (Fleming, *René Girard*, 141).

[147] Though, this does not exclude from his theory other material causes, like the technological accelerations and discoveries of the fifteenth century onward (*EC* 246).

[148] "In our society religion has been completely subsumed by economics, but precisely because economics springs from a religious matrix . . . . It is nothing but the secularized form of religious ritual . . . . Trade was [originally] an offering to the foreigner, in order to placate the foreign god, who was seen as a possible threat" (ibid., 248).

[149] *EC* 13; *TOB* 97f. See also Wolfgang Palaver, "Hobbes and the Katéchon," 57–74. Agamben reads *katéchon* in relationship to 2 Thessalonians 2: "the mystery of lawlessness": "The *katéchon* is therefore the force – the Roman Empire as well as every constituted authority – that clashes with and hides *katargesis*, the state of tendential lawlessness that characterizes the messianic, and in this sense delays unveiling the 'mystery of lawlessness.' The unveiling of this mystery entails bringing to light the inoperativity of the law and the substantial illegitimacy of each and every power in messianic time" (Agamben, *The Time That Remains*, 111).

[150] *BTE* 131. Dumouchel adds that these changes stem not only from the spread of biblical ideas but of *practices* like unconditional charity and forgiveness: while benevolent, they

We have already noted above, with Nietzsche, that revelation of the scapegoat mechanism involves potentially apocalyptic consequences – that "this biblical change of perspective has undermined the pagan ways of containing violence forever."[151] By "apocalypse" Girard does not mean predicting a divine intervention at the end of the world. Quite the opposite: humanity has been deprived of its ancient safeguards and a sense of divine, retributive management. The subsequent cultural decay and increases of violence will be our own violence, not God's[152] – for which we must learn to take responsibility or suffer the consequences.

Post-revelation, the world is now dangerously experimenting with how to live without gods, as monotheism has blocked our ability to make new ones. Nietzsche lamented this: "almost 2,000 years, and not a single new god!" – for humans have "contradicted their instincts."[153] The biblical heritage has desacralized us and is at the root of the modern "recession of the sacred" or the "loss of transcendence."[154] While a convincing case can be made that the modern world is in fact precisely one of secular *enchantment* – transfixed with mammon and the sacred status of the state[155] – Girard nonetheless joins a chorus of those who see the biblical tradition as nonetheless disenchanting and secularizing our world, exorcizing the gods.[156] This results in intensified feelings of the *absence* of the god, in contrast with a certain at-home-ness in ancient religions.[157] While we are tempted to see Christianity as dying, as part of this slow death, Girard counters this is only because Christianity is destroying religion wherever it spreads: "Christianity is not only one of the destroyed

---

undercut the traditional safeguards of reciprocal solidarity and the duty to vengeance (Dumouchel, *The Barren Sacrifice*, xxvii).

[151] Palaver, "The Ambiguous Cachet of Victimhood," 72

[152] *BTE* x; *EC* 112.

[153] Nietzsche, *The Antichrist*, § 19.

[154] Assmann is among the many who share this assessment. Jan Assmann, "Cultural Memory and the Myth of the Axial Age," (hereafter *CMA*), 371. See also Robert Bellah, "Religious Evolution"; Charles Taylor, *A Secular Age*.

[155] Eugene McCarraher, *The Enchantments of Mammon.*

[156] See, e.g., Max Weber, Eric Auerbach, Marcel Gauchet, and Hans Blumenberg.

[157] Cowdell, *René Girard and Secular Modernity*, 12. "Togetherness and personal security are typically rooted in a violent compact and its mythico-ritual reinforcement, so that the price of liberation for a future of genuine humanity and self-determination is the risk of isolation, exposure, and emotional flatness. This is because the false sacred has been punctured. Disenchantment is thus the price of Christian maturity and closeness to God." (Cowdell, *René Girard and Secular Modernity*, 13, 179).

religions but it is the destroyer of *all* religions." The atheistic sense of God's death comes *from* Christianity.[158]

Christianity's secularizing force leads Dumouchel to quip that, for Girard, "Christianity is a religion that should not exist."[159] Christianity seems *incompatible* with human culture because it keeps re-presenting and thereby problematizing the hidden connective principle of humanity: the scapegoat. Counterbalancing such anarchic Christianity is the "sacrificial misreading" of historical Christendom, what some call Constantinianism. Such a cultural-dressing of Christianity has enabled it "to build a culture which somewhat resembled ancient cultures"[160] and thereby assume the ancient role of containing violence. This turning of Christianity into a sacrificial religion, inheriting Roman political power, helped slow down the gospels' dissolution of cultures and differences.[161] But with the decline of sacrificial Christendom today, we enter a further stage of accelerated, globalized secularization and the dissolution of cultures.[162]

Thus, modernity's problem is not merely the existential malaise of divine absence but a political problem of our ability to authoritatively, legally contain violence. In the framework of archaic religions, Girardian exegete Gil Bailie argues, collective expressions of violence produced their own legitimation and assent – through terror, unity, fear, and fascination. This generated and sustained the difference between evil violence and the legitimate violence that contains it. But now, we are experiencing a world of more simmering, protracted, ubiquitous conflict because "violence has been shorn of much of its once shimmering moral and religious prestige."[163] Official and legal violence is undergoing a slow delegitimization due to the corrosive seepage of the biblical sensitivity to victims. For, as Girard observes, we have in the Passion the representation of the

---

[158] *EC* 257.

[159] Paul Dumouchel, *Violence and Truth*, 17. According to Girard, "the biblical exposure of the scapegoat mechanism undermines all culture. This means that a culture based on the Bible is ultimately impossible" (Palaver, "Hobbes and the Katéchon," 59, 61; *TH*, 249–62).

[160] Palaver, "Hobbes and the Katéchon," 61.

[161] Ibid., 62, 67.

[162] "For me globalization is mainly the abolition not only of sacrifice, properly speaking, but also of the entire sacrificial order: it is the encompassing spread of Christian ethics and epistemology in relation to every sphere of human activity" (*EC* 245). We are in a "historical situation that is without precedent: the death of all cultures," for which Christianity is responsible (*TH* 441).

[163] Bailie, *Violence Unveiled*, 72–3; 53, 64.

supposedly highest legal apparatus in the world "in the service not of justice but of injustice, systematically warped by distortions of persecution."[164] And as we will note in analysis of Jesus' trial (Chapter 7), this narrative of juridical injustice inspires not an affirmation of our world's forms of justice but a radical "undecidability" and a crisis in the containment of violence.

The biblical siding with victims coincides with a growing awareness that what we used to consider "good violence" might really be persecution. Animated by this sensitivity, our contemporary world is far from abandoning absolutes; the concern for victims has become the new absolute; *"it is the absolute.* One will never see anyone attacking it."[165] Wolfgang Palaver agrees that the biblical siding with the victim is at the root of our "modern concern for human dignity and our eagerness to overcome all forms of victimization." But he adds that this sensitivity has also "enabled human beings to increase tremendously violence and destruction."[166] Instead of this concern for dignity simply improving the world, it "may indirectly worsen the relationship between antagonists."[167] As such, our sensitivity toward siding with victims against persecutors can easily lead to a new form of persecuting persecutors, scapegoating scapegoaters. The defense of victims can disorder society. It does not necessarily have to arise in conjunction with forgiveness, mercy, and love of enemies. "One can persecute today only in the name of being against persecutors."[168]

This unleashed capacity for violence may be seen in contrast with how the archaic sacred not only expressed violence but entailed esteem, even awe, toward enemies, shaping and restraining conflicts.[169] The scapegoating encoded into humanity through the evolutionary transit of natural

---

[164] Girard, *The Scapegoat,* 201–2; *GR* 18, 282; René Girard, "The Logic of the Undecidable," 20.

[165] *EC* 258.

[166] Palaver, "The Ambiguous Cachet of Victimhood," 79.

[167] Ibid., 71.

[168] *EC* 258. "Never before in history have people spent so much time throwing victims at one another's heads as substitutes for other weapons. This can only happen in a world that though far from Christian to be sure, is totally permeated by the values of the gospels" (René Girard, "Generative Scapegoating," 140; *ISS* 158, 164; *TOB* 82).

[169] Palaver, "The Ambiguous Cachet of Victimhood," 70. The divinization of enemies (or seeing them as "cosmic enemies") corresponds readily with political enemies, like Rahab for Egypt (Isa 30:7; Ps 87:4). This, in other words, is the equation of political enemies with cosmic enemies, regularly attested in ancient myth cycles (Mark S. Smith, *The Early History of God* [hereafter *EHG*], 58).

selection was calibrated in imbuing violence with both frightful evil and benevolent necessity. It mixed hatred with respect; scapegoating manifested through demonization mixed with divinization. But monotheism, Girard argues, interferes with this double transference to the extent that scapegoating has been reducing to only the demonization. Now we remain capable only "of hating our victims; we are no longer capable of worshipping them."[170] With a contemporary world animated by an unmoored, rampant demonization of enemies, "modern scapegoaters are aiming at the annihilation of the enemy because they are no longer able to divinize their victims .... The protective side of the old pagan sacred has completely disappeared."[171]

The shift from sacred-enemy to an inhuman-foe can be described in not only monotheism's symbolic interruption but more broadly in what Palaver and Elias Canetti call "religions of lament," which all too easily turn victim-sensitivity into vengeance for the victim. These would include religions where a victim is centralized, for example, Adonis, Tammuz, Attis, Osiris, Christ, and Husain (Shia Islam). These religions urge one to "side with a persecuted victim in order to expiate their own guilt as persecutors."[172] They center their myth around an unjust killing, perhaps an unjust trial, and "attach themselves to one who will die for them and, in lamenting him, they feel themselves as persecuted." Animated and justified by this victimization, "the hunting or baiting pack expiates itself by becoming a lamenting pack," which is really a war pack.[173] One calls to mind how, even if many Psalms excel in their narrating the victim's perspective, many also cry out loudly for violent vengeance;[174] one might see parallels in the flood in Genesis, where the survival of the persecuted coincides with the drowning of the violent.[175] Osama bin Laden claimed to be acting in defense of Muslims killed by the United States and even the victims of Hiroshima and Nagasaki; much of twentieth-century fascism

---

[170] *TH* 37; *EC* 262. "Victims are still demonized, but no longer divinized: 'Medieval and modern persecutors do not worship their victims, they only hate them" (Palaver, "The Ambiguous Cachet of Victimhood," 71; Girard, *The Scapegoat*, 38).

[171] Palaver, "The Ambiguous Cachet of Victimhood," 72; Mark Juergensmeyer, *Terror in the Mind of God*, 171–86; Mark Juergensmeyer, "Religion the Problem?," 30–1.

[172] Palaver, "The Ambiguous Cachet of Victimhood," 74.

[173] Ibid., 74; Elias Canetti, *Crowds and Power*, 168–71.

[174] René Girard, "Violence in Biblical Narrative," 388. Also, the terrorist cult Aum Shinrikyo justified its terrorist bombings as in defense of victims. See also Charles Taylor, "Notes on the Sources of Violence," 36.

[175] *TH* 143.

was animated by laying claim to victimization, and so forth.[176] Nietzsche called all of this an inability to properly and powerfully love enemies: in the biblical reification of God in the image of the weak, and its resentment of the strong, it constructs an absolute "evil enemy," "the *Evil One*."[177] This can be regarded as temptations toward "scapegoating reduced to its demonizing side,"[178] shorn of divinizing. By contrast, Canetti intriguingly found how the Pueblo people, who suppress lament in their tribes, saw little war and hunting.

In light of these problems, Girard suggests that a proper "conversion" to biblical revelation requires not merely being scandalized at how other people are scapegoaters – which only repeats the pattern of accusation and expulsion – but "recognizing that we are persecutors without knowing it."[179] Repentance is scapegoating in reverse. This was the repentance of Peter and Paul in admitting their mob guilt; this is the Jewish moral traditions that refuse to demonize one's enemy.[180]

As for how and whether other religions and cultures have also participated in this reconfigured relationship to victims over the centuries, Girard is willing to grant them some place but not nearly as central a place. The ancient Greeks critiqued group victimage, particularly the tragic poets. But, that Sophocles never explicitly did away with a justified expulsion of the victim in his plays suggests, for Girard, that Sophocles intuited such a removal would have sealed his own expulsion. Jainism and Hinduism, indeed, had an internal critique of sacrificial mechanisms, but this never became thoroughly developed.[181] Islam may critique sacrifice at

---

[176] Palaver, "The Ambiguous Cachet of Victimhood," 76.

[177] Nietzsche, *The Genealogy of Morals*, §1.10.

[178] Palaver, "The Ambiguous Cachet of Victimhood," 73.

[179] *EC* 198; 173, 223. Conversion means coming "to see oneself as a persecutor" (*TOB* 60).

[180] E.g., Ex 23:5; Prov 25:21–2. See Marc Gopin, *Between Eden and Armageddon*, 41–2, 78–9.

[181] *EC* 212; 201. See *Sacrifice* for Hinduism commentary and *EC* for the relative similarity with the Orphic and Gnostic traditions (Girard, *Sacrifice*, 165; *EC* 257). On Buddhist critique of sacrifice: *Sacrifice*, 87–95. On the innocence of victims in antiquity, like Socrates, Antigone: Girard, *The Scapegoat*, 199. For interreligious critique, see Leo Lefebure, *Revelation, the Religions, and Violence*, 21f; Mark Wallace, *Fragments of the Spirit*, 109–11.

That other cultures may have given strong voice to innocent victims and the guilt of crowds begs for more comparative analysis – a line of analysis we cannot pursue here. Lawrence Wills draws on Burkert to note how the "gospels are no more oriented toward the victim's point of view than is the *Life of Aesop*" (Lawrence M. Wills, "The Death of a Hero," 82; Walter Burkert, *Structure and History in Greek Myth and Ritual*, 64, 70). Also Hector Avalos, *Fighting Words*, 75–8.

points, but Girard sees its refraining from explicit representation of Christ's crucifixion as suggestive of why it has not entirely dissolved animal sacrifice wherever it spreads.[182]

E. CONCLUSION

In that last portion of his theory, a dramatic sociology of history stems from the hypothesis about what biblical symbols and religion have done, perhaps unwittingly, to the cultures where it has spread. My interest here is to not grapple with that sociology of the Common Era but to return to the core biblical and theological claims that informed his ambitious reading of history. Monotheism's political consequences concern the rejection of the victim-divinizing mechanism. This idea of his remains underdeveloped and a hasty conclusion for the unconvinced.[183] His sui generis monotheistic revelation appears, to critics, as almost mythical, coming out of thin air. Is this monotheistic "refusal to divinize victims" accurate with respect to its historic emergence in the ancient world? These questions invite us to go outward from his theory to explore scholarship –

[182] In a Docetist escape at the last moment, akin to the *akedah*'s replacement of Isaac with a ram, it only "seemed" Jesus was killed and was instead immediately assumed (Quran Sura 4:157–8). Girard has noted some "prophetic insight in Muslim tradition into the role of sacrifice" (Cowdell, *René Girard and Secular Modernity*, 150; VS 4–5). And yet, "the Muslim religion has not destroyed the sacrifice of archaic religion the way Christianity has. No part of the Christian world has retained pre-Christian sacrifice. Many parts of the Muslim world have retained pre-Muslim sacrifice" (Robert Doran, "Apocalyptic Thinking after 9/11," 20–32).

[183] James Alison concurs: "Girard's presumption of the effect of revelation is grossly under-demonstrated, is true" (Personal correspondence, August 11, 2016). Girard's oeuvre contains only about a half a chapter on monotheism specifically, along with some other scattered commentary (*ISS* ch 9; *EC* ch 6). He briefly mentions how religions that "prohibit all images" ought to be analyzed with respect to "doubling" and "rivalry" (*TH* 14). He does not interact with virtually any monotheism scholars. Girard's chief Jewish interlocutor, Sandoor Goodhart, who nonetheless emphasizes the importance of monotheistic "anti-idolatry" for mimetic theory, does not offer a detailed investigation of monotheism (e.g., Sandoor Goodhart, *The Prophetic Law*).

Mark S. Smith responded to my inquiry of his analysis of Girard's concept of monotheism: "I don't think I recognize the polytheism that Girard presupposes about the ancient near east. I think one should study something about the gods before accepting something that sounds so reductionist. There is a category of dead gods in Mesopotamian religion that differ from other gods (for the most part) and I'm not sure how Girard would deal with these (as far as I can tell Girard does not deal in any concrete manner with the facts about polytheism on the ground). It seems to me that Girard's theory makes polytheism into a scapegoat, not to mention a fantasy of his imagination" (Personal correspondence, August 25, 2016).

particularly that of Jan Assmann and his critical extension of Freud – on monotheism's relationship to its polytheistic context, violence, and the political order.

But before proceeding, some observations relevant to the overarching thesis of this book should be noted. Girard and Mouffe both identify human association as marked by a paradoxically inescapable "sacrificial" dimension. All human association is marked by something of an originary division: the formation of a "we" has long been constitutively forged through the formation of a "they." This pattern has sedimented into human culture – indeed into our bodies – through various manifestations of the victim mechanism. But, on this originary division, both Mouffe and Girard have two layers concerning its *escapability*. In one sense, it is inescapable: "the political" for Mouffe refers to the grammatically ineliminable dimension of exclusion in all sociality (i.e., inclusion contains exclusion, and tolerance contains intolerance; liberalism does not escape the political dimension of democracy). A politics-beyond-hegemony is thus mistaken. Girard likewise urges that "sacrifice" is unavoidable: you either join culture's containment of violence or you potentially get sacrificed by it. Thus, in one sense, peace-beyond-sacrifice is mistaken. For both authors, the unavoidability of the political means there is no neutral ground, foreign to exclusion, available to us. We suffer, in Colborne's gloss of Girard, from "a political, religious, and cultural problem without a political, religious, or cultural solution." For any attempt to remedy our violence – whether through laws, consensus, inclusive procedures, religion, taboos, public shaming, etc. – seems to be yet another concealed iteration of exclusion, rivalry, and scapegoating.[184] Are we forced to conclude that *any* participation in politics, religion, or even culture itself is de facto participation in scapegoating? How can we operate against injustices, then, without becoming ensnared in yet further rivalry?

But, at another layer, both authors seek to deconstruct sacrifice as contingent, not a requisite essence of who we are – you might say, "unnatural." For Mouffe, we must unearth how society is "the product of a series of hegemonic practices . . . that conceal the originary act of their contingent political institution and which are taken for granted as if they were self-grounded." This mythic order, while often striking us as sacred and solid, must be unveiled as "temporary and precarious,"[185] requiring agonistic intervention. The political is unavoidable; but politics are

---

[184] Nathan Colborne, "Violence and Resistance," 116–7.
[185] Mouffe, *For a Left Populism*, 88.

transformable. Girard also argues that our perception of social objectivity is mythically grounded on originary exclusions. He adds we must learn a pacific mode of mimetic relation to the Other that has rarely been experienced since our origins – with rare exceptions in Christ and sages. There is a peace possible that, currently, surpasses our understanding. Far from arguing that the "primordial division" in society's scapegoat mechanism is the essence of humanity, revelation invites us to historicize and denaturalize it. We must expose our sociobiological evolution as a contingent, mistaken chain of events that *did not have to happen the way it did*. The doctrine of original sin is homologous with our critique and exodus from it.

In both authors, the invitation to critique (to, say, enact hegemonic interventions on neo-liberal hegemony), the call to change, requires not the abandonment of intolerance but its creative reconceptualization. In Mouffe's political idiom, our predicament requires embracing the positive "intolerance" of liberalism's inclusivity even while its promised land can never be reached: it must be worked out, incompatibly, through the hegemonic exclusions of democracy. This is expressive of a deeper apophatic intolerance, of refusing the illusion that we could ever attain a non-hegemonic social unity, refusing any terminal representation of society's Absolute. Such openness must take shape as political agonism shorn of antagonism: respect toward adversaries with whom one differs in interpreting shared founding principles while nonetheless fighting for the victory of one's own interpretation.[186]

Those insights on improving the earthly city, as it were, are illuminative in conceptualizing the heavenly city's theological agonism. Even if the concepts do not perfectly translate, the coming chapters take Girard as pointing us toward a Jewish monotheistic intolerance that "separates" God from the political sphere – rendering them incompatible – in a way that is both radically dangerous and potentially liberating. But this separation cannot be understood as *depoliticization*, some kind of universal faith beyond hegemony that pretends to escape public, political existence. By Chapter 7, I come to describe the practical embodiment of this intolerance in Christ's agonistic love, so "separate" from the sacrificial mechanism that he engages and undergoes its violence so as to render it inoperative. My coming chapters thus turn to examining the emergence of this monotheistic intolerance.

---

[186] *AG* 7.

3

Monotheism and the Monopoly on Violence

Freud and Girard

I started with Mouffe reconceptualizing the intuitive connections between inclusion and pluralism. She clarified how the hegemonic nature of every social order is not overcome through consensus or some universal open-mindedness; rather, we must think in light of the exception, the inescapability of the political. In such a light, liberalism's benevolent but dangerous intolerance should not be abolished; it must be counterposed with an apophatic intolerance that repudiates illusions of ever attaining a non-hegemonic social unity. Her theory, by extension, invites us to rethink simplistic approaches to monotheism as either a harbinger of universal tolerance or malignant anti-pluralism. Monotheism, I will show, involves an intolerant negation of the Absolute and is crucial to conceptualizing pluralism today. Mimetic theory contributes toward this rethinking by conceptualizing monotheism as an intolerance that critiques idolatrous unity – the unwitting worship of the scapegoat – and reorients our relation to marginalized victims.

Whatever the merits of Girard's theory of religion, violence, and biblical revelation, it surely entails a contrastive, dialectic method, wherein a line between true and false religion is drawn. As such, his theory provokes reflection on what Egyptologist Jan Assmann terms the Mosaic distinction. This is a distinction wherein biblical revelation is seen as a discontinuous and superior religion in contrast with the "falseness" of other religions. Given the biblical violence toward idolaters, this distinction is easily viewed as a "murderous distinction." Theologians have long been inclined to soften, dissolve, or at least inject greater tolerance into this true/false antagonism. But Girard paradoxically retains the intolerant distinction precisely on account of concern over violence: all human religions and cultures since the foundation of the world stand on the "false" side of this distinction in their mythic misapprehension of the scapegoating mechanism. Monotheism, for him, is "true" in that it reveals, through *separation*, the archaic sacred's falsity: "devictimizing God," "refusing to divinize victims," and "dedivinizing the social order." Can any of these grand, cryptic, and triumphalist claims stand up to a historical investigation of monotheism and its roots?

For this we must turn to contemporary monotheistic scholarship, particularly that which lingers around the analyses of violence, intolerance, and even Egyptology. Jan Assmann is a crucial and often misinterpreted scholar at this nexus. Analysis of monotheism naturally concerns Egyptology because the Mosaic distinction of true vs. false is most familiar to us in the biblical theme of "Israel vs. Egypt." Biblical monotheism narrates its origins as an exodus from pagan, enslaving "Egypt," even if this is shorthand for the many cultures that Judaism sought to distinguish itself from over many centuries.[1] Breaking down that antagonistic barrier and returning to a more tolerant framework would seem to diffuse the hubris of biblical "superiority." Assmann's work has not only investigated the relative validity of this distinction between the true Israel and false Egypt, but he has explored the many historical attempts at mitigating it. Any introduction to his oeuvre or that mitigation-discourse requires orientation with Sigmund Freud's *Moses and Monotheism* (hereafter *MM*, published 1939), the aim of this chapter.

When Freud stepped into the Egypt vs. Israel discourse with his *MM*, he did not simplistically take sides or try to do away with the intolerant distinction. He indeed theorized Israel as birthed from Egypt, and that Moses was Egyptian, thus blurring the historical lines between Israel and Egypt. To his critics, this seemed as if he was trying to abolish the Mosaic distinction. But this was not the case: Jewish monotheistic intolerance for Freud involved a profound "advance in intellectuality." He thus situated himself as a qualified *defender* of monotheism. In sum, monotheism for him involves a profound psychological grappling with humanity's primordial relationship to despotic power and alpha males. It involves the beneficial suppression of both violence and the instinct for material

---

[1] This polemical "Egypt" trope has manifold expressions. See K. A. D. Smelik and E. A. Hemelrijk, "Who Knows Not What Monsters Demented Egypt Worships?," 1908ff. They explore numerous biblical, rabbinic, and Christian examples: e.g., rejoicing in Egypt's destruction; Ishmael is of Egyptian descent; Egypt as abomination; Egypt's excessive sensuality; opposing alliances with Egypt; religious condemnation; Jerome determines Egypt's etymology as "to be narrow, oppressed," etc.

representation, with God as transcendent and image-less. Understanding the strengths and weaknesses of Freud's position in this chapter will lead us, then, to see how Jan Assmann builds upon and corrects Freud.

A. FINDING MONOTHEISM IN EGYPT?

While the word monotheism does not emerge until around 1660 (through the philosopher Henry More), debates on the intolerance stemming from the notion of a one true God emerges at least around the Jewish Maccabean revolution, in the second century BCE. This revolt was seen by Seleucids as a failure to get along with Hellenic culture, to put it mildly, echoed again in the first- and second-century Jewish revolts against Roman occupation of Palestine. Celsus of the second century CE saw biblical monotheism as stubbornly antisocial in its refusal to join in the Mediterranean political community. Its denunciation of other gods as false or demons posed a problem to the empire's flexible "One God" that could tolerate many subordinate gods or the diverse manifestations of the One God, just as one Caesar had to manage many diverse regions.[2] (We will describe this as "henotheism" in Chapter 4.)

But the biblical monotheistic opposition to other gods, however, soon won a privileged position in the political administration of Western civilization, inheriting the throne of the empire's high God, famously in Constantine and Theodosius. With Christian monotheism holding court, it was now the *plurality* of gods and nations that were regarded as a threat to the Christian political order.[3] At the popular level, numerous Christian pogroms and iconoclastic violence asserted their triumph with great bloodshed.[4] And at the political level, the following centuries of medieval inter-state conflicts often overlapped with inter-religious conflicts, both between Christian sects and against Islam – where intolerance of heterodoxy often coincided with restraining political division, revolt, or invasion. To be fair, the Roman Empire's "inclusive" imperial religion had not exactly been pacific, containing the extravagant violence of its domain. But it is not unreasonable to ask if the infusion of Christian

---

[2] Origen reconstructs Celsus' now lost work in his *Contra Celsum* (see 1.24; 8.35).

[3] For Constantine-friendly theologians like Eusebius, the monotheistic unity of God was tied to the unity of the empire. Thus the "unifying" wars and Pax Romana of Caesar Augustus providentially prepared the way for a unity that could receive its true monarch, Jesus Christ. See Erik Peterson, "Monotheism as a Political Problem."

[4] Guy Stroumsa, *End of Sacrifice*, 106.

monotheism diminished whatever tolerance Rome practiced, enflaming society with religious intolerance. While one could try to make the alternative case that biblical values somehow made Western civilization more tolerant or sensitive – say, in dissolving slavery or child exposure – it could also be argued, as religious historian Guy Stroumsa does, that "the boundaries of freedom and action and of religious thought were undeniably curtailed in the Christianized empire."[5]

With this historical tension as a backdrop, theologians for the last several centuries have tried to mitigate monotheistic intolerance. Perhaps, many thought, the problem is not with the pagans or heretics but with this whole biblical habit of denouncing pagans in the first place. Jan Assmann notes how many theologians around the Renaissance, trying to disarm the religiously inflected conflicts of their day, suggested returning to a seemingly more tolerant pagan theology. This was sometimes done by arguing that monotheism was born not in Israel but in Egypt, thus showing that monotheism was not unique to Israel. Or, to go further, some argued monotheism was a common, natural, default theology held by *all* peoples since the beginning of humanity.[6] With Israel's uniqueness thus softened – and all the competing feelings of superiority and indignation fueled by it – monotheism could then be regarded as a more universally shared, less antagonistic worldview. With the One God as transnational, Israel's special revelation and superiority complex can dissolve. But the defenders of biblical monotheism would, in response, reinforce the unique biblical difference and the monotheistic revelation as stemming from Israel alone. Or, at least some might try to strike a more compromising, compatible tone: "the Supreme Being of the primitive

---

[5] Ibid., 97.

[6] The Renaissance's "diffusion theory of truth" tried to conceive of an originary, inclusive monotheism – which spread via a Noah-styled dispersion of early humanity – seen also in Plethon, Ficino, Pico della Mirandola, Steuco (*PM* 70, 77–8; *ME* 18, passim). Reinhold regarded Israel's negation of gods as merely about the hidden secrecy of divinity, not uncommon to pagan religions. Or, Schiller saw Moses as not promoting a new idea but simply popularizing it (*ME* 126.) See also Patrizi's "convergence theory," that all religions converge toward the truth (*PM* 78ff). See also Spencer, whose De *legibus Hebraeorum ritualibus et earum rationaibus* (1685) argued that Mosaic ritual law was simply borrowed and translated from Egyptian religion. He applied Maimonides' idea that many Israelite laws are really derivative: they are "normative inversions of the abominations of the other cultures into obligations and vice versa" (*ME* 31). Others include Tindal, Reinhold, Schiller, etc. (*ME* 75, 91–2, 100).

By the seventeenth and eighteenth century, we begin to hear more counterargument, that the pagans had in fact stolen biblical knowledge. E.g., Cardinal Huet argued for monotheism's Mosaic uniqueness against Spinoza (*PM* 83; *ME* 71).

culture is really the God of monotheism"; the default high god of all human cultures is just made explicit and fulfilled in the biblical Yahweh.[7]

Throughout this discourse, Moses has been a key suspect under investigation. For he straddles the polytheistic world of Egypt and the monotheistic world of Israel. The scholarly discourse that emphasized how Moses was *Egyptian* aimed "to deconstruct 'counter-religion' and its implications of intolerance by blurring the basic distinctions as they were symbolized by the antagonistic constellation of Israel and Egypt. 'Revelation' had to be (re)turned into 'translation.'"[8] That is, Moses could be a bridge to connecting biblical monotheism to pagan religion, making it like them, with a similar high God but just a different name. In the nineteenth century, this discourse gained much grist for the mill through the archaeological excavations of an Egyptian city, Tell-el-Amarna. Unearthing strong signs of monotheism there, a cascade of publications argued that monotheism first arose in Egypt, further dulling the Mosaic distinction.[9]

Freud entered this stream of publications with his own synthesis of the archaeological findings and a unique psychoanalytic spin on how to relate "Egypt" and "Israel." Instead of Moses as monotheism's first midwife, he argues it was a great Pharaoh, Amenhotep IV, who later changed his name to Akhenaten – named after the only God, the sun disc, Aten.[10] Around 1350 BCE, he forced a severe monotheistic revolution upon his country. He shut down the temples, banned worship of (most) other gods, effaced old inscriptions on temples, prohibited sorcery and magic, and banned the cult of Osiris, the old god of the dead. The diversity of Egyptian cults was monopolized at a newly built city, Amarna. Sudden, violent, and strict, Akhenaten's religious revolution faced resistance, lasted for only his reign, about eighteen years, after which his name was erased from virtually all records and his revolutionary city buried.[11]

---

[7] Rodney Stark applauds the apologetic value of this position, as it suggests a rational foundation to theism, a shared, universal revelation (Rodney Stark, *Discovering God*, 62). My book takes the imperial nature of the high god concept – or simply, the violent sacred – shared in so many cultures as little cause for its celebration as the validation of some natural, reasonable, universally shared "religious impulse."

[8] *ME* 147.

[9] E.g., John G. Wilkinson, *Manners and Customs of the Ancient Egyptians* (1822); James Henry Breasted, *De Hymnis in Solem sub Rege Amenophide IV. Redactis* (1894); Eduard Meyer, *Die Israeliten un inhre Nachbarstämme* (1906).

[10] James Hoffmeier, *Akhenaten and the Origins of Monotheism*, 204, 206, 237.

[11] The Boundary Stela at Amarna references the "evils" and "offensive things" against which Akhenaten had opposed his reign (Hoffmeier, *Akhenaten*, 161ff).

Records resume a few years later with the reestablished order and more tolerable religion under the leadership of Horemheb.

Akhenaten's revolution may have been in the making for decades through an increasing cultivation of worship of an old high-god, Aten/Atum/Re.[12] It is no coincidence that a supreme sun God emerged in Egypt while it also became an expanded, massive superpower, the first large territorial state in human history.[13] Erik Peterson once argued the thesis that "the ultimate formulation of the unity of a metaphysical construction of the world is always co- and predetermined by a decision for a particular political conception of unity."[14] When it comes to Egypt in the centuries preceding Akhenaten, this is no exception; Freud's citing of the great Egyptologist J. H. Breasted concurs, seeing their solar "monotheism" as nothing but "imperialism in religion."[15] This is to say that symbols of metaphysical unity tend to reflect the political "monopoly on violence" – the state as the consolidation of the legitimate expression of violence and power.[16] And to the extent that Girard's thesis holds true, that the containment of violence is homologous with "the sacred," we can likewise see how Egypt's unifying imperial order was reflected in its metaphysical and religious conceptions of Unity.

And yet, though political expansionism may have prepared the way for Akhenaten's revolution, his regime manifested as a discontinuous break with the past. His was – so far as we know – the "first attempt" in world history to install, basically by coup, worship of an "Only God." Assmann calls it the "first conflict between two fundamentally different and mutually exclusive religions in the recorded history of humankind ... not only the first but also the most radical and violent eruption of a counter-religion in the history of humankind."[17]

As for Freud's accuracy with respect to the history of Akhenaten, there is no major controversy worth noting here. Akhenaten did indeed install a religious-political revolution centered on only one God and expunging other gods. Debates continue as to how and whether Akhenaten abolished or in fact absorbed the other gods, and so on. But Freud's unique and controversial interpretation of Egyptian monotheism concerns, first, how Israel may have inherited monotheism through an *Egyptian* Moses,

---

[12] *MM* 22, 24–5, 72–3, 80, 108, 137; James Breasted, *Dawn of Conscience*, 275.
[13] *MM* 72; *ATM* 53.
[14] Peterson, *Theological Tractates*, 71.
[15] James Breasted, *Development of Religion and Thought in Ancient Egypt*, 315.
[16] Tony Waters and Dagmar Waters, eds., *Weber's Rationalism and Modern Society*, 136.
[17] *MM* 24–5; 21, 73.

and second, mapping this monotheism onto an evolutionary, psychoanalytic theory concerning violence and despotism since human origins.

B. FREUD'S MOSES, THE ATEN-WORSHIPPING EGYPTIAN

Moses is undoubtedly an Egyptian name, made of the root "born of."[18] Along with other reasons to posit Moses as an Egyptian, Freud argued the following hypothesis: Moses lived during the reign of Akhenaton and was greatly inspired by his movement. He may have worked for Akhenaten as a governor in the border provinces, overseeing Semitic tribes.[19] In any case, he was "a man of great importance in the land of Egypt" (Ex 11:3). In the political vacuum subsequent to Akhenaten's death, Moses was inspired to use his authority to take up Aten's lost cause. Heading out of Egypt, now hostile to the Aten religion, he took his retinue with him, the first Levites.[20] And like Akhenaten, he forced a new religion upon people from his region.[21]

Moses' "speech impediment" (Ex 4:10) signals he spoke a different language than the acquired people, requiring translation.[22] In the desert, there were many "grave revolts" against this alien despot; the people twice nearly stoned Moses to death (Ex 17:4, Num 14:10), which he put down in divine wrath. The aggravation at his chafing rule eventually resulted in a similar outcome as it did for Akhenaton: they could not bear his religious despotism and they killed him in a rebellion at Shittim, the threshold of entry into the Promised Land. If not, he was still the domineering Superfather – the alpha male who demands unconditional obedience – whom the people at least *wanted* to kill.[23] Freud is drawing on Ernst Sellin's hypothesis that this murder of Moses was repressed in early Jewish tradition and survived only in the dark recesses of memory, within the rabbinic tradition (in no less an authority than Rashi), memories of

---

[18] *ATM* 63f.
[19] Josephus suggested that Moses was an Egyptian field marshal while Strabo had also suggested Moses was an Egyptian priest who, disappointed with local religion, founded a new religion with an emigrating group (Jan Assmann, "The Advance in Intellectuality," 13).
[20] *MM* 45f.
[21] Ibid., 57, 166.
[22] Ibid., 58.
[23] Ibid., 86.

the killed Prophets (esp. Isa 52–3; Neh 9:26; Lk 13:34; Acts 7:52f), and the above passages of revolt.[24]

Having lived through the double trauma of now two cast-off regimes, the extant Levites and the group still had to carry on somehow.[25] Given their association with Akhenaton's infamous regime and religion, they could not return to Egypt. Before long they encountered an Arabic tribe, the Midianties,[26] who worshipped a volcano god named Yahweh. An agreement between these two tribes emerged, forming into one people and one god what had in fact been two.[27] The mediator between the two parties was the son-in-law of the Midianite priest Jethro, who – in the legacy that follows – was imputed with the name "Moses."

The two religions had to negotiate the merger. They retained Akhenaten's prohibition of the underworld cult of Osiris – explaining why Jewish tradition shows little sign of belief in an afterlife. And Aton, variant of Aten, may (or may *not*)[28] echo in the Torah as *Adonai*: "*Shema Yisrael Adonai Eloheinu Adonai Echod.*"[29] But, any good Egyptian, if they truly wished to be part of a holy nation, needed to retain the custom of circumcision (which archaeology suggests would have come from Egypt, not Abraham's Mesopotamia).[30] Forcing circumcision upon the Midianite tribe, who still comfortably wore their foreskins, was not an alluring option. So, if the Egyptian faction wished so strongly to keep this custom, they would have to allow Yahweh to have pride of place over

---

[24] Sellin sees such memory traces in the suffering prophet of Isa 53 (Ernst Sellin, *Mose und seine Bedeutung für die israelitisch-jüdische Religionsgeschichte*, 73–113; MM 42). See also the Psalm on Moses' death at the threshold of the promised land: "[Our fathers] provoked God's anger at Meribah, and Moses suffered on their account" (Ps 106:32). Sellin later downgraded his thesis that they merely "wished" to kill Moses (*ATM* 65).

  Rabbi Rashi of the eleventh century read the passage around the Golden Calf incident (Ex 32:6) as the "codified indication of murder and debauchery," while the request for Aaron to "make us gods, which shall go before us" (Ex 32:1) "associates the death of the leader with the totem that replaces and represents him." And the unknown whereabouts of his tomb (Deut 34:6) is one of the many clues that point in the direction of the murder-hypothesis (Rojtman, "The Double Death of Moses," 108, 113).

[25] MM 65; 84.

[26] Ibid., 39; 75–6.

[27] Ibid., 64; 54.

[28] Assmann rejects any connection: *ME* 22–4.

[29] MM 27–8; 12, 19.

[30] Ibid., 29–30. The Atenists tried to disassociate circumcision from appearing of "Egyptian" origin, wanting to differentiate themselves from the stubborn Egyptians who could not handle the Aten religion (ibid., 53). Freud sees the Jewish swine prohibition as also an Egyptian import: the god Seth, as a black pig, had wounded Horus (ibid., 34).

Aten.[31] Thus in merging the founding legends, Yahweh precedes the Egyptian religion – hence the Canaan-centered, pre-Moses patriarch myths. Thus both parties have a shared interest in repressing any memory of the murder of an Egyptian Moses, though for different reasons.[32]

In subsequent Jewish history, in which there is constant internal tension between Aten and Yahweh, Yahweh comes out on top, while Aten remains a constant subterranean pressure. Freud sees the mixture of volcanic-paganism of Yahwism with Aten's enlightenment as a "retrograde development" that will mire the Jews in pagan, ritualistic religion for centuries. Yahweh is the narrow-minded, tribal, bloodthirsty god who was useful for the early, violent conquests of this group.[33] By contrast, Aten is too intellectually superior, too universal, for a primitive people. The sun disc by which Aten was worshipped is not direct and idolatrous but the manifestation of that source of all things which the sun represents.[34] In contrast with the volcanic violence of Yahweh, Aten is a pacifist god who traffics in ethics and justice.[35] Aten marks the more "spiritual conception of God, a single God who embraces the whole world, one as all-loving as he was all-powerful, who, averse to all ceremonial and magic, set humanity as its highest aim a life of truth and justice."[36] This enlightened spurning of sorcery, magic, sacrifice, and rituals reemerges in time through the prophets, who are the champions of reviving Aten worship and ethics – though not by name – against the constant drift to Yahweh. It is not until around the reforms of Ezra/Nehemiah, when Aten's theological superiority seems to have been finally sealed in Jewish religion, even if not in name. In all, the subterranean Aten influence imbued in this people a deep psychological "progress in intellectuality," spiritual endeavor, and a disinclination toward violence rooted in critical insight.[37]

A key element in this progress concerns its "dematerializing of God"[38] – the elevation of reason and rationality over physicality,

---

[31] Ibid., 47.

[32] Ibid., 85.

[33] Ibid., 61; 77, 159.

[34] Ibid., 23.

[35] Ibid., 78.

[36] Ibid., 61; 80, 142; ethical vs. ceremonial: 84; magic and ceremonial: 82; ritualistic rules: 81; anti-sacrifice: 62.

[37] Ibid., 109, 144–5, 147, 158. Given that Freud strictly contrasts *Gesitigkeit* with mysticism, Assmann finds it best to see this flexible word translated as "intellectuality" and not Katherine Jones' "spirituality." Assmann, "The Advance in Intellectuality," 17.

[38] *MM* 147.

visibility, and senses. This means grasping the ungraspable God, beyond material representation. The epitome of this, of course, is the prohibition of images in which God would have "neither a name nor countenance ... in this, I suspect, Moses was outdoing the strictness of the Aten religion."[39] This renunciation of sensual instincts and the instinctual need for visible representation was, for Freud, a triumph, "unquestionably one of the most important stages on the path to hominization."[40] Assmann summarizes Freud here: "far from owing our most impressive cultural achievements to instinct, we have the suppression of instinct to thank for them."[41]

+++

Before proceeding, we should note that Freud admits his hypothesis of the exodus, Moses, his murder, and the genetic connection between Egypt and Israel enjoys little evidence.[42] He admits Moses' religion may have been more like "monolatry," the exalting of one god above the rest, rather than strict monotheism.[43] But, while these admissions would seem to be lost on some critics, his goal is not exact historical reconstruction. I have foregrounded here what I see as his deciphering – which I will critique later – the psychology at the roots of the antinomy between Egypt and Israel. Some see in his hypothesis a larger speculative exploration of the roots of anti-Semitism in the West, as represented by Nazi Germany in Freud's day. A Jew himself, Freud wants to explore the structure and origins of the Jewish mind, what charged that people of such long-term survival, to consider "how the Jew became what he is and why he attracted this undying hatred."[44] These points contextualize why *MM* comes to Judaism's defense against Christian polemics of "carnal

---

[39] Ibid., 144.

[40] Ibid., 113.

[41] *PM* 88; Sigmund Freud, *Beyond the Pleasure Principle*, 36. Kant also viewed the second commandment as key to this progress in both Judaism and Islam: Immanuel Kant, *Critique of the Power of Judgment*, 156.

[42] Further, as Jacqueline Rose notes, we can reject Sellin and *Totem and Taboo*'s flawed historical arguments while still "accepting the underlying thesis that there is no sociality without violence. What binds the people to each other and to their God is that they killed him" (Edward Said, *Freud and the Non-European*, 75).

[43] *MM* 61.

[44] Assmann, "The Advance in Intellectuality," 13. Robert Wistrich judges *MM* ultimately as "a psychoanalysis of antisemitism." Robert Wistrich, "Sigmund Freud's Last Testament," 62; Guy Stroumsa, "Myth into Novel," 207.

Israel."[45] Edward Said also notes how Freud's emphasizing the Egyptian/pagan origin of Israel helped undermine doctrinal efforts to found purist Zionism to the detriment of Palestinians – as became a crucial issue in Freud's era onward.[46] In any case, more important than the historical reconstruction of Moses is a complex of historical, political issues regarding intolerance.

C. THE EVEN DEEPER AIMS: THE HISTORICAL TRUTH OF RELIGION

We must now center upon how Freud sees this monotheistic progress of intellectuality as related to despotism and murder – not just an especially spiritualized God. For Freud, this brings us to contemplate the major patterns of power in human evolution. This is the deeper layer of *MM*, entering us into clear links with Girard's theory.[47] After having considered the hypothesis of an Egyptian-Moses and his murder, Freud layers on a second hypothesis regarding murder catalyzing human evolution. This notion, drawn from his earlier work in *Totem and Taboo*, suggests the earliest proto-humans lived in small groups, each dominated by an alpha male, a singular strong man who would put down all challengers and owned all the women. This alpha-male submission pattern was the primal dominance pattern, and, being operative for so long in proto-human existence, it left a deep instinctual mark upon our species' intuition and habits. And, as the omnipotent sovereign, the Father of the group, it is the originary psychological conditions of unconscious monotheism.

But he argues we killed our way out of this dominance pattern. At some point the brothers formed a horde to kill the alpha male and then eat him. Their cannibalism was their identification with the "Father," whom they had wanted to become. The following instability eventually resulted in a new social pattern. Freud calls this the "first form of social organization," the beginnings of morality and law. And, being animated by the tenuous relating to the slain Father, these proto-institutions are all

---

[45] Assmann, "The Advance in Intellectuality," 16.
[46] Said, *Freud and the Non-European*, 44f, 51.
[47] Guy Stroumsa regards Freud's work as not only about Judaism and anti-Semitism but also "the 'historical truth' about religion – about religion in general ... which he claims to have discovered" (Stroumsa, "Myth into Novel," 206).

characterized by the *"renunciation of instinctual gratification."*[48] Specifically, this would include renouncing the grasp for obtaining the former authority position of the Father. (After having killed off his alpha-dominance, who would want to exalt themselves to that position and also get killed!?) This group refusal to retake the Father's position marks the transition into the hominid's apparently longest-standing social mode, already noted: aggressive egalitarianism.[49] Research from Richard Wrangham suggests the transition into egalitarianism through killing off alpha males is not entirely unreasonable. As anthropologist Melvin Konner summarizes Wrangham's hypothesis, "cooperative killing of incurably violent individuals played a central role in our self-domestication ... our ancestors killed men who were guilty of repeated acts of violence."[50] In other words, egalitarianism in the wake of the slain alpha may have meant those who exalted themselves were indeed humbled, fatally.

The killed Father is still to be worshipped but through its substitute – first through a sort of strong animal or totem, conjoined by a feast upon flesh, humanity's rudimentary form of religion and the site for revisiting the Father-cannibalism through repetition.[51] In the course of evolution, other replacements include not only animals but heroes and humanized deities, with a spectrum in between – including the mystifying animal-

---

[48] This involved "subordinating sense perception to an abstract idea ... a triumph of spirituality over the senses; more precisely, an instinctual renunciation accompanied by its psychologically necessary consequences" (*MM* 144).

[49] Ibid., 153. Robert Bellah argues that this egalitarianism characterized early humans for at least hundreds of thousands of years. He also outlines the transition from this to our much later statist-monarchies: "The elevation of rulers into a status unknown in tribal societies went hand in hand with the elevation of gods into a status higher in authority than the powerful beings they were gradually replacing.... The establishment of the early state ... destroyed the uneasy egalitarianism of hundreds of thousands if not millions of years of hominid evolution" (Robert N. Bellah, "What Is Axial About the Axial Age?," 69.

On another front: "Well-armed egalitarians will not allow enough authority to develop for alpha-style peacemakers to step in and stop hot conflicts, so, if peacemaking is to succeed among these hunter-gatherers or tribesmen, it must be attempted at an early stage of the conflict. When humans became egalitarian, such interference disappeared, while lethal self-help [taking vengeance into one's own hands] developed as a form of negative reciprocity that could be readily engaged in by male kinsmen of homicide victims" (Christopher Boehm, "Retaliatory Violence in Human Prehistory," 522, 527f).

[50] Richard Wrangham, *The Goodness Paradox*; Melvin Konner, "A Bold New Theory Proposes That Humans Tamed Themselves."

[51] *MM* 104, 168.

human hybrids we often find in early art.[52] In the emergence of the humanized deities, the maternal deities probably came first, then later male ones, who first emerged as sons of mothers.[53] These religious shifts corresponded with political shifts, wherein matriarchal structures were replaced by patriarchal structures, even if "the new fathers, it is true, never succeeded to the omnipotence of the primeval father."[54]

Killing off the alpha-male social pattern did not make for liberation from rules but new and noninstinctual ones. Renouncing the alpha male's regime gave birth to a sacred social canopy of taboos, obligations, and institutions deemed sacred. These include renouncing the Father's possessing of the mother or sister – the origin of exogamy and the taboo on incest.[55] Akin to Girard's notion of the sacred as protective misapprehension, Freud insists that these taboos, even if they emerged unconsciously in humanity, should not be regarded as mindless superstition. They are safeguards, renunciations of dangerously violent instincts, rules that protect the group, the establishment of authority for keeping order.[56] Human culture in this view was born in containing violence – through taboos, renouncing instincts, and rituals that rearrange violence after having killed off the old dominance pattern. In each stage of the emerging religiopolitical changes, unconsciously latent under the deity is the dead alpha male, whose imagined will is "the sacred." Primitive religion is ultimately relating to the will of the slain Father.[57]

The instinctual renunciations that surround the traumatic violence of the Father-murder, even if beneficially protective, come at a psychological cost. Memory of the murder of the Father is repressed in the human unconscious within the matrix of culture. As Freud knew from his therapy clients, people repress and manage their memories through various defense strategies, such as repetitively reviving a trauma so as to enact certain defenses against it. Such "fixation" can include compulsive avoidance, phobias, and inhibitions.[58] The farther the actual memory becomes disconnected from any conscious, rational management, the more trauma enters a "latency." The memory is then even less explicit, perhaps even unconscious underneath the fixations, which are no longer cognitively

---

[52] Ibid., 105, 171.
[53] Ibid., 64.
[54] Ibid., 105f.
[55] Ibid., 104.
[56] Ibid., 144, 152.
[57] Ibid., 253, 156, 165.
[58] Ibid., 95.

linked to the originary trauma, manifesting in neurosis. What can inter-rupt this entrenched latency is the "return of the repressed,"[59] when some event(s) resemble the original traumatic experience. When such retrigger-ing is accompanied by a weakening of the ego's defenses, the latent can more acutely return to the conscious, usually with great irrational force or terror.[60]

On an individual level, this seems to be common sense: psychological problems can likely be traced to traumas that haunt us in varying degrees. But Freud applies this to *collective* trauma, to *mass* psychology, and the transmission of unconscious memory traces *over generations and in groups*.[61] He argues, somewhat in the Lamarckian epigenetics frame-work, that experiences, traumas, repressions, latencies, and thought-dispositions can be transmitted genetically and culturally over time. Humans are not born as blank slates but as carriers of a messy mixture of phylogenetic inheritances that are not only bodily morphological but psychological and cultural.[62] Critics of Freud's Lamarckianism[63] today face some scientific challenges, as transgenerational epigenetic and phylo-genetic research has corroborated some of Lamarck's position. One such important study demonstrates how mice transmit traumatic experiences to their offspring genetically, without any interaction with the parents.[64] There is no reason to doubt that some such transmissions occur in humans too. And, given the entirely culturally embedded nature of humans, this can reasonably include our cultures and their transmission over generations.[65]

For Freud, it is not that religion *can* be neurotic. Rather, religion *is* the expression of fixations, latencies, and neuroses stemming from human-ity's deep-seated trauma. Religion is the word to describe the violence management and trauma stemming from the father's murder, repressed

---

[59] Ibid., 101, 107, 164, 170.

[60] Ibid., 121.

[61] Ibid., 87, 128, 163. Unconscious memory traces: 120, 170.

[62] Ibid., 120, 125, 127.

[63] Yosef Hayim Yerushalmi, *Freud's Moses*.

[64] Brian G. Dias and Kerry J. Ressler, "Parental Olfactory Experiences Influences Behavior and Neural Structure in Subsequent Generations," 1–9. Assmann seems to not factor in such research when he writes that "cultural memory is not biologically transmitted ... group memory has no neurological basis" (Jan Assmann, *Cultural Memory in Early Civilization* [hereafter *CMEC*], 72).

[65] "[Animals and humans] carry over into their new existence the experience of their kind; that is to say, that they have preserved in their minds memories of what their ancestors experienced" (*MM* 129).

since our origins.[66] Religion mediates the fact that humans "have always known – in this particular [unconscious, repressed] way – that once upon a time they had a primeval father and killed him."[67]

D. RESTORING THE PRIMAL FATHER

Akhenaten's despotism involved a supreme reenthronement of over-whelming magnitude, matched by conflict, rebellion, and resistance to it. This was doubly echoed out (hypothetically) in Moses' despotism that was put down in murderous revolt. Seen in an evolutionary framework, "monotheism" is the restoration of the paternal Father of his historical rights. Monotheism is the religion of the primal alpha-figure, the return of the one and only father deity whose power is unlimited.[68] The *credo quia absurdum* that so characterizes monotheistic religion is precisely the powerful return of the repressed trauma of the murder of the dominant patriarch.[69] Only with monotheism "was the grandeur of the primeval father restored; the emotions belonging to him could now be repeated."[70]

But, just as the murderous transition from a proto-human alpha-male pattern to egalitarianism involved repressions of instincts, so too danger and violence is repressed and contained in Mosaic monotheism. Moses' theological regime repressed any expressions of Father-hate; this was to be replaced by the guilt of one's own sin or Israel's sins.[71] As the Jews encountered national collapse, invasion, and exile over the centuries, any mistrust in the Father's providence was silenced and eclipsed by a pervasive guilt.[72] (As we will find in Chapter 6, this inwardly directed guilt was expressed through an available cultural-linguistic form: the imaginary of violating a political loyalty oath with a despotic overlord like the Assyrians.)

---

[66] Ibid., 71.

[67] Ibid., 129.

[68] Ibid., 106–9.

[69] Ibid., 107, 151.

[70] Ibid., 172; Sigmund Freud, *The Future of an Illusion*, 19. Utterances of certain Gods as "Father" litter the Iron Age, while Akhenaten addressed himself to his divine father as "your son" in the great hymn (Hoffmeier, *Akhenaten*, 53–4, 122).

[71] *MM* 172. Regina Schwartz notes a second repression with Moses' murder as *an Egyptian*: "you slay your *Other* to forge your identity – not your father" (*CC* 111).

[72] *MM* 172. And yet, the eventual collapse, one by one, of the imperial oppressors – Assyria, Babylon, the Seleucids, Rome, etc. – dimly confirmed the father's providence.

To manage this feeling of guilt, ascetic and spiritual practices increased over generations, drawing upon Atenic transcendence.[73] This makes for a feedback loop of ascetic, instinctual renunciations, resulting in the afore-noted "progress in intellectuality" – of which the ban on graven images is the outward cultic sign, and this ascetic, ego-strengthened, instinctual renunciation is the inner psychology. "Every renunciation of instinct now becomes a dynamic source of conscience and every fresh renunci-ation increases the latter's severity and intolerance."[74] By this unique combination, the Jews attained "ethical heights that had remained inaccessible to the other peoples of antiquity."[75]

With my larger goal of defending the Mosaic distinction in mind here, we must emphasize how Freud does not condemn this severe "intoler-ance." Indeed, it is precisely this intolerance that mediated the unique Jewish intellectual breakthrough. And yet, this enlightenment has its costs for Freud: the satisfaction of having renounced one's instincts feeds the ego – the by-product of which is the mirage-fantasy of "election" or "chosenness," of the Father having bestowed special favor.[76]

But latent within this increased intellectual rigor, under the increased asceticism, under the pride in having renounced instincts more effectively than the idolaters, under the deflected father-hate that we all bear, is the primal, repressed memory of the Father's founding murder. Why would this have particularly emerged among Israel? The repressed returned to their consciousness because of conditions that resembled the originary deed: the murder of the Father-like despot, Moses.[77] (Though he does not emphasize this, Akhenaten's despotic revolution and its rejection would also be another key moment within this return of the repressed.) So, while the conception of an almighty Father God was not exactly unique to the ancient near east, its combination with a repressed murder and an alpha-despotism made for a "reanimation of primeval experience in the human family that had long ago faded from the conscious memory of mankind."[78]

Provocatively, Freud argued that monotheism emerged through the trauma and repression surrounding collective murder of the alpha: "It seems as if the genesis of monotheism would not have been possible

[73] *MM* 109.
[74] Peter Gay, ed., *The Freud Reader*, 760; *MM* 128, 149.
[75] *MM* 173.
[76] Ibid., 79; 108–9, 135.
[77] Ibid., 140–3, 192.
[78] Ibid., 167.

without these events."[79] Though Judaism sometimes bore no consciousness of the Moses-murder trauma, it remained latent in the wish-fantasy
of a Messiah who would return from the dead and finally usher them into
the Promised Land.[80] Ideally, the doctrines of Moses, which prophesied
the father to whom they are subject, might have been "a stimulus to their
memory." But his teachings were met not with remembrance but rather a
repetition of the primal act of patricide. Centuries later, Christianity's
murdered Messiah again resurfaces the repressed murders of Moses, the
first messiah, and his subsequent prophets. Christ is not only the resurrected Moses but ultimately the return of the "primeval father of the
primitive horde"; only this time he is transposed, "as a Son in the place
of his Father."[81] One might surmise Freud would exegete Jesus' "the
Father and I are one," and "no one comes to the father except through
me" as rendering their seemingly separate murders as homologous: we
cannot expiate our guilt of the Father's founding murder except
through admitting to the Son's murder today. The repressed murder
returns with intense force when the memory trace is awakened in Paul:
"the reason we are so unhappy is because we killed God – if only we
would admit it."[82]

But just as under the Mosaic regime any father-hate was replaced by an
internalized legacy of guilt and a bolstered ego (the fantasy of election), so
too, in Freud's reading of Christianity, the attention devoted to the
traumatic murder was diverted and distorted. While Freud appreciates
Paul as having "correctly traced" humanity to its murderous source, Paul
doesn't quite represent the murder rightly, but more as a "fantasy of
expiation," wherein facing the trauma of the murder is diverted into the
sense of guilt in original sin.[83] By this diversion, Christ is more the leader
of the brother-horde who receives the due punishment for our uprising,
thus propitiating the Father's wrath and will. Through this propitiation –
and Freud unfortunately does not elaborate well here – the Son now
stands in the position that the brother-horde had coveted; the brother
now *is* God; whereas Judaism was a religion of the Father, Christianity
becomes the religion of the Son.[84]

---

[79] Ibid., 129f.
[80] Ibid., 43; 57.
[81] Ibid., 114.
[82] Ibid., 174; 113, 115, 176.
[83] Ibid., 110.
[84] Ibid.,175.

For Freud, Paul's expiation fantasy is yet another failure to maintain Judaism's "lofty heights of spirituality," gained under Aten.[85] This is evident in Paul's abandonment of circumcision – which had symbolized the primal castration-threat of the Father, to which Egypt's sons submitted.[86] And all of Freud's complaints against the ritualistic primitiveness of Yahweh are repeated in accusing Christianity of regression into magic, ritual, and superstition. In Christianity, the gods are re-enthroned in thinly veiled ways, like its mother of god.[87] For all of Christianity's enlightenment, in explicitly returning the repressed founding murder to our consciousness, its regression into paganism is for Freud really the "priests of Amun returning vengeance yet again upon the children of Akhenaton" to bury once again the higher spirituality. The true "progress in spirituality" abides in the Jewish spirituality of the dematerialized God, its instinctual renunciations, and its ethical heights.

Freud's praises of monotheism's "progress in spirituality" are measured. When we glance upon this drama of a killed primal Father and imagine how its repression has returned to consciousness – through Atenic monotheism and the Christian representation of murder – he indeed appraises both these religions as unparalleled breakthroughs to truth.[88] But he demurs from seeing such breakthroughs as verifications of the "eternal Truth" of some Father-God, Supreme Being notion. However lofty a concept this is in one sense, such a "Being" is for him idealism at best, but more a mode of neurosis.[89] Such a God concept, as a projection of the Primitive Father's sovereignty, he regards as a distortion of thought, "a delusion." But, "in so far as it brings to light something from the past, it must be called truth."[90]

E. WHAT TO DO WITH MOSES AND MONOTHEISM?

Freud's *MM* made quite a stir in academia and thus earned its own version of repression. His hypothetical "founding scenario" of an alpha

---

[85] Ibid., 111.

[86] Ibid., 112.

[87] By which I imagine he means Mary/Jesus as an iteration of the Isis/Horus cycle, for example – or perhaps other King/Queen of Heaven pairings, as in the Ugaritic Ilu/Athiratu or the Canaanite El/Asherah.

[88] This does not exclude Islam, which for Freud is a repetition of the Mosaic revolution in its own way (*MM* 118).

[89] Ibid., 157; Peter Gay, *A Godless Jew*; Wistrich, "Sigmund Freud's Last Testament," 52.

[90] *MM* 167.

male murder, however speculative, underwent an unfortunately premature censure in anthropological studies – through a series of misunderstandings about its non-falsifiability, detailed by anthropologist Richard Smith.[91]

A philosophical husk that can obviously be discarded with Freud's theory is the dualistic oppositions of enlightenment versus religion/ritual/magic, or spiritual immateriality versus materialist hedonism, or logic versus myth. This disenchantment-dualism is visible in his hard distinction between the universal, anti-ritualistic pacifist god, Aten, and the superstitious, ritualistic, violent volcanism of Yahweh. This echoes out in his denouncing Christianity, in its magic-sacramentalism and reestablishment of pagan mother gods, as having lusted for the fleshpots of Amun's Egypt. In this dichotomy, Freud's project can be seen as flirting with a certain Enlightenment deism that may shipwreck upon hard, empirical reality far more nuanced than dualism. For he blatantly calls black white: we have a Pharaoh sitting atop one of the largest violent imperial agglomerations in history and a lavish temple system of over 2,000 offering tables at Amarna[92] – and Freud dares call it pacifist and averse to ritual.

We need not dwell long here on the countless ways this rigid distinction between intellection and ritualism can be put to rest, as I will return to it in Chapter 7, seeking to moderate both the myth/history, primitive/enlightenment antinomies and interpret Christ as a total separation from, and yet engagement between, God and the victim-mechanism. We can simply note here the *impossibility* of such an epistemological optimism: there is no non-ritualized, non-mythic space in human thought and culture. Ritual, myth, and narrative are fundamental modes of human thought and speech. There is no escape into pure non-mythical thought. Rational thought is an extension of, not an opposition to, mythical thought. "Ritual, when thrown out at the front door, returns at the back door: there are even anti-ritual rituals," as Robert Bellah notes.[93] Seeing past the simplistic antinomy, one is reminded of how many Jews have cultivated what Betty Rojtman calls a non-idolatrous *"material spirituality."*[94]

---

[91] Richard Smith, "Freud and Evolutionary Anthropology's First Just-So Story," 50–3.

[92] John Wilson, *The Culture of Ancient Egypt*, 207; Hoffmeier, *Akhenaten*, 143, 150; *NOG* 169.

[93] Bellah, "What Is Axial?," 85.

[94] Rojtman, "The Double Death of Moses," 107. I may not give Freud sufficient credit on this point, as he does not see monotheism as a "pure" breakthrough in enlightenment, but

As for the biblical, theological content of his book, one can understand its weak reception, and not merely due to a defensive bias of theologians. Since Freud's time, it has become clear to archaeologists and historians that the link between Akhenaten and Judaism is much weaker than he suggests. A leading Egyptologist, Donald Redford, writes that we have little or no evidence to support the linkage. "The monotheism of the Hebrew Bible and the New Testament had its own separate development – one that began more than half a millennium after the pharaoh's death."[95] If anything, the Phoenician scribal tradition, not some Aten-priest, may have carried some pieces of Egyptian texts and ideas into Israelite tradition (maybe like Psalm 104, which reflects Akhenaten's Great Hymn, etc.).[96] Assmann simply writes, "the two religions are worlds apart," with the exception of their both rejecting the other's gods.[97] As we will explore, Jewish monotheism took a significantly different trajectory than an Aten-influence would suggest.

But, while some aspects of Freud's thesis have been critiqued or falsified, scholarship on his thesis has seen a recent increase in over a dozen monographs.[98] One could even regard Girard's work as one such critical redeployment of Freud's originary murder hypothesis, even if Girard disavows that it was an ingredient in his mimetic theory. Girard saw in the representation of Christ's Passion an urge to "get back to origins and look once again at constitutive acts of transference so as to discredit and annul them."[99] No theory I have read to date more closely resembles Freud. The notion of resurfacing a founding murder – that has latent reverberations in our culture – and "admitting" to it, is a shared, crucial aspect in their theories. When asked of his take on Freud's *MM*, Girard affirmed it as comprehending religion "better than anyone," highlighting

---

rather a complex insight that transitions us into a new tension, *a new pathology* – with its own, real footholds on truth – not a release from pathology. At times, Freud seems to admit that the notion of a pure release from pathology is itself a delusion; one cannot speak from the position of neutral observer and simply reject this new tension.

[95] Donald B. Redford, "Aspects of Monotheism." A minority opinion holds that Atenism may have influenced Israel: William Propp, "Monotheism and 'Moses,'" 539; Hoffmeier, *Akhenaten*, 246.

[96] *NOG* 173; *IR* 40f.

[97] *ATM* 64, 68.

[98] See a catalog in *PM* 85, 134 n1. In post-revolution Egypt (2012), Akhenaten has been embraced by Muslim leaders and has elsewhere served as a diffuse global symbol of revolutionary rebirth, as "marginalized groups around the world, ranging from gay-rights activists to Afrocentrists, have gravitated to the figure of Akhenaten" (Peter Hessler, "Akhenaten," 142–3).

[99] *TH* 153; *EC* 141; *ISS* 137.

how the themes of an inevitably resurfacing murder ultimately validate mimetic theory.[100] Yet, he sought to expand Freud's thesis of Moses' lynching – which he affirms as "more authentically biblical than it seems" – beyond the biblical frame. Girard would have us remember that similar rumors of murder surrounded "Romulus, Zoroaster and most foundational religious figures …. All these stories resemble the story of Moses, as interpreted by Freud, but he never related them, and that is why he was not able to discover the scapegoat mechanism."[101]

Girard also often critiqued Freud as too rigidly fixed on the psychology of the "father" or "mother" figures, insisting instead on a more generalized mimesis that can attach to any model. Desire for the mother, if it is common, is simply mimetic desire conducted through its most commonly on-hand model, the father. Oedipal desire is merely a species of mimetic desire, not a basic instinct.[102] This grants mimetic theory greater flexibility in interpreting the variety of ethnographic data on how mimesis can arbitrarily work in groups and lynch mobs.

Girard's preference for a more generalized mimesis than Oedipal desire, however, also means a more generalized, random scapegoat. The broader, more arbitrary aims of mimesis inclines Girard to not draw the dramatic link Freud does between monotheism and the re-enthronement of the sovereign primeval father. Girard thus does not offer much commentary on Freud's (underdeveloped) observation that Christianity's Divine Son finally fulfills our primevally forged desire to "take the place of the father." Some connection may be in Girard's brief and provocative assertion that we killed Christ because we wanted to be him.[103] As such, Christ's murder represents the primally slain father, whom we also wanted to be. But Girard has tended to emphasize not an analysis of sovereignty with respect to symbols of father and son but how the mimetic processes of demonization-lynching-divinization affects our cultural psyche. The mimetic process can be enacted upon any scapegoat – outsiders, insiders, people too unlike the group, exceptionally normal people, etc. – not just a powerful father figure. It is a machine into which anyone can be thrown and come out a god. As such, monotheism is for

---

[100] *EC* 186.

[101] *EC* 204.

[102] See *VS* chs 7 and 8.

[103] "Cannibalism is the essence of sacrifice. Cannibalism means that you eat the sacrificial victim in order to be your victim, because you want to be that victim. The reason you killed him is you want to be him" (Rene Girard, "Afterword," in Michael Hardin, *Reading the Bible with Rene Girard*; *EC* 217).

Girard less about "reenthronement of the father," or the "son taking the throne with the father" – or any such variation – and more of "a refusal to divinize victims" and a devictimization of God. In any case, one sees numerous, under-explored lines of inquiry at the intersection of mimetic theory and the monotheistic scholarship of which Freud is but a part.[104]

By mimetic theory's lights, I think, the more interesting idea in *MM* is less the connection between Moses and Akhenaten and far more the connection between monotheism and the monopoly on violence. By this monopoly, I refer to how violence is used, consolidated, and represented in groups, vested in a "legitimate" or sacred center. As noted, such a violence-monopoly over a region is often regarded as the most basic feature of what makes a "state." As Robertson-Smith wrote, "What is often described as a natural tendency of Semitic religions toward ethical monotheism is in the main nothing more than a consequence of the alliance of religion and monarchy."[105] This becomes interesting insofar as monotheism coincides with the emergence of large states and monarchies, marking a relatively recent (in evolutionary terms) resurgence of the long-since abandoned alpha-male dominance pattern. The resurgence must be seen in great contrast with the much longer hunter-gatherer history of violently enforced egalitarianism. In monotheism, conjoined with the state's monopoly of the legitimate use of violence, Freud sees a return to the earlier alpha-submission patterns.

In the state's monopoly on violence, the relationship between monotheism and "peace" is *radically* ambivalent. Having monopolized violence, the state insists and enforces that all subjects are duty-bound pacifists, with the law never to be taken into one's own hands. That is, "vengeance is mine" saith the state, police, and judiciary. Although we will explore and ultimately affirm the notion that monotheism somehow separates God from the political theologies of archaic states, we must bear in mind how this process could have been partially shaped by the growth of imperial power, the development of a judiciary, and the outsourcing of violence-containment into a distinct police force. These political changes – and not merely *choosing*, through ideational conviction, to distinguish God from the political order – may be correlated with the emergence of monotheistic religion. The radical ambivalence of this development

---

[104] E.g., Goodhart, *The Prophetic Law*; Kathryn M. Frost, "Freud, *Moses and Monotheism*, and the Conversation between Mimetic Theory and Psychoanalysis"; Thomas E. Reynolds, "Beyond Violence in Monotheism."

[105] W. R. Smith, *The Religion of the Semites*, 74.

concerns how the state's consolidated "peace" – its "reabsorption of alterity into oneness," per Mouffe – may at points feel deceptively non-coercive, especially when its daily constraints are as small as a pinch of incense, taxes, or periodic public executions. (Or, in the modern era, its violence becomes even less visible as punishments decreasingly serve as public spectacles.)[106] This will call to mind Mouffe's critique of a depoliticized liberalism, which becomes forgetful of its own exclusions and sees itself as a non-hegemonic unity. Under a consolidated monopoly on violence, one is tempted to see the political order as nonviolent, if only incidentally violent. We might call this a pacifism "from above," which would have naturally permeated cultures where archaic states increasingly monopolized legal violence into a judiciary and police force.

It would seem reasonable in such an analysis, yet entirely wrong, to cynically regard the commands to "love your enemies" and "leave vengeance to God," as nothing more than a by-product of the emergent state. While the ancient state's increasingly ubiquitous monopoly on violence may have made possible a certain kind of enemy-love and restraint upon retribution, such "pacifism from above" seems the photographic negative of what we can call a love of enemies "from below." It stretches credulity, for example, to see Christ's command to walk a second mile (or other commanded acts of creative nonviolence) as a mere by-product of servility to the Roman occupation – when it obviously violates its regulations.[107] Or, more recently, one should doubt that Gandhian pacifism was a mere reflex of the pacifying effects of English empire, or that the civil rights movement's nonviolence was mere cowering to the United States' institutionalized white hegemony. Rather, we see in such provocative (even "divisive") peaceableness a nonviolent problematization of the state that, at the same time, does not enter into direct conflict with it. Perhaps the argument could be made that the growth of archaic states and law constructed a sphere of relative safety amidst subordination, making *possible* new kinds of imaginaries with respect to violence – for example, a growing trust that some *other* entity ("the Father" = "the State") will avenge transgressions, thus diminishing some pathways of vengeance. But the above examples of nonviolence strike me less as instances of submitting-to-the-Father-viz-the-state and more the *refusals* of such idolatrous unity. They reserve the Father, as it were, a space unrepresented in the State. They offer a very *different* vision of unity, manifesting in fact as

---

[106] Michel Foucault, *Discipline and Punish*, 7.
[107] Walter Wink, *Engaging the Powers*, 175ff.

rabble-rousing disturbances to public order. We thus must be able to conceptualize very different kinds of relations between "monotheism" and the political monopoly on violence – those of symbiosis and those of political apophasis. As will emerge in the coming chapters, we must be able to imagine how there could be "two radically opposed yet formally similar modes of divinity."[108]

If Girard is an "implicit" theorist on Freud's linkage between murder and monotheism, the leading *explicit* theorist on *MM* today is Jan Assmann.[109] Assmann, informed by the century of Egyptological scholarship since Freud, picks up where Freud left off. And, more specific to the concerns of this book, he treats monotheism with special attention to our concerns of violence, intolerance, and political theology. Though one Girardian, Wolfgang Palaver, cites Assmann as yet another simplistic accuser of monotheism's special penchant for violence (like the New Atheism's Richard Dawkins et al.),[110] and Joseph Ratzinger and Mark S. Smith see Assmann's "Mosaic intolerance" as univocally a slur against biblical revelation, we find a more subtle and complex account once we read him closely. For, not only Freud, but Assmann too affirms the intolerance of the Mosaic distinction as the source of its "progress of intellectuality." If nothing else, Freud is very *obviously championing* the importance of the Mosaic distinction by praising the enlightenment of Atenism and battering the regressive falsehoods of Yahwehism – even if his speculations are schematic, simplistic, or even shots in the historical dark.

Insofar as Assmann develops upon Freud, he will supplement the monotheistic rudiments in Girard's theory. To clarify my goals, we are not in search of the exact lineage and activities of the historical Moses (if he even existed) or his hypothesized murder. Rather, my search centers upon what one can accurately say of the epochal changes monotheism wrought in the polytheistic world with respect to the political order, gods, and victims. What did the world incur through these revolutionary changes? Adding to Freud's "progress in intellectuality," Assmann argues monotheism radically alters not only our conception of God but also human nature and politics itself. This monotheism, forged over centuries, ultimately emerges, in the midst of the ancient world, as an unprecedented breakthrough.

---

[108] *TOB* 43f.
[109] "The most comprehensive attempt so far to locate Freud's *Moses and Monotheism* on the spectrum of the history of ideas has been pursued by Jan Assmann" (Schäfer, "The Triumph of Pure Spirituality," 35).
[110] Palaver, "The Ambiguous Cachet of Victimhood," 74, 81.

4

Containing Violence and Two Entirely Different Kinds of Religion

Freud broached several topics central to Assmann's investigation of monotheism. These include the notion of humanity's culturally transmitted complex relationship to power, murder, and instinctual renunciation; the emergence of intolerant monotheism in Akhenaten's Egypt prior to Israel; and, finally, Judaism's "progress in intellectuality" with respect to these histories. The following chapters will explore how Assmann ultimately discerns in these topics a break between the "political theologies" of polytheism and monotheism. As noted in my Introduction, I am using political theology here to refer to the way a society configures and represents the relations of God, gods, rulers, administrators, legitimacy, and political power. The argument that emerges in coming chapters is that polytheism "contained" violence, whereas monotheism releases or unleashes violence. In subtler form, I argue that monotheism rearranged the polytheistic symbols of sovereignty to begin dividing God from the ancient religiopolitical order.

I will present that argument by first distilling from Assmann and related scholarship a framework for categorizing different kinds of religion and violence. This involves separating out two major ideal types or *genera* of religion – those compacted with the sociopolitical order and those separated from it. I will then introduce Assmann's concept of the "translatability" of religions. Translatability, in brief, refers to whether one can exchange a god's name or religion into the god-names of other religions and cultures – that is, a certain comparability or parallelism between religions. Chapter 5 then explores a brief case study of political theology in ancient Egypt, to be later contrasted with the biblical gestation of monotheism.

A. DIFFERENT KINDS OF RELIGION

The outline that follows is my distillation of Assmann's categorizing different kinds of religions. It contains the two large *genera* of "primary" and "secondary" religions, customary categories for historic analyses of religion.[1] Violence and translatability are then overlaid, making for three different species of religions. Assmann uses such classifications as Weberian "ideal types" – simplified categories to make sense of what are, in reality, blurry phenomena.[2] As such, we should keep in mind that the rubric used here is specifically for methodological purposes in discussing violence, intolerance, and monotheism, and are not meant to exhaustively classify religions.

(1) **Primary religions:** locative (place-based), cult oriented, immanent-cosmotheistic religions (these religions and cultures "contain" four kinds of violence: raw, legal, political, and ritual):

    (a) *Nontranslatable* tribal religions

    (b) *Translatable* (thus "polytheistic"), state-based, archaic religions[3]

(2) **Secondary religions:** world/utopian (not place-based), book oriented, invisible-transcendent[4] (these religions introduce the new possibility of "religious violence")

    (c) *Nontranslatable*, generally "exclusive monotheism" religions. While first attempted by Akhenaton, a border case between primary and secondary religions, the key historical instantiation is found in the Mosaic distinction. This is set in a larger context of axial age religions and cultures around the world, catalyzed by changes in writing technology and the construction of canonical texts.

i. Primary and Secondary Religions

Primary religion refers to a cultural mode of being that dates back to even our pre-human context. Such religions are specific to a local culture and

---

[1] One will notice a rough similarity with Girard's common usage of "archaic" religion in contrast with "biblical" or revealed religion.

[2] GG 110.

[3] Bellah similarly discusses the homology of sociopolitical and religious realities in tribes and archaic states, wherein "supernature, nature, and society were all fused in a single cosmos" (Bellah, "What Is Axial?," 70).

[4] Henri Bergson used the classes of "static" and "dynamic" religions, which correspond with Assmann on the distinction between *immersed* ("conciliatory") and *distanced* ("redemptive") religions (*PM* 126).

place, and are marked by the centrality of cult, ritual, and illiteracy. They draw no distinction between true and false religion. Here "religion" does not really exist – that is, it is not a distinct category of life but inextricably coextensive with culture. "There were no 'religions' in pagan societies, only 'cults' and 'cultures.' 'Religion,' like 'paganism,' is an invention of monotheism."[5] This is all the more evident in tribal societies without a distinct police force or judiciary; taboos and rituals embedded in the culture do the work of containing group violence.

In such intimate contact between culture, gods, and violence-management, one does not "believe" in the gods. Gods are not objects of "faith," but one "knows" about gods in a way that may strike us today, who live in a world saturated by monotheism, as oddly matter of fact or intuitive.[6] The gods are as *real* as the political body with which they are associated. One does not believe in gods any more than one believes in the police or judges. Instead of entailing a distinctly secular world as contrasted with a singularly transcendent God, primary religions instead live in "a world of gods,"[7] bequeathing meaning and order. Whatever the limitations or seeming superstitions of primary religions, in an evolutionary scope their structuring of meaning is still a crucial achievement and organization of human thought. For it conceptualizes humanity as woven into a divine cosmic network in which society and politics cohere in a field of "order, truth, and harmony."[8]

Secondary religions, by contrast, are global (less place-based) religions, centered on texts more than a locative cult. These coincide with a general decline in (or a replacement of) sacrificial cult.[9] Such "book-" or "founded-" or "revealed-" religions include the Western monotheisms of Judaism, Christianity, and Islam, as well as Jainism, Sikhism, and, even with its complex relationship to theism, Buddhism – all founded, in some form, on a canonized scripture.[10] And though these all build upon primary religions, they typically draw up some sort of distinction from or

---

[5] *GG* 10. In ancient Egypt, for example, "Cult and political identity are aspects of one and the same concept of divine presence and communication" (ibid., 15). Also Daniel Boyarin, "The Christian Invention of Religion."

[6] *PM* 15.

[7] For Assmann, polytheism has three elements: a world of gods, humankind, and society. The divine difference of monotheism, which separates the world and God, adds a fourth: God, the cosmos, humankind, and society (ibid., 40).

[8] *CMA* 395.

[9] *PM* 104, 109.

[10] Ibid., 104; *ATM* 88. All secondary religions, he notes, follow either the example of the Buddhist or Hebrew canon, the two original innovators of religious canon (*CMA* 390).

denunciation against primary religions as pagan, idolatrous, or superstitious.[11]

Secondary religions draw a distinction between "faith" and "knowledge" that simply did not exist in primary religions. This is a revolutionary new kind of truth: absolute, revealed, metaphysical, exclusive, or fideistic truth, which does not stem from empirical observation and experience.[12] Instead of "knowing" God, one instead "believes" in God.[13] As such, secondary religions entail a radical transformation of the primary sacred from a localized culturally identical mode – in which gods are known and the sacred is more immanently manifest in the world – into a mode that is detachable from a society and transplantable.[14] Perhaps overstating this ideal type, Assmann writes that, for secondary religions, "the sacred is no longer to be found in the world,"[15] migrating from the cosmos, cult, and king into scripture. (But even in ideal form, this would seem quite odd, given the largest secondary religion's position on sacred presence in Catholicism.) If religion in this secondary mode doesn't entirely destroy sacrifice, it at least turns it into more an act of optional "faith" than collective, civic obligation.[16] In the Girardian sense, the violence contained in the archaic sacred does not disappear in secondary religions but fractures, migrates, and is outsourced to the spheres of law, politics, and sports, while "religious" phenomena – often privatized and decoupled from the civic realm – begin to fade from their role and capacity in containing violence.

Faith in secondary religions, besides involving a new kind of "interiority,"[17] are *against* primary religion, requiring individual conversion.[18] Indeed the counter-religious disposition against paganism is "structurally related to conversion" and the obligation to remember – so as to avoid relapse.[19] Here the command that you shall have no other gods means one has to commit to "love God with all one's heart" (Deut 6:5): "In the frame of this partnership, man grows individualistic and God grows

---

[11] *PM* 1.

[12] Ibid., 15; *ATM* 58. This adds another species of "truth" to what Assmann regards as the already existing pagan list of truths: the truths of experience, mathematical truth, historical truth, and truths conducive to life. Secondary religions add "religious truth."

[13] *PM* 15; *MPC* 146.

[14] *PM* 105.

[15] Ibid., 106.

[16] Stroumsa, *The End of Sacrifice*, 89; *PM* 108.

[17] *GG* 110.

[18] *CMEC* 184; *ME* 7, 24; *PM* 15.

[19] *ME* 216.

monotheistic."[20] By contrast, Cicero, writing in what may be called a primary mode of religion, speaks of religion inextricably within the political collective, not an individual's commitment: "no one shall have gods to himself, either new gods or alien gods, *unless recognized by the State.*"[21] One does not "convert" to a religion in the world of primary religions. In its stronger forms, the conversion spirit of secondary religion retains the purity of an event, the un-institutionizable holy, which cannot be mediated by culture, rituals, or seasonal rhythms. The vigilance toward conversion allows no such "auto-pilot," no serene stability; its spirit is "countercultural." Its zeal is expressed less in cult, much less the state; its spirit "can only be guaranteed longevity as a textual corpus, not as an institutionalized religion, at least not in absolute strictness, purity, and consequentiality."[22]

Consonant with this sense of "conversion," secondary religions do not see themselves as the result of a slow evolution of the many toward the One but rather as a revelatory "revolution."[23] Even if biblical monotheism or other secondary religions may have, in history, slowly evolved out of polytheism, in memory they tend to represent and conduct their religion as if they were a revolutionary break from polytheism, excluding it. For example, the Jewish proclamation "The Lord is One" had many ancient parallels in exaltation of the One Creator above/behind the many gods and created things (like the Egyptian proclamation "Amun is One"). But the Jewish variant is very different in what follows: the *exclusivist* religious commandment, "You shall have no other Gods." Regarding this exclusive against-ness, "there is no parallel in the religions dwelling on the theme of divine oneness."[24] Primary religions may have drawn distinctions between purity/impurity, sacred/profane; but the notion of "false" religions is foreign to them.[25] In sum, unlike the primary religions, secondary religions *know that they are religions*, and they tend to look at

---

[20] *CMA* 397.

[21] Cicero, *De legibus*, 2.8.19, italics added.

[22] "Counterreligion is an aggregate state that no religion can sustain in the long run. None of these secondary religions has ever been able to avoid (and perhaps even wanted to avoid) incorporating into itself elements of the very primary religions it proscribes as pagan" (*PM* 34f).

[23] *GG* 107; *CMA* 369–70. "Correct, embellish, and complete Baal and Astarte as you will, you will never make the God of Moses out of the gods of Canaan" (De Lubac, *The Discovery of God*, 34).

[24] *GG* 108; *PM* 34; John F. A. Sawyer, "Biblical Alternatives to Monotheism," 175.

[25] *GG* 84.

other religions as being false or at least lacking truth.[26] Israel's construct of "pagan Egypt" is the most famous example.

Though lumping all religious forms into these two large *genera* can appear too crude to supply any meaning, it is at least better than seeing "religion" as always referring to the same, one kind of thing. Rather, "religion" can mean at least two very different kinds of things. Using two major ideal types helps us consider entirely different arrangements between the "political" and "religious" spheres, or we might say between violence and the sacred. There is a primary mode of religion in which divinity coincides with state, cosmos, and culture; and there is a secondary mode in which it is somehow different from the state, cosmos, and culture. Secondary religion thus entails the epochal separation between Church and State, religion and politics. And this separation can be negotiated in numerous ways – for better and worse.

Once we find that secondary religions derive their symbols *from* primary religions (like faith, allegiance, jealousy), as we will see in these chapters, we can expect even secondary religions to display a messy mixture between political and "religious" symbols. In this sense, primary and secondary categories are perhaps better regarded as *dimensions* or *layers* of religion. While secondary religions indeed critique the primary form, certain primary elements inescapably remain. Secondary religions may critique primary elements of cultic sociopolitical obligation and place-based cult, but they cannot *escape* elemental social features like ritual, myth, inclusion/exclusion – ultimately, the political. Counter-religions and countercultures inevitably embody a political, cultural, or institutional dimension. This notion of inescapability calls to mind – and I go beyond Assmann here – parallels with Mouffe's social theory. She saw in liberalism, in its pursuit of a society beyond exclusion, a transcendent, intolerant, and critical movement that resembles "secondary" features: its agitation against all hegemony, all exclusion makes it *counter-political*, as it were. It invokes an intolerant distinction of societies being wrong or deficient insofar as they fail to enact liberal values. But, she adds, this movement cannot ultimately escape the exclusions and decisions of the political – the "primary," constitutive dimension of all human association, as one finds in democracy or *any* kind of association. And yet, despite the apparent incompatibility and friction between these layers, she does not advocate abandoning the transcendent, liberal layer.

[26] *PM* 112.

Put differently, the primary/secondary classification offers a hermeneutic for the interlaced roots and genes between political and religio-theological symbols. Carl Schmitt, for example, argued that "all significant concepts of the modern theory of the state are secularized theological concepts."[27] But this primary/secondary classification adds that the reverse is also true; much of what counts now as "religious" or theological was once homologous with the political realm and only later hived off into this secondary sense. Assmann thus rejoins: "The significant concepts of theology are theologized political concepts."[28] Even if secondary religion involves some separation of religious and political spheres, they left a lot of residues on each other. One cannot easily say whether the concepts of "faith" or "allegiance" are fundamentally political or religious concepts.[29] Seemingly non-religious things, like capitalism or nationalism, might be regarded as "religions" in the primary religion sense of a socially binding mythos. It depends on whether one is referring to the primary or secondary kind of religion. Even secular polities involve "faith."

Distinguishing two major kinds of religions also helps us take more seriously the major transformative impact that literacy and written technologies have had on human subjectivity and cultural representation, especially pivoting around the great transformations of the first millennium BCE. Attention to such shifts from primary to secondary religions is housed within axial age theory, a hypothesized era of religious and intellectual revolution where three major centers of civilization virtually simultaneously underwent radical innovations in thought – in the Mediterranean/Mid-East, India, and China. This is an era not merely associated with material innovations but with what some call a revolutionary "leap in being" that divides time into a before and after, an "estrangement" from the past that its predecessors may not have known.[30] This leap emerged partly due to the substantial effects of writing technologies on culture and thought,[31] creating the intellectual world that we now recognize more as our own. Prominent axial theorists include Jaspers, Voegelin, Habermas, Bellah, and Eisenstadt – as well as

---

[27] Carl Schmitt, *Political Theology*, 36.
[28] Jan Assmann, *Herrschaft und Heil*, 20; Giorgio Agamben, *The Kingdom and the Glory*, 193.
[29] Carolyn Marvin and David Engle, "Blood Sacrifice and the Nation."
[30] *CMA* 375.
[31] *ATM* 85ff.

Assmann.[32] The axial age is usually defined around 800 BCE to 200 BCE, though this is strongly disputed. For example, Assmann's emphasis on how writing helped restructure human thought and the critique of mythic thinking leads him to diffuse the period to a time frame 5,000–6,000 years ago and hold the theory much more loosely.[33]

Assmann argues that many axial theorists like Weber or Voegelin over-emphasized similarities between these cultures of the first millennium BCE while excessively thinking the changes were driven by *ideas*.[34] By contrast, Assmann emphasizes the close relationship between intellectual *and historical processes* (material forces, politics, culture, etc.). For him, although monotheism – a key axial movement – was undoubtedly mediated through ideas and human agency, its rise may have been more a *by-product* of historical changes and events. As we will discuss in detail, Israel's "breakthrough" to monotheism is for him more a result of their national breakdown.[35] We also do well to bear in mind other massive material forces surrounding this theoretical axial age: the metallurgy transition from bronze to iron affecting farming and warfare; or changes toward market economies that destabilized traditional patterns; or advances in literacy technologies, just to name a few.[36]

ii. Translatability and Political Theology

A more detailed layer that Assmann adds to this primary/secondary classification is the notion of "translatability." This concept refers to whether a religion (its gods, ideas, rituals, culture, politics) can say of another religion or political group, "same god, different name" or "different god, similar functions." Herodotus, for example, understood the

---

[32] Root theorists begin at least around Abraham Anquetil-Duperron (1731–1805) and Alfred Weber (1868–1958). Samuel Eisenstadt, "The Axial Conundrum between Transcendental Visions and Vicissitudes of Their Institutionalizations." Karl Jaspers, *The Origin and Goal of History.*

[33] *CMA* 380, 383, 389; *ATM* 81.

[34] *ATM* 94.

[35] See also Eric Weil, "What Is a Breakthrough in History?" Both Bellah and Weil see Israel's "revolution in mythospeculation," compared with its neighboring cultures, as the most pronounced (Bellah, "What Is Axial?," 89). Voegelin discusses Toynbee's notion of the biblical history as a by-product of *disintegrations*: Abraham from the disintegration following Hammurabi, Moses from the disintegration of Egypt's New Kingdom, the Prophets from the disintegration of Syriac civilization, and Christianity from the disintegration of Hellenic civilization (*OH* 120).

[36] Bellah, "What Is Axial?," 74; *NOG* 253–5.

Greek gods as imported from Egypt and then translated into different names, tasks, and ornamentation, identifying Horus with Apollo, Osiris with Dionysius.[37] Cicero similarly equated Thoth with Hermes.[38] And while gods could be translated according to their functions, so too could a singular supreme God be translated: Varro, Porphyry, Symmachus, Celsus, Plutarch, Seneca, and Pliny the Elder all spoke of a One behind the many, whose specific name didn't so much matter, given their shared, singular, ultimate referent.[39]

By contrast, monotheism's intolerant "untranslatability" is quite different. We know from the prophetic injunctions and numerous passages of monotheistic violence against the idolaters that the biblical texts regard other religions as a kind of disloyalty to Yahweh or false; they are not translatable with Yahweh's religion. Outsiders of that religion, too, like the Greek philosopher Strabo (b. 64 BCE), understood the Mosaic religion as a counter-religion that could not translate with the other religions.[40] And as noted in Chapter 3, it has been the aim of many theologians for centuries to soften this counter-ness and untranslatability in light of its apparent intolerance or potential for conflict. Assmann regards this exclusive untranslatability as crucial to the transformations that radically shaped the ancient world; and it is still with us today, lingering amidst the problems of "religious violence" and "intolerance." "Translatability" roughly manifests itself in three religious forms (again, as ideal types):

(1) "Primitive" and "tribal" religions exist in small, face-to-face groups. While varying greatly, these religions are generally *not translatable* with other religions and are "by necessity, ethnocentric."[41] The most extreme cases would be tribal religions that regard outsiders as not even human.[42] Contact and interaction with other groupings are shunned or at

---

[37] Herodotus, *Histories*, 2.144.

[38] *De Natura Deorum*, 3.22.56; *GIT* 252f.

[39] *GG* 56; *PM* 19f. See, e.g., Pliny the Elder, *Natural History*, 2.15: deities are a matter of "different names to different people" (*GIT* 243). Or, Apuleius of Madaurus, *Metamorphoses*, 11: "my divinity is one, worshipped by all the world under different forms, with various rites, and by manifold names."

[40] *ME* 38; Richard J. Bernstein, "Jan Assmann," 5.

[41] *PM* 24.

[42] Girard writes of this: "In many archaic societies [like the Mundurucu] there are no human beings outside the tribe: they represent themselves as the only humans" (*EC* 115; Irenäus Eibl-Eibesfeldt, *Love and Hate*, 99–100; R. F. Murphy, "Intergroup Hostility and Social Cohesion," 1028).

least carefully controlled. Untranslatability here is a safeguard against the dangers of potential violence of the unknown other, and it corresponds with the lack of shared cultural presuppositions and norms that might mediate safe encounters.

As for Girard's mimetic theory, he focused more often on the ethnographies of tribal religions and spent little time distinguishing them from the following translatable religions of archaic states. And yet, of crucial concern for him was the difference between societies with a judiciary (which operate more through "reactive" and precise vengeance) and tribal societies (whose religious taboos and sacrifices serve more as preventatives to vengeance). For Girard, a key feature of tribal religions is how they contain violence through sacrifice, whereas sacrifice languishes in societies with a judiciary.[43] For a judiciary subsumes many of the former violence-containment functions of sacrifice and taboo in tribal religion; and law's codification enables a society to risk a greater social osmosis as they expand beyond an intimate group. Nontranslatable tribal religions will not retain the center of this book's attention.

(2) With the growth of archaic states and larger settled societies in the last several thousand years – increasingly composed of larger populations of strangers – there emerge translatable religions. Generally regarded within a meta-system of "polytheism," these religions and gods are more translatable across cities and cultures, accommodating greater intercultural exchange and trade. For example, our earliest documents of international law, dating back to the third millennium BCE, contain god-lists, glossaries of translated god-names of ancient empires. Peace treaties and alliances across city-states or empires were written up with reference to their gods who are translatable according to their cosmic, biological, or cultural functions (i.e., a city's storm god, its god of craftsmanship, war, magic, etc.).[44] Often, these gods serve as "an international divine council" as witnesses to the treaty's terms.[45] In this case, intercultural theology was

---

[43] VS ch 1. Whereas sacrifice used preventative means to quell and divert vengeance, Girard sees the judiciary as using more accurate, strict, reactive, and curative vengeance through the state's monopoly on violence. After the judiciary's slow but successful establishment in the ancient world, then, ritual sacrifice would slowly become an appendix so far as politics is concerned. For religion no longer *contains* violence in the same way it used to.

[44] The glossaries equated Sumerian and Akkadian words and lists of divine names across languages (GG 54f; cf. GIT 42, 169 n139; Joseph Ratzinger, *Truth and Tolerance*, 219).

[45] GIT 57.

a matter of international jurisprudence.[46] Also, many of these deity-lists were "directly related to sacrificial practice," while "a deity's own land was generally the appropriate site for her or his cult."[47] We can regard these as clear signs of the gods' embedded sociopolitical function across societies, almost always with a "national god" as preeminent among them.[48] It is not difficult to see how the merging and translation of gods was a matter of statecraft in the imperial consolidation of regions.[49]

We can thus understand how a certain state-based "monotheism" coincided with the first millennium BCE's immense imperial consolidations and the concomitant reductions of "gods" in pantheons. Here we see that the sociopolitical meaning of polytheism is not in its numeric theology of "many gods"; polytheistic translatability serves social cohesion and unity and tends toward the notion of the One High (or Highest) God behind all other gods, governing all others.[50] Assmann writes, "God's oneness is not an invention of monotheism, but the central theme of polytheistic religions as well."[51] The pagan Celsus, for example, seems to have been even more *numerically* "monotheistic than the Christian Origen."[52] Theologies emphasizing a One God were ascendant in politically consolidating Mesopotamia throughout the first millennium BCE, just as Egypt saw an increasing consolidation of its pantheon, centuries prior, under Amun.[53]

In a One God theology, the many gods may be mere manifestations of the One or exist distinctly as administrators. Such Oneness theology is still polytheistic,[54] often regarded by the name "henotheism," where one

---

[46] *GG* 55; *GIT* 80, 111. See Judges 11:24 as a passage of international relations with the equation of national warrior gods (in Chemosh for the Moabites, Molkom for the Ammonites, and Yahweh for the Israelites – i.e., not yet "the whole earth"). The first hard evidence of universality in Judaism appears in the sixth century in the Khirbet beit Lei inscription "Yahweh is the god of the whole earth" (*GIT* 178; *EHG* 149: 2 Kgs 5:15; 1 Kgs 17:14; 19:15; 2 Kgs 5:1; 8:13; Ps 47:2; cf. Pss 8:1; 24:1; 48:2; 95:4; 97:5; Isa 6:3).

[47] *GIT* 64.

[48] Ibid., 45, 119.

[49] *NOG* 165–6. Over time, pantheons shrunk from the Late Bronze Age into the Iron Age, once populated by hundreds or dozens, down to usually a handful of deities for a polity's pantheon, "largely revolving around national gods" (*GIT* 128, 170). "While more than two hundred deities are attested at Ugarit, the texts for the first millennium states in the region attest to ten or fewer deities" (*EHG* 25).

[50] Greek: *Hyposistos*, "The Highest One," or *Heis Theos* (*PM* 31).

[51] *PM* 30.

[52] Stroumsa, *The End of Sacrifice*, 5.

[53] *GIT* 19, 245.

[54] Ibid., 158f.

deity is the sum of the reality of the other deities. This could involve the worshipping of single gods, with each god – say, of storms, or fire, or water, etc. – manifesting as supreme, absolute divinity. This one supreme deity is, as biblical scholar Mark S. Smith puts it, the "realization of functions or aspects of divinity traditionally associated with the other deities."[55] Similarly, Voegelin refers to "summodeism," wherein the numerous gods, which may have distinct existence, are administrators of the High One who stands above the many as an expression of a political sovereignty.[56] In the late Classical era, henotheistic Oneness theology could be expressed in a high god who was called by different names like Zeus, Sarapis, Helios, Marduk, Iao (sometimes regarded as the Greek equivalent of Yahweh), and so forth. "One Zeus, one Hades, one Helios, one Dionysus, One god in all gods,"[57] reads a Classical text. Or, the Rigveda (1.169): "they call it Indra, Mitra, Varuna, and Agni ... but the real is one, although the sages give different names." Egyptian wisdom literature could often speak simply of a singular *god* "instead of specific gods ... the only god that really counts."[58] Because such "oneness" includes the idea of plurality, it can also be referred to as "inclusive monotheism."[59]

By contrast, the monotheism of secondary religions *excludes* such plurality. As we will explore later, Judaism's exclusive monotheism emerges from the germ of Israel's occasional "monolatry." Monolatry denotes the exalting of one god while the worship of other gods, who are presumed to exist, are prohibited. This practice may be interpreted, to a

---

[55] Ibid., 166, 292.
[56] *OH* 34, 46–7, 73–4, 267, passim. Assmann notes how C. S. Lewis mistakenly conflated an inclusive monotheism (as the natural evolution of thought toward unity – a polytheistic Oneness theology), with biblical, exclusive monotheism that must *reject* the other gods (*ATM* 57; C. S. Lewis, *The Allegory of Love*, 57).

See Michiko Yusa, "Henotheism," 3913. De Lubac distinguishes "two kinds of monotheism" (De Lubac, *The Discovery of God*, 29–31): first, an imperial kind that reflects political conditions and metaphysical speculation, where variety rationally suggests unity (seen in Babylon, Egypt, Hellenic, etc. empires). "It is right that whatever everybody worships should be considered one thing: we behold the same stars, the heavens are common to us all, the same world embraces us" (Symmachus, *Relatio*, 10). The second monotheism is "exclusive jealousy," where there is "no God but God."
[57] *GG* 55.
[58] *GG* 63. Assmann clarifies this as a "monotheism of perspective," or again henotheism. It can be seen in "the God" in both Egypt and the Akkadian version of the treaty between Hattusilis III and Ramses II – denoting the "chief god of each party."
[59] *ATM* 57; *GIT* 165; Theodore M. Ludwig, "Monotheism," 9.6157; Jan Assmann, "Theology, Theodicy, Philosophy," 531–2.

great degree, as related to the political energies of local patriotism and the partisan spirit. In the ancient near east, we find many cases of monolatry – although, the *entire exclusion* of all others gods is very rare.[60] The outstanding such case is again in preexilic Israel, which, in its unique, covenant-shaped monolatry, Assmann also calls a "monotheism of loyalty": for it speaks not of a "one and only God" but this exclusive loyalty to its particular god.[61] Otherwise, phrases like "the Lord is one" or "God is one" are common utterances in a polytheistic framework, in that they exalt the political claims of one god above the other gods. Assmann notes, for example, that there are "hundreds of assertions such as 'Amun is one [unique].'"[62] Such phrases mean "the only one," in the sense of the god's sovereign power. They are monolatrous if they exclude the other gods; they are henotheistic if they absorb, include, and allow worship of the other gods.

The political value of "one God" is most evident in the concept of "divine Monarchy." Monarchy, meaning "one first principle," was a crucial political symbol of the classical world, in both biblical and Hellenistic circles. Monarchy refers to the metaphysical simplicity that corresponds with political orderliness in states. As anyone can look upon politics and conclude that no two constituencies can agree upon the same law, so the logic goes, the perpetual drift toward division and revolution must be curbed by a singular reign. And yet this singular sovereign needs many others to administer and govern. "The king reigns but does not *govern*": for governing the single reign is a task for many, in serving the collective. If Girard's theory was correct in asserting the archaic sacred is homologous with violence, it is again no surprise that the ancient development of a "one high god" theo-political concept coincided with the annexations and consolidations of political sovereignties into larger states and empires. Henotheism suggests cosmically inflected nationalism in correspondence with imperial governing structures.[63] The many gods are increasingly seen as administrators or functionaries of the One, just as smaller polities were absorbed into empires. That is, "empire informs

---

[60] Morton Smith, "The Common Theology of the Ancient Near East," 138–9. Examples of monolatry include Mesopotamia: Ashur, Bel, Ishtar; Egypt: Thot, Re, Amon; Hittite: Arinna, Uliliyassis. King Apophis' worship of no god "except Seth" is much closer to exclusive monolatry. Mesha of Moab's exclusive devotion to Chemosh, or Atrahasis to Ea are other more exclusive examples.

[61] *IR* 83–4.

[62] *GG* 107. *GIT* 145: e.g., the Akkadian "one" connotes "unique, outstanding."

[63] *NOG* 170.

the degree and nature of translatability."[64] As such, henotheistic political theology mirrors the Empire-Province, Emperor-Satrap political arrangement, whereas summodeism and monolatry would have been more fitting theo-political concepts in smaller, polycentric political conditions. In Mesopotamia, for example, where the polycentrism of city-states eventually merged into centralization, Marduk is praised with fifty deity names, seemingly coinciding with the absorbed pantheons of subordinate regions, regarded as aspects or manifestations of the singular power. In all, monolatry, summodeism, and henotheism (inclusive monotheism) may be analyzed as a "spiritual byproduct of processes that belong to the practical and political sphere."[65] We can classify religions of a "one high god" among the religions of translatable polytheism, even if they appear *numerically* monotheistic, insofar as they resolve plurality into an ultimate unity.

To the extent that a high god can be "translated" with the high god of another political sovereignty, we might regard this as analogous to how global state powers today recognize one another as legitimate within the "higher" international political order.[66] Mark Smith identifies such international recognition as pronounced in the Late Bronze Age, where "translatability ... is a function of an imperial *ecumene* of relative equals."[67] Here kings are inclined to address one another as "brothers," not due to affection, but because their relation is neither domination or vassal but parity. But, as to a "highest" order that stands even above such relations – like the United Nations today – this is a contestable position, all the more so in the ages of political fragmentation. Correspondingly, it is not surprising that explicit ancient attestations of *"the* supreme god," prior to the first millennium, are rare, given the more fragmented sovereignties of the Bronze Age. But in times when an empire has almost ubiquitously absorbed all neighboring regions and cultures, when it is tempted to see itself as the *only* power, henotheism can sometimes evince a certain "non-translatability."[68] This seems best interpreted not as exclusive monotheism but as chiefly a political epiphenomenon coinciding with

---

[64] *GIT* 180.

[65] *GG* 57.

[66] F. M. Cross, *From Epic to Canon*, 49; Ron Hendel, "Israelite Religion," 7:4742.

[67] *GIT* 61, 77.

[68] The neo-Assyrian and neo-Babylonian empires "engulfed regional translatability." As such, "parity no longer worked conceptually" (*GIT* 157; Baruch Levine, "Assyrian Ideology and Biblical Monotheism," 411–27). Some have argued that the idea of Yahweh as a cosmic creator "is a response to the Babylonian image of Marduk as

the expansive, imperial monopolies on violence. Imperial monotheism could entail non-translatability because empires can grow so large and annex all competitors to such an extent that no other "valid" gods or sovereignties remain – just barbarians.[69] Monotheisms from above, such as Amun or Marduk, may have a "hidden God" because the sphere of violence containment has grown so ubiquitous it is no longer perceived. By contrast, in contexts of political fragmentation, Smith observes that many "one god" expressions are *inner*-cultural and not *cross*-cultural; they express the polity's singular internal cohesion, its patriotism.[70] That there could be numerous one high gods should not trouble our logical minds. As Voegelin notes, the notion that a large state coincides with the entire cosmos, "remains undisturbed by its logical incompatibility with the existence of rival powers outside the cosmic analogue."[71]

At the heart of "One God behind the many" is an overarching conception of the god-world relation, intimately relevant to the political sphere. "God" in the polytheistic framework is compacted with the universe in what Assmann labels "cosmotheism" or a "world-of-gods that *is* God": God's being is inextricably tied with the cosmos such that it is the body of God.[72] This cosmotheism can even include a capacity for "negative theology," which negates any visible analogy of the world with God by asserting divinity's transcendence and inaccessibility.[73] *But*, even in this view, the cosmos is still a *process*, maintained through human attention to the gods through cult. Cosmotheism operates in the primary religion assumption that "that the universe would suffer, or even come to an end, if the rites ceased to be observed in the prescribed fashion."[74] Once we draw attention to this god-world relation, we see that the deeper sociopolitical-psychological meaning of polytheism is not that "God is many," or even that "God is One," but instead that "God is *all*." All patterns, all cults, all events, all gods, all administration of violence are

---

world creator. Jeremiah also borrowed the Babylonian idea that the creator deity also had a plan for the entire world" (*NOG* 82).

[69] *GIT* 324.

[70] *GIT* 55, 246, 325.

[71] *OH* 26.

[72] *PM* 41f. Cosmotheism is "the religion of an immanent god and a veiled truth that shows and conceals itself in a thousand images that illuminate and complement, rather than logically exclude, one another" (*PM* 43). See also *OH* 41, 44: "the world is not created by the gods, but the gods are massively the world itself."

[73] *OH* 86f.

[74] *PM* 105; 15.

part of a singular system – an encompassing God. This is of such crucial importance for Assmann that he prefers to use cosmotheism to more accurately describe what is usually meant by polytheism.[75] For, what is politically important is not numbers but this god-world relation, of a cosmogonic compaction of the gods with the cosmos, the political realm, and kingship. (I will tend to use the more familiar "polytheism" while implying this cosmotheistic denotation.)

(3) Our third ideal type of religion, and the subject of Chapter 6, is non-translatable religion: *exclusive monotheism*, or biblical monotheism, or for simplicity, "monotheism." If translatable cosmotheism meant God's compaction with the cosmos, in an intuitive religiopolitical compatibility, untranslatable exclusive monotheism means God's division from and incommensurability with the cosmos. We do not have here cosmos-as-the-body-of-God. Nor do we have here "a god of water," "a storm god," or even the god of the king, or any other *societal function* that could be translated across polities and religions. Divinity is not "completed" by any ritual or political procedures. Though words fail me here, it is as though God here is *functionless*:

A transcendent God has no cosmic function that could serve as a common denominator function for equating him with another God. [Yahweh] did not say, "I am the Sun," or even "I am all that is, was, and will be," like the Egyptian god ... but "I am that I am."[76]

Unlike the many interlocking functions of divinities and cults in primary religion, this revelation means an entirely untranslatable God: "The world owes its continued existence, not to the performance of any rites, but to the preserving will and workings of a transcendent god."[77]

While the cosmotheistic One High God is numerically inclusive amidst its singularity, here it is religious *exclusivity* that makes for "a totally different kind of monotheism," emanating most "specifically from Palestine."[78] This exclusive monotheism means *nontranslatability* with,

---

[75] Or "cosmogonic monotheism." Jan Assmann, "Religion and the (Un)translatability of Cultures," 24:00f. Stroumsa likewise discusses "the non-pertinence of an opposition between the concepts of monotheism and polytheism" (Stroumsa, *The End of Sacrifice*, 5). Emperor Julian also saw the mono-/poly- difference as "trivial" (Christoph Markschies, "The Price of Monotheism," 110).

[76] Assmann, "Religion and the (Un)translatability of Cultures," 42:00f.

[77] *PM* 104f.

[78] *GG* 107.

and intolerance of, other gods and religions.[79] In such an ideal type, Yahweh cannot be translated with Jupiter, Amun, Zeus, or Assur – even if other religions tried to make such a translation.[80] While many other religion-cultures translated their gods, there is – to be mild about it – a "relative lack of translatability for many Jewish and Christian authors."[81] For theirs is a *counter-religion*; exclusive monotheism understands itself as *not polytheism*; it is ultimately *anti-polytheism*.[82] "The distinction between true and false religion pertains solely to this exclusive monotheism."[83] This is a theoclasm that "blocked intercultural translatability. False gods cannot be translated."[84] So the crucial distinction of monotheism is not that there is only one god but the exclusivity "that alongside the One True God, there are only false gods, whom it is strictly forbidden to worship."[85] Polytheism is again not characterized by the assertion of the plurality of gods in contrast with divine oneness but that there is a *compatibility* between there being one god *and* that this god is manifested, served, even worshipped through subordinate gods.[86] The monotheistic distinction concerns the nontranslatable and *exclusive* fidelity to its particular God, crystallized in the command, "thou shalt have no other gods."[87] Thus Assmann includes the above-noted monolatrous "monotheism of loyalty" as Israel's crucial base layer of such exclusive theology; and only later, exile onward, does it accrue a more numerical and universal layering of a "monotheism of truth," wherein the other gods do not exist;[88] these two layers of *loyalty* and *truth* ultimately forge an "indissoluble bond" and abide together in the Bible. The resultant monotheism is

---

[79] *PM* 19. Mark Smith writes that "the history of ancient Israelite religion involved both translatability and its eventual rejection ... the conceptual shift in this period involved a sophisticated hermeneutic that retained older formulations of translatability within expressions of non-translatability and monotheism" (*GIT* 8).

[80] Many philosophers and cults tried to translate Yahweh with Dionysius, Zeus, and Jupiter (*GIT* 276f). Assmann regards Macrobius' translation of Iao (Yahweh) as the "supreme god of all gods" as part of the Greco-Roman "quest for the sole and supreme divine principle beyond the innumerable multitude of specific deities" (*ME* 51).

[81] *GIT* 283; Martin Goodman, "Trajan and the Origins of Roman Hostility to the Jews," 11–2.

[82] *PM* 39; 22.

[83] Ibid., 36.

[84] *ME* 3.

[85] *PM* 34.

[86] *GG* 108. "There has never been a religion that defined itself with reference to the concept of plurality, one that adopted *polloi theoi* (many gods) as its motto instead of *heis theos* (one god alone)" (*PM* 31).

[87] *GG* 110.

[88] *IR* 834.

most distinct not on the matter of divine oneness but that this God is not part of the world of gods, the world's all-ness. In the compaction of primary religion, "the divine cannot be divorced from the world. But monotheism, however, sets out to do just that. The divine is emancipated from its symbiotic attachment to the cosmos, society, and fate and turns to face the world as a sovereign power."[89] In light of these nuances and radical distinctions, Assmann qualifies that the terms mono- and polytheism are less useful, and we do better to refer to exclusive and nonexclusive theologies.

Given these substantive differences, we are speaking of a different *kind*, a different *genus* of religion altogether from what was known in primary religion, entailing a unique conceptual framework and lexicon. It generated previously inconceivable categories we only now call "polytheism" or idolatry – along with heathens, pagans, gentiles, unbelievers, idols, heretics. All these are really only post-facto constructs of exclusive monotheism.[90] These novel distinctions suggest it is pointless and anachronistic to speak of ancient polytheistic religions as "tolerant." For among them, Assmann writes, "the criterion of incompatibility is missing. As far as other peoples' religion is concerned, there is nothing that would need to be 'tolerated.'"[91] Put differently, we could say that intolerance and incompatibility were *already decided* in the ancient world, subsumed within the encompassing hegemony of the religiopolitical realm.[92] In primary religions, it was inconceivable for untranslatability to be hived off and applied in the sense of a secondary religion. (Similarly, it is anachronistic to speak of ancient religions having a notion of divine "immanence" in the world. For the word immanence "presupposes an understanding of 'transcendence' that is not yet achieved.")[93] This should give us great pause when theologians, in critique of exclusive monotheism, speak about the "tolerance" of polytheism. This may be akin to stating, by analogy to the political sphere, that the United States is very tolerant for acknowledging France is a country. This is a meaningless assertion in that nontranslatability between the two countries is not really

---

[89] *PM* 41f.
[90] *MPC* 141, 149.
[91] *PM* 18.
[92] We will recall that polytheistic religions entailed plenty of state regulation, exclusion, discipline, and persecution. See, for example, Peter Garnsey, "Religious Toleration in Classical Antiquity." Here we find the selective imperial inclusion of various gods was an effect of them having been made subject to Roman imperialism.
[93] *OH* 84.

an option available to our common sense. Even more, if there is any such "tolerance" between the two countries, it is a result of the sedimentation of a violent, complex history of treaties stemming from wars and the battles for global dominance. Mark S. Smith thus reminds us that the translatability and tolerance of ancient polytheism was really a matter of imperialism.[94] Again, per Mouffe, tolerance or translatability do not escape the political. The hidden exclusivity of international translatability becomes more apparent if we consider the prospect of the more powerful UN countries recognizing not France but Palestine as a sovereign authority. For in this case, we can at least see how power relations are still constitutive to translatability, just as "consensus" – however "tolerant" or inclusive – is still an exclusive form of hegemony.

As we will detail in Chapter 6, Assmann largely associates untranslatable counter-religion with the Mosaic distinction, a movement within a complex, originally polytheistic Israelite religion. This monotheism is more like an "event" in the sense that it cannot be easily institutionalized, and it emerges only in fugitive spurts. The exclusive monotheism that eventually took shape in Judaism, again, differs far more from Akhenaton's kind of exclusive monotheism than Freud speculated. Nonetheless, Akhenaton's revolution, because it was indeed *against* the other gods, still counts at least partly as a species of exclusive monotheism.[95] The Mosaic distinction means a type of "counter-knowledge" that knows itself as not-polytheism, applying the true/false distinction in relation to religion, just as the Greek Parmenidean distinction applied the notion of true/false to science and logic. The Greek-scientific as well as the Mosaic-religious "true/false distinctions" are both intolerant counter-knowledge in that they know what is "false" or "*not* true" and exclude them.[96] (The invoking of true/false does not preclude that there is room for subsequently drawing up reentries or subdistinctions. These could include non-true, less-than-fully-true, etc.)[97] We will see how the nature of this distinction in Israel's religion is not abstract but stems more from the idea of *fidelity/adultery* or *loyalty/treason* to Yahweh's covenant.

---

[94] *GIT* 89.
[95] While he retained the compaction between religion and politics, "Akhenaten was the first in the history of mankind to apply the distinction between true and false to religion . . . . He was also the first to formulate the principle of exclusive monotheism, namely, that there be 'no gods but god!'" (*GG* 81).
[96] *PM* 12–3.
[97] *ME* 1ff.

With counter-knowledge comes a different potential for violence and enemy-making: "the truth to be proclaimed comes with an enemy to be fought."[98] Thus we now turn to mapping different kinds of violence-potentials onto these different kinds of religions. As we turn to the violence dimension here, we should remember how translatability does not simply mean pacifism and tolerance, nor must untranslatability denote an arbitrary, malignant intolerance. In fact, we will see in Chapter 6 how ancient Israel, as Smith asserts, "developed a critique of translatability as an act of resistance against empire," and that "translatability does not offer a model of tolerance for the modern world," nor is it "a proper model for encouraging tolerance of others."[99] This invites us to again reconsider the models of tolerance too simplistically applied to monotheism today, noted earlier in Schwartz et al. – wherein polytheism (or at least an open, universalistic revision of monotheism) is seen as an antidote to the dangerous intolerance of monotheism.

B. DIFFERENT KINDS OF VIOLENCE

Assmann classifies five different kinds of violence that we can map onto this religious taxonomy. These are again "ideal types" and they concern how varieties of violence involve differing motivational sources, symbolic or rhetorical legitimations, and social functions. The first kind is "raw" or affective violence: this violence is motivated by anger, revenge, fear, or greed, and it has no legitimizing or authority reference other than its being done "in one's own name" or interest, as it usually has no legal basis or referent to the social order. In cases of greed, its justification is at most "might makes right"; in cases of fear, such violence is motivated by self-defense or preemption.[100]

A second kind of violence is "legal" violence, seen as counter-violence against raw violence, done in the name of a law, devoid of affective passion. "The aim of legal violence is the creation of a sphere of law and justice in which raw violence is excluded."[101] Such violence is often today obliquely referred to as "force," suggesting its normative and legitimate difference from raw violence. "Force" is good and just, but "violence" is bad and unjust – even though we know that "force" is

---

[98] *GG* 7; *PM* 4.
[99] *GIT* 28f, viii.
[100] *GG* 142.
[101] Ibid., 143.

indeed violence. This difference between good force and bad violence is central to societies sustainably containing their violence.

A third kind of violence is "political violence," which founds or establishes new political order outside of law and legal violence. It tends to be done in the name of a ruler or "the people," and the anti-affective, cool spirit of legal violence is shed here; rather, emotion and fervor are essential to the cause. All revolutions, for example, which of course do not ask for legal permission to revolt and thereby birth a nation, are engaged in political violence. Political orders emerge and exert themselves, that is, in a state of emergency or exceptionality to law. Law derives from what is outside law. For political violence *creates* law; it cuts open a space that delineates friend and enemy.

"Ritual violence" is done in the name of some specific god or religion. This is most commonly exemplified in immolative sacrifice, though ritualized mock warfare, sports, duels, sacralized interstate warfare, or ritualized raiding are also fitting examples. Insofar as these rituals of violence serve to annex land, persons, or territory and create or extend a political unit, ritual violence overlaps with political violence.[102] In the ancient near east, for example, where religion and politics are largely homologous, we see how the Assyrians justified their violence toward unfaithful vassals in the name of the national god Assur. Assyria would attack the "enemies of the god Assur" for their breaking political loyalty oaths sworn in his name.[103] But the religious justification of such violence is about primary, not secondary religion. It is not about how the vassals were "religiously" faithless (in worshipping false gods) but how they were politically faithless in serving other immanent enemy groupings. We mistakenly view these as cases of "religious" rivalry, when in fact the religious representations are indistinguishably woven with the political realm. Ancient accounts of massacres disguised as "plagues," or myths wherein conflicts between the gods evidently reflect political conflicts, may also be categorized as ritual violence.[104] Numerous biblical passages of divine violence closely resemble that of their polytheistic neighbors on these counts.[105]

---

[102] Egypt's annexations by war, for example, could be classified political violence even while they also served an almost magical or "ritual function to ward off the peoples and tribes that surround Egypt" (ibid., 28–30).

[103] *PM* 19.

[104] *GG* 52.

[105] *IR* 87. Consider when Phineas murdered the idolater and thereby stopped Yahweh's violent plague that killed 24,000. Assmann writes, according with Girard, that violence disguised as a plague "is normal, so to speak, in the ancient world." But what is different

Ritual violence shares some of the politically ordering ends of legal violence. For example, the ritual violence of human sacrifice, Girard emphasized, is not a mere spasm of superstition but a channeling, redirecting, and containment of raw violence – selected not by human choice but natural selection – which may in fact order the community. Though ritual violence might seem to have vanished from our world, the migration of ritual violence into other spheres of society is a crucial topic of inquiry, as we see in Taylor's *A Secular Age*, for example.[106] Interpreters of modernity may analyze, for instance, how sports are secularized ritual violence, how the state sacralizes itself through rituals of pledging allegiance, how we still worship through "sacraments" like flags and tombs to unknown soldiers, how we still tell founding myths of unity, and how we profess creeds of "faith" in political metaphysics.[107] If these constitute "civil religion," should the legal and political violence contained in modern states also be categorized as "ritual violence"? If seemingly "secular" rituals bind a populace together, directing joint attention upon acceptable targets and ends, they at least serve a similar *function* as that of formerly religious ritual violence. Such a line of inquiry suggests that "faith," again, is not a term to be reserved for secondary religions but an inescapable category of political existence – that "in terms of faith [the modern state] is often as 'religious' as any medieval or ancient community was."[108] In other words, the violence-containing functions of primary religion may be seen as having separated out and migrated: the sacred now abides more natively not in "religion" but within the state apparatus and its symbolic habitus. Or: the violent sacred remains in the political realm as it always has; but "religious" representation has been hiving off into distinct separation.

Given that the first four kinds of violence are native to a polytheistic context, Assmann asserts that "polytheism contains violence"[109] in the double sense of the word, akin to mimetic theory.[110] It takes this containment for granted the way it takes its gods as real. "Tolerance" and

---

is "the deed of Phinehas, who intervenes spontaneously for God: this is new, even revolutionary, and would have been impossible, I assert, in any other ancient culture" (*ATM* 118).

[106] Charles Taylor, *A Secular Age*, 648–75.

[107] Marvin and Engle, "Blood Sacrifice and the Nation."

[108] Niebuhr, *Radical Monotheism*, 69.

[109] *GG* 52.

[110] *EC* 204. "Pagan violence stems from the indistinction between state and religion" (*GG* 29).

"translatability," far from being pacific concepts, both restrained and expressed violence in ancient polytheism. And it is crucial to see how theologies of metaphysical oneness – in henotheism or summodeism – were often little more than imperial metaphysics. Derrida's remark on Oneness thus serves as something of a warning label over tolerance and translatability concepts: "The gathering into itself of the One is never without violence. As soon as there is the One, there is murder, wounding traumatization."[111] Nonetheless, when compared to tribal/primitive religions, we might consider archaic polytheistic translatability as still a relative "advance" in facilitating some pacific intercultural exchange. At the same time, the "tolerance" of the polytheistic framework is always already a system of political power relations that implicitly reference the threat of violence. Such "tolerance" contains not only varieties of ritual and legal violence but the political decision of whether a difference is a threat to order and if it should be repelled or killed. Translatable gods are not particularly pacific; they can be used as the pretext and interpretation for war or vengeance, and they are of crucial value in imperial expansionism and management.

This "positive" containing- and ordering function of violence can go unaccounted for in some canonical "peace studies" classifications of violence. For example, whenever Johan Galtung speaks of "violence," whether direct or structural, it is unequivocally *unjust* and to be rooted out, without sufficiently theorizing what could count as just or legal violence.[112] One is thus left wondering if removing all violence can be done without more violence, or without replacing or redirecting the order-producing violence. Without accounting for violence-containment, such theories of violence can suffer from what Mouffe called depoliticization, of avoiding political decision and exclusion so as to appear on the side of a neutral, pacific humanity – leaving the door open to *liberal violence* – a form of violence not discussed by Assmann (perhaps akin to political violence) but discussed in Chapter 1. Such violence, again, does not sanction itself with respect to a legal order, a polity, or a god, but "humanity," executed in a posture of possessing the universal position.

---

[111] Jacques Derrida, *Archive Fever*, 78, 106.

[112] E.g., Johan Galtung, "Violence, Peace, and Peace Research." He experiments with defining violence as "the cause of the difference between the potential and the actual" (168). Boulding critiques Galtung's rhetorical "taboo on violence" in Kenneth Boulding, "Twelve Friendly Quarrels with Johan Galtung."

While raw, legal, ritual, and political violence are native to tribal and archaic religion-societies, Assmann's fifth is "religious violence," unique only to exclusive monotheism. This classification is necessary due to monotheism's "disembedded" or "distanced" relationship between the political order, religion, and gods. Within a polytheistic system, by contrast, its legal, political, and ritual violence all share in the archaic sacred. But because exclusive monotheism separates God from the political order and the cosmos, it makes possible their rejoining in a novel explosion. This is what we mean by religious violence being different from the various kinds of violence contained in polytheistic religions. So, ritual and political violence in a polytheistic context could indeed be done in the "name of God" or gods; such violence was largely indexed to the cultic distinction between pure and impure. But the "religious violence" potential of monotheism, by contrast, is when the novel distinction between true and false religions (or religious loyalty and betrayal) *becomes re-applied to or conflated with the political distinction* between friend and enemy. Religious violence "is directed against pagans, unbelievers, and heretics, who either would not convert to the truth or have defected from it and are therefore regarded as enemies of God."[113] So, what is new in monotheism is not violence; archaic religions since time immemorial had plenty of religiously interpreted and legitimated violence. "What is new, is the religious motivation of violence – the idea of killing a person or starting a war for the sake of God, to fulfill his will and orders, acting as God's executioners."[114]

In other words, whereas the first four kinds of violence can be done *within* the polytheistic system, and thus regarded as intra-systemic violence, "religious violence" is by definition "*extra*-systemic" violence. The pagan is outside the threshold of conversion. "You can integrate an enemy into the polytheistic system. But the idolater and heretic are dealt with by extra-systemic integration and conversion."[115] Even though religious violence is theoretically directed against "paganism," Assmann notices that, in practice, religious violence has been typically directed "against the 'pagan within' – and not against political enemies."[116]

A symbol at the heart of monotheistic religious violence is "Sinai," where Yahweh reveals the true religion. Sinai, by rabbinic interpretation,

---

[113] *GG* 144; *IR* 82–3.
[114] *MPC* 142.
[115] *GG* 31.
[116] Ibid., 29.

means "hate."[117] That Mosaic mountain symbolized a novel boundary of hatred or envy descending in the world. Assmann reminds us that this is, of course, not the *origin* of hate, which of course is a far older demon. But it is a new *kind* of hatred: the monotheist's hatred toward the old gods and the idolaters who wrongly worshipped them and the hatred harbored by the excluded, denigrated idolater toward the elect.[118] Though Assmann will argue that hatred and "religious violence" are in fact a distorted application of mature exclusive monotheism, not fitting with its evolved, normative ideals, it is nonetheless a real and unique potentiality opened up by exclusive monotheism.

But we must again be very careful here: to analyze "religious violence" as unique to monotheism does not imply one must regard the latter as intrinsically belligerent. For in the archaic compaction between religion and the political sphere, violence is inextricable from the ritual/religious ecosystem; in itself, there is no point outside it by which to radically critique it. When the gods of primary religion are as *real* as the political body with which they are associated, phrases like "religious violence," "religious justifications for violence," or "sacred kingship," Girard would remind us, are tautologies. For, to the extent that "religion" – as some distinct institution – does not really exist in primary religions, they do not have *religious* violence. The sacred isn't used to "justify" violence; violence *is* the sacred, and vice versa. Likewise, kingship at the primary level is not *imbued* with the sacred – as if it were *another thing*. Rather, the violence centered in kingship *is* the sacred.[119]

Whenever monotheistic religions execute violence "in the name of God," Assmann argues this has to be classified as a regression into "sheer pagan violence." Defined this way, monotheistic "religious violence" is paradoxical: it is only possible due to monotheism's differentiation of God from the political; but its violent actualization occurs only through them returning to homology. Monotheism reverts to paganism insofar as, through religious violence, it smashes back into the political realm, becoming co-identified with it. It becomes "pre-axial" – or really *worse* than pre-axial. For it is an explosive re-mixing of a potent "secondary religion" zeal, which otherwise has its merits when distinct from the

---

[117] Babylonian Talmud, Sabbat 89a.

[118] *PM* 67.

[119] Or, one might hear of "religious-based accusations," which at the *primary* level is again tautology for Girard. Accusation doesn't "use" the sacred; it is the sacred. This is why "Satan" (the prosecutor, the spirit of accusation), for Girard, is not the "cause" of the scapegoat mechanism, but *is* it.

political realm. But such religious violence brings it back into the political sphere with a vengeance, after having cultivated a zeal in depoliticized conditions.[120] That is, monotheism can turn polytheistic swords into plowshares; but plows can still be re-weaponized. But again, as I'll later show, despite this volatile potential, Assmann regards monotheism as gestating an urge toward nonviolence through a distancing from the political realm. Such a claim, which regards monotheistic violence as more an accidental distortion/regression than an inherent characteristic, is a hard sell.[121] He does not pronounce some absolute "essence" of monotheism; but he will nonetheless point toward its pacific *telos* or maturation. Does this too easily excuse the extreme violence narrated in biblical monotheism? Adjudicating this problem requires exploration of the complex political-religious history of Israel, to be explored in Chapter 6.

I explore in the coming chapters how the *in*tolerance within exclusive monotheism, in contrast with polytheism, is a potentially liberating critique against these varieties of violence. Namely, that while polytheism and cosmotheism contained violence, "many of these forms were domesticated, civilized, or even eliminated altogether by the monotheistic religions as they rose to power, since such violence was perceived to be incompatible with the truth they proclaimed."[122] Crucial to those changes is how an intolerant untranslatability mediates a new relationship between politics and religion. The mere numeric aspect of theology, in poly- or monotheism is far less important. Having honed terms of religious *genera*, translatability, and violence, we can now explore a specific case of cosmotheistic Egyptian political theology, over a range of time that contextualizes Akhenaten's supposed monotheism. This will then serve as a backdrop by which to explore Mosaic monotheism in Chapter 6. Between the two we can detect changes with respect to political theology and victims, supplementing Girard's account of monotheism as a refusal to divinize victims.

---

[120] Stroumsa, *The End of Sacrifice*, 98.
[121] Bernstein critiques Assmann for deeming nonviolence the "true" mission of monotheism. "Such an antiseptic view of monotheism fails to underscore how over and over again the Mosaic distinction has been used *to justify and legitimize* physical violence. Once we zealously commit ourselves to *our* god as the one and only true god, we have the *strongest* possible justification for destroying infidels" (Bernstein, "Jan Assmann," 24).
[122] *PM* 16.

5

Polytheism and the Victim in Ancient Egypt

Having set up a framework by which to analyze what is at stake in different political theologies – of how divinity, politics, and violence are configured – we turn to a concrete case of ancient Egypt. As noted, "Egypt" was one of the most common foils of choice when Israel sought to critique and rhetorically distinguish itself from neighboring religions, a metonymy for idolatry and false religion. But is there any validity to such a distinction? While this and Chapter 6 detect numerous similarities between Israel and its neighboring ancient cultures, Assmann argues that there is a fault line of divergence between them at the level of relating divinity and the state. To understand this difference, he writes, it "must be reconstructed and interpreted in terms of political theology."[1] We thus do well to explore the outlines of Egyptian political theology.

To be sure, the long politico-religious history of Egypt is dynamic. But that does not preclude Assmann from constructing some synchronic observations about its political theology. The center of his attention, and ours here, concerns the mythologies of violence-containment, the rituals of divine kings, the Pharaonic office, and the existential threats to it. For if God and cosmos are intimately linked in polytheism, it is in divinity's relation to the king that this linkage is most pronounced and dramatized. There, "the divinity of the ruler assures the link between the divine world and human society," wherein "'reigning' counts among the sacred actions."[2] Egyptian divine monarchy is as clear a case as any for

---

[1] GG 77.
[2] ATM 9. A divine Pharaoh need not mean strictly incarnate divinity – which is a more specific, if rare, species in the ancient world. More likely one finds the king as the *analogy*

observing this linkage and the political theology of polytheism. In exploring the mythologies and political rituals surrounding Horus, Osiris, and Seth, and even the religio-politics of Akhenaten, we find a compaction between divinity in politics that is strongly contrasted with what is to emerge in Jewish monotheism.

A. THE GOD-KING COMPACTION: A CASE STUDY IN EGYPTIAN POLITICAL THEOLOGY

Egyptian political theology was rooted in a long lineage of remembering its kings. The ancient historian Herodotus noted that the Egyptians had accounted for an impossible 11,340 years of their own history and kings, an epoch during which "they said no god had ever appeared in human form." And yet, before this long history, Herodotus adds, "Egypt had gods for its rulers, who dwelt upon the earth with men, one being always supreme above the rest." Overthrowing the god of chaos, Egypt's last god-king was "Horus, the son of Osiris (also seen as the son of Re), called by the late Greeks Apollo."[3] In some Atum myths, the gods had withdrawn from directly ruling humans in reaction "to a rebellion of mankind against the aging sun god"[4] – according with mimetic theory's notion of a founding crisis resolved through an expulsion, cementing the social order. And so as early as the fourth millennium BCE, it is in the gods' absence that the Egyptian state mediated divine presence. The Pharaoh ruled over the earth "as the representative of the creator god,"[5] in analogy with Re's reigning over the gods. As divine deputy, the Pharaoh "reigns as god, first as the incarnation of the god Horus and then also as the son of the sun and creator god Re."[6] In other words, the ruler was the "image of God," a common royal epithet.[7]

---

between divinity and the cosmos, or a manifestation of divinity. Voegelin notes how Egyptians "were fully aware that their Pharaohs died like all other human beings" and that they were "a man in whom a god manifests himself ... not a god who has assumed human form. As such, the god remains distinct from his manifestation" (*OH* 72).

[3] Herodotus, *Histories*, §II 142–3.

[4] *GG* 61.

[5] Ibid., 16; *PM* 68.

[6] *GG* 60-1. Hoffmeier, *Akhenaten*, 7, 9; Ellen Morris, "The Pharaoh and Pharaonic Office," 204.

[7] *GG* 62. It is not uncommon, however, for other humans and animals besides the king to be regarded as "images of God" (ibid. 29; *PM* 68). E.g., *The Instruction for King Merikare*, wisdom literature in early second millennium BCE, writes of creatures, "His images are they, having come forth from his body."

The pharaohs of early Egypt were some of the world's first emperors to reign with an expansive sovereignty that reached beyond the horizon. In this context, as we saw in Freud and Breasted, the religious sun god worship of ancient Egypt corresponds with the encompassing power of the emperor.[8] The supreme Sun God, having created the world and its many gods, corresponds with the Pharaoh's political dominion over lesser beings. That is, theological "creation" is the analogue of political "dependence."[9] Creation is the foundational power relation; this chain of relations ends with Atum-Re, who is not created, but "originated by himself," and is thus sovereign.

Though the gods had fled, with royal deputies left in their absence, the gods nonetheless would regularly return in the form of citywide feasts, mock battles, and processions. These performative advents of the god were essential to the common life of ancient Egyptian cities; to be a citizen in such a city meant participation, with unanimous assent, in the gathering. These rituals would dissolve the common metaphysical boundaries between the god and the citizenry, reuniting heaven and earth. Whereas the temple usually contains the presence of the god, in the processions the god is paraded outside the temple, through the city, in a festal, if grave, state of exception. One of the oldest Egyptian processional songs reads, "The god comes; beware, earth!"[10] As we will see, these events often involved sacrificial immolation, whether in effigy or animal; and they could involve the bringing together the many disparate pieces of a god's torn up body. We can see some correspondences in the processions with Girard's conceptualization of ritual: the reproduction of a public crisis of distinctions for the sake of its resolution, the gravity of unanimous participation, sacrifice, and dis-/rememberment. The sacred presence is distributed outside the temple, and there is a gathering into a form that, in other circumstances, might resemble a mob.

Resembling Girard's notion of kingship as originating in human sacrifice, the Egyptian Pharaoh was often one who – even though a *representative* of the god in one sense – must apologize *to* the god for any of his sins that may have caused problems in the city. For example, king Mursilis had to confess any sins he could imagine so as to end a pestilence crisis, lest he be killed; he even dug up his father's sins from

---

[8] GG 18–9.
[9] Ibid., 60f.
[10] Ibid., 16–7; ME 26.

twenty years prior.[11] We can see here signs of a scapegoat-king, a conse-crated victim who reigns against the horizon of his immolation – and preparedness to sacrifice him in case of an unresolved crisis. Indeed, the earliest coronation rituals we know from the Old Kingdom, as mimetic theory would predict, are virtually identical with those found in mortuary texts.[12] Voegelin was perhaps correct to marvel at, and not decide on, the debate as to whether these are coronation or mortuary rituals: for Girard has offered good reasons to see both phenomena as stemming from the mimetic containment of violence, transformed over time into political office. The earliest attested coronation rituals admonish the king to stand on "the primeval hill."[13] The connection between Pharaohs, these hills, and the iconic pyramids again suggest some subterranean linkage between the king and his immolation. For Girard, burial by stone-heap and pyramid ultimately stems from "the collective stoning of the original lynching" and its ritual reenactment upon surrogates.[14] This may help contextualize why, in some Egyptian texts, a god is coidentified with the primeval mound itself, which then turns into a small pyramid in which the god dwelled.[15] Sometimes heaps of stones served as representations of gods and "witnesses" to ancient pacts, which are frequently accompanied by sacrifice.[16] And in cosmogonic myths and rituals – so frequently centered upon a group killing – we find references to a primeval hill or mound, which could have simply been a rough earth pile on which temples and their altars were built.[17]

Such speculation does not at all mean that scapegoating would have been explicitly experienced, much less understood, as a root meaning of Egyptian kingship. In Girardian terms, there is forgetfulness and misap-prehension within memorial, myth, and funerary. It follows that, despite ancient Egypt's enthralling processions, vast amounts of monuments, and

---

[11] *GG* 24–5.

[12] *OH* 76f.

[13] "The ascension of the king to the throne repeats the ascension of the god to the hill of cosmic order . . . the ascension to the throne can blend intelligibly into the ascension of the dead and reborn king" (*OH* 77).

[14] *EC* 165; *ISS* 91–2; Simon Simonse, *Kings of Disaster*; Walter Burkert, *Homo Necans*, 55 n29. The primeval mound was the first element of creation, central to the Pharaoh's resurrection-renewal ritual. In many pyramid designs, a human sized mound served as the foundation for a temple. The "Holy of Holies" in such architecture is literally "the holy place of the first occurrence" (Hoffmeier, *Akhenaten*, 10–3).

[15] *Pyramid Texts* 587, 600.

[16] *GIT* 105.

[17] Herman Kees, *Ancient Egypt*, 155.

elaborate king-lists, Assmann concludes this grandiosity seems to have acted less as sparking critical historical insight and more a tranquilizer against it.[18] "What can the Egyptians learn from their well-documented hindsight over thousands of years? Simply that nothing has changed ... the lists of kings open up the past, but they do not invite us to look any further .... This intensive preoccupation with the past ... served to halt history and strip it of any semiotic value."[19] If divine monarchy is indeed an unconscious and forgetful by-product of the scapegoat mechanism, Egypt's Pharaonic office is an extravagant example of this phenomena. It was both a pole that oriented and organized the imaginary of the populace and a dam against violence.

i. Osiris and Seth: Gods Who Contain Violence

The god of kingship and the sky, Horus – with his iconic falcon head – was a central figure in the political theology of the Pharaoh. But a violent drama mythologically precedes and gives rise to Horus: the conflict between Osiris and Seth. They represent different aspects of the victim-god theme, dramatizing the violence in social order and disorder. And their mythological cycle is a key cosmotheistic element that, while translatable in other ancient cultures, has no analogue in mature Jewish monotheism. For cosmotheism includes more than just the sublime; its political embeddedness involves the *containment* of evil and violence. Seth provides an example of this containment, in contrast with a political theology of exclusive monotheism wherein God is separated from the cosmos, the land, and the victims of the political order.

The myths suggest Osiris "actually" reigned in Egyptian prehistory, by which Assmann surmises this god represents something of an actual event, a king killed in very early Egypt. In any case, his myth lived on as a root symbol in Egyptian religiopolitical mythology for centuries. Once upon a time, so his mythic cycle goes, Osiris' brother Seth was jealous of his brother's reign. And, in mimetic rivalry over the throne, Seth killed Osiris, cut up his body, and scattered it all around Egypt. Where Osiris' dismembered body parts were buried corresponded with the regions of Egypt. In eras when Egypt comprised forty-two nomes, Osiris had been cut into forty-two pieces (at other points, fourteen pieces/nomes). Thus,

[18] *CMEC* 51, 56.
[19] Ibid., 57–8.

Egypt was often imagined as the "Body of Osiris."[20] Osiris' sister Isis –
she who "drives off foes" and "stops the deeds of the disturber" –
gathered up his scattered body parts and reanimated him. She had intercourse with the resurrected Osiris to beget the god Horus, whose deputies
are the Pharaohs.[21] Osiris' cycle shows its origin and function not only in
this myth form but in the material, practiced cult of the Pharaohs. That is,
the Osiris myth and its cult "grew out of the royal funerary ceremonial."[22] In such rituals, Osiris is the prototype of the deceased, buried,
mummified king, and his son Horus is the living king. The killed god is the
analogue of the alive king.

Insofar as the slain Osiris is raised to a new transcendence in the
resurrected son Horus, who is the prototype of all kingship, we have here
clear signs of the divinization of the victim. In cultic practice, representation of this myth took shape, as noted, in annual festivals where each sub-
state brought their own regional canopic jar containing some part of
Osiris' body, and the forty-two priests from each region processed with
said jars through the city. This public co-re-membering and resurrecting
of Osiris's body served to reconstitute the Egyptian political body and
land, which is the body of its founding victim.[23] (As a foreshadowing, if
the land and polity is the body of the victim, it is very significant how
Israel's monotheistic political theology gestated most powerfully *in exile*,
without a land.) Egypt as the remembered land-body-politic of a victim
provides a crucial bridge between Girard's victim-foundation hypothesis
and Assmann's idea of cosmotheism containing violence. It is a fairly
generic thing to say that Egypt is the body of God, or that the whole
world is the body of God; metaphysics here feels like a picturesque, if
superstitious first draft at cosmology. But it is quite another, striking thing
to say the world is the slain, dismembered body of Osiris. Or, even more:
Egypt is the *process* of Osiris' dismemberment and re-membering, in
which humanity participates. Here, religio-metaphysics shows itself less
as proto-science and more a grammar of violence management.

This political mythology of cosmogony through Osiris' murder and
reunification corresponds with numerous creation/founding stories, as
noted in Chapter 2. These included the creation-dismemberments of the

[20] *GG* 42; Assmann cites Girard's mimetic theory on explaining this "primordial fratricide"
     (*GG* 34).
[21] Miriam Lichtheim, *Ancient Egyptian Literature*, 81, 83.
[22] John Gwyn Griffiths, *The Origins of Osiris and His Cult*, 5, 35; Smith, "Dying and Rising
     Gods," 525.
[23] *GG* 42.

victim gods Purusa, Tiamat, Omorka, and so forth.[24] As Girard writes, "practically every story of origin or foundation myth states that society was founded upon a murder."[25] The victim Osiris as the body of Egypt is a key building block – indeed a victim foundation – in the Egyptian god-world compaction, and it fits within the mimetic theory framework that the religiopolitical sphere is the expression of the scapegoat mechanism.

In the ritual-mythological legacy of Seth's slaying of Osiris, Seth served as the antitype for the dangers of violence, political dissolution, and death itself. In Carl Schmitt's framework, where "the political" is characterized by the always-possible threat of an enemy – that which must be prepared for and repelled or killed when necessary – Seth is Egypt's most common narrative construction of the political. Seth's slaying of his brother Osiris symbolizes the dangers of violence that must be contained. In the public ritual life of Egypt, ritualistic violence was regularly conducted against representations of Seth, purveyor of malignant danger, contrasted with the good Horus, the avenger of Osiris.[26] This corresponds with the political distinction between good force and bad violence: Seth, as bad violence, becomes the target and symbol of good, ritual, collective violence. Seth is homologous with death itself, which remains a perpetual threat of national destruction, of tearing the Egyptian body apart. "The restitution of life and honor to Osiris is acted out primarily by inflicting ritualistic sacrificial violence on Seth. Seth is the prototype of [and identified with] the sacrificial animal."[27]

In sum, through publicly containing violence in the anti-model of Seth, Osiris and Egypt's political unity is revived and protected. In times when Egypt suffered extreme political turmoil and foreign invasions, Seth merged with another cosmic foe, Apep, only further evidencing Seth as

---

[24] *OH* 44f. See also Nintura hymns in which the cosmos is the body of the deity (*GIT* 174).

[25] *EC* 163.

[26] *GG* 40.

[27] Ibid., 35–6; *ATM* 74. Dating back at least to the third millennium BCE, there was a ritual of overthrowing Seth: "Let a figure of Seth be brought made of red wax ... bind it with the sinew of a red bull ... stamp on it with the left foot ... hit it with a spear ... cut it with a knife ... spit on it many times in the fire" (*GG* 49). Many other similar accounts are directed toward internal or external political enemies, involving the smashing of pots or figurines inscribed with their names, burying them, etc.

"If the ceremonies for Osiris are neglected ... the country will be deprived of its laws. The plebs will abandon their superiors and there are no orders for the masses. If the foe is not beheaded that is at hand made of wax ... then the foreign countries will rebel against Egypt and civil war and revolution will rise in the whole country" (*GG* 50, citing *Papyrus Jumilhac*).

a god who contains disorder and order. Seth "is the violence that rips apart order which then founds the world"; and yet at the same time "he is also the one who holds back the cosmic foe Apep."[28] Societal dangers and foes – and those who decide upon such crisis – are thus constructed and resolved through ritual procession and immolation of the Seth surrogate. This is the pharmacology of ritual violence containing raw violence, of the virus of violence being used in small ritual doses to thwart the disease.[29]

Seth may symbolize, as the antitype of Osiris, a scapegoat who was slain at the foundations of Egyptian culture and demonized/deified in time. The difference between murderer and murdered, however, is not entirely important for practical purposes: that Seth is "guilty" of murder is only the proximate accusation that serves to unite the people in a pole. The religiopolitical system that formed around him was protected and strengthened by cultic attention upon his dangerous memory, as it galvanized attention against the ongoing threat of societal dissolution. Such representations were perhaps naturally selected for their survival value. Seth, as demon/god, binds Egyptian society together through being both a personification of disorderly violence, to be repelled, and the recipient of ordering violence – and thus a source of resolution and peace.[30] Seth's "badness" and violence is "integrated into a holistic concept of sovereignty, combining death and life, violence and law."[31] Even as a demon, Seth is still an ambivalent, good/bad, chaos/order figure: "He represents *an evil that is necessary to keep the world going* ... that must simultaneously be controlled and contained because it threatens the world."[32] So, just as the demon Seth could politically symbolize violence and reconciliation, so too could Egyptian political theology incorporate reason and

---

[28] *GG* 36; Burkert, *The Orientalizing Revolution*, 67ff. In one of Egypt's representations of kingship, the unification of two Egyptian kings in a peace treaty is sometimes pictured as Horus and Seth tying together lily and papyrus. In Plutarch's writings, Seth is translatable with the demon Typhon.

[29] The connection between raw and ritual violence is visible, for example, in how redheads in times of Egyptian crisis were more likely targets for human sacrifice, as red was the color representing Seth (*GG* 41, 43).

[30] Recall how Girard regards the societal violence-containment function as crucial to mythological cycles: e.g., "Culture does not proceed directly from the reconciliation that follows Victimage; rather it is from the double imperative of prohibition and ritual, which means that the entire community is unified in order to avoid falling back into the crisis, and thus orients itself on the model – and the anti-model – which the crisis and its resolution now constitute (*TH* 32). Osiris/Horus is the model, Seth the anti-model.

[31] *GG* 40. See parallels in other theo-political systems in *OH* 39, *et passim*.

[32] *GG* 34, emphasis added.

force, justice and violence in its application of legal and ritual violence.[33]
Seth is a necessary "process" or function of violence containment.

ii. Was Seth Translatable in Israel?

Given that every society contains violence, it is not surprising to find that
Seth was "translatable" in neighboring countries. For Seth entails the
translatable societal function of containing violence. The neighboring
Hyksos, for example, translated their god Ba'al with Seth at their Avaris
cult, wherein both were seen as the same storm god by a different name.[34]
The Ba'al cycle, certainly within ancient Israel's religious watershed, was
also rooted in royal funerary and symbolized political threats, displaying
Seth-like elements: a founding murder, an intervention from sisters, an
awakening from death, the defeat of the enemy (the sea), followed by the
building of the divine palace for the divine warrior and concluding with
the vanquishing of the enemy, death.[35] And, by extension, the Babylonian
conflict between gods Marduk and Tiamat, was arguably modeled on the
Ba'al cycle.[36] There, public New Year's processions attacked Tiamat in
effigy to renew the cosmic cycle of defeating the enemy.[37] These parallels
are visible elsewhere in the ancient near east and Hellenic era.[38] That the
roles between murderer and victim are dizzyingly convertible across
various cultural translations again suggests not that these are rational,
metaphysical speculations on good and evil but that they serve a social
function of cohering the group's violence containment.[39] They narrate the
cyclic benefits of ritual and legal violence casting out chaotic violence.
(This parallels Girard observations on the ambivalence of kingship:
whether a reviled scapegoat or an adulated king, the point is their galvan-
izing joint attention.)

---

[33] Ibid., 39.

[34] *GIT* 71.

[35] "Baal is being modeled on the perceived fate of Ugaritic kings who descend to the
Underworld" (Mark Smith, "The Death of 'Dying and Rising Gods' in the Biblical
World," 296, 307; *EHG* 58; *NOG* 119, 150ff).

[36] Smith, "The Death of 'Dying and Rising Gods,'" 271; *EHG* 42, 54, 58.

[37] Peter Machinist, "How Gods Die, Biblically and Otherwise," 189–240, 234.

[38] See also the Greek Gorgon cycle: Zeus – whose monarchy coincides with imperial order –
triumphs over chaos of the Titans (Burkert, *The Orientalizing Revolution*, 85f). Dumuzi-
Tammuz seems to be a "divinized human" behind whose death "may lie the influence of
royal funerary cult" (Smith, "The Death of 'Dying and Rising Gods,'" 275, 277, 285).

[39] The roles may shift in translation: Ba'al, as killed, may resemble Osiris more than Seth
(Smith, "The Death of 'Dying and Rising Gods,'" 271).

The Seth-like Ba'al cycles, in a patchwork of mythology undergirding the Ugaritic dynasty and Levantine cultures, left residues in ancient Israelite religio-politics. Ba'al's victory over enemies is reflected in biblical texts proclaiming Yahweh's violent victory – including feeding on the flesh of captives, drinking the blood of victims, and wading in the blood of the vanquished.[40] Psalm 82, for example, appears to be a declaration of Yahweh deposing or killing off the other gods.[41] Some rabbinic and Christian literature carry forward these motifs, wherein the defeat of Sea, the building of the heavenly palace, and the destruction of death belong to the future divine transformation of the world.[42] There is likewise good reason to see Ba'al imagery at the roots "of the 'Son of Man' figure in Daniel 7 or Michael in the book of Revelation."[43] Simply, the religions that converged around Yahweh do at times have a sense of cosmic enemies, common to ancient myth cycles, even if they are not always directly correlated with political enemies.[44]

But these residues fade in Israel's traditions in proportion to its losing political sovereignty. Admittedly, in early Israel Yahweh had a monarch for a deputy, just as Horus was deputized by the Pharaoh.[45] And, as we will see in Chapter 6, Yahweh at times had cultic enemies all too obviously mirrored in political enemies. But what happens when there is no monarch, no state? This is the political context that helps illuminate what it meant that Yahweh became untranslatable with other gods, like Ba'al, Seth, and others. The idea that the land or cosmos are the body of a slain god seem to disappear in Israel; or rather, as we will see in coming chapters, the whole idea of land and sovereignty is creatively reconfigured. Exilic Deutero-Isaiah, for example, is conspicuously devoid of an originary conflict cycle when it speaks of creation, like we find in Seth. Rather, the divine Word replaces "combat as the rationale for the high god's universal dominion."[46] It appears that in Israelite religion slowly

---

[40] *EHG* 61ff; Isa 34:2, 49:26; Deut 32:43; Pss 58:11; 68:24; 110:6; Joel 3:13; Rev 14:14–20; Jdgs 8:1–2; 20:44–6; Jer 6:9; Deut 32:42; LXX Zech. 9:15; Num 23:24. "The battle with the sea was connected to Yahweh's creation of the world and was celebrated in the autumnal New Year's festival" (*NOG* 119).

[41] *NOG* 181.

[42] E.g., Rev 21:1–4.

[43] *NOG* 245. In one Greco-Egyptian text Seth and Yahweh seem to be translatable to each other through donkey imagery. And Plutarch writes that Seth, after killing Osiris, fled to Palestine, where he had two kids named Judah and Jerusalem (*IR* 36–8).

[44] *EHG* 58; Isa 30:7; Ps 87:4.

[45] E.g., Ps 2.

[46] *GIT* 177; *NOG* 208, 261.

losing state functions, evil and violently containing it became less and less a necessary cultic-political function, a necessary aspect of the cosmic pantheon as seen in Seth or Ba'al. Even if Seth may show traces of translation in the biblical landscape through Satan, Belial, or Ba'al Zebub, this figure is decreasingly treated as a personified divine opponent, an object of ritual violence, "an evil necessary to keep the world going" – and increasingly distilled in rabbinic tradition as simply the inclination toward evil.[47] (Perhaps Hajj rituals of "stoning of the devil" are one instance of its survival in Abrahamic tradition.) With the state-based violence-containment function slowly fading, there were less and less ritual means, no necessary sacrifices, by which to keep the world going. The Jewish God becomes, in a sense, removed from the cosmic process. This is a crucial front in which the monotheistic God becomes untranslatable with the "victim mechanism."

B. AKHENATON'S BORDERLINE CASE: NONTRANSLATABLE, BUT STILL COMPACTED GOD-KING

In the preceding, we have sketched a general Egyptian polytheistic political theology and its conceptualization of sovereignty and violence, with Osiris-Seth as a centerpiece. Importantly, in such political theology, we see the ambivalent conceptualization of victimage and violence-containment. And we can reasonably aver similar parallels or "translations" in ancient religion-politics, without presuming precise correspondences. One finds here something of a dark confirmation of Nietzsche's suspicion about the biblical concern for victims – that our species and our polities depend upon the necessary sacrifice of certain individuals. Cosmotheism not only takes for granted its gods, but it takes for granted its "need" for a Seth, a reified enemy; it must narrate why (and enact how) "force" is good and "violence" is bad.

But the difference between Egyptian polytheism and Mosaic monotheism is not entirely simple, with a gradient between these ideal-types. The specific case of Akhenaten's revolution, with which Freud acquainted us, is the most important such borderline case between primary and secondary religion. It bears many signs of the compact between God and King but also a strong sense of untranslatability. Thus, it is something of a historic forerunner in manifesting the Mosaic distinction. It will serve us

---

[47] Will Kynes, "Satan."

well to understand Akhenaten's revolution within the context of Egyptian political theology drawn up here.

Preceding Akhenaten, Egyptian political theology entailed the "oneness" characteristic of henotheism, with a very strong sense of divine unity behind the many. Atum was the preexistent primordial One, who was represented in the sun, the god Re, the creator and king of the gods and all cosmic elements. Indeed, stemming back to at least 3000 BCE, this strong divine unity can still be detected, with its emphasis on the state of Egypt as coextensive with the cosmos (i.e., Egypt *is* the world), as it emanated from and was ruled by the sun and the Pharaoh. But from 1500 BCE on, the theological parochialism widened along with its political borders. A chain of foreign invasions and wars of liberation put Egypt into an increasingly global and interconnected position – often above or at least beside other large states. As such, a more universalist political theology began to emerge: "Egypt was no longer seen as coextensive with creation in the sense of an ordered world surrounded by chaos but just part of a far more comprehensive world containing many comparable nations and civilizations."[48]

We thus have a parochial unity-theology gaining a universal character in the period leading up to Akhenaten. Even more importantly, the prevalent sun worship of this period mediated a theology in which, "The [sun] god confronts the world in sublime solitude. The distance between god and world has become extreme."[49] Thus a pre-Akhenaten hymn: "You have settled very remote, very far away; you have revealed yourself in heaven in your aloneness."[50] Theologically speaking, we *seem* to see an intensified transcendence, emphasizing an "invisibility of which no immanent visible order can be a proper analogue." And yet, crucially still cosmotheistic, the visible sun god represented in the Pharaoh remains "the Egyptian political god par excellence, deeply affecting the structure and durability of the imperial order."[51]

Akhenaten's religious revolution (*c.*1360–1340 BCE) intensified this divine distance from the world in a strongly universal theology. Of Aten we hear, "O sole god, beside whom there is none! ... there is no other

---

[48] *ATM* 53; *CMA* 377. Assmann calls this increasing "internationalism" a hallmark of the Late Bronze Age (1500–1100 BCE). There is a stela hailing Thutmose II as "Lord of every foreign land," with Amun-Re as his patron (Hoffmeier, *Akhenaten*, 58).

[49] *GG* 67.

[50] Ibid., 66.

[51] *OH* 69f.

except him."[52] In his hymns we hear of this sole God who made the world and all its foreign lands, all peoples of different skins, and sustains them all.[53] Despite the striking universality, with its nation-transcending divine, however, this religion was not yet properly monotheistic by Assmann's reading. The Aten religion may have been more universal in divinity than any preceding religion, but it remains in the cosmotheistic classification in that it was ultimately a henotheistic expression of empire while the god remains politically representable.[54]

And yet Akhenaten's "universal" God still radicalized the unity theology that had preceded it. He did not merely notice one God over all other nations; his revolution *abolished* all other gods.[55] This is the earliest evidence (so far) of a *nontranslatable* religion that sought to "abolish a whole religious tradition in the name of truth,"[56] attacking and deleting the gods through despotic political repression. This was the "most radical and violent eruption of a counter-religion in the history of humankind."[57] As such it can partially be categorized as "exclusive monotheism," somewhat sharing a place with a later Judaism. But as Akhenaten did not say "thou shalt worship no other gods," his religion does not have the same degree of againstness as the coming Mosaic religion. Rather, he "simply abolished the other gods and did not consider them worth mentioning after that, nor even for polemical purposes. Their exclusion took place on a practical rather than on a discursive and theoretical level."[58] Stemming from his idea of total cosmic dependence on the sun – which generates all things, even time – the other gods were for Akhenaten nonexistent deceptions. By contrast, the Mosaic religion sought to carve out a *people* from the world, bound to its Lord, "not a new cosmology . . .. What Akhenaten takes to be a mistaken worldview is for Moses evidence of disloyalty or, more precisely, a breach of contract."[59]

Akhenaten's abolishing the other gods radicalized Egypt's prior henotheism. His religion imagined that a "solitary god and a godless

---

[52] *GG* 81.

[53] Hoffmeier, *Akhenaten*, 223.

[54] *ATM* 13; see also *OH* 108.

[55] *PM* 64.

[56] *GG* 47.

[57] *ME* 25; Hoffmeier, *Akhenaten*, 199, 203.

[58] *PM* 30.

[59] *PM* 37f. Notably, "the rejected tradition is never mentioned in [Akhenaten] text" – i.e., it didn't develop "an antagonistic construction of the discarded tradition," the way the Mosaic distinction constructed "Egypt" or "paganism." The Mosaic form, however, "depends on the preservation of what it opposes" (*ME* 211).

world face each other in a relation of continuous creation and animation .... The world originated not once in primeval time from the sun, but is constantly emanating, albeit without gods, deprived of any divinity of its own."[60] So there is here some sense of a dedivinized world that, somehow, simultaneously retained a pantheistic notion of participation in the divine: the multitude of things in the world are but transformations, manifestations, or forms of the One: "You create millions of forms from yourself" reads one prayer.[61]

Akhenaten's religion also remains a primary and cosmotheistic religion in that it retained an extreme linkage between the God and King, with the Pharaoh as Aten's co-regent. Akhenaten's God-King compaction was so intense that he installed an exclusive and extreme form of state- and emperor-worship, much *un*like the Jewish monotheism that will, in time, emerge.[62] Far from altering the primary homology of religion and politics, he was worshipped as the deified king, the exclusive mediator between the sun god and humanity, revered as the object of personal piety.[63] And with Aten as a visible, cosmic God, he offered virtually nothing new in spiritual or ethical content; "he is strictly heliomorphic. Freud did not understand this."[64] The monistic political theology of the Amarna era thus is squarely located in the cosmotheistic compaction we discussed above, even if Aten effaced all the other gods and is untranslatable. Akhenaten's religion is more imperial henotheism, a despotic "monotheism from above," in Gnuse's phrasing.[65] By contrast, in Chapter 6, we will explore how a mixture of monolatry and monotheism from above in Israelite religion made possible a "monotheism from below."

With the Pharaoh as co-regent with Aten, his revolution ought to be regarded as a supreme connection of political and religious salvation. The potential for redefining the god-king link may have begun, even while the two remained intimately linked. With the notion of false religion having emerged, the relation between the king and salvation is radically

---

[60] Jan Assmann, "Jan Assmann, Ramesside Theology and Its Place in the History of Religion," 10:58.

[61] *GG* 67.

[62] *PM* 46; *OH* 109.

[63] *GG* 81f. Jan Assmann, "Axial 'Breakthroughs' in Ancient Egypt and Israel," 145; Hoffmeier, *Akhenaten*, 87. In Mesopotamia, some similarities: "the sun-god Marduk is appointed as the ruler over all the peoples, and his earthly analogue, Hammurabi, rises like the sun over the people and lightens up the land" (*OH* 26). Vassals address Akhenaten as "my god" in the El Amarna letters (*GIT* 14, 74).

[64] *ME* 210.

[65] *NOG* 22, 94, 170–1; Gnuse, "Breakthrough or Tyranny," 85, 90f; *IR* 43.

redefined: unlike previous Pharaohs, Akhenaten did not "represent" the absent god; rather both he and the god "*reign together*, one as a cosmic, the other as a political and moral power. Here, too, then, the connection between dominion and salvation is strengthened, even as the two are distinguished."[66] Put in terms of the god-world relation, Akhenaton's god is, in fact, not really transcendent or eternal, but the sun. This religion suggests the cosmos, the land, the political apparatus, and the king are all compatible.[67] Per Mouffe's theory, this is not a recipe for harmony but totalitarianism[68] and false unity, a "complete reabsorption of alterity into oneness," resistant to intervention, self-reflexivity, and improvement.

Akhenaton's religion of the sun disc, Assmann insists, is *not* the model for the later Jewish prophets,[69] contrary to Freud's speculation that the prophets were ultimately restoring Aten worship against Yahwist primitivism. The few ancient accounts that associate Moses with Akhenaton's revolution appear as a distorted conflation of historical memories. We find this conflation, for example, in Manetho, an Egyptian priest around the third century BCE. He wrote of a long-ago revolution of atheist lepers who rose up against Amenophis III – one of whose leaders took the name "Moses."[70] The impious lepers prescribed all that was forbidden in Egypt, refused to worship any god, and forbid intercourse with outsiders. Joining forces with the Hyksos of Jerusalem, they tyrannically ruled until they were cast off.

Manetho's account suggests memories of Akhenaten's revolution were likely conflated, over time, with the Jewish exodus story. Assmann catalogs several other similar Egyptian versions of the Hebrew exodus that also recall a political revolution of impurity, trauma, atheism, and theoclasm.[71] But these legends err in "retroactively interlinking" Aten's religion with Moses' exodus. As some of the earliest versions of anti-Semitism, they project Egypt's many historic traumas (including the Hyksos tyranny) onto the Jews, wherein iconoclasm – dissimulated as

---

[66] *PM* 47f, italics added.

[67] *ATM* 55; cf. Hoffmeier, *Akhenaten*, 225.

[68] Emily Teeter, *Religion and Ritual in Ancient Egypt*, 182–96.

[69] *GG* 161.

[70] The Moses element may have been a later interpolation reflecting encounters between Hellenic-era Egyptians at Manetho's time and Jews, who were likely seen as threats to the Egyptian sense of religious stability. As such, the story conflates a feeling of threat to national religious stability, the repressed trauma of the Amarna period, and Jewish iconoclasm (*PM* 59f; *ME* 32; *GG* 46).

[71] *ME* 35ff; *PM* 62.

unclean, godless "leprosy"[72] – symbolizes the danger of political and religious persecution that Egypt suffered under Akhenaten and from neighboring powers in the centuries after him.[73] He was remembered namelessly as "the criminal of Amarna";[74] and the memory of his impure iconoclasm may have bled into the symbol of Seth, who "rejoices in separation, who hates fraternity, who relies only on his own heart among the gods."[75]

It is important to ask how these blurred Exodus/Aten histories, which paint Israel's exodus derisively, have colored our reception of the Mosaic traditions since its origins. That is, the Mosaic distinction, from an Egyptian perspective, was seen in a very negative light and likely colored its reception history. We do well to carefully sift out what may be conflations with Akhenaten's despotism. These conflations suggest, at least, we have reason to be suspicious of too strongly linking, as Freud did, Akhenaten's and Israel's monotheism.

C. AFTER AKHENATON IN EGYPT: A MIDDLE-WAY COMPROMISE

After Akhenaten the gods returned. Egypt's theologians retained a strong emphasis on divine, hidden unity that was manifested in diversity.[76] In a greater compact between God and the universe than even before Akhenaten, God as invisible begets himself into the millions of visible manifestations of the cosmos. In this sense, the cosmos is *creatio ex deo*, the body of God; God is like the hidden soul that animates a visible body of the universe. God *is* the world in this intensified cosmotheism.[77] This involves compatible dualities of double layering: hidden/manifest, One/many, esoteric/exoteric religion. God was hidden and ineffable as ever,

---

[72] *GG* 47. Manetho seems to conflate the commandment to worship no other gods with a ban on worshipping any gods at all (*PM* 60, 111; *GG* 47; *ME* 57–9).

[73] *PM* 57, 59f; Smelik and Hemelrijk, "Who Knows Not What Monsters Demented Egypt Worships?," 1911.

[74] In court proceedings forty years after Akhenaten's death, he is avoided to be called by name: simply, "the enemy of Amarna," or over fifty years later, "the rebel" (Hoffmeier, *Akhenaten*, 244).

[75] *GG* 48; Hoffmeier, *Akhenaten*, 243.

[76] *PM* 33, 26.

[77] *GG* 68–70; *PM* 73; *ATM*, 19. Or "hypercosmism."

while the visible Pharaoh could receive, as a representative, this devotion.[78]

This form of cosmotheism will live on for some centuries and undergo transformations with the Hellenic upheavals centuries later. Its double layering is retrieved much later in the Enlightenment's nostalgia, evident in secret societies (the Illuminati, the Free Masons),[79] who – in the wake of Napoleonic adventures abroad – saw themselves as rediscoverers of this Egyptian legacy: an enlightened, esoteric, pure, spiritual pantheism for the initiated, on the one hand, and a banal, exoteric religion of animal-gods for the plebeians on the other.[80] For the Enlightenment rediscoverers, this theology mirrored their own social context, "with its exterior face of Church and absolutism and its interior of deism and enlightened philosophy."[81] Freud's simplified approach to ritual and enlightenment reflects some of this dualism.

Akhenaten's revolution left behind traumatic memories of kingship turning evil, criminal, and against the gods. As a result, religious piety began to migrate from explicit attention upon the visible Pharaoh into an increasingly private, personal form of piety toward the god. One would no longer pray to the Pharaoh for providential protection but to the "God alone." Devotional language usually at home in the *religiopolitical* sphere – of pleading to the Pharaoh – transposed into a distinctly "religious" sphere of "prayer." "God" came to no longer coincide exactly with the king who saves. After Akhenaten one can find many prayers like: "I have not sought for myself a protector among men, God N is my defender," resembling biblical language of trusting alone in God.[82] In such prayers, "God" now plays the role that Pharaohs and former patrons had played. This all ushered in an increase of what Assmann calls "explicit theology," wherein religion began to receive more distinct reflective attention in writing and teaching than in previous centuries, creating a "country of theologians." To some extent, then, a more personal, proto-depoliticized "religion" that transcends the political realm, slowly begins in Egypt – though we will find a more intense iteration in

---

[78] E.g., a post-Akhenaten utterance: "People fall down immediately for fear if his name [Amen] is uttered knowingly or unknowingly. There is no god able to call him by it" (*GG* 65).

[79] See Cudworth, *The True Intellectual System of the Universe* (1678); Schiller, *Die Sendung Moses* (1790).

[80] *ATM* 97.

[81] *ATM* 104.

[82] *GG* 82. E.g., Ps 20:7; 33:16; Ams 2:14; Hos 10:13.

Israel. Notably, in both cases, this change does not happen merely through "ideas" and rationalization but through national breakdown, disappointment, and tumult.

The above is a transposition of "protection" from the political sphere to a newly distinguishing and transcendent religious sphere. In other words, this is part of Assmann's overarching thesis that what we think of as "religious" concepts are in fact genetically "theologized political concepts." As another example, Assmann observes a similar kind of transposition had taken place in Egypt a millennium prior, with respect to "judgment" and the afterlife: whereas the divine Pharaoh used to hold a monopoly on judgment (including burial and immortality), traumatic breakdowns of the political order and the vast destruction of tombs all served to detach judgment from kings toward a transcendent Osiris.[83] By Assmann's appraisal, "this is the first instance of the transposition of an idea or institution from the earthly sphere involving the social and the political to the transcendent sphere of the divine."[84] Whereas divinity had been inextricably compacted with the political sphere, we have here the dim beginnings of a *distinct* religious sphere, separating from a compact with the political.

A certain resultant cosmotheism permeates Egyptian religion from Akhenaten into the Alexandrian era, amidst an increased synchronicity with Greek influences. In it God and royalty are simultaneously distinguished yet intimately compatible, in a hidden/manifest duality. We can imagine Egyptian henotheism as being annexed into new, but not incomprehensible Hellenic themes, of Aristotle's Unmoved Mover, Rome's pantheon, or in Neoplatonic theologies of a God Beyond Being. Amidst its transformations, with the exception in Akhenaten, Egypt's cosmotheistic God remained *translatable*. At times, there is no need for a name of the One Hidden God, as this God is One and behind all.[85] By contrast, Assmann argues it is Judaism that truly reconfigures ancient political theology through an *untranslatable* God, radically transcendent to the cosmos and royalty. Judaism will use "Egypt" as its symbol for the religion out of which it escapes and opposes itself. Notably, it will do so not from the pinnacle of political power, as Akhenaten did, but at the bottom of a chain of historical traumas and descending into subsovereignty.

---

[83] *GG* 80.
[84] Ibid., 79; *ATM*, 20; *OH* 56f.
[85] *PM* 20.

6

A Political Theology of the Mosaic Distinction

The Development of Apophatic Intolerance

The many layers of the Hebrew Bible evince centuries of conflict between parties who disagree on Israel's proper religious form – ranging from a common polytheism to an intolerance oriented by the distinction between true and false religion. This latter Mosaic distinction never showed itself as a stable, unanimous force in Israelite religion, manifesting unevenly over centuries. But between these differing parties, the final version of the Tanakh that we now have largely reflects the winning party's interpretation of history. It displays strong signs of intolerance and at least fantasized violence, and its narrative centerpiece is the exodus. This legend, in Assmann's analysis, symbolizes the transition from polytheism to monotheism, the shift from primary to secondary religions, "supplanting, absorbing, and extinguishing everything that went before."[1]

And yet, we will find, it is this unstable font of intolerance that bequeaths to us a unique and profound critique of divinized kings and ancient royal theology – slowly dissolving the ancient compact between God and the political order. For one of the chief metaphysical consequences of the Mosaic distinction, Assmann argues, is the separation of God from the cosmos, while its chief political consequence is the separation of religion from the political sphere.[2] As such, the Mosaic distinction marks one of the most crucial intellectual and cultural breakthroughs in civilizational history. It is precisely through its intolerance that Judaism came upon a form of life that Assmann sees as potentiating "emancipation": it breaks open humanity from its "embeddedness in the

---

[1] *ATM* 42.
[2] *PM* 48.

world and its political, natural, and cultural powers," while liberating the
"divine from mundane immanence."[3]

Drawing upon Assmann and adjacent scholarship for clarity and supplement, this chapter will argue the following: Jewish monotheism
emerged through the multi-century collective experience of undergoing
threat, brutalization, and displacement from various powers. In response,
generations of "intolerant" branches in Israelite religion cohered around
the exodus story. This narrative mediated, in part, a jingoistic monolatry
not entirely uncommon in the ancient world, while those outside it were
perceived as seditious or idolatrous. But, over time, this exodus story
redirected the covenantal loyalty owed to their imperial overlords to
Yahweh alone. This total devotion to *no other gods* resulted in a unique,
reconfigured theological imaginary that became (potentially) incompatible with any political order.

This zeal, comingled with historical traumas, created in its devotees a
very unique sort of acid, as it were – like the kind that develops
photographic film, inverting whites to black and vice versa. It is an acid
composed of numerous ingredients, each briefly reviewed in the several
sections of this chapter: subjugation to imperial covenants, occasional
monolatry, a king-critical prophetic tradition, exile, the development of
memory-techniques and canon, and a ban on divine representation. While
each ingredient was not entirely unique in itself, their accumulation
resulted in a novel compound. This acid slowly "developed" the outer
forms of ancient political theology from their negative into their positive.
While the outer forms remain somewhat identical (namely, zealous alliance to a divine Lord), their meaning and substance inverts. Ancient
political theologies that founded a political order were transformed into
a refusal of any political representation of God. Through this, the potentiality of ancient Israel's "intolerance" transposes over time from
political-power ambitions to the possibility of messianic patience. (The
metaphor is my own, but its method and content are derived from
Assmann and others noted here.)[4]

This transformation of intolerance bequeathed to us both liberation
and danger. It opened up entirely new ways to view politics, God,

---

[3] *ATM* 42.
[4] The metaphor, I think, fulfills Assmann's insistence that – while the process involves
historical similarities – one must not regard it as a mere evolution, continuous with its
surroundings: "Nothing would be more wrongheaded than to assume that biblical
monotheism has evolved from particularist monolatry to universalistic monotheism"
(*IR* 84).

religion, and the world itself, breaking up the cosmotheistic worldview. In Girardian terms, it separated God from the sacred, from the victim. In Mouffian terms, it opened up an allegiance incompatible with any political order. Strikingly, this monotheistic breakthrough emerges through Israel's breakdown – a complex history of the battle for political sovereignty and the fall from it. Exploring these changes helps us, among many things, answer the critical question that was posed to Girard, regarding "what peculiarities in the ethical organization of the Hebrews made them, among all the peoples of the ancient world, the 'chosen' discoverers/inventors of monotheism."[5]

A. ISRAEL AS ORIGINALLY POLYTHEISTIC

Israel's early archaeological record gives little signs of a revolutionary uniqueness or Mosaic distinction in its religion.[6] Israel likely began not with an influx of Egyptian refugees on exodus[7] but simply the indigenous of Canaan, for whom intermarriage with surrounding tribes and city-states was common.[8] It was likely a loose confederation of polytheistic Canaanite tribes, even down to the Davidic monarchy (~1000 BCE), when it was still more of a "well developed chiefdom" than a state. An Israelite state didn't truly emerge until around the eighth century BCE.[9]

El was one of Israel's earliest chief gods, among several others.[10] Yahweh likely entered into Canaan from the nearby southern highlands along with a tribe that slowly intermixed with Canaanites.[11] Yahweh seems to have been originally a more solitary god, without a divine family, and not integrated into a pantheon; this may have supplied some monolatrous potentiality as Yahweh became integrated into the Canaanite pantheon.[12] Early visual representations of Yahweh included

---

[5] Eric Gans, "René et moi," 23.
[6] The earliest artifact testifying to the existence of "Israel" dates around 1208 BCE, in a pharaonic monument celebrating Egypt's power over Syro-Palestine (*EHG* 5; *GIT* 100; Merneptah stele, line 27).
[7] *EHG* xxxi.
[8] See 1 Kgs 11:5; 2 Kgs 23:13; Jer 11:13; Ezk 8. *EHG* 145.
[9] *NOG* 200.
[10] *EHG* 7. Other names would include El-Elyon, -Shaddai, -Bethel, -Roi, and -Olam (*NOG* 182).
[11] Hoffmeier, *Akhenaten*, 258; Deut 33:2; Jdgs 5:4; Ps 68:8, 18; Hab 3:3, 7; *GIT* 96; *EHG* 25, 32–3, 81; *NOG* 194.
[12] Rainer Albertz, "Monotheism and Violence," 376; *NOG* 196.

the calf,[13] and it was not until around the time of Hosea (eighth century BCE) that we find any critique of representing him visibly, in the Golden Calf legend. In Israel's earlier periods, Yahweh was likely translatable with El and worshipped alongside other gods, including Ba'al, the sun, the moon, the stars, and the female deity Asherah.[14] Generally speaking, a plurality of gods and translatability was as normal to early Israelite religion as it was to its Levantine neighboring religions.[15]

During the monarchy period, Yahweh slowly subsumed El, wherein the latter becomes one of Yahweh's titles.[16] Similar to neighboring state religions in Mesopotamia and Egypt, Yahweh served as the divine, national king, accumulating in himself the attributes of other Israelite gods.[17] Yahweh thus ruled – not unlike Babylon's Marduk, Assyria's Assur, Egypt's Amun-Re – as the head of a small pantheon, presiding as warrior god over his polytheistic religio-state well into the seventh century.[18] There would have been relative tolerance toward subordinate gods and cults inside Yahweh's borders and recognition of the supreme gods outside its borders. With Yahweh as the sponsor of Israel's monarchy, foreign gods were "tolerated" as the respective divine kings of other nations, so long as they kept themselves out of Israel's borders.[19]

Such a summodeistic Israel included the classic arrangement of a king who is a representative or an analogue to the supreme deity. El had also served earlier in Ugarit as a royal god with whom deified kings would merge at their death.[20] Israel's monarchs, too, as adopted sons of Yahweh, were perhaps thought to "participate in" Yahweh's reign and

---

[13] Although, the golden calf may have symbolized "Egypt" and its bull Apis (*NOG* 187; *EHG* 23). Polemics against images: Isa 2:8; 10:10; 30:22; 31:7; 40:19; 42:19; Jer 1:16; 8:19; Mic 1:7; Nah 1:14.

[14] Moloch worship, via infant sacrifice, up until Josiah's reforms, is also arguably part of the religious milieu (*NOG* 118, 187f, 191). Condemnations are clearer here: Jer 2:23; 7:31; 19:5–6, 11–4; 31:30; 32:35; Isa 30:33; Mic 6:7, and Ezk 16:20–1; 20:26; 23:37–9. *EHG* 146.

[15] *GIT* 96, 98, 102, 129. See, e.g., El's identification with Yahweh in Ex 6:3. *NOG* 87; *EHG* 25.

[16] *GIT* 142; Ex 6:2.

[17] Ps 10:16; Ex 15:18; 1 Sam 8:7; Ps 47:9; 93:1; 96:10; 97:1; 99:1; 146:10; J. A. Soggin, "The Davidic-Solomonic Kingdom," 361–3, 370–3; *EHG* 55f; 1 Kgs 20:23; *NOG* 197.

[18] *CMEC* 181f.

[19] Mark S. Smith, *The Origins of Biblical Monotheism* (hereafter *TOBM*), 162–3.

[20] Becking Van der Toorn and Van der Horst, eds, *Dictionary of Deities and Divinities in the Bible*, 1725.

his sovereign claims to the land.[21] And just as Seth cosmically symbolized Egypt's political enemies, the divine enemies of Yahweh were analogues of the king's opponents.[22]

Though redactors apparently attempted to efface this original polytheism, its residues remain in the biblical text or are even at times explicitly acknowledged.[23] An earlier textual stratum shows signs of Yahweh's polytheistic genes: El and Asherah had divine kids, one of whom was Yahweh, who inherited the land from El (Deut 32). Or, some texts suggest an earlier version of polytheistic translatability, which became partially effaced in redaction – wherein El is entirely supreme and the gods are reduced to nothing.[24]

On these historical matters, Assmann aligns with the scholarly majority on Israel's originary polytheism and the emergence of monotheism, even if his approach to the intolerant Mosaic distinction is a point of controversy and misunderstanding. The extreme end of the spectrum regards Israel as monotheistic from its birth – originating with a historical Moses or the judges era in a revolutionary and normative Yahwism.[25] On the other end, monotheism is only a very late, *postexilic* achievement (538 BCE onward), perhaps centuries after; and prior Israelite religion was entirely and indistinguishably polytheistic. In between the two positions is the scholarly majority, roughly put: early Israel slowly evolved from a relatively common polytheism, occasionally expressing monolatry through the *no other gods* imperative; but through this it eventually gestated a unique monotheism around Josiah of the late monarchy and especially the Babylonian exile; and it solidified these religious

---

[21] *TOBM* 159. Bernard M. Levinson, "The Reconceptualization of Kingship in Deuteronomy and the Deuteronomistic History's Transformation of Torah," 512. 1 Chr 29:20 entails people bowing to Yahweh and the king as if one, or Ps 68:25 draws God and king identifications. Margaret Barker also traces from Qumran texts the liturgies of the first temple, wherein the King "underwent an apotheosis and was venerated as the Lord in the midst of his people" (Patrick Chatelion Counet, "The Divine Messiah," 47; Margaret Barker, *The Great High Priest*; *EHG* 146; 2 Kgs 11:17; 2 Sam 23:5).

[22] *TOBM* 157.

[23] E.g., the Book of Kings acknowledged Asherah worship, or Jeremiah's "Queen of Heaven" (*GIT* 143).

[24] E.g., Psalm 82 appears to critique translatability in an attempt to dissolve plural gods, even while its original text may have been polytheistic: the other gods had been gods of nations, but in the psalm's ending, El inherits authority over everything. Machinist, "How Gods Die, Biblically and Otherwise," 234; *GIT* 139.

[25] E.g., G. Mendenhall, "The Monarchy"; J. Bright, *A History of Israel*.

transformations after the exilic period.[26] We in the West are more familiar with the cleaner version: Israel was originally normatively monotheistic but it periodically regressed into polytheistic syncretism. Majority
scholarship, however, sees any signs of monotheism prior to the exilic
hinge as reflections of a smaller movement or textual retrojections, propaganda of later centuries.[27]

Emphasizing polytheism as native to Israel not only puts a check on
simplistic varieties of biblical triumphalism and uniqueness, betraying a
history more complex than the brochure, but it raises an important
analytic question: Why do we see in Israel a movement that, unlike its
neighbors and its own history, eventually condemns the worship of other
gods? Why does this people remember its history not only through an
exodus liberation but as a violent revolution against idolaters?[28]

B. EXODUS AND THE *NO OTHER GODS* MOVEMENT

Answers to these questions are complex, but crucial ones linger around
the exodus legend and its "covenant," symbols, which served at various
times to consolidate Israel's political unity.[29] As to the historical status of
the exodus, we have no material evidence; it may be the combination of
several histories.[30] But the important question is *why* was this story being
told?[31] This story seems to emerge, partly, through a rift not simply

---

[26] *ATM* 52. Hoffmeier attests to Assmann's location in the prevailing view (Hoffmeier,
    Akhenaten, 265). See also Rob Gordon "Introduction to Israel's God."
        There are about only twenty-five declarations of full, strict monotheism in the Bible:
    "most of them in the Old Testament, and virtually all of them are Deuteronomic or
    Deutero-Isaianic ... (e.g., Deut 4:35; 32:39; 2 Sam 7:22; 1 Kgs 8.60; Isa 45:5–6, 14, 18,
    21). The same applies to passages in which other gods are dismissed as 'nothing' (e.g., Jer
    2:5, 11 [and chap 10]). The few exceptions like two Psalms passages (86:10; 18:32 =
    2 Sam 22:32) are hard to date and do not affect the general conclusion that in ancient
    Israel monotheism was not explicit or emphasized until the sixth century BC" (Sawyer,
    "Biblical Alternatives to Monotheism," 173). See also *EHG* 15.
[27] *EHG* 81.
[28] *EHG* 150; *MPC* 147.
[29] *NOG* 77.
[30] *ATM* 26, 61, 67. Assmann's suggested historic ingredients in the exodus legend include a
    several-century period: the regional traumas of the Hyksos, Akhenaten's revolution, the
    regional plague following his regime, the experiences of the Habiru, slave escapes, and the
    large-scale migrations of "the sea people." *IR* ch 2.
[31] Assmann calls this method, which asks about how the exodus story was transmitted
    throughout Israel's history, "mnemohistory." Such a historical method asks: who was
    retelling this story, to whom, when, and why – and what did it do to them? *CMEC* 180;
    ME 2; *MPC* 148; *ATM* 39.

between Israel and Egypt but between the Northern and the Southern Kingdoms. (The former is often denoted as "Israel" – although that word too connotes the historical construct of Yahweh's people and the entire biblical story line – and the latter as "Judah.") If 1 Kings is reliable, the exodus legend at least corresponds with a northern critique of the imposing, toilsome Temple construction in the South – forced on the region by Solomon and Rehoboam in the tenth century. Under the northern leadership of Jeroboam I, a South-critical secession exalted Yahweh as their liberator from such tyrannical enslavement.[32] The movement was perhaps inspired by anti-colonial cultural memories dating back to Egypt's domination over Canaan.[33] But, just as the exodus legend narrates regression of the liberated, Jeroboam too is remembered as an idolater: though freeing them in one sense, he depicts Yahweh with two golden calves and establishes shrines to foreign gods with non-Levitical priests.

The exodus legend also intersects with King Asa of the ninth century.[34] Asa, his son, and the prophet Elijah supposedly enacted sweeping and harsh religious reforms and persecuted Ba'al priests, temples, and idols, using the exodus as a basis: just as Yahweh had taken them out of Egypt and commanded them to do away with idols, so must the people of Asa's day do away with their idols.[35] And yet we suffer layers of distance from this story. While Asa was supposedly invoking an exodus event that preceded him by centuries, the stories about him are being told *centuries later*, in Ezekiel around the sixth century. Furthermore, it is difficult to know how much Ezekiel's text is a product of later redactive agendas.[36] The same could be said of a later king, Hezekiah, who, inspired by prophetic warnings about worshipping foreign gods, centralized the Judean cult and prohibited worship of any god but Yahweh (710–700 BCE).[37]

---

[32] 1 Kgs 12:14–28; *IR* 51.

[33] *IR* 44, 64; Ronald Hendel, "The Exodus As Cultural Memory."

[34] Albertz argues that "the exodus tradition was well known at least in the northern kingdom of the 10th century (1 Kgs 12:28–9; Rainer Albertz, *Orthodoxy, Liberalism, and Adaptation*, 40).

[35] For the purge, see Ezk 20, 36–8. Asa reigned circa 911–870 BCE.

[36] *NOG* 258: "much of the language in the prophetic books may be the product of the exilic and postexilic redactors who created the books in their final written form." Again, "The narrative material of the Hebrew Bible pertaining to the Iron I period dates largely from the latter half of the monarchy, removed at least two or three centuries from the events of the Iron I period that the texts relate" (*EHG* 3).

[37] 2 Kgs 18:2; 2 Chr 29–30. As for Hosea, Micah, and Amos, see Stephen Cook, *The Social Roots of Biblical Yahwism*. For Hezekiah, see *EHG* 155, 160.

In any case, sometime in these centuries, between Asa's and Hezekiah's supposed centralizations, we can postulate the beginnings of a *no other gods* movement,[38] likely originating from a secessionist North while its attention eventually coheres around a unified cult in the South. The core text of this theological tradition comes down to us in the form of Deuteronomy.[39] This was a prophetic minority movement, whose size and popularity are disputable, in conflict with Israel's original polytheism.[40] The early stages of this movement were not monotheistic, in the numeric sense of disbelieving that the other gods *exist* or that they are "false." Rather it was a monolatry – or again a "monotheism of loyalty" – in which Israel should have *no other gods*, condemning allegiance to any other gods, just as matrimony condemns taking other lovers, who nonetheless exist.[41] Its crucial rhetorical mode is not truth/untruth but loyalty/betrayal, the worship of other gods as adultery. This exclusive allegiance is a crucial ingredient in what later, by the end of the monarchy and the onset of exile, accrues a more numeric and universal "monotheism of truth," which stems in from Deutero-Isaiah, postexilic prophets, Daniel, and others, for whom there simply is no other god.[42]

One of the early expressions of *no other gods* monolatry is Elijah, who, in the name of Yahweh, attacked the priests of only a certain *kind* of Ba'al gods, the ones from the North. Notably, Elijah left the worship of other gods untouched – like the asherim and other local Ba'al cults.[43] Elijah's political context is telling as to why: he was objecting to the northern Israelite Omride Dynasty who, under pressure from the Assyrian Empire, syncretized their cults and forged trade partnerships, thereby ensuring some economic ascendancy and stability. But this Omride boon came at a cost to many, who saw the dynasty as corrupted and compromised by foreign influence.[44] Objecting to the costs of such an arrangement, Elijah campaigned for a more protectionist Israel and, with Elisha, executed a violent coup against the dynasty and a destruction of its Ba'al temples.

---

[38] *CMEC* 182; *EHG* 155.

[39] *CMEC* 192; *GG* 115; *PM* 33.

[40] E.g., Bernhard Lang, *Monotheism and the Prophetic Minority*; Morton Smith, "The Yahweh Alone Movement and the Making of Jewish Monotheism"; *GIT* 124.

[41] See Juha Pakkala, *Intolerant Monolatry in the Deuteronomistic History*.

[42] *IR* 83; *EHG* xxviii. Israel's eighth-sixth century monolatry, which entails some non-translatability, fits with Smith's time line that "non-translatability in Israel may predate its explicit expressions of monotheism" (*GIT* 147).

[43] *GIT* 115, 122; 1 Kgs 18; *NOG* 79, 186, 200.

[44] Albertz, "Monotheism and Violence," 380. Albertz suggests the more solitary character of Yahweh could be part of this isolationist policy.

Their isolationist monolatry desiccated the state and its economy. When the Deuteronomistic historians later recounted this history, however, they stressed only the religious dimensions of the rebellion, even though the conflict "may have been more political than religious."[45] While Albertz sees in this event an early instance of "monotheistic" intolerance,"[46] Assmann reads it as political-ritual monolatrous violence common to the ancient world. For the other gods that Elijah attacked were as real as Assyria and the Omrides. (It is only much later, with the Maccabean revolt in the second century BCE, as we will see, that Assmann detects true monotheistic, religious violence.)[47]

The *no other gods* movement more clearly emerges through prophets like Amos, Hosea, and Micah around the eighth and seventh centuries BCE.[48] Like Elijah, they wrote under the pressures of Assyrian dominance and invasion in the North, though the situation had only worsened. Assmann calls this time for Israel a "state of emergency," which clarifies the meaning of their monolatry: politically establishing who is the enemy corresponded with theologically exalting the god who will save. Under the threat of absolute servitude to Assyrian overlords, these prophets reached back in time, calling upon the covenant established in exodus, to consolidate Israelite identity.[49] "But I am the LORD your God ever since Egypt; you know no God but me, and besides me there is no savior" (Hos 13:4). In this era, employing a golden-era founding legend was not entirely unique to Israel. Many cultures of the first millennium BCE were nostalgically retracing founding stories that marked the transition from the Late Bronze Age into the Iron Age to establish aesthetic and legal norms, with Homer's Trojan war as a most famous example among many.[50] Israel was looking back to revolutionary events of the fourteenth or thirteenth century in Rammeside Egypt.

---

[45] *NOG* 76, 183.

[46] Albertz, "Monotheism and Violence," 381.

[47] Rodney Stark, by contrast, sees Zoroastrianism (dating its contested origins roughly around the seventh-sixth century BCE) as perhaps the first such "religious violence" (Rodney Stark, *Discovering God*, 167).

[48] *ATM* 27; Mic 6:4, Hos 11:1, Ams 2:10. Dating later, around 520 BCE, see Hag 2:1–5. "Hosea appears to be the first 'Yahweh aloneist' among the prophets (750 BCE)" (*NOG* 76).

[49] See Assmann, "Myth As 'historia divina' and 'historia sacra,'" 13–24.

[50] Homer of the eighth century is looking back to Mycenaean Greece of the thirteenth and twelfth centuries. The neo-Assyrian Renaissance was particularly archaeologically nostalgic as it dug for this golden age under Sargon of Akkade of the twenty-fourth and twenty-third centuries. Or in Egypt, the Saite Dynasties (of the seventh and sixth

This prophetic legend of an exodus covenant conveyed that the Israelites were once slaves and had been chosen in an exclusive alliance with a liberating god. But Hosea's twist suggested a unique response to the catastrophic Assyrian terror in his day. Unlike the natural temptations toward either resistance or submission – that is, make alliances with neighbors to fight, or beg forgiveness for ever having considered disloyalty to Assyria – Hosea rejected both options. For the prophet, Israel was suffering domination because it had been disloyal to Yahweh for their having allied with and worshipped foreign gods. The Assyrian despotism was only mediating the punishment of Yahweh himself.[51] This is an odd move. It suggests Yahweh, only seemingly overpowered by Assyria, was in fact transcendent to their power. This is very rare to have a god working not only beyond one's own government but through another one to discipline his own. Moreover, this serves to locate not only the deity, but one's identity, as transcendent to any of the available political options. The prophet was redirecting the loyalty demanded by Assyrian tyranny – which we will examine in Section C, "Covenants" below – and displacing it into a different register. Israel's liberation required neither insurrection nor sheer abrogation. The exodus claim on Israelite loyalty required an inward purification not a political solution.

Hosea's move is very awkward to modern readers, as it seems typical of abusive relationships: an abusive tyrant who provokes servile self-accusation. But David Carr, sensitive to the workings of trauma, sees this as not so simple. The prophet, admittedly, partially suggests a loathing and a misogynistic deity, mirroring the Assyrian despot. But at the same time, this opened up an alternative to a total annihilation of meaning amidst the Assyrian onslaught. There lingers in Hosea an underdetermined hope in the exodus liberation. Hosea's self-blame "offered Israel a way to see itself as empowered in an otherwise helpless situation ... Israel could change its behavior and regain control over its situation."[52] If Assyria's violent threat suggested the red-hot pincers of torture to extract their allegiance, Hosea is redirecting their use to pull out the log in their own eye. We might see this as a first instance of Israel turning swords into plows. It is despotism in reverse.

centuries), in their own renaissance, were looking back to the Old and Middle Kingdoms. *CMEC* 77; *ATM*, 32f.

[51] David Carr, *Holy Resilience*, 27, 35.
[52] Ibid., 32–3.

Moreover, Hosea's focus on Israel's internal guilt made possible a self-reflexive relationship to their collective past that was apparently uncommon to the ancient world (and, we might add, the partisan, chauvinist spirit today). Whereas ancient cultures tended to represent their histories through self-adulation and deprecation of outsiders, this notion of guilt makes possible a certain exit from the "scapegoat mechanism" in its redirection of the accusatory impulse. For the worshippers of "false religion" here are, in a sense, themselves. As Gerhard Lohfink observes of this self-critical spirit: "There is no people in the world that has interpreted its own history in this way, as an unending succession of uprisings and rebellions against God; and there is no people that has so uncompromisingly revealed its own lack of faith and fidelity."[53]

C. A COVENANTED PEOPLE

Covenants were political agreements, vassal-treaties, or loyalty oaths, commonly used by archaic states and lords in the near east in the second millennium BCE and after.[54] They provide a fascinating key to understanding monolatry, in that the formula "thou shalt have no other gods besides me," is not originally "religious" but *political*. *No other gods* is a variation of common covenant phrasing "thou shalt have no overlords besides me."[55] Similarly, the imperatives to "love the Lord with all your heart" or "to love X as oneself" were common vassal-treaty formulas to love one's king in full loyalty, seen in Hittite and Assyrian treaties.[56] Under constant threat and pressure from Assyria, it is likely that some of Israel's kings would have been impelled to use such covenant language to swear their loyalty to these foreign powers.[57]

But while one can find in Israelite scriptures formulas that seem word-for-word copies of, say, Esarhaddon's loyalty oaths, they were not simply

---

[53] Gerhard Lohfink, *Does God Need the Church?*, 94f. Or, "instead of cursing the enemy, the prophets condemn their own nation" (Abraham Heschel, *The Prophets*, 12).

[54] See also Moshe Weinfeld's notion of vassal-treaty transposition: *The Place of the Law in the Religion of Ancient Israel*. See *GIT* 151. For a complication of Weinfeld's parallels regarding covenants and ancient near east treaties, see Gary N. Knoppers, "Ancient Near Eastern Royal Grants and the Davidic Covenant," 670–97.

[55] *ATM* 49; *GG* 113; *IR* 85, 345 n54.

[56] Moshe Weinfeld, *Deuteronomy and the Deuteronomic School*, 351; Ada Taggar-Cohen, "Political Loyalty in the Biblical Account of 1 Samuel xx–xxii in the Light of Hittite Texts," 258; *GIT* 78.

[57] *GG* 113.

borrowing and repeating common covenantal expressions. The *no other gods* movement evidently transposed or displaced this covenantal loyalty, from a political oath owed to Assyrians into a prior loyalty to Yahweh and his covenant established in exodus. The religiopolitical relations of god-king-subject were not *translated* into another context; rather, they were transpositioned into a distinctly "religious" register. The role of Assyrian overlord demanding loyalty is transposed onto Yahweh as the liberator offering a covenant. This notion of "a political alliance between a god and a people is an absolutely new, unheard of, and unprecedented concept."[58]

But this transposition comes at a cost; political unity symbols bear violent baggage. Political loyalty oaths often demanded intense surveillance of one's neighbors, even one's family members, of denouncing and prosecuting any who expressed disloyalty. The experience of this terror under the Assyrian regime may have served as the model of the Deuteronomistic command that one should kill even one's family members who entice one to worship other gods.[59] But now, applied in a new way, Yahweh takes *"the place previously occupied in the collective mind of the nation by the feared, almighty king of Assyria,"*[60] becoming the despot demanding surveillance. Perhaps a mimetic analysis renders monolatry's zeal more intelligible: the threat of foreign violence, whether potential or actualized, invites mirroring within the group: monolatry may be a mimetic internalization of despotism. In any case, one can conclude from the array of covenant scholarship that the violent demands of covenantal loyalty, originally a feature of polytheistic political theology, is a – if not *the* – key port of entry where violent zealotry was smuggled into early monotheism and remained as a potentiality over time. Thus, the early signs of the Mosaic distinction between true/false religion emerged from – and retained residues of – the more primordial distinction between political friend and enemy. For the intense violence and jealousy surrounding the religiopolitical realm became redirected into a new, extra-political, distinctly "religious" positioning, creating a new potentiality for religious violence.[61] This helps account for the strikingly bellicose biblical accounts of monotheistic violence in its founding.

---

[58] *ATM* 119; 28, 49.
[59] *GG* 113; Ex 32:27–8; Deut 13:7–10. *GIT* 160.
[60] Simo Parpola, "Assyria's Expansion in the 8th and 7th Centuries BCE and Its Long-Term Repercussions in the West," 99–111; 105, italics original; *GIT* 161.
[61] *ATM* 118, 126; *ME* 211; *IR* 86.

In light of this transposition, we can dismiss how Sloterdijk or Cliteur critique monotheistic violence: they argue that monotheism's zeal supplied the ingredients for monolatry.[62] The historical case is simply the opposite: violent zeal and loyalty remain as residues in monotheism because it emerges *from* the political registers of lord-vassal subjugation. Monolatry and subjection to imperial covenants share similar political genes: they are both the archaic sacred that cohere subjects into a unity that contains violence. Both Israel's early monolatry and its experience of imperially demanded loyalty supply the ingredients that, in time, became depoliticized into (secondary) "religion" and "monotheism."

That political language could become distinctly "theologized" (or detached from its political structure) is not entirely unique to Israel. We already saw, in Chapter 5, how pleading to the god's kingly representative became detached, via public catastrophes and diminished trust in the protection of Pharaohs, into a more private, personalized mode of prayer and piety. And again, we saw how the idea of "final judgment" became detached from Pharaonic competency, into a distinctly theological register, with Osiris' judgment in the underworld.[63] Despite some of these other ancient parallels in the theologization of political realities, the Jewish transposition of covenantal loyalty, Assmann argues, took a more radical hold because, first, it emerged through an unsurpassed form of historical trauma. Freud's hypothesis of trauma and guilt about Moses' murder is superfluous compared to Israel's collective retention of centuries of imperial threat and violence.[64] Secondly, Israel recast the political covenant concept to *a whole people*, and not just a land, a state, a priestly caste, or king. The priestly class that one can find in, say, the cultures of

---

[62] Sloterdijk aligns with Assmann's notion that a "new moral quality for killing" was birthed in the monotheistic concept, in that killing for an idea/principle, and not merely the tribe, becomes central. But Sloterdijk errs in arguing that "One consequence of monotheism is monolatry," when it seems obvious that monotheism is a by-product of numerous ingredients, one of which is monolatry (Van Riesen, "A Violent God?," 173–93; 182; Sloterdijk, *God's Zeal*, 26; Paul Cliteur, *The Secular Outlook*, 216).

[63] Assmann, "Axial 'Breakthroughs' in Ancient Egypt and Israel," 137f. See also J. G. Griffiths, *The Divine Verdict*; Daniel Steinmetz-Jenkins, "Jan Assmann and the Theologization of the Political," 511–30.

Mimetic theory argues that the originary "theologization," as it were, was in perceiving an endogenous process of human violence as an exogenous divine force, the sacred. The victim was the site of theologizing the physical into the superphysical, from the immanent to the transcendent. The original theo-political "analogue" is between the body of the victim and the body of god.

[64] GG 83; Jan Assmann, "Freud, Sellin, and the Murder of Moses," 149.

Egypt, now applied to a whole populace.[65] While the Moabite national god would become angry with "his country," Yahweh was always furious with "his people."[66] That is, there are no ancient parallels of a god directly choosing a whole people as his vassals, from out of the world, to form a treaty that transcends the country's sovereign status. (We should also note that covenants were cut exclusively between males. Therefore, Israel's re-use of covenant incurs the inheritance and negotiation of archaic patriarchalism.)

This new covenantal model birthed "a new genus of society,"[67] a shift from the representative, "indirect" theocracies of the ancient near east into a mode of "direct" theocracy.[68] In polytheistic political theology, the high god rules among the gods, among metaphysical equals, in analogy with the human king ruling over humans; as such, the god rules indirectly through his political representative. But in Israel's configuration of covenant, Yahweh *directly* rules a whole people – less and less through the kingly intermediary. Such theology speaks of an ideal in which no monarch, "no son shall rule over you," and "the Lord alone shall rule over you." It valorizes a time in which "there was no king in Israel" and remembers the movement to install a monarch (in Saul and David) as a rejection of God's direct rule: "it is me that they have rejected as their king." Indeed, for 1 Sam, the demand for a human king is correlated with the serving of other gods, evoking memories of the Egyptian exodus.[69]

Such an alliance with a God unmediated through a king, sub-deities, or administrators is a genuinely different kind of political theology: it "draws God more intimately into human affairs than had been the case in Mesopotamia and its neighboring civilizations . . .. Nothing of this sort is to be found in Egypt, at least not until the Late Period."[70] While ancient

---

[65] Deut 14:2; *CMEC* 185.

[66] Albertz, "Monotheism and Violence," 377; Num 11:1, 11. The Hebrew Bible concept of "a holy people" (Ex 19:6) is not present in the Egyptian lexicon (*CMA* 406).

[67] *OH* 113.

[68] *MPC* 158. Assmann notes a certain mode of imperial "direct" theocracy emerging in Egypt around 1000 BCE, which seems more a semantic novelty, in that the king still mediated this theocracy. Although he does not rule out its influence on the Deuteronomic tradition (*IR* 47).

[69] Jdg 8:23; 18:1; 1 Sam 8. Notice, per Girard, how the demand for a king, in 1 Sam, bears something of a mob-like form, in which – almost akin to the trial with Pontius Pilate – the structure entails a single person trying to reason with a crowd. Mimetic theory suggests there is little essential difference between a mob mimetically demanding a king and one demanding crucifixion.

[70] *GG* 26–7. While Egypt and Israel narrated their golden-era communion as lost, Egypt attempted to heal this break precisely by means that Israel condemned as idolatry.

covenantal politics were often directly linked with the fate of a state, this more intimate and direct morphology of covenant could outlive Israel's monarchy amidst foreign invasions, oppression, and deportations in the centuries to come.[71] For these covenanted exodus-people owe their Lord fidelity irrespective of the sovereign status of their state or any royal mediator. This shifting of political loyalty into a more intimate register perhaps helps contextualize why prophetic denunciation of covenant-breach is cast less in terms of sedition and treason and more in metaphors of lost marital fidelity, prostitution, and adultery.

This "absolutely new, unheard of, and unprecedented concept" requires explanation and a background story; and this is why the exodus was told, Assmann argues. The *no other gods* counter-narrative consolidated Israel amidst the decay of its monarchy, making it less and less "translatable" to its neighboring nations and their gods. Eventually, the only religious translatability left in Israel was its reaching back in deep time to translate the exodus God into the present.[72] This recovery involved effacing Israel's original polytheism with a mythological origins story driven by a single deity, against which any other gods were new and false.[73]

This covenant with Israel's highest God only later grew into a numerically singular, Only God.[74] What is at stake here is less the numerical divine oneness – common in various ancient political theologies – and more the compatibility between the divine and the political. Whereas the political theology of Assyria, for example, stressed the "inseparable unity of the divine and the political," the *no other gods* theology "stressed the categorical separation of these two spheres."[75] It is not covenant per se,

---

"Herein lies the crucial difference between Israel and Egypt. Yahweh's 'dwelling' (*shekhinah*) is never symbolic but always directly present, though changeable and inaccessible." (*CMEC* 176 n5). See also *OH* 124: "Israel alone constituted itself by recording its own genesis as a people as an event with a special meaning in history, while the other Near Eastern societies constituted themselves as analogues of cosmic order."

[71] In Egypt, the symbols of origin, god, and religion all stem from the locality itself, where the "primal hill" is the house of the god. The exodus God, by contrast, is "extraterritorial," ultramundane, and "had no temple or place of worship." This religion remembers itself as *preceding* "the acquisition of a homeland" and "remained universally valid no matter where in the world the Jews find themselves" (*CMEC* 180; *GG* 83f).

[72] *GIT* 147.

[73] Deut 32:17. Israel "chose *new* gods" (Jdg 5:8; cf. Ps 44:21).

[74] Albertz, "Monotheism and Violence," 377; *MPC* 148f.

[75] *GG* 84.

but the "subversive inversion" of covenant, as Mark Smith notes, that began distinguishing Israel from ancient religiopolitical structures.[76] What is new here is not just "exclusivism" or "jealousy." For violent jealousy was native to ancient political bodies, subjugation, and loyalty treaties. What is new is a once-political exclusivism morphing into a zeal that transcends political status. An originally *political* treaty inverted, making possible a politically detachable *religion*, a theologized "exclusive allegiance" attached more to a people and a God than a state. This transcendence increasingly materializes as Israel's national hopes are crushed, forcing Yahweh's people out of the political, land-based nest.

D. PROPHETIC CRITIQUE

Another crucial ingredient in the emergence of Israel's monotheism is its intensified prophetic movements. Amidst the decline in the North and South, the prophets who called upon the exodus covenant often spoke in critical denunciation of almost all the kings – elevating, first, a certain notion of justice and, secondly, severing the divine and royal wills.[77] In the first case, for Israel's prophets justice became more central to and intimately linked with theological-religious meaning than it was in any neighboring cultures.[78] This is not to say that justice was a concern unique to ancient Israel. Justice was a matter of extensive attention and devotion in cosmotheistic cultures, and nearly all of them advocated some kind of "righteousness greater than that required by law."[79] In Egypt, for example, we hear of the "lord of justice ... who rescues the fearful from the overbearing, who judges between rich and poor."[80] And there we hear of how the character of the upright is more important than the sacrifices of the evildoers. Full portions of Proverbs' wisdom seem to be lifted from Amenemope.[81]

The difference in Israel is not simply a concern for justice but that it gestated a prophetic tradition that uniquely elevated justice as *central* to

---

[76] *GIT* 166.

[77] *CMEC* 179; *EHG* 150.

[78] *PM* 43, 45.

[79] Smith, "The Common Theology of the Ancient Near East," 144; *CMA* 396. Stephan Seidlmayer, "The First Intermediate Period (c. 2160–2055)," 118–9. *EHG* 99; *ATM* 19; *OH* 24; *NOG* 231, 249f, 351.

[80] *GG* 64.

[81] Hoffmeier, *Akhenaten*, 247, 255–6; James B. Pritchard, ed, *Ancient Near Eastern Texts Relating to the Old Testament, passim.*

religion, as sacred duties, all the while in critical friction with political rulers.[82] "No other society took the literature of dissent and placed so much of it into a sacred text, which in turn provided the blueprint for religious and social life."[83] So, even if, say, the cause of justice in the biblical Sabbath and Jubilee years seems to be adopted from Babylonian Amorite edicts, nevertheless, the Jews under prophetic injunction sought to render these more radically religio-culturally normative. In all, the prophets "theologized justice" more so than had been done in neighboring cultures, elevating it to the status of religious truth. But there is a religious-intolerance cost to this: when "justice becomes the epitome of true religion," lawlessness and indecency become cast as the hallmark of paganism. This only further galvanizes the Mosaic antinomy of true Israel against immoral, idolatrous Egypt.[84]

Secondly, besides uniquely elevating justice to a religious duty, this prophetic tradition, related as it was to the direct covenant with Yahweh, made law a more directly divine matter. By contrast, when we noted how Egypt transposed "judgment" from the pharaoh to a transcendent god, the god was still not a *distinct lawgiver*. For the god's and the king's wills were still imagined to be the same. But the royalty-critical prophetic tradition severs the linkages between the will of the king and the will of God. Assmann writes, "only in the context of a religion in which god appears as both lawgiver and judge does the thought first become thinkable that man's judgment and god's can diverge significantly. That is the authentic innovation of biblical monotheism."[85] This prepares the ground for a different kind of political imagination, involving incompatibility between the now separated religious and political spheres: God, now as a direct, legislative sovereign, enters into friction with the king, eclipsing or usurping his sovereignty.[86]

Although other countries of the ancient near east also harbored concepts of justice (and also suffered their own foreign threats and invasions), they never experienced such a sustained, dramatic, king-critical, prophetic schism with its ruling elite.[87] Once we appreciate how acerbic and emphatic much of this criticism was, we also begin to see the potentially liberating nature of this "intolerance." Gnuse, for example, outlines how

---

[82] *PM* 53; *NOG* 250.
[83] *NOG* 256, 259.
[84] *PM* 52.
[85] Ibid., 55.
[86] Ibid., 52; Assmann, *Herrschaft und Heil*, 46–52.
[87] *GG* 83.

modern sources of anti-tyranny, like *The Federalist Papers*, for example, often cited the prophetic intolerance of tyranny.[88]

E. KING JOSIAH'S REFORMS TOWARD SOVEREIGNTY UNDER ASSYRIAN RULE

Israel's fall from sovereignty happened in stages. Assyria destroyed the ten tribes of the Northern Kingdom in 722 BCE, subjugating or deporting its inhabitants, and it dominated the Southern Kingdom as a vassal state.[89] But a century later, during King Josiah's sub-sovereign rule of the South (625–609 BCE), the ascendancy of the Babylonians weakened Assyria's power over Israel. With Assyria's grip loosened, Judah of the South could try to regain the lands of the North.

Josiah seized this opportunity through calling on fidelity to the god of the exodus. This is described in 2 Kings 22–3, with the "discovery" of a lost scroll during Temple renovations, recounted as the return of forgotten cultural memory. From the scroll's contents, the discoverers and listeners became convicted they had backslid from its Yahweh-alone origins into syncretistic idolatry. In worshipping other gods (like Ba'al, Asherah, the sun, the starry hosts, etc.), they had forgotten their founding covenant. Realizing from what fidelity he and his compatriots had fallen, King Josiah rent his garments in repentance, publicly renewed the covenant, instilled Passover observance, centralized the cult at Jerusalem, and enacted sweeping reforms with a harsh violence reminiscent of King Asa's supposed reforms and Akhenaten's revolution.[90]

The originally plural identities, multiple regions, and syncretistic religions of Palestine were trimmed into the singular exodus narrative. The syncretistic majority was portrayed as having forgotten the exodus and its demanded fidelity. Josiah's enemies – including everyone from banal worshippers to temple prostitutes and those sacrificing children to Molek – were painted as deviant idolaters, even though their religions

---

[88] Robert Gnuse, *No Tolerance for Tyrants*; NOG 253.

[89] James Alison, *Jesus the Forgiving Victim*, 144–5.

[90] The reforms are of unsure historicity given that "neither Jeremiah nor Ezekiel make any detailed reference to them" (*CMEC* 194). While the Deuteronomic historian records no massacres in Jerusalem, "more brutal seems to have been the destruction of Bethel, the competing Yahweh sanctuary off the former northern kingdom (2 Kgs 23:15–18). [Bethel] was the model for the story of the golden calf ... but that is to be regarded as a warning example, written during the period of exile, and has never been reality" (Albertz, "Monotheism and Violence," 383).

were common in Israel's own history and indeed all cultures of the ancient near east.[91] Idolatry and forgetfulness are here symbols of assimilation to Assyrian influence. Those who had succumbed to foreign influence were like those who had entered the Promised Land only to forget. They had grown soft in decadent comforts, in the milk and honey of cultural assimilation, breaking the Law. They were the complainers in the desert of exodus, longing for the fleshpots of Egypt. True fidelity to Yahweh, on the other hand, is in the desert, at Sinai, as wanderers, exiles from Egypt.

The scroll may have been an early version of Deuteronomy, materials of the *no other gods* movement, a core element to the emerging Torah. Or, it may have been freshly minted propaganda to underwrite Josiah's reforms and campaign of independence from Assyria.[92] For all we know, the figure of Moses may have secured his importance sometime around these reforms, as a contrast figure to foreign despotism and a unifying bond to its past and its god.[93] Whatever the case, the resultant message is that Judah's subjection to Assyria now had an explanation, akin to Hosea: it was divine punishment for their forgetting and violating the exodus covenant.[94] This polemical contradistinction between memory/forgetfulness would emerge again after the South's destruction and exile: the vigilant fidelity of those who suffered deportation contrasted with the forgetfulness of those who stayed and assimilated. The implicit valorization of the desert in such exodus themes hints at why entrance into the Promised Land is not included in the Torah. The land, like the vassal-treaty, was becoming theologized. The Promised Land, charged now with the notions of forgetfulness/idolatry and remembering/fidelity, is turning into something that cannot be definitively stabilized, that "cannot be conquered within history."[95]

F. ROYALTY DISAPPEARS

While some amount of authority rested on the Judean King Josiah, the aura of divinity could not. Nor could it rest upon any subsequent Jewish kings. Just as the symbol of the desert was displacing a statist, religiopolitical dynasty of Yahweh, so too the Deuteronomic movement

---

[91] *CMEC* 204–5.
[92] *CMEC* 182.
[93] Alison, *Jesus the Forgiving Victim*, 155; *IR* 44.
[94] *NOG* 73, 76, 121; *CMEC* 194.
[95] *OH* 114.

reconfigured the god-king compaction, dissolving Israelite royalty. Not only was the covenant concept usurping allegiance to any mediating royal institution (Israelite or foreign), any residual royalty in Israel was becoming subordinate to and relativized by a divine lawgiver. The authority of the nascent law of the Torah was replacing the sacred aura of kingship – subjecting the latter to the former. Josiah repenting before the judgment of the scroll is an exemplary image. In all, through the confluence of the several factors we are outlining, in Judaism "royalty disappears."[96]

Pace the critiques that monotheism is a univocal sacralizing of political absolutism, we see here the opposite being made possible. For the divine royalty emerging here opens up critique of the great metaphysical error in polytheism's indirect theocracy, its royal "idolatry." This error, as Halbertal and Margalit put it, is "the cumulative illusion of power that blurs the boundaries between the human and the divine and traps the powerful person in the myth of his own power."[97] Or, we could rather say that in cosmotheism such "boundaries" between the human and divine ruler were *always* blurred, such that they had never quite existed. Those boundaries were constructed and galvanized through a novel (anti) political theology: a divine kingship no longer mediated by human royalty.[98]

This replacement of human kingship with a scriptural and interpretive tradition becomes pronounced when Babylon destroys the South in the sixth century and scatters thousands of Judeans into exile. With the Temple destroyed, many deported, and the Babylonians dominating, whoever counts as Yahweh's people at this point no longer even enjoyed sub-sovereign rule as they did under Assyria. And yet, counterintuitively, this depoliticized context served to *intensify* the notion of Yahweh as direct king – at least among those who cultivated it. Jewish kingship and sovereignty migrated away from the body of a king (or the *body of the land*, as Egypt's Osiris suggested to us), into a portable fatherland of the Torah. Yahweh was outgrowing his role as a state god. His country was transforming into a "religion," Judaism.[99]

Freud saw monotheism as a re-enthronement of the primal father. But the above suggests something more like a dethronement. In a

---

[96] *GG* 96; *PM* 48; *ATM* 125; Deut 17:18–20.

[97] Moshe Halbertal and Avishai Margalit, *Idolatry*, 221.

[98] James W. Haring, "The Lord Your God Is God of Gods and Lord of Lords," 18–9; Eric Nelson, *The Hebrew Republic*, 26–56.

[99] "Pure monotheism does not recognize national gods," Assmann writes, a conviction emerging from conditions of exile and foreign domination (*MPC* 149–50).

cosmotheistic framework, the analogues were relatively clear and sensible: to defeat a country and its king was to defeat its divine king.[100] But here a once enthroned Yahweh now turns homeless and sub-sovereign. Or rather, Yahweh remains sovereign despite all political signs to the contrary. While the material prospects of the country deteriorated, Yahweh's status increased.[101] This "inverse correlation," as Haring terms it, between decreasing political power and increasing theological elevation of Yahweh, is a genuinely "new formulation or interpretation of religious reality."[102] Contrasted with the metaphysics of Seth, wherein divine foes correspond with political foes, there is now no human, royal agent who mirrors rivalry with the divine king.[103]

The textual epitome of this inverse correlation between divine power and royal power is in Deutero-Isaiah's Suffering Servant. Its several passages on Yahweh's kingship contain no references to the royal covenant with David. True kingly power is invested not in any exalted royalty but instead in the humbled, beaten, and despised one.[104] Whether this mysterious figure is somehow a symbolic reference to Israel as a whole, a messianic individual, or an eschatological inflection, Deutero-Isaiah doubles down on the inverse correlation: his notion of Yahweh's universal dominion is no longer the expression of political hegemony. As an inversion of the partisan spirit, Yahweh's universality – akin to Hosea – entails chastising his *own* people through using *foreign* powers as a tool, like Cyrus the Persian.[105]

In this inversion, the common imperial henotheism of a high God undergoes development like that of a photographic negative: a similar outer form takes on opposed inner content: symbolism suited to a monotheism from above (a god whose reign extends beyond their borders)[106] takes on inverted content as a monotheism from below. Gnuse argues that we find in this a first genuinely universal deity, capable of transcending the political sphere. Put more specifically, "The Jews did not invent the

---

[100] Haring, "The Lord Your God," 15.
[101] *TOBM* 165. See also how Ezekiel "frees this divine rule from its ties to an earthly king or dynasty" in contrast with Marduk's reign via Nebuchadnezzar (Dale Launderville, "Ezekiel's Throne-Chariot Vision," 362, 367; Haring, "The Lord Your God," 20).
[102] *TOBM* 193; Haring, "The Lord Your God," 16.
[103] *TOBM* 170; Haring, "The Lord Your God," 19.
[104] Haring, "The Lord Your God," 21; Isa 49:7; 52:1–53.
[105] *NOG* 260; Isa 45:1–3.
[106] *GIT* 159. One can find several gods who had extensive power "beyond their own lands," or even rule all the world and humanity (Smith, "The Common Theology of the Ancient Near East," 140). See also Amos 9:7.

concept of a universal deity. But they were the only people who could express it 'from below,' strip it of political pretentions."[107] It is no coincidence that we find Judaism express its most explicit monotheistic formulations either under threat from, or subjugation to, empire. Israel's monotheism emerged less as the expression of imperialism and more a sort of "resistance" to it.[108]

To sum up thus far, we can see in ancient Israel both an evolution and a revolution. It accrued common, political-theological elements but in a unique recasting. Several realities converged in time: the reconstrued vassal treaty, an idealized originary legend, an elevated prophetic critique severing the royal and divine wills, a series of political breakdowns, etc. This contingent mixture resulted in the symbols of hegemony being recast, perhaps unintentionally, into what Smith calls a "form of inverse hegemony."[109]

G. BAN ON IMAGES AND POLITICAL REPRESENTATION

Another crucial ingredient in the dissolving of Israelite royalty – lending it a virtually *anti-state* character – is the ban on graven images.[110] The core meaning of idolatry and the ban on divine images concerns, for Assmann, not ethereal, mystical art theory but rather "the legitimization of rulership in terms of divine representation."[111] Whenever precisely the intolerance of images appeared in Israelite history,[112] its political implications are crucial. For the attack on "false religion" coincides with an attack on the

---

[107] NOG 260–1; GIT 178; TOBM 149–66.

[108] GIT 180; 222.

[109] GIT 183.

[110] PM 103; MPC 158. See also Halbertal and Margalit, *Idolatry*, 220: "in the biblical conception ... the monarchy is not an institution rooted in the cosmic order, and it is not part of the primordial structure of the world."

[111] Assmann, "Axial 'Breakthroughs' in Ancient Egypt and Israel," 151.

[112] When precisely aniconism and anti-idolatry emerges in Israel's history is disputed. It may have been a minority position like the *no other gods* tradition; some of the early monolatrous prophets, like Hosea, show signs of anti-idolatry of the calf. We can also surmise that the lack of a temple for exilic Yahwists – with a dearth in money and artisans – may have abetted aniconism. Aniconism certainly shows up strongly in and after the Maccabees (second century BCE), who violently rejected any cultic translatability between the Jewish god and Hellenic gods. GIT 283–6; 126, 304. Cultic translatability in this context clearly "served the purposes of foreign, royal power." 1 Macc 1:11–5, 43, 52; 3:15; 2 Macc 5:15. "Morton Smith notes that before the Maccabean revolt Yahweh was identified in Jerusalem with Zeus and Dionysius" (GIT 284).

very basis of ancient political legitimacy, cutting at the linkage between political and religious representation.

The ban on images runs counter to archaic politics' representative theocracy. Ancient states, such as Egypt, Assyria, and Babylon, represented their power and mediated their divine linkage through images, statues, ceremonies, and symbols. But, as Assmann observes, the Bible deems this idolatry. "From the viewpoint of Egypt, however, it is precisely for this that the state was created." Here the opposition between cosmotheistic and monotheistic political theology is pronounced: "it is precisely the category of representation that points up the falseness of Pharaonic politics with respect to religion in its most obvious and abhorrent form, namely, the sphere of kings, images, and sacred animals."[113] As we have seen, Israel had been birthing a unique direct theocracy, bypassing royal mediation. The ban on images must be seen as a corollary to this, in that it refuses immanent mediation and representation. The divine could now operate independent of political institutions and withstand statelessness and exile.[114] Cosmotheistic cultures had never clearly distinguished the political from the religious. For they had never rejected, as the Jewish ban does, the "claim to represent the divine sphere and to act on earth as a representative of the creator."[115]

In the ban on images, Assmann sees not a "'religious arrogation of political power' but quite the opposite, a blocking of such arrogation."[116] This blocking expresses what I have called apophatic intolerance, and it bears powerful liberative potentials. For the exodus paradigm narrates and exposes the hidden connectivity between idolatry, collective delusion, and slavery. Exodus prophesies a liberation from political oppression that coincides with God's emancipation from political representation.[117] By contrast, Akhenaten's iconoclastic monotheism was the supreme expression of political sovereignty, a union of the political and religious. Israelite monotheism becomes virtually the photographic negative, wherein the

---

Similarly, the history of Israel's divine (anti)anthropomorphism is not entirely clear. Even while Israelite religion seems to have slowly reduced anthropomorphic depictions of Yahweh, still "the avoidance of anthropomorphic imagery was by no means a general feature of Israelite religion after the Exile" (*NOG* 212; *EHG* 100, 102; e.g., Dan 7; Isa 27:1; cf. Zech 14:4; 1 Enoch 14).

[113] *GG* 87.
[114] Ibid., 99.
[115] Assmann, "Axial 'Breakthroughs' in Ancient Egypt and Israel," 149.
[116] *PM* 131; Albertz, "Monotheism and Violence," 386.
[117] *GG* 85.

transcendence of the deity does not found, but *precludes*, representation in a ruler.[118] While Akhenaten may have effaced many images of the gods, his iconoclasm underwrote a tight god-king relationship; it resembled nothing like a prophetic "resistance movement"; it had no critical relation to royalty; it never kept its religion alive as a stateless society of exiles. Ultimately, it did not weaken the link between political dominion and salvation, as the Jewish ban did.

We should not jump to regard this ban on images as a depoliticization, a sheer *escape* from politics, nor even a *direct opposition* to or replacement of competing polities – as if Jewish monotheism simply aimed to found another state that is uniquely intolerant and devoid of art. Rather, this is more an inversion of political representation. Even though Israel was reconfiguring statist symbols, monotheism meant not so much the founding of a state as getting "rid of the oriental principle of statehood" or birthing "*a kind of counter-society* in which the principle of statehood or kingship is permitted only minimal importance."[119] Instead of simply replacement politics, we have born in Jewish monotheism something of a new form of life where there is "perhaps for the first time in history a clear-cut distinction between state and society."[120]

H. EXILE, MEMORY, AND THE BIRTH OF A CANON

If the monotheistic transformation of political symbols must be seen as an acid of many ingredients, we must add "memory" as a key part of this compound. National destruction and exile incurred the loss of crucial memory markers of land and temple and thus the danger of forgetfulness. We already saw how Josiah's revolution cast idolatry as "forgetfulness." To avoid relapsing into idolatry, therefore, required intensified practices of remembering. Intensive cultural memory techniques and the birth of a canon replace what is lost in Israel's political breakdown.[121] The Jewish attention to memory, Assmann insists, constitutes the unique *cultural* achievement of monotheistic Judaism. Yahweh's people, lest they

---

[118] *PM* 47; *GG* 77.

[119] *GG* 85; *PM* 45. We thus see why Isaac Deutscher refers to the Jews' embrace of the nation-state as "the paradoxical consummation of the Jewish tragedy" (Edward Said et al., *Freud and the Non-European*, 52; Isaac Deutscher, *The Non-Jewish Jew and Other Essays*, 35, 40).

[120] *GG* 85; 75. Assmann, "Axial 'Breakthroughs' in Ancient Egypt and Israel," 149.

[121] *CMEC* 90.

assimilate into their host cultures, co-evolved with and through use of new memory techniques to keep their covenant.

The notion of a people who must never forget their founding covenant made for an intense, "all-embracing framework" of life that could no longer rely on the common, place-based memory markers of temples, monuments, tombs, political territories, etc. Rather, "all these places were transferred from the exterior to the interior"[122] – that is, from the locative to the utopian mode, from cultic to textual, as axial theory described secondary religion. Exile, in the sixth and fifth centuries BCE, provided the crucible and catalyst for such a transference.[123] While Israel's state functions were absorbed by the Babylonian and Persian Empires, monotheism emerged through resistance to cultural and memory absorption. This was made possible through increasingly attending to study of the Torah.

The cultural marginality wrought by exile is crucial to these developments.[124] To remain faithful to the covenant requires creating a remembering culture, opting for a certain cultural isolation and anti-assimilation. While the ancient world was already honing the arts of memory on a more individual level and cultic settings, Assmann argues, Yahweh's command to remember the exodus covenant through one's entire life results in a novel mode of *collective*-memory techniques that "had and has had no parallel in human history."[125] This collective remembers itself as elected by God, independent of a city or political unit. "No one could conquer or burn their chosenness like one could burn a city. No one could seize and deport or kill their chosenness like one could a king .... No empire could deport or execute their divine king."[126]

Ancient covenants not only involved surveilling the political loyalty of neighbors; they also required frequent public remembering.[127] For example, Syrian kings regularly required subordinates to publicly remember and pledge their loyalty – lest they treasonously "forget" their oaths. For example, the Sarsaru oath-ritual of Esarhaddon: "you speak in your hearts: Ishtar, she is close. But then, you will go back to your towns and districts, eat bread, and forget these oaths. However, when you drink

[122] *CMEC* 191; *EHG* 151.
[123] On a scholarly consensus that exile catalyzed monotheism: Hoffmeier, *Akhenaten*, 257.
[124] *NOG* 213–4.
[125] *CMEC* 193, 204f; *IR* 60.
[126] Carr, *Holy Resilience*, 122, 140.
[127] Hittites and Assyrians would regularly read treaties publicly; and Babylonians would curse false copyists of legal agreements (*CMEC* 199–200).

from this water, you will remember and observe these oaths."[128] So too must the exodus covenant be regularly remembered. The Deuteronomist tells us that such remembrance required obligatory scriptural memorization, continued teaching, inscription upon doorposts and body, public recitation at holidays, etc. – and, the memory technique par excellence, the Seder liturgy.[129] The imperative to remember the exodus covenant and partake in the Seder, lest they forget like the assimilated, is likely a variation of political memory-rituals like the Sarsaru oath-ritual.

But while some outer forms of Seder are evidently borrowed, Assmann argues that its Jewish adaptation has no ancient parallel in its attention to detail, narrative, and elaborateness. While the preexilic prophets had used exodus imagery, it was the exilic communities onward that began deepening it into "an art of memory that is based on the separation of identity from territory ... outside the Promised Land."[130] This memory work (re)constitutes a stateless people through transforming the distant past of the exodus people into "our past."[131] This is how memory and monotheism reciprocally deepened through exile and diaspora. Yahwism no longer enjoyed locative, state supports and was now standing, as it were, on its own two feet.

A life saturated by attention to covenantal memory is intimately linked with the notion of living a life based on canonical scriptures. Holy writings, of course, were not new in the world. But the notion of centering and basing collective life on interpreting them "was a new phenomenon in the history of writing as well as that of religion and civilization generally .... No pagan religion had ever made similar claims."[132] As we saw, the exodus covenant had been established between Yahweh and a *whole people*, not just its ruler, or scribes, or priests. Thus, *everyone* is responsible for remembering and keeping the oath of the people. As such, the Jews became an exegetical people en masse. With the crystallization of canon as a shared property of the people, the common interpreter, not just a king or priestly caste, begins to interpret the will of God.[133]

The imperative against forgetting coincides with canon: not adding, changing, or subtracting anything from the founding story and

---

[128] *CMEC* 201, 203; Deut 8:7–19.
[129] *CMEC* 53, 196f.
[130] *CMEC* 192; *NOG* 90.
[131] *GIT* 305.
[132] *GG* 120–1.
[133] *GG* 99f.

covenant.[134] Like other ingredients in this chapter, Judaism did not invent "canon"; this was a common textual technique for making ancient legal contracts unchangeable and closed. But Judaism transposed this technique into a distinctly "religious" realm. Canonization further galvanized the Mosaic distinction, layering into it the distinction between the canonical and the apocryphal.[135] Living in the horizon of a canon through rigorous memory practices is a novel form of life in the ancient world, stemming from the diasporic enclave cultures whose practices likely contributed to the crystallization of the Tanakh.

While all ancient societies had some amount of or retrospective obligation to preserve its past, exilic Israel onward developed an extreme and vivid narrative form. And while many polytheistic scriptures made demands upon human action, there are no other ancient examples of scriptures so taking hold of the totality of a group's life.[136] The development of an elaborate set of canonized laws, to be regularly interpreted, would have been incomprehensible in primary religions where the divine is more self-evident. By contrast, "whoever lived according to these laws could not forget for one minute who he was or where he belonged."[137] Such extreme attentiveness crosses the threshold into "secondary" religions with a notion of "conversion" and "commitment" foreign to primary religions. The character of such commitment is *countermemory*: a refusal to forget a people-wide commitment.

I. POST EXILE

The Persian Empire released several thousand Jews from Babylonian captivity around 536 BCE, at which point they were granted a territory that would remain subordinate to the Persians. As the new overlords until 323 BCE, Persia may have facilitated the canonization of the Torah.[138] But whatever form the Torah took around that time, it was not a sovereign, territorial, legal constitution, but more a semi-depoliticized "wisdom literature." So, while postexilic Judaism could never

---

[134] Deut 4:2; *CMEC* 200; *GG* ch 5.

[135] *CMEC* 78–80.

[136] *CMEC* 87–90; *MPC* 145.

[137] *CMEC* 185.

[138] Ezr 7:14. Indeed the Persian Empire was likely responsible for a sea change in canonization in that era, through their imperial guardianship of many local traditions and their attempts to rule diverse local cultures at distance.

comprehensively execute a distinctly sovereign Mosaic law (and many parties certainly tried to, culminating in a few liberation revolts to be discussed),[139] its sub-sovereign way of life became a crucial point of conflicting interpretations. A chief contention was between the communities of Jews who had for generations suffered deportation and exile from Assyrian or Babylonian Empires, and the "Jewish" communities who had remained in the land, forming mixed marriages with neighboring/conquering cultures on the other.[140] We use scare quotes surround "Jewish" here because the exilic parties, who mostly won the debate in forming the canon and harbored the *no other gods* intolerance, saw these groups precisely as not true Jews – for they evidently had no loyalty to Yahweh alone. They were painted with the brush Josiah had used: the assimilated idolaters. Only now the conflict was exaggerated by the growing importance of canon.[141]

Thus, the more boldly emerging Mosaic distinction in postexilic Judaism produced a fissure of at least two contending Jewish positions concerning neighboring cultures and religions: (1) the Deuteronomic tradition and the *no other gods* movement, as roughly traced above, played the more rigorist role, while (2) the more syncretistic parties were painted as the idolaters. The former was constituted more by the literate, priestly, and upper classes that Babylon selected for deportation, while leaving the "poor of the land" in Judah, seen as no threat to the empire's order. Atop these divisions, the destruction and exile had left gaping differences in experience: those who had not undergone exile did not so stridently think of themselves as God's elect or that their normal life was idolatrous and had caused a divine punishment of exile.[142]

These battle lines left traces in the biblical text. The book of Exodus, for example, appears to have been useful to the rigorist party in this debate, in contrast with the Patriarchal out-of-Mesopotamia narratives of Genesis. Assmann sees the antinomies of this era playing out as follows, with the Exodus-rigorist emphasis first, and Patriarchal-laxist narratives second:

- Strict observance of law vs. Genealogical belonging (circumcision)
- Conquest of land vs. Purchase/Coexistence

---

[139] See, for example, Jeremiah Cataldo, *Breaking Monotheism*.
[140] *CMEC* 188. He also suggests that the rigorist party may have *provoked* the growth of the more generous and syncretistic accounts of Jewish identity.
[141] *CMEC* 183.
[142] Carr, *Holy Resilience*, 132.

- Non-contracts with outsiders vs. Contracts
- Exclusive vs. Non-exclusive[143]
- Aggressive vs. Pacifist
- Particular Liberator vs. Universal Creator
- Alliance with a people (the chosen people of exodus) vs. An individual (Abraham)
- Nontranslatable religion vs. Melchizedekian translatability

Though the categorization is simplistic, it helps us identify how and why differing rigorist and laxist agendas could coexist within the same scriptures. The Priestly strata appears to have synthesized the two into a larger narrative, reconciling these apparently irreconcilable camps.[144] The emulsifier was the Joseph legend, which narrated how the patriarchs got to Egypt, thereby creating a shared, single, long-term saga between the two postexile parties.

The Torah's combination of these apparently incompatible parties is a unique and complex achievement. Indeed, Assmann argues, the Bible contains not only some different versions of a religion, but *two different genera of religion* – primary and secondary[145] – making it, therefore, so infamously difficult to interpret. And yet it is precisely this internal volatility that Assmann urges has been the crucial ingredient to its staying power.[146] It combined into one narrative the existential themes of being "strangers and aliens" in this world, with all of its separatist rigors, as well as the cosmotheistic feeling of being "at home" in the world, with its translatable inclusions. In placing these incompatibilities in perpetually unresolved canonical relation, Judaism made possible a unique configuration of ancient political theology. Through a sort of suspended mode of identity, it spawned a new genus of society, wherein "zeal" was redirected from the sphere of state-creation and maintenance into an alternate mode of allegiance.[147] As such, the cosmotheistic religiopolitical hives off into now distinct religious and political spheres, "whose relationship had to be

---

[143] Contrast Ruth's cross-cultural marriage with the Ezra/Nehemiah policy of forced divorce with foreigners.

[144] Assmann reads the priestly strata of the Torah as cosmotheistic, emphasizing a one universal god, and "scarcely differing" from the primary religions of that day (*PM* 8–9). *IR* 57, 69, 72.

[145] *PM* 8.

[146] *PM* 10.

[147] *GG* 125.

laboriously negotiated and whose reunification could be achieved only through force."[148]

J. ZEAL, ACTIVE AND PASSIVE

Such a forceful reunification of the religiopolitical is especially evident in the Maccabean revolt (167–160 BCE).[149] Assmann classifies the Maccabean revolutionaries as the first executors of uniquely "religious" violence. While it is true that many pagan heroes killed and died for their religiopolitical units, the whole Maccabean notion of "dying for God was something new."[150] The zeal for *no other gods*, as we have seen, may have somehow resulted in detaching religion from the political sphere, but this made possible a new kind of violence: the violence once reserved for those violating political boundaries is transformed into violence toward those outside the truth of the canon. Such violence is foreign to the polytheistic system in that it fights on a new front: the boundary between religious truth and falsehood. Although it is an "extra-systemic" violence, attacking those falling outside the monotheistic line, it is more often directed against coreligionists who "have fallen out of the system. It is extra-systemic but mostly introverted violence."[151]

Harkening back to a scriptural ideal, the revolutionaries emulated the intolerant zeal in the Deuteronomistic history and sought to fulfill the canon. Mattathias, taking passages from Numbers and Deuteronomy more literally than the founding events perhaps were in actual history, refused Hellenic assimilation and took up arms: "he was seized with the passionate zeal for the Law and he did what one Phinehas did to Zimri" – that is, kill idolaters during the exodus.[152] The texts celebrate such violence and valorize the captured Maccabees who died, under pain of torture, with the scriptures on their lips.

While this revolt might be considered "the first religiously motivated resistance movement known to history,"[153] we should notice its extensive killing of fellow "Jews." The war aimed not merely at the destruction of the Seleucids but the cleansing of Jewish apostates and collaborators, for

---

[148] Ibid., 86; *NOG* 104f, 150.
[149] *CMEC* 188.
[150] *MPC* 144.
[151] *GG* 32.
[152] Ibid., 119; *ATM* 121.
[153] *MPC* 143; *CMEC* 64; *ATM* 120.

whom a special violence was reserved.[154] Echoing the canonical imperative, the Maccabees massacred entire Hellenic-friendly Jewish towns. This easily overlooked fact suggests the revolt was more a religiously motivated civil war with the dressings of an anti-assimilation political revolt.

In any case, the Hasmonean regime following the Maccabees was eventually crushed by Roman invasion, under which Jews remained subject until the dual destructions of 70 CE and 135 CE, subsequent to revolts. Jewish statelessness, for the most part, can be seen as effectively sealed thereafter – wherein most Jews found ways to imagine covenant fidelity without reference to a political kingdom.[155] No longer having a Temple, faithfulness to practicing covenant sacrifice did not so much disappear as transform into prayer and study of the Torah. And for the Christian sect of Judaism, sacrifice became a mixture of martyrial- and Eucharistic sacrifice, often linked in symbolism.[156] As such, the active, Maccabean zeal of dying for God, could transform into a more nonviolent, passive zeal, valorizing not the violator but the nonviolent. (Although, for some Christians this could be inflected through a certain masochism.)

We can regard these Jewish and Christian reconfigurations of sacrifice as crucial to the epochal redefinition of religion, the axial shift from primary to secondary religion.[157] Assmann concludes that we see in such shifts a maturation in which monotheistic intolerance does not imply zealotry. The majority rabbinic tradition, he suggests, overlooked or reinterpreted violent passages against the idolaters as regressions, not consonant with the mature potentiality of monotheism.[158] Taking the Maccabean and bar Kochba revolts as exceptions from the much larger implications of Jewish political theology, he concludes, "Judaism is the only [monotheistic religion] that has never turned the implications of violence and intolerance into historical reality precisely because it has relegated the final universalizing of truth to eschatology and not to

---

[154] *IR* 87. This may have left traces in the redaction of Joshua, wherein the conquest of Canaan legends suspiciously resemble the geography of the Maccabean revolution: Joshua's "neighboring tribes" (now the Seleucids) were treated with the common ancient warring practice of taking booty and slaves, while complete annihilation was reserved for those living nearest to Palestine (Jews collaborating with Seleucids). *GG* 118; Carr, *Holy Resilience*, 131.

[155] Mack, *The Christian Myth*, 134.

[156] Stroumsa, *The End of Sacrifice*, 75; Daniel Boyarin, "Martyrdom and the Making of Christianity and Judaism"; *GG* 126.

[157] Stroumsa, *The End of Sacrifice*, 77, 80.

[158] *ATM* 124.

history."[159] Such maturation, we must note, is not the abrogation of intolerance but its deepening and ripening, in what I have called apophatic intolerance: a refusal of the catharsis of enthroning God in an immanent regime, a refusal (a la Mouffe) of the representation of the Absolute. For the mature monotheist, God is no longer the symbolic ground for political representation. "True religion" refuses idolatry, which is false precisely in its illusory unity, its correlating divinity with the political. This maturation of monotheism understands existence as marked by a perpetually unresolved tension, an incompatibility that never achieves final release. The intolerant refusal of divine representation is a crucial element of this messianic dimension of Judaism, which Scholem calls a "life lived in deferment."[160] Such messianism eschatologically postpones political fulfillment of its religious ideal in a sort of anti-totalism. Assmann hears this too in Christ, whose "kingdom is not of this world" and who speaks of rendering to Caesar and God their due – while, importantly, these are not the same.[161]

While the Maccabean, active, persecutorial intolerance is egregious, we must recognize how it shares certain formal structure with a mature, "passive" – or rather pacific – intolerance. If there is revolutionary value in monotheism, it comes through its intolerance. The challenge of seeing this similarity-yet-radical-difference is, again, analogous to the development of a photographic negative while the external forms might remain similar.[162] This is especially manifested in the drama of martyrdom and its relation to a violent, persecutorial spirit. Admittedly, the energies have genetic relations, namely, in their fervent intolerance. But the two are frequently and wrongly conflated when, say, suicide bombers are described as "martyrs." The word is rather best occasioned when, in witnessing to peace through the refusal of injustice, one *incurs* but does not execute violence. While it remains a matter of conflicting interpretations as to what constitutes an injustice worth suffering for – and that

---

[159] GG 111; Gideon Aran and Ron E. Hassner, "Overview of Religion and Violence in Jewish Tradition." Assmann's position here is in tension with his own admission that the fall of the fortress at Masada now serves as a foundational story for the modern state of Israel and its creeping extrajudicial annexations (*CMEC* 59). He rightly clarifies in *IR* 88.

[160] Giorgio Agamben, *The Time That Remains*, 69.

[161] Matt 22:21; Mk 12:17; Lk 20:25; Jn 18:36; *ATM* 126f.

[162] *ATM* 122. See also Ithamar Gruenwald, "Intolerance and Martyrdom." Erlewine nuances Assmann, arguing he fails to appreciate how monotheistic martyrdom can involve far more than mere rejection of the Other but precisely the love of the Other and truth (*Monotheism and Tolerance*, 173–4).

there can indeed be misled martyrs – this should not obscure the altruistic importance of this kind of intolerance. This is exemplified not only in Jesus' love of enemies (and the many nonviolent Jewish movements around his time)[163] but also the modern peaceable activism of, say, Indian decolonization, the United States' civil rights movements, Lehmah Gbowee's Liberian movement, and so on. In such cases, peaceable means and ends remain tightly united, without any of the dark calculus of attaining peace through violence.[164] The sacrifice in these works of justice is indeed costly, severe, and animated by a kind of "intolerance" – though radically opposed in content to that of religious persecution. It suggests, as Christian activist Shane Claiborne often says, that "there are things worth dying for but none worth killing for." Martin Luther King Jr's notion of "extremists for love" captures a similar "intolerant" spirit.

This suggests the more essential issue about managing the Mosaic distinction is not just how it distinguishes Israel against polytheistic pagans but more about this noted distinction between a monotheism from above or from below.[165] The former is banal theological imperialism, while the latter is potentially liberative – even if the cost of this liberation, Assmann admits, is the possibility of religious violence and absolutism.[166] It is right to warn that this danger should be mitigated by maintaining the separation of church from state, as Albertz et al. have noted.[167] But this should be admitted through recognizing the more fundamental paradox: it was monotheism itself that helped *birth* this very separation of religious from political power.

Assmann argues that we should not reject but in fact "hold fast to" the inherited intolerance of the Mosaic distinction; but we must sublimate and humanize its energetic conviction into political patience. Sounding like Mouffe, he sees this involving the transformation of antagonism into

---

[163] See Richard Horsley, *Jesus and Empire*.

[164] Walter Benjamin regarded the calculus of means and ends as "the most elementary relationship within any legal system" (Benjamin, *Reflections*, 277).

[165] *NOG* 125. A problem with Gnuse's assessment however, is he thinks the Mosaic distinction animates only monotheism "from above," as if the "from below" somehow sheds that intolerance. He simplistically regards a monotheism "from below" in a more liberal democratic frame – centered upon "the people," entailing "dignity, toleration, and peace." He retains nuance when admitting that sometimes, in Jewish history, it was rather the educated religious elite that held back the mob violence of "the people" in their monotheistic, if misguided, religious zeal (ibid., 90).

[166] *ATM* 126.

[167] Albertz, "Monotheism and Violence," 386.

dispute and dialogue and even the practice of courageous nonviolence.[168] The parallels go further: we will recall that Mouffe emphasized, in my gloss, a beneficent, cataphatic intolerance of the liberal tradition: its right/ wrong distinction about universal human rights, its agitation toward an exclusion-free politics. These can indeed turn into liberal violence, just as they have violence embedded in their origins. But the answer, she insisted, is not to abrogate liberalism's intolerance. It must be matched with what I have called apophatic intolerance. This requires negating "the very idea of a complete reabsorption of alterity into oneness and harmony," refusing to "claim any mastery of the foundation of society," admitting "full objectivity can never be reached"; we must come to terms with our "lack of a final ground and the undecidability that pervades every order."[169] At the heart of these observations is the admission of the ultimate incompatibility between liberalism and the political sphere. I see this admission as deeply resonant with the monotheistic incompatibility between God and the political order described in this chapter. For the political implications of the Mosaic distinction concern the rejection of political oneness-mythologies and refusing, to any one, mastery over the foundations of society. The Mosaic distinction ultimately results in a division of God from political representation. Such a separating of divinity from political power situates monotheism at the roots of, not opposed to, "secularism":[170] monotheism critically distances the political sphere from the divine in refusing to immanentize the Absolute, relativizing all politics against a greater eschatological horizon.

Monotheism offers no guarantee of a healthy, perfect, sustained division of God from the political order. Wherever monotheistic religions have insisted on the violent political realization of religious truth and collapsed religious salvation with political dominion – like we saw in Akhenaton or the Maccabees – Assmann regards these as regressions from the potentiality of monotheism. This is also evidenced in "theocracy, Byzantine caesaropapism, or the usurpation of profane authority by spiritual leaders."[171] He identifies this corruption also especially in

---

[168] GG 114. He adds this involves no longer grounding truth in indisputable, inaccessible revelation but making it an "object of incessant reflection and redefinition" (*PM* 120; GG 126; Kirsch, *God against the Gods*, 89).

[169] *DP* 33; *AG* xi, 2, 17, 19, 22.

[170] See Eric Voegelin, *The New Science of Politics*, 100. Wolfgang Palaver, "Carl Schmitt's 'Apocalyptic' Resistance against Global Civil War," 69–94; 92. Also, John Ranieri, "What Voegelin Missed in the Gospel," 125–59.

[171] GG 89; 29, 86; *PM* 47f.

Christianity and Islam when they "universalize" the Mosaic distinction and paint those outside their religions as categorically outside of "truth," paving the way for religious violence.[172] Overall, Assmann's theory suggests that when "religion" becomes a distinct sphere from the political, it incurs a perpetual liability of volatility: they can slam back together with greater force than before. This possibility of violent relapse is the price of monotheism. And yet Assmann reminds us for what this price has been paid. Monotheism indeed means exodus; it means liberation from "the omnipotence of political power."[173]

K. CONCLUSION: MONOTHEISM IS WORTH THE PRICE OF ITS INTOLERANCE

Through national breakdown, Israel may have lost the world, but it gained a soul. It lost political sovereignty to its overlords, but its collective memory held onto a uniquely theologized king, to whom they ultimately owed fidelity apart from national fortunes. Particularly among a movement energized by a *no other gods* theology, fidelity meant refusing for centuries to translate this sovereign god with any other gods while resisting political alliances and cultural assimilation. This sovereign Yahweh could not be represented through the translatable signs of a political sovereign, dividing the homology between divine and political power. This made possible a new genus of religion that was less a projection of religiopolitical power and more a potential exodus from it.[174] This rendering of God as incompatible with the political sphere, dividing God from the cosmos, is not a universal idea that always existed. It was birthed through a contingent course of events, even, at times, as an unintended by-product of breakdowns.

We can admit of these liberative potentialities while acknowledging that this monotheism has in its genes the common, violent, political notions of monolatry, henotheism, and monotheism from above. One cannot fail to note the irony here, and we need not univocally valorize

---

[172] *PM* 18.

[173] *GG* 125, 145.

[174] *GG* 75; *GIT* 160, 327. Or: "Israel articulated nothing radically different from other ancient Near Eastern religions about Yahweh. Israelite religion came to be unique more in terms of 'recognition of what God was not.' God was not in the forces of nature, not to be represented by human or animal form, nor to be found in a multiplicity of forms" (*NOG* 82).

this God with special pacific, universal, liberal qualities. We must bear in mind that the covenant structure was rife with threat, terror, and patri-archalism; much of Yahwism may have looked like isolationist populism; and the monotheistic utterances of Deutero-Isaiah may stem from some inherited spirits of chauvinistic monolatry.[175] Israel's early germs of monolatry were statist in orientation, and its later monotheism had elements not entirely unlike imperialistic henotheism. The Deuteronomist strata and *no other gods* movement evidently sought to seize state control and political dominance, at times, with a fervent intolerance evidenced in the supposed efforts of Asa, Elijah, Josiah, and Ezra-Nehemiah.[176]

And yet my study suggests it is crucial to conceive how a possible break with these varieties of intolerance could be afforded through a reconfigur-ation of this very energy. Covenantal intolerance, refracted through col-lective trauma amidst national breakdown, had the effect of separating out a prior "religious" loyalty from socio-political-national loyalty in an inversion of ancient political theology.[177] As such, it became possible for "intolerance" to become something like a counter-political power. The later Jewish sect centered upon Christ crucified affirms and clarifies what is suggested in the Suffering Servant: the Mosaic distinction between true and false religion takes on a clarified meaning in the distinction between divinities who oversee empires and one who suffers under them.

Given Assmann's appreciation of both the cost and value of the Mosaic distinction, we can put to rest some of the critiques of his theory. In sum, Assmann's critics have read him as arguing that monotheism's intolerance and untranslatability is simply "bad," while polytheism's translatability is the kind of good tolerance we need for a pluralistic world. Mark Smith lodged this criticism in his *GIT*, which is framed as a rejoinder to Assmann and any who claim that god-translatability and polytheism are a more pacific theology. I have shown, however, that this is a position Assmann clearly does not hold. Smith's *GIT* is thus an exquisitely detailed and informative shot at a wrong target when he critiques Assmann by refuting mostly his book- and chapter *titles*, not his content. He considers Assmann as lodging a "polemic against traditional Christianity" because the title *The Price of Monotheism* suggests that monotheism has "taken a terrible toll." And Assmann's chapter "Abolishing the Mosaic

---

[175] Smith, "The Common Theology of the Ancient Near East," 147.
[176] NOG 84, 100–1, 258.
[177] GG 84.

Distinction: Religious Antagonism and Its Overcoming" only means to Smith that Assmann has hostilely taken "sides in the contemporary debate over theism and belief" and that he is extolling polytheistic "translatability as a model of religious tolerance."[178]

But in that book and chapter, Assmann argues quite the *opposite* of any abolition of the Mosaic distinction. He argues that monotheism's price, though high, has been *worth it*; and any theological efforts to abolish the Mosaic Distinction are in fact mislead and futile.[179] If anything, Assmann's appraisal of Mosaic intolerance could be critiqued as too *optimistic* about monotheism. For, even while Assmann emphasizes the originally violent semantics of exodus/conquest/Asa/Josiah/et al., he largely dismisses these cases as likely merely fantasized violence and residues of monolatry, only realized in the exceptional revolts noted above. If anything, Assmann downplays monotheistic violence as mostly that of a *potentiality* and a relapse, not an essence.

Joseph Ratzinger in *Truth and Tolerance*, like Smith, also critiqued Assmann as trying to abolish the Mosaic Distinction and thus misses Assmann's point.[180] When Ratzinger tells us "the gods were by no means always peaceful and interchangeable. They were just as often, indeed more often, the reason for people using violence against each other,"[181] we can simply agree and move on, knowing that Assmann agrees and has more subtle points to argue about the value, costs, and political consequences of Mosaic intolerance and untranslatability.[182]

Assmann's position is *not* trying to abolish the Mosaic distinction for its intolerant exclusion of polytheistic gods. As we have seen, the Mosaic distinction for him inaugurates a *different genus of God and religion*, a novel stratum of thought, which radically divides and reconfigures

---

[178] *GIT* 28, 326. Smith's inability to countenance a liberative meaning of "intolerance" limits his work, inclining him into an unnecessary emphasis on how Israel's monotheism had tolerant and translatable underpinnings, or was at least ambivalent.

[179] Smith also wrongly presumes Assmann thinks the Mosaic distinction characterized Israel from its origins (*GIT* 324).

[180] Ratzinger has the excuse of having released his book the same year as Assmann published clarifications in *PM*. Sloterdijk (*God's Zeal* 151–4) and Cliteur (*The Monotheist Dilemma*, 191–4) also wrongly classify Assmann as a mere critic of monotheistic violence (Van Riessen, "A Violent God?" 186).

[181] Ratzinger, *Truth and Tolerance*, 219.

[182] Erich Zenger also characterized Assmann as arguing for the abolition of the Mosaic distinction on account of its violence (*PM* 6). Similar misunderstandings pervade a compendium of commentaries on the subject: Erik Borgman, Maria Clara Bingemer, and Andrés Torres Queirga, eds., *Monotheism*.

politics and religion. In Girard's terms, it divides God from the sacred – separating the holy from the containment of violence. Assmann is not repeating the Enlightenment attempts at dulling or erasing the Mosaic distinction. Assmann admits he initially and mistakenly saw such a gesture in Freud's *Moses and Monotheism*.[183] But, while Freud's efforts were too speculative and simplistic, he nonetheless upheld monotheistic intolerance as something we must learn to appreciate and sublimate. Freud and Assmann both point us toward integrating the intolerance and zeal of monotheistic anti-political theology today, amidst contending plural communities and democracy. This "progress of intellectuality ought not to be relinquished, no matter how dearly it may have been purchased."[184]

Regina Schwartz was half-correct in critiquing monotheistic transcendence for gestating absolutist certainty, jingoistic pride in having the "true religion," and pathological ownership of truth.[185] But as we have shown above, the Mosaic distinction has helped open up a critical perspicacity toward the political realm that relativizes all political imaginaries in light of an absolute truth that we do not possess. Quite opposed to the notion that divinity, the political order, and the cosmos fit together in a continuous, harmonious package,[186] the above suggests precisely a growing awareness of incompatibilities, irresolutions, and discontinuities. We must appreciate this weighty apophatic intolerance embedded in monotheism, which reveals our own relative grasp on that absolute, that we do not *possess* this truth nor can it be represented in the political realm. This is in fact the very gift of monotheistic intolerance.[187] Paradoxically, such an absolute and exclusive truth – as housed in the idea of a "true religion" – relativizes our grasp on this truth. The Absolute, yes, can

---

[183] *PM* 86; *ME* 5.

[184] *PM* 120; 13, 86; *MPC* 143.

[185] *CC* 48.

[186] Vine Deloria Jr., *God Is Red*, 290. He rightly critiques the "logically pleasing" monotheism that is averse to imagining the universe's "discontinuity" with divinity. This study affirms this discontinuity. Although, for him, this discontinuity somehow opened up the possibility of a refraction of divinities.

[187] As Voegelin notes, "The break with early tolerance results … from the profounder insight that no symbolization through analogues of existential order in the world can even faintly be adequate to the divine partner on whom the community of being and its order depend …. The horror of a fall from being into nothingness motivates an intolerance which no longer is willing to distinguish between stronger and weaker gods but opposes the true god to the false gods" (*OH* 1, 9).

absolutize; but it can also relativize. This sense of "truth" knows that it does not know.[188]

The chief question, then, is not whether to abolish the Mosaic distinction but how to conceptualize it. That is, if the Mosaic distinction refers to "true religion," what is truth? On this point, on the *content* of the Mosaic distinction, Assmann devotes little attention. He briefly draws on Lessing and Mendelssohn's "weak" notion of truth: a permeable openness, an ongoing pursuit of truth through reasoned discourse.[189] This means that one cannot ground religious truth only in "revelation," without any parlay with reason. Rather, Lessing wrote, "the development of revealed truths into truths of reason is absolutely necessary if the human race is to be assisted by them."[190] Without this leaven of reason, monotheistic faith ossifies into what Sloterdijk calls a monotheism of "personal suprema-cism," where our reason plays the role of servile vassal in an "extreme will to obey the most rigid laws and commandments," however arbitrary (i.e., an extremist Divine Command theory).[191] But beyond this notion of weak truth, Assmann is largely silent on conceptualizing the content of the Mosaic distinction. His passing remarks on Christianity mostly emphasize its penchant for violent politicization and repeat Freud's critique: that it is a regression from monotheism into mythological ritualism. I take this as a reason, therefore, to use Chapter 7 to sketch, using Girard and others, a Christian theology of monotheism, conceptualizing what counts for "truth" in the intolerant Mosaic distinction.

The Mosaic distinction for Girard, we will see, is not arbitrary or mystical, but in fact a critical, anthropological insight: it is the victim distinction, the truth of the foundational role of the scapegoat in human culture and thought – and siding with her. "True religion" unveils victims while false religion occludes them. The division of God from the victim mechanism corresponds with the Mosaic division of God from the political realm. This truth of the victim is revealed not through triumphant chauvinism but only in the process of it being cast out by our violent

---

[188] Hence, when the apostle Paul wrote "now that you know God" he immediately qualified: "rather, are known by God." This is a revelation of occultation – that we "see through a glass dimly" (Gal 4:9; 1 Cor 13:12).

[189] *GG* 145; *ATM* 127.

[190] Toshimasa Yasukata, *Lessing's Philosophy of Religion and German Enlightenment*, 107.

[191] By contrast, Sloterdijk refers to a preferable "impersonal supremacism" within monotheism, which treats reason as not the antipode of but a participation in the divine (Van Riessen, "A Violent God?" 184).

blindness.[192] Girard echoes Assmann in appreciating how this distinction is indeed dangerous and intolerant, but it is nonetheless worth it. The truth of the victim – however much Nietzsche was correct that it courts apocalypse – should not be relinquished.

But if we are to speak of monotheism separating God from the victim mechanism, how does this square with the evident re-unification of God with the victim in Christ? Does this not relapse into polytheism? We saw this critique in Freud, and it stands in Islamic and Jewish traditions, concerning Christ's divinity and the Trinity.[193] Chapter 7 will synthesize Girard's attempted solution to this problem while developing upon it, considering how dividing and re-uniting God with the scapegoat mechanism makes for a movement of simultaneous transcendence and immanence, of incompatibility with the world and dangerous engagement with it.

[192] *TH* 235.
[193] E.g., Quran 4:171; 5:73, 116; 18:88–93; 23:91; 112:1–4.

7

Jesus Christ and Intolerance

Toward Revelation without Rivalry

What is most distinct and consequential about monotheism is not the unity of the divine but the *division* from the political. The Mosaic distinction's untranslatability made possible an incompatibility, both liberating and dangerous, between divinity and the political sphere. But how do we conceptualize this separation?[1] A paradigmatic Christian scripture on this, as Assmann noted, is Christ speaking of his kingdom being "not of this world." Do we take this to mean not *in* this world, in an other-worldly, transcendentalism – a neutralization? Not only would such a two-world metaphysics seem to pave the way for the desacralization and spoliation of the earth's ecosystems, it would seem to result in what Mouffe called *depoliticization*, a pretention to having escaped the political.

At the same time, Christianity seems to show many signs of the ancient *politicization* of religion: while monotheism supposedly does away with deifying kings, what do we make of Christ the divine king? With the Son of God hanging from crucifixes do we not regress from the unrepresentable God into an idolatry of a divinized victim?[2] Is not "Jesus Christ the

---

[1] Bypassing, here, the immense Jewish reflection on this question, I speak in interpretation of my Christian tradition – which is of course derivatively Jewish. The vast field of Jewish (and Muslim) commentary on political theology not only exceeds the constraints of this book but my own capacities. Starting points for such reflection would need to include Hermann Cohen, Jacob Taubes, Franz Rosenzweig, Leo Strauss, and a catalog of others that one sees digested in Paul Nahme, Judith Plaskow, Robert Erlewine, Lenn E. Goodman, and, say, the edited volume: Randi Rashkover and Martin Kavka, eds., *Judaism, Liberalism, and Political Theology*.

[2] *TOB* 39, 59.

one true Lord" a return to the dictatorial politicization of the divine? In unearthing the parallels between Christ and, say, Osiris' murder and rising, it would seem Christianity is less a separation from the cosmotheistic victim and more a return to it. Do we not have in Christianity, as Girard asked, a badly disguised polytheism, a myth "that is not essentially different from the ancient myths of death and resurrection?"[3] In Christianity's inheritance of monotheistic division, we seem to face the extremes of both depoliticization and politicization.

Let us introduce, in rough ideal types, two ways Christianity has managed this "separation" of religion from the political sphere. One is evidenced in the history of Christianized empires from Constantine onward, which simply repeats what Jonathan Z. Smith called the ancient distinction between power and purity: the king is powerful but impure (the container of violence, the executioner, etc.), while the priest is powerless yet pure.[4] This configuration allows for a pseudo-separation of religion and politics that conceals their deeper compatibility. This is visible in Eusebius' imperial theology, wherein the divine Christ is the transcendent sovereign, arrayed in purity through ecclesial representation, while Constantine serves as his political analogue and deputy.[5] Even though the emperor is dedivinized in Christian empires, the religiopolitical compact abides, is even strengthened, under the false pretense of separation. The "two swords" of spiritual and temporal authority are separated but compatible.[6]

One might alternatively separate religion from politics in a more explicitly *depoliticized* manner. Monotheism, in such a view, is a pacific universalism that sheds political division, invokes an inclusivity beyond exclusion, a Church or society beyond hegemony, a movement beyond particularist identities, beyond violence, beyond hierarchies, beyond religion, beyond us-versus-them thinking. This is present in varying degrees in Schwartz and other authors noted in Chapter 1 who, sensitive to creating a belonging beyond all differences, argue for an inclusive monotheism (or polytheism). Monotheism here, while seemingly conciliatory, means a sheer dialectic break with primary religion, freed of the political. Girard regarded this inclusivist approach to monotheism as seeking to

[3] *ISS* 121–2.
[4] Mack, *The Christian Myth*, 130, 143, 172.
[5] Eusebius Pamphilius, *Church History, Life of Constantine, Oration in Praise of Constantine*, 1.37–41.
[6] See, e.g., the papal encyclical *Unam Sanctam* (issued 1302 CE). See also Joerg Rieger, *Christ and Empire*.

"move God so far away from any involvement in the scapegoat mechanism that they view with suspicion any contact with it in religious thought and symbolism."[7] This spirit of definitive separation is especially appealing for many in our age, wherein institutional, hierarchic Christendom lurches toward extinction through the exposure of its abuses and cover-ups.

The first, politicized mode sees enemies defined through the triumphant truth of Christ; the second mode says the problem is having enemies in the first place. The first's theological motif is Christ the cosmic monarch; the second's is "neither Jew nor Greek, slave nor free, no longer male and female." The first is institutional; the second is anti-institutional. The first, Christ's death is the ultimate sacrifice, founding the true Kingdom; the second, Christ's death is an anti-sacrifice that dissolves all forms of belonging from which conflicts stem. In the first, the Kingdom of God is an analogue of continuity with archaic religio-polities through fulfilling them; in the second, God's *kin*-dom is a dialectical break from all hierarchical *king*doms, abandoning the archaic sacred. The first is a coup of the world; the second, an escape from it.

Both manners of "separating" religion and politics, however, fail to conceptualize a creative, benevolent reconfiguring of monotheistic intolerance. In the first, politicized case, monotheistic intolerance is little more than a continuation of the jingoism inherited from henotheism and monolatry. Its intolerance remains the *libido dominandi* with simply a new *dominus*. This fails to see the apophatic intolerance of monotheism – the radical incompatibility between God and the political order, as evidenced in Chapter 6. Lacking this, such a faux-separation ironically lends itself to a *privatization* of faith through subordinating Christ's teachings to "common sense" – ultimately, the political expedient of containing violence. In Christendom this was often evidenced in downgrading Christ's commands on enemy love and "do not resist an evil person" from having public, binding import for all Christians to being a matter of private comportment. Martin Luther, for example, laudably insisted that the counsels of perfection must be obligatory for all Christians, not only clergy; but, he blinked, if "do not resist an evil person" were applied publicly this would be ruinous to civic order and court anarchy; ergo, all Christians should love enemies in private but restrain them in public (you can love the enemy through killing them); forgo even self-defense on a

---

[7] *EC* 211.

personal level, but in public one must bear the sword for the benefit of neighbors.[8] One could rightly investigate the political history of the West using this pseudo-division as a hermeneutic. A recent striking example – besides Christian institutions remaining largely silent, if supportive, while its members deployed to wars deemed unjust, like the 2003 Iraq invasion – is in a figure of the US Religious Right, Jerry Falwell Jr. He has long argued for a surgent Christian America and bringing evangelical "moral- ity" into politics. But when asked to explain his trenchant support for President Trump, Falwell clarified the ironically privatized results of politicization: "I don't look to the teachings of Jesus for what my political beliefs should be."[9]

But in the second case, monotheistic intolerance is disavowed, aban- doned, in a depoliticized desire to transcend all differences and conflicts. But, as Mouffe would point out, such an abolition of intolerance, pre- suming to have spoken from a position of neutrality beyond hegemony, retains a clandestine, dishonest intolerance. It is not so much a wolf in sheep's clothing as a wolf who has convinced itself it is a sheep. Losing sight of the inescapability of the political, this mode loses touch with its own cataphatic intolerance, its own fervent claims and exclusions. One calls to mind King's notion of the "white moderate," as noted in Chapter 1, who is "not divisive" yet thereby safeguards deeper injustices and divisions. In the face of divisive conflicts about racism, they calm us all down with the reminder that "all lives matter" and ensure the continu- ation of structural racism. Again, all polities and groupings inescapably express their own particular intolerance. Monotheism, as explored in Chapter 6, entails a unique reconfiguration of common political intoler- ances of the ancient world. It was this particular, intolerant exaltation of an exclusive god – *not* the speaking from a position of abstract, inclusive universality – that helped catalyze divinity's incompatibility with worldly authority. Attempts to abolish intolerance not only reiterate a covert intolerance, but they lose touch with a positive, prophetic distinction.[10]

---

[8] Luther, *Selected Writings of Martin Luther*, "Temporal Authority." Dostoyevsky, in his scene of the Grand Inquisitor interrogating Christ, portrays the Church as the chief restrainer of the holy anarchy of its nominal Lord. A similar critique is in Kierkegaard, who saw Christendom and Christian scholarship as largely conspiracies in justifying the avoidance of Christ's commands.

[9] Scott Michels et al., "How Evangelicals Gained Political Power."

[10] E.g., Rousseau's inclusivity seems blind to its own anti-pluralistic intolerance: "whoever dares to say, *no Salvation Outside the Church*, has to be driven out of the State" (Rousseau, *Rousseau*, 151; Robert Erlewine, *Monotheism and Tolerance*, 26).

This idealized antinomy is not merely a problem for religionists but a fundamental issue concerning the human hope to overcome antagonism, intolerance, violence, and oppression without simply reiterating them. That problem was broached through Mouffe on the matter of liberalism; and it has been reconstructed – but left open to interpretation – concerning the monotheistic division from the political sphere. I want to end by exploring how the political symbolism surrounding Jesus Christ entails a nuanced response to this issue. The apostle Paul, in Giorgio Agamben's reading, saw in Christ a subtle movement to overcome the powers of law, the "principalities and powers." But Christ did not simply fulfill or take the throne of such powers, nor did he enter into rivalrous antagonism with them. And yet, at the same time, he had no pretention to neutrality: he sought to "render them inoperative." This messianism does not simply replace, attack, or escape the political, which would again only re-establish new powers and rivalries. It seeks to de-activate the powers without somehow re-activating them.[11] This chapter conceptualizes how Christ as the divine scapegoat-king is a complex model of "intolerance," a living response to this problem. Such an example involves navigating the "division" between monotheism and archaic religions through both continuity *and* discontinuity, analogy and dialectic, conciliation and attack.

To describe this, Section A will, first, elaborate on axial theory, introduced in Chapter 4. This theory concerns the matter of divine-political separation in that it deals with the transition from myth to logic, or from primary religions to secondary religions. Axial theory helps us speak of a genuine monotheistic difference while also not falling into naïve categories of pure discontinuity or anti-mythology. It suggests secondary religion involves critical reconfiguration of the symbols of primary religion, but it does not simply *escape* them – a nuance profoundly grasped by Girard's notion of sacrifice.[12] I then apply, in Sections B–D, that axial-informed hermeneutic in interpreting some key political theology symbols, evidenced in cosmotheism but reconfigured in Christianity: sovereignty and land. Sovereignty here will include the symbols of Jesus' trial, crucifixion, and resurrection. Just as in Egypt the land was also the body of a victim,

---

[11] Giorgio Agamben, *The Time That Remains*, 24, 27, 97–9. He notes the linguistic link between deactivation and fulfillment, between abolishing and conserving.

[12] Girard considered mimetic theory as aiming precisely to interpret this transition "from one type of religion to another. Beyond that, [mimetic theory] does not claim to exhaust the innumerable forms this transition has assumed in human history" (*TOB* 113).

I will explore the New Testament's redeployment of "land" as the symbol of Christ's body and his "reign." In exegeting such symbols with the help of Girard and others, I conceptualize a monotheism that avoids both politicization and depoliticization through the creative redeployment of cosmotheistic political theology.

A. AXIAL THEORY: NOT ESCAPE BUT RECONFIGURATION

Axial theory concerns, among many historical topics, the shift from primary to secondary religions in the ancient world. Again, speaking in ideal types, primary religions are central to tribal groups and archaic states, wherein religion and politics, divinity and society, God and cosmos are roughly homologous. Secondary religions break up this compaction. With Judaism as a key example, they stem from an era, often framed as the first millennium BCE, of eruptive sociopolitical changes – for example, the transition from tribes and smaller city-states into larger, more imperial, cosmopolitan regions; the growing prevalence of writing technologies and market economies; iron overtaking bronze, exacerbating conflicts; the increasing centralization of divinity and pantheons into imperial henotheisms, etc.

Through a complex array of such factors, this era was marked by what the sociologist Robert Bellah calls a Eurasian-wide "political legitimation crisis." This crisis provoked the rethinking of the very "religio-political premises of society itself" – evinced among Jewish prophets, Plato, Buddha, and so on.[13] In these small but concentrated pockets, axial theorists see a theme of critically stepping back from the world, in a benevolent alienation and transcendence. While the "mechanisms of social domination" were increasing significantly in the first millennium BCE, axial theory concerns how protesting them, in both renunciation and denunciation, "for the first time becomes possible."[14] Partly catalyzed by such protest, the cosmotheism of primary religions begins to give way to secondary religions and their theo-political differentiating of God from the cosmos and political order.[15] Cosmogonic myths that once combined the foundation of the cosmos, the origins of the state, the birth of the gods, and history were slowly broken up into philosophy, history,

---

[13] Robert Bellah, "Heritage of the Axial Age," 460.
[14] Ibid., 450.
[15] See *OH*; *GG* 88; *PM* 125; Bellah, "Heritage of the Axial Age," 462; *CMA* 370; Assmann, "Axial 'Breakthroughs' in Ancient Egypt and Israel," 151.

theology, political science, etc. Speaking in ideal types, secondary religions all share this disposition, even if they differ widely in their respective details and forms.

The most consequential feature of these pockets of axial critique, Bellah and others concur, is in the "rethinking of sovereignty." For the sovereignty embodied in archaic states grew from a particular feedback loop of the violent sacred: the king – who Girard would remind us emerged from the scapegoat – emerged as a manifestation of the god. Thus, the most consequential breakthroughs in the axial age were at the level of rethinking, reconfiguring, or breaking the god-king linkage. Bellah sees the recurring, fundamental question asked in the first millennium BCE as: Who is the true king, "the one who really reflects divine justice"?[16] As explored in Chapter 6, Jewish monotheism, forged amidst various crises, posed and answered this question in its division of God from the cosmos and king, its covenantal "direct theocracy" with a Lord not mediated by royalty or government. Christ's paradoxical kingship, with his crown of thorns and his throne a cross, is also a striking extension of this new relationship between God and king, as we explore in this chapter.[17]

But, lest we myopically emphasize the biblical revolution to the ignorance or negation of others, axial theory invites us to situate these biblical breakthroughs amidst many other cultural-religious transformations. In Greece, for example, Bellah notes the shifts in emphasis from Achilles the hero-prince to Socrates the stonemason. In China, Confucius and Mencius were the itinerant, unrecognized, and uncrowned kings. In India, Buddha the prince abrogated his kingdom for his politically irrelevant enlightenment. Temiya (a Buddha incarnation) "ruled" over an "empire of renunciation," involving the abstention from violence and sex, in a reign that could never be realized on this earth.[18] In Egypt, in response to generations of political subjugation, an eschatological religious messianism emerged.[19] In Plato, the truly good king would not

---

[16] Robert Bellah, "What Is Axial?," 71–2. Mack refers to Christianity's important turning to "symbols of sovereignty" as a response to the "breakdown of societies in the Greco-Roman age" (Mack, *The Christian Myth*, 136, 142).

[17] Voegelin contrasts Egyptian divine kingship with Christianity by the latter's centering upon a man of low status (*OH* 74).

[18] Bellah, "The Heritage of the Axial Age," 460, 462.

[19] E.g., "the *Potter's Oracle* and the Demotic *Prophesies of the Lamb* ... foretell the return of a messianic king who, after a long period of oppressive foreign rule, will establish a new time of glory by restoring the Pharaohs" (*CMEC* 64).

want to reign and would be killed by the unenlightened mob.[20] Aristotle was an alien, not a citizen, who couldn't buy land for his "school of renouncers."[21] In Ramayana, the Hindu epic, the ideal king is radically alien to this world. In Islam, the Prophet is, in Bellah's words, "a king and not a king." While all these cases each have their own unique qualities, Bellah identifies a common thread: "The old unity of God and king was broken through dramatically in every case, and yet reaffirmed paradoxically in new axial formations."[22]

The dividing of God from the political evoked new tensions and new equilibriums between the transcendent and the world. The question becomes how to bridge or relate these two increasingly differentiated modes of thinking.[23] In other words, as religion broke up from its homology with politics – losing touch with ancient traditions, institutions, and meanings – there emerged different *kinds* of religious and political structures of thought, necessitating new relationships between them. Axial theorist Eric Voegelin sees in this epoch an increasing distinction and friction between transcendent and immanent modes of thought, necessitating negotiation. This is accompanied by a "dualistic structure of existence," as one might find in the Augustinian distinction between the earthly and heavenly city, or, simply, the church and state.[24] The mature philosophical resolution to these new tensions, for Voegelin, is attained in admitting the *tension yet inescapable contact* between the transcendent and immanent. Breakthroughs in thought may introduce a radically critical spirit – a "love of being which inspires intolerance," a critical intolerance of the insufficiency of the old religions and ideas. But such transcendence must learn to "compromise with the conditions of

---

[20] Plato, *Republic*, §347c–d, 521a–b, 540.

[21] Bellah, "The Heritage of the Axial Age," 463.

[22] Bellah, "What Is Axial?," 72. However, Voegelin notes, Confucianism, because it entailed no radical incompatibilities with the available order, did not break up the religiopolitical linkages. This made it ripe for imperial utilization (*OH* 62). See also Schmel Eisenstadt who, speaking generally about Axial shift, but with its most dramatic example in ancient Israel, writes, "The king-god, the embodiment of the cosmic and earthly order, disappeared, and the model of secular ruler appeared .... Similar concepts emerged in ancient Greece, in India, and in China – most clearly manifested in the concept of the Mandate of Heaven" (Eisenstadt, "Destructive Possibilities," 280).

[23] Bellah, "What Is Axial?," 81.

[24] *OH* 11. Burton Mack: "there is no debate about the fact that the early Christian experiments did create a split view of the world in which the structures of each half did not easily mesh and were hardly expected to do so" (Mack, *The Christian Myth*, 118).

existence."²⁵ Without this compromise, the sense of an intolerant and critical breakthrough is tempted toward a violent schizophrenia that is both alienated from the entire world and yet prone toward seizing this world through coup and replacement. For millennia now, Voegelin argues, varieties of this alienation have been tempted toward violent manifestations, such that the only way to heal the divide – between this world and the lost "original" from which it has strayed – is to destroy this world to make room for the new one.²⁶ Voegelin's word for such antagonistic substitution is Gnosticism (though this is not the only way to define its diversities). Such a view can involve the creation of an idealized "second reality"²⁷ that becomes not just otherworldly but *over*worldly: it can see the only way forward as "abolishing the constitution of being, with its origin in divine, transcendent being, and replacing it with a world-immanent order of being, the perfection of which lies in the realm of human action."²⁸ (He saw this especially in political communism of the twentieth century.) Opposed to such alienated Gnosticism, Voegelin argues we must regard "the new" (i.e., critical transcendence, the love of being that inspires intolerance) as an "addition" to the old, not its destruction or substitution.²⁹

The problem with Gnosticism is not that it is "too radical" or too much of a secondary religion. Rather, precisely through trying to destroy and replace the old world, it paradoxically regresses into it, *reproducing* it. As such, its rivalry ultimately offers nothing *new*, no break from the stifling compaction of the divine with the world; for in the rivalrous replacing of the old gods it becomes the new one. The revolution becomes the regime. (This is where one observes in political communism the indistinction between atheism and the radical immanentization of divinity.) It is possible for a certain mode of radicalism to be ultimately conservative through its reiterating what it critiques.³⁰ This calls to mind the inescapability of the political: even the most tolerant attempts to

---

²⁵ *OH* 11.
²⁶ *SPG* 8–9, 11.
²⁷ Ibid., 35.
²⁸ Ibid., 100.
²⁹ *OH* 11.
³⁰ Erik Peterson calls Gnosticism's political theology one in which "the government of the demiurge is always wrong." Of this two-tiered political metaphysics, "the sovereignty of God is truly good, but the regime of the Demiurge (or demiurgic 'Powers,' usually seen as officials) is bad: in other words, the regime is always wrong" (Peterson, *Theological Tractates*, 71 n15. See also Agamben, *The Kingdom and the Glory*, 77).

construct a "politics without a scapegoat" can re-entrench a concealed intolerance. We cannot lose sight of Mouffe's observation, that even if some ideal society-beyond-hegemony were ever to become instituted through a politico-juridical form, it would paradoxically no longer be pluralistic, inclusive, and open.

Likewise, we might be tempted to regard the axial shift from primary to secondary religions as a pure replacement of "myth" with "logic." But, for all the historical evidence of genuine epistemological shifts in the axial epoch, to conceive of logic as replacing myth is misleadingly simplistic. We already saw in Freud a faulty dualism between Yahweh as mythical, superstitious, ritualistic, violent and Aten as anti-mythic, enlightened, anti-ritual, pacific. But myth and logic – indeed the gambit of simplistic antinomies like ritual and spontaneity, nature and revelation – do not work as poles but more like layers. Logic does not supplant myth; rather, logic extends, supplements, or reconfigures mythical thought. Narratival or mythological thinking is not de facto irrational; even more, all logic is narratival in nature. Even the most analytic of words and theory do not displace mythic and narratival thinking but add to them.[31] Logic does not escape from myth but is its leavening, its creative reconfiguration. In parallel with Mouffe's critique of depoliticization, logic that presents itself as having entirely escaped myth simply becomes the new myth.

"Mythical" thought, in ideal types, can sometimes be described as "analogical" in form, prevalent in "compact," "cosmotheistic," and "mythic cultures."[32] In such a mode of thought, the world and all its processes and functions are analogues for the world of gods, the cosmos – which ultimately *is* the one body of God. Inclusive translatability reigns here. And, by contrast, secondary religions, in their declaration of all other religions as false, can be characterized by their tendency toward a "dialectic" mode: in an exclusivist break from analogical thought, the revealed, untranslatable God cannot be known by any analogy in the natural world. Such a dialectic mode of thinking involves an epistemological divide from God. We saw the crucial aspects of this in Jewish monotheism, wherein nothing can represent God; in the Christian tradition it shows itself in a wide range of utterances from the fathers of the Church to Barth. Irenaeus wrote, "No one can have any knowledge of

[31] Bellah, "What Is Axial?," 79, 86.
[32] *CMA* 372.

God unless God teaches him."[33] Or Hilary of Poitiers, "God himself is our authority about God; otherwise he is not known."[34]

This dialectic epistemology, which would seem to coincide with monotheism's distinguishing God from the cosmos, sees the cosmos not as the begotten body of God but as secular, created, and understandable on its own terms. As noted in Chapter 6, God in this secondary-religion sense is not one of the cosmos' functions; God is functionless, beyond being. That is, God is not a *process* that any ritual or act in the cosmos completes. Under monotheism's exclusion of the gods, the subordinate gods who administer the nature-functions of the universe are demoted to angels, eventually reduced further to two basic poles of Manichean good and evil, drifting perhaps – with God fully functionless – toward what seems like atheism.[35] But as to whether the cosmos (among whose processes includes the political sphere) reveals anything about such an utterly transcendent God, the logic of monotheism would seem to suggest this is now de facto impossible: between creature and Creator there can be imagined no greater ontological difference. This is one way of describing what I am referring to as "dialectical" thought in contrast with "analogical" thought – roughly coinciding with secondary and primary religions.

But if we bear in mind that logic is not the replacement or destruction of myth but its extension, we can see how, by extension, secondary religions do not simply replace but reconfigure primary religious symbols. Secondary religions do not cleanly escape primary religions any more than logic escapes myth. Dialectic thought does not and cannot escape analogical thought just as, by extension, tolerant liberalism cannot construct a politics without a founding exclusion. When Voegelin discussed this relationship between myth and logic, he suggested the axial revolution opened up a mode of thought where myth is not replaced by, but interpenetrated with, logic. He called this "mythospeculation." It is an important and real step in critical perspicacity but not absolute. Such thinking knows that rationality, while it helps in deconstructing and challenging the sedimented structures of society, is nonetheless still inescapably constituted by myth. It does not pretend to be simplistically "myth-free," to replace myth, or to have absolute knowledge. Rather, it

---

[33] St. Irenaeus, *Adversus Haereses*, IV, vi, 4.
[34] St. Hilary, *De Trinitate*, V, I, 21. See also Keith Johnson, *Karl Barth and the Analogia Entis*.
[35] Sawyer, "Biblical Alternatives to Monotheism," 176. Agamben, *The Kingdom and the Glory*, 286; Gnuse, "Breakthrough or Tyranny," 8.

knows that it is "myth with an element of reflective theory in it," having *added to* myth.[36] In other words, one must conceptualize how to integrate without collapsing – in a hypostatic union, as it were – the two distinct denotations of the word "myth": the exclusivist notion of "a story that is false," and the inescapable notion of "a story to live by."

We might describe this interpenetration at the level of primary and secondary religions. No matter how much secondary religions are characterized by counter-religion, rejecting primary religion as falsehood and idolatry, they do not and cannot simply replace or supersede primary religion. In the least, secondary religions always minimally retain some residue of primary religions by remembering them as the reified opponent (e.g., "Egypt" as the symbol of Israel's idolatrous origins). But, more fundamentally, primary religion coevolved with the political, with the inescapable, mimetic, constitutive features of human sociality since our origins: inclusion and exclusion, "us" and "them" constructs, association/disassociation, reciprocity, taboo and restraints, rituals and myth, loyalty/faith, and so on. Mouffe and Girard each clarified in their own way how these features cannot be simply abandoned without somehow, in turn, repeating them. Assmann too notes how, because so many primary religious elements concern these inescapable dimensions of human life, the transition from primary to secondary religion is rather "a complex process of repudiation and symbolic reintegration," wherein "the vital elements of primary religious experience are integrated and fused into a new synthesis." This syncretism is "both inevitable and unobjectionable."[37] This means for Assmann the counter-ness of secondary religions incurs a price: they bear within themselves elements of primary religion that they supposedly reject. This makes secondary religions partly dishonest, "duplicitous." Creating in us a new form of unconscious, the elements of primary religion "constitute a kind of 'crypt' in the edifice of secondary religions, a subterranean realm no longer illuminated by the light of consciously cultivated religious semantics."[38] One identifies here a resonance with Mouffe, in that liberalism, for all its potentialities in the ideal of transcending exclusion, incurs a price of potential duplicity: it always bears within itself the dimension of the political that it supposedly rejects.

---

[36] Bellah, "What Is Axial?," 81.
[37] *PM* 109.
[38] Ibid., 109–11.

Chapter 6 demonstrated how monotheism – despite all its claims to distinction – has numerous polytheistic, political building blocks in its crypt. Jewish monotheism's foundation includes stones hewn from common ancient norms of justice, law, covenants, and memory rituals; it reused, but made uniquely religious, the growing trend in canonizing normative texts; even the notion of an *only God* was not entirely unique. But, a complex repudiation amidst integration was evidenced, for example, in the transposing of the violent, jealous zeal contained in archaic political loyalty oaths into a distinctly "religious" zeal. As such, the intolerant allegiance of the political sphere was not evacuated but transformed into a potentially nonviolent "intolerance," while nonetheless retaining residues that make possible a new kind of "religious violence." In all, while ancient Judaism may have been an exodus from archaic "myth," it did not and could not, in cultural linguistic practice, escape from myth into a pure rationality unlike anything prior to it.[39] It instead modified and critiqued myth in its own unique and liberating, if ambivalent, adaptation.

But when it comes to Christianity inheriting this creative intolerance, Freud declared that it ultimately regressed from monotheistic logic into pagan myth. Rejected with some qualification, he admitted that Christianity's victimage-symbols bore an enlightened, if muffled, return of the repressed. It brought before our eyes the primal scenario of murdering the alpha male and dramatized his reenthronement; this drama invites us to admit our guilt in humanity's founding murder, opening up and airing out humanity's repressed crypt as it were. But, despite its dwelling on such weighty images, Freud also argued that Christianity turned this crypt into a gift shop, so to speak, averting awareness of our founding murder with mythologies of atonement and fantasies of expiation. Freud praised Aten's monotheism as pacifism, intellectualism, and a-ritualism, while reviling Christianity's "ritualism," "superstition," and "magic."

Echoing and mostly affirming Freud, Assmann too agrees that Christianity's mythical modes of thought, like the "theology of incarnation," regrettably "reopened the doors to images, sacramental magic, and other forms of religious life."[40] Unfortunately, Assmann doesn't

---

[39] On this "reconfiguration" or "mixing" theme: William Dever, "How Was Ancient Israel Different?"; Gnuse, "Breakthrough or Tyranny," 79.

[40] GG 105.

elaborate enough to make this a substantial, instructive rejection on his part.[41] But such a curt exodus from mythical symbols, I argue, seems not only epistemically naïve, in its putative escape from myth and religion. But it also implies a kind of monotheism Girard critiqued as too alienated, too aloof in enlightenment from the inescapable problems of scapegoating, ritual, and myth. Assmann leaves the Christian theologian asking again how exactly to relate monotheism to an apparent Christian regression.

B. GIRARD ON THE TRANSITION FROM PRIMARY TO SECONDARY RELIGION

Girard offers, by contrast with Assmann, a better framework for interpreting Christianity's relationship to monotheism, relating myth and logic, crypt and edifice. For Girard, Christianity's dialectical, revelatory discontinuity from archaic religions is mediated *through* its analogous continuity with them. The more similar Christianity appears to myth, he writes, "the more clearly it becomes a radical rereading of myths."[42] For Girard, the path to subverting violent falsehoods within archaic religion is not by external attack or escape but by internal subversion.

Girard has, at times, lacked emphasis on this, speaking of Christianity in almost purely dialectical tones: Christianity is an anti-religion that, in theory, should not even exist, given its attack on the fundamental, sacrificial features of human association: Christianity is non-sacrificial, an attack on myth, an attack on religion and human culture itself.[43] But, at his more nuanced points, he plied a more interpenetrative, mythospeculative understanding of the change from primary to secondary religion. As such, he emphasized Christianity as discontinuous with archaic religion through its continuity with it; Christianity is an "*exit*

---

[41] In an under-developed flourish, Assmann regards monotheism's trauma and murder as comingled with its enlightenment: both stem from its killing off, first, pagan gods, and then killing the "God" of monotheism itself. This "theoclastic violence" involves negative theology and the death of god as part of the progress of intellectuality (*PM* 97).

[42] *EC* 178f.

[43] One can hear the dialectician in Girard: "by submitting to violence, Christ reveals and uproots the structural matrix of all religion" (*TH* 178–9). "Christianity is destructive of the type of religion that brings people together, joining them into a coalition against some arbitrary victim, as all the natural religions have always done, except for the biblical ones" (Vattimo and Girard, *Christianity, Truth, and Weakening Faith*, 25).

out of religion that is offered *from within* the demythified religion."[44] Christianity for Girard is a "myth in reverse," retaining the subtle combination of the two denotations of myth as story and myth as falsehood.[45] This combination did not soften the distinctive discontinuity of Christian revelation for Girard. It in fact retains the distinction precisely because, paradoxically, any simplistic *opposition and radical break* between archaic and revealed religion would reiterate the very mimetic rivalry one hopes to abolish.[46] That is, Girard sought to mitigate the antagonism of the Mosaic distinction while not abandoning any notion of difference and revelatory critique. Instead, he interpreted the discontinuity through continuity. "If biblical texts resembled myths less than they do, they could not differ from myths as much as they do."[47]

His theory required this nuance because he recognized, as noted, that key features of archaic religion are largely homologous with human culture itself. That is, things like myth, ritual, taboo, funerals, education, rites of passage – all of these "derive from sacrificial practices" and yet social life without them is "unimaginable."[48] Unable to abandon or supersede these inescapable elements, Girard imagined we could somehow reconfigure them, hollow them out from within their sacrificial violence. How to conceive of this transformation again requires familiarity with the Mouffian insight: while inclusivity can reshape and expand

---

[44] *BTE* 25, emphasis added. He admits of having spoken with exaggeration and that he wanted to "rectify the error of the so-called anti-sacrificial argument I made in my first writings on this subject, especially in *TH* ... [bringing] my perspective into closer alignment with traditional theologies" (*TOB* xi; 42).

[45] This approach attends to both discussed "layers" of the Mosaic distinction. The monolatrous "monotheism of loyalty" layer concerns gods as real and inescapable: we all inevitably worship some god, just as we all live according to a story. This is Bob Dylan's "gotta' serve somebody" dimension of human culture, which is also inescapably mimetic; we all worship gods, just as we all imitate models. As to deciding which one, this layer concerns not the *true* or "universal" god but *loyalty* to a particular one who liberates the oppressed.

In a distinct idiom, a "monotheism of truth" universally declares all gods illusions in contrast with the One True God. This is a grammar not of fidelity but of "insight and knowledge" (*IR* 84). On this point, Girard clarifies how "truth" in religion concerns not arbitrary squabbles but matters of anthropological insight.

Mythospeculation, if I may use that here, takes both of these as important grammars of thought. It may also explain why god and G̲od capitalization seems so haphazard in this book: it is not an editing error but an effect of the intermingled layers of loyalty and truth: myth as story and myth as falsehood.

[46] *EC* 204.

[47] *TOB* 38.

[48] Ibid., 126.

boundaries of exclusion, it never ultimately abolishes them – just as expunging myths and sacrificial rituals only creates new ones.[49]

For Girard, this important problem is symbolized in the dense word "sacrifice." Girard defined sacrifice as "an effort to revive the conciliatory effects of unanimous violence by substituting an alternative victim for the original scapegoat." Sacrifice connotes the practices of how societies contain violence, securing peace through some cost. Such containment may involve restrictions (in taboos, myths, and rules) or explicit violence, including ritual sacrifices that channel attention to an animal, human, or effigy. Sacrifice is well-expressed in the tragic calculus that "it is better that one man should die than many." In light of this violence, Girard initially saw in Christ's nonviolence, love of enemies, and nonresistance precisely the diametric *opposition* to sacrifice, a non- or anti-sacrificial death. Far from his suffering being a supreme sacrifice, per the habit of Christendom, one must instead conclude: "So great is the distance between the sacrifice of Christ in this sense and archaic sacrifice that a greater one cannot be imagined."[50] Just as we may find everywhere today the desire to construct a politics without exclusion, some theologians similarly seek to construct a theology without "sacrifice." For the word suggests violence, exclusion – ultimately a regression into archaic religion's homology with the political.

And yet Girard came to regard the relation between Christ's nonviolent death and archaic sacrifice as simultaneously "entirely other" and yet "inseparable." Christ's exodus from sacrifice came through undergoing it. For if one refuses to sacrifice or do violence to others, one must be prepared to be sacrificed themselves. Sacrifice for Girard is thus akin to what we defined as the political in Mouffe, the exclusions and decisions constitutive of human association. Even for the most inclusive of cultures, sacrifice shows itself as largely inescapable. Sacrifice and the political can be spoken together in the word "victim," given how *decision* bears an etymology of cutting off, delineation, even slitting the throat of a sacrificial victim.[51] To see the victim is to see the exception. This is the paradox of Christ's non-sacrificial "sacrifice," in his refusal to sacrifice others: "Use of the same word in each case dispels the *illusion of*

---

[49] It is thus instructive that Girard, who admitted his scholarship was initially animated by the avant-garde deconstruction of religion, ended up a practicing Catholic who submitted himself to its rituals.

[50] *TOB* 40f; *ISS* 131; Girard, *Sacrifice*, 81.

[51] Wolfgang Palaver, "A Girardian Reading of Schmitt's Political Theology," 56; Wolfgang Palaver, "Europe and Enmity," 281.

a neutral ground where violence is nowhere to be seen."[52] To abandon violence incurs possibly suffering it. "There is the sacrifice of the other, and self-sacrifice; archaic sacrifice and Christian sacrifice. However, it is all sacrifice ... absolute knowledge is not possible."[53] That is, the inescapability of sacrifice coincides with the unavailability of absolute, non-mythic reason.

For Girard, Christ's "sacrifice" – dramatized in his cross and resurrection – is not so much an escape from, or an attack on, the myths of the archaic sacred. Nor is it a mere repetitive analogue of archaic dying and rising myths. It rather reveals the mythic misapprehension of the sacred from within it, through similarity-amidst-radical-difference. The violence contained in the sacred is both prefiguration and antithesis of Christ's sacrifice. God in Christ "reuses the scapegoat mechanism, at his own expense, in order to subvert it." The irony is that we are dealing here with two radically opposed relationships to violence while they are yet called the same name. They both go by the name sacrifice, yet they "exhibit odd mirror effects in relation to violence." One of which would rather be sacrificed than sacrifice the other; it is rooted in a pacific "love that surpasses our understanding and our powers of expression." The other mode is a preparedness to sacrifice the other, rooted in fear. Christ's love, taking the position of the victim, refusing to violate the evildoer, and forgiving even his torturers, reveals to us that, in all sacrificial cultures and his own sacrifice, we find "two radically opposed yet formally similar modes of divinity."[54] On this point, Girard aligns with his Jesuit interlocutor, Raymund Schwager, who saw the theological consequences of mimetic theory's suggesting the gods stemmed from scapegoats. If the sacred is homologous with humanity's misapprehension of its own violence, Schwager concludes "the true God" will be revealed most fully precisely where such "violence also is most decisively contrasted to him ... as a person where this mechanism is most radically unmasked."[55]

Here we see why the "separation" of divinity from scapegoating is symbolized precisely through the "unity" of divinity with the scapegoat. The "opposition" to sacrifice emanates from the sacrificed. Thus, for Girard, Christianity's using the same word "sacrifice" for formally similar

---

[52] *TOB* 43, emphasis added.

[53] *BE* 35; *TOB* 71f: "Everything is summed up in this idea .... There is no way out from sacrifice. There is no purely objective knowledge."

[54] *TOB* 43f.

[55] Schwager, *Must There Be Scapegoats?*, 134.

but substantially opposed realities "paradoxically hints at going beyond the opposition between them."[56] As such, the sacrifice of Christ involves simultaneous continuity and yet a break with the sacred. This complex interplay involves the attempt to dispel violence; and yet it does not speak from the position of the neutral, objective observer who simply condemns violence, "as if we were by nature strangers to violence."[57] Such a direct condemnation or attack on violence does not reveal but repeat it. That is, we must not merely *abolish* swords but redeploy them as plowshares. We saw an example of this in ancient Israel, in how political zeal could be turned into a critical revelation against political absolutism. We must imagine how the sword could become the medium of the revelation against the sword, how Christ's lynching becomes the salvific medium of the deactivation of the scapegoat mechanism.

This mythospeculative approach led Girard to abandon the apologetic search for a "symbolically manifest difference" between biblical revelation and archaic religion. Instead of finding the revelatory nature of Christianity in sheer discontinuity with primary religious symbols, it is found precisely in its critical reconfiguration of them. This involves not a destruction of myth and sacrifice, or a rivalrous opposition to them, but myth and sacrifice *in reverse*. That is, Christianity bears all the structures of myth, particularly in its murder and rising trope, even while the myth's *content* (victim-guilty, group-innocent) is profoundly inverted. Concerning the resurrection, for example, he drew special attention to this similarity and difference: the fact that Christ is depicted as divine *preceding* the Crucifixion indeed "introduces a radical rupture with the archaic" – for, unlike the common scapegoat mechanism pattern, his divinity is not a dependent *result* of his lynching. But, he added, Christ's resurrection is undoubtedly, symbolically "in complete continuity with all forms of religion that preceded it. The way out of archaic religion comes at this price."[58] While Girard admitted the resurrection may have been some kind of miracle that somehow marks its discontinuity from other religions (in the sense of a "prodigious transgression of natural laws"), what is most consequential to us is its overcoming of the powerful bio-psychological mimetic contagion at the foundation of all human evolution and culture. Or better, we should say that *is* a miracle. For the resurrection enables the disciples "to recognize what they had not

[56] TOB 43.
[57] EC 218.
[58] BTE xv, 126.

recognized before . . . . They acknowledge the guilt of their participation in the violent contagion that murdered their master."[59] I will offer further commentary on the resurrection later in this chapter.

Girard's approach opens a theological method that can be confessional while not avoiding the comparative, naturalistic "history of religions" methods that have done so well to point out Christianity's archaic parallels. It also offers a way of treating the dense reality of "sacrifice" with no pretention to a depoliticized, neutral, objective, non-sacrificial position. This in turn leads to seeing sacrifice as a self-implicating reality for which we must respond, personally and normatively, in a way that neither abets its violence nor escapes it. His approach suggests that attempts to abolish "sacrificial Christianity" on account of its violent history or to redefine sacrifice more pacifically using "gift" concepts, as some theologians are inclined today, too easily takes the position of being a stranger to violence through rhetorical escape.[60] And yet, Christianity is certainly not yet another "sacrificial" religion. Nor is it in the tepid middle. We must imagine both a severe dialectic against, and an analogy with, sacrificial religions.[61]

This interpenetrative approach conceives the transition from primary and secondary religions as indeed revelatory, affirming Mosaic distinction concepts like superior/inferior, true/false, intolerance of falsehood. But it also opens up the possibility of a revelation without antagonistic rivalry, without scapegoating primary religions. There is a nonviolence to this method in that it treats revelation as an "internal subversion rather than external assault."[62] For, an external assault upon "false" archaic religion and its misapprehension of sacrifice would again simply repeat the scapegoating mechanism of expulsion in another mimetic rivalry, another religion. One must rather imagine how to "supersede" sacrifice "while

---

[59] *ISS* 189; Brian Robinette, *Grammars of Resurrection*, 318.

[60] For an overview of literature in this frame, see J. Denny Weaver, *The Nonviolent Atonement*. On constructing a more pacific definition of sacrifice and "cooperation," see Sarah Coakley, *Sacrifice Regained*. She misreads Girard in referring to his position as "mandated violence" (25), or a simplistically "negative theory of sacrifice." She treats "cooperation" as a univocally positive concept without considering how scapegoating, too, is cooperative.

A similar misreading is in Grace Jantzen, "New Creations." She sees Girard as arguing *for* violence and that conflict resolution *requires* scapegoats. Girard "leaves no room for generosity of spirit rather than rivalry and incessant struggle" (285). This misses the virtually pacifist dialectic in Girard's approach (e.g., *BTE* xiv, 63).

[61] For discussion of both discontinuities and continuities, see *TH* 401–2, 445.

[62] Cowdell, *René Girard and Secular Modernity*, 99.

leaving it intact," as Chris Fleming notes.[63] "Indeed, any straightforward 'destruction' of the old system through force – supernatural or otherwise – would have been simply its *continuation*."[64] Attacking archaic religion repeats archaic religion. With this in mind, Jesus' nonviolence is structurally essential to his mission. Nonviolence does not soften the Mosaic distinction. Rather, it suggests the *content*, the *meaning* of the Mosaic distinction concerns the scapegoat and the misapprehension of victimage.

Girard thus reframed the relation between archaic- and Mosaic religions in a way that centers not rivalry but "figural" or "typological" concessions.[65] In such theologies, archaic religions are usually regarded as a prior "shadow" or prefiguration of the eventual revelation of Christ. While such theologies can often take on a tone of monotheistic supremacy, Girard viewed pagan, polytheistic religions as "part of the revelation in a figural sense" and argued that archaic religions served as "a prior moment in a progressive revelation that culminates in Christ."[66] This is a more conciliatory perspective on the exodus from primary to secondary religions, while not abolishing the liberating dialectic of an exodus. It affirms the positive value of archaic religions, which were the "educators of mankind," which helped "lead us out of archaic violence." Contrast this figural approach with, say, Karl Barth, who dialectically opposed the Word to polytheism and false religion. He abhorred the idea that "idolatry is but a somewhat imperfect preparatory stage of the service of the true God."[67] The interpenetrative approach I am instead sketching here suggests we must, in the least, appreciate how idolatry or polytheism contained violence in human evolution, helping us objectify our apprehension of and control over our own violence – even if misunderstood as an exogenous divine agent. (We see resonances in Mendelssohn here, for whom "even idolatrous, superstitious systems often serve as pillars of the social order, the destruction of which would do more harm than good.")[68] Monolatry and henotheism served as the *medium by inversion*

---

[63] Chris Fleming, *René Girard*, 181; Robert Hamerton-Kelly, *Sacred Violence*, 60.

[64] Fleming, *René Girard*, 132.

[65] Girard mentions "figural" interpretation seven times: EC 180–1, 204, 207–9, 255.

[66] Ibid., 216–7. Henri De Lubac similarly noted, "the victorious God takes over and uses to his advantage all that is true [I might add here, "and all that is false"] in the thought and worship that had gone astray. The phase of opposition is succeeded by a phase of absorption" (De Lubac, *The Discovery of God*, 35; 23, 36). For him, then, a truly transcendent God cannot be reduced to dialectic, synthesis, or antithesis – affirmation or negation, integration or contrast.

[67] Clifford Green, *Karl Barth*, 158.

[68] Erlewine, *Monotheism and Tolerance*, 73.

for revelatory monotheism. Likewise in Christianity, it is through the one undergoing the archaic sacred's violence that "God becomes victim in order to free man of the illusion of a violent God, which must be abolished in favor of Christ's knowledge of his Father."[69] Here, the figural notion of archaic religion as shadow involves both analogy and dialectic; they have structurally similar forms/outlines even while their content is virtually opposite. Or, again, the relation is likened to that of a photographic negative and its development into its opposite. This metaphor supplies a sense of "reversal," though without connotations of complete difference or detached opposition. Appreciating this interpenetration helps steer us away from the potential vice of the Mosaic distinction: revelation as rivalry.

Having laid out this nuanced relation between primary and secondary religious symbols, we can apply it in brief reference to some Christological symbols, seeing in them not a regression into cosmotheism but a continuation of Jewish monotheism: trial, crucifixion, resurrection, and land. On each of these topics, I have selected vignettes of Christ from a variety of scholars who may be situated more in a confessional theology (Lohfink, Robinette) or more religious studies– or philosophical approaches (Miller, Agamben, Marcus). But each case, considered through the above method, evokes a revelatory "rethinking of sovereignty" without succumbing to mere politicization or depoliticization.

C. TRIAL: JUDGMENT IN REVERSE

Sovereignty is manifest in decision, in judgment. Similar to the way in which monotheism divided God from the cosmos, Giorgio Agamben's *Pontius Pilate* argues that Christ's trial critically separates two incommensurate forms of authoritative judgment: the worldly and heavenly. He turns especially to Augustine, who was among the earliest writers to have observed a critical feature of the Passion's court proceedings: they conspicuously lack any legal ruling or judgment. It is only after numerous backroom discussions, in the back and forth of indecision, that Pilate finally sits on the ruling bench. This signifies "that the entire preceding debate had not a procedural value but a private one."[70] And in the end

---

[69] *EC* 217; "The archaic, is prophetic of Christ in its own imperfect way" (ibid., 215; Girard, *Sacrifice*, xi).
[70] Giorgio Agamben, *Pilate and Jesus*, 24.

Pilate refuses to judge, limiting himself to "handing over."[71] But a trial without a judgment is not properly a trial. Augustine saw how this representation of a judicial hoax implicated Pilate and the courts in what was really a crime under mob pressure.[72]

This comports with Girard's reading of the Passion, that its distinctive point is not that it represents God harmoniously working through the execution of law – for the sake of delivering him up to the divinity requiring an ultimate sacrifice. Nor is it distinctive in representing a victimization through a coalition of worldly powers, which is a trope continuous with the ancient world, at the root of all mythology. Rather, its distinction is in representing law's unjust snowballing through unconscious mimetic rivalry. Unlike narratives that bind groups in unanimous submission to the coalition's verdict, the distinguishing element is in its denouncing the verdict as "a total mistake" and a "perfect example of nontruth." For in the representing of persecution from the view of the victim, it provokes a "crisis" "in every representation of persecution from the standpoint of the persecutor."[73] And it is in the continued representation of this total mistake, throughout its reception history, that Christ makes "sacrifice unworkable, at least in the long run, bringing sacrificial culture to an end."[74]

Agamben confirms this in writing that the trial under Pilate, by its ignominy and failure of judgment, is "the most severe objection that can be raised against the juridical order."[75] In the Passion we see not so much a condemnation as a murder, unveiling that the foundation of law is not cool reason but mimetic ochlocracy, the state of exception from which the mob generates law. (This clarifies the meaning of Christ revealing a justice outside the law, per Rom 3:21.) Rather than representing a harmonious partnership between human and divine administrations, we see that between Christ and Pilate, the human and the divine kingdoms, the temporal and the eternal stand in inconclusive confrontation.[76] By insisting upon the incompatibility of these judgments, the Passion iterates a monotheistic division between the two: thus, "every possibility of a Christian political theology or of a theological justification of profane

---

[71] Ibid., 37, 47; Mt 27:26; Mk 15:15; Jn 19:16.
[72] Ibid., 48–9.
[73] Girard, *Sacrifice*, 114f.
[74] GR 18.
[75] Agamben, *Pilate and Jesus*, 51.
[76] Ibid., 14, 37.

power turns out to fail."[77] Akin to Girard's notion of the Passion damaging sacrifice's legitimacy and workability, Agamben sees that it has rendered "unfathomable" any final compatibility between the heavenly and earthly judgments, leaving us to constant undecidability. (In some pluralism discourse "undecidability," per Connelly, connotes how the realm of "criminal responsibility is now recognized to be one in which a subterranean injustice seeps into the practice of justice."[78] Or, in Mouffe's idiom, we begin to face how "conflicting points of view are confronted without any possibility of a final reconciliation.")[79]

This critical, eschatological separation of worldly from heavenly judgment has often been lost in the Christian tradition. Pascal and Dante are, for Agamben, popular examples of having missed this separation – although Eusebius' attempts to construe Christ and the empire as compatible is another striking example. Dante imagined that Christ, coming amidst the Roman Empire, supplied the providential context for suffering a proper judgment of a lawful earthly judge.[80] Therein the "lawfulness of the whole Roman Empire" is symbolically levied against Christ in compatible alliance with, or in analogy to, the heavenly will.[81] Jesus' registration under Caesar's census symbolically sanctioned his Passion with the "seal of the law."[82] So too for Pascal, "Jesus Christ did not want to be killed without the forms of justice, because it is much more ignominious to die justly than through an unjust sedition."[83] By this logic, with Pilate as the earthly executor of divine justice, and the legitimacy of mission assured, Christ would then not want to escape the trial.[84] Adhering to this myth of being "justly" and legally killed is also why Martin Luther regarded Pilate's wife's dream – which suggested something was wrong with killing the evidently innocent Jesus – as a demonic interruption.[85]

According to the logic of Eusebius, Dante, Luther, and Pascal, Pontius Pilate directly administered God's sovereign judgment. They understand the ignominy of the cross but not the incompatibility of divine and human judgment. They understand a transcendent God who can "ordain

---

[77] Ibid., 57.
[78] Connelly, *Why I am Not a Secularist*, 122.
[79] AG 92.
[80] Agamben, *Pilate and Jesus*, 38.
[81] Ibid., 39.
[82] Ibid., 56.
[83] Pascal, *Pensées*, §790.
[84] Agamben, *Pilate and Jesus*, 31.
[85] Ibid., 30.

governing authorities" (Rom 13); but most of them seem to inadequately grasp how God providentially uses these authorities despite their godlessness, error, and evil. They understand some notion of salvation "through" the cross; but they do not grasp how this through-ness is also its against-ness, its opposite: exposing the cross's mistake and injustice. We must see the dialectic amidst this seeming continuity: Pilate's sword is beaten into a plowshare by Christ's weak power. It is not Pilate's judgment, as some sign of righteous law, but the unveiling of its ochlocracy that is salvific. Salvation in the Gospels does not mean a legal death according to the forms of justice.[86] Such atonement theory misses what Augustine saw – this is not a just and valid judgment but precisely a representation of the world's falsity and incommensurability with divine judgment. The crowd's delusional judgment to "crucify him" – thinking they were doing God a favor (Jn 16:12; 1 Cor 2:8) – is the photographic negative of God suffering crucifixion. We see odd mirror effects between Pilate as judge and Christ as a king and sovereign "judge": the word is an analogy dialectically opposed.

Christ's trial unveils a different kind of "royal judgment." This is not a rivalrous *attack* on Pilate's judgment and law – nor a replacement of it, a fulfillment of it, or even its alternative. Nor is it in an apolitical escape from judgment. Standing before Pilate, his is a silent-judgment from the position of the judged; it is judgment in reverse, incompatible with the world's judgment. But this incompatibility does not utter the depoliticized "my kingdom is not *in* this world" – but rather that it is not *of* this world. This "king" speaks a language the political cannot speak; for it speaks through its being expelled by the political. Instead of rendering a new judgment, Christ's judgment unsettles all judgment.[87] It is fitting, then, that Agamben concludes "the radical critique of every judgment is an essential part of Jesus' teaching."[88] Such radical critique is evidenced, of course, in the command, "judge not." Here Christ critiques criticism, questioning how we point out the speck in another's eye, when we have a log in our own (Mt 7). Paul similarly judged judgment, noting how, in our passing judgment on others, we condemn ourselves (Rom 2). We also find this in the peculiar "judgment" in the parable of the Sheep and Goats. There, as a "king" seated upon his glorious throne, the true judge renders a verdict, not from on high but from below, as the Son of Man. There,

---

[86] Ibid., 51.
[87] See also Rowan Williams, *Christ on Trial*.
[88] Agamben, *Pilate and Jesus*, 37.

judgment speaks through the mouth of marginalized victims or the judged ones. This is the unsettlement of all judgment in that one can never determine one's relation to this victim: not only did the goats not understand their neglect of the divine victim, but even the sheep did not understand their relation to him.[89]

This kind of "judgment" is not a linear escape from critique or a movement beyond judgment – in some depoliticized transcending of the violence of the political. His agonism fervently critiqued the world with great political consequence: denouncing the principalities and oppressive religious hypocrites, freely healing in violation of sacred boundaries, cleansing the temple of its Mammon, etc. This critique has historically spread, as Girard notes, in our increasingly critiquing worldly power from the perspective of the victim. But as dangerous as this critical spirit can become, he adds, we should not do away with that intolerance. Rather, we must grasp the paradox of how critique works and thereby "purify" it with nonviolence. The paradox is that critique offers no escape from critique; indeed "critique embodies part of the same violence – it is always in the same circle of violence." That is, we must see the mimetic "*circularity*" of the psychic space in which we live. We must critique; but that critique remains susceptible to critique – a critique that also remains open to critique, and so on. By contrast, we wrongly intuit judgment as linear – paradigmatic in the judgment that decides upon the expulsion of wicked. Such a logic fails to see our mimetic situation, our inextricably interdividual nature: such judgment "always wants to turn the other into something that would be *solidly posed*, there in front of you and separate from you, because you are good and they are bad. And in a judicial affair, you have a physical separation between the two." But, stemming from Christ's judgment, "*Christianity is constantly abolishing this separation.*"[90] Akin to Mouffe's agonistic pluralism, we are afforded no escape into an objective perspective from which to definitively found and stabilize a social order. This demands of us, yes, a certain pluralism; but it is not one of mere inclusivity-beyond-judgment but rather ever-open, agonistic, forbearing critique.

One is reminded of the Nazi defector, Franz Jäggerstätter, whose trial is dramatized in the film *A Hidden Life*. His dominant response to

---

[89] Another line of inquiry concerns the similarities and difference here between the parable with Gautama Buddha's dictum that, "whoever tends a sick person, as it were, tends me" (*Mahavagga*, VIII, 26).

[90] René Girard, "Interview with David Cayley," 12:00ff, emphasis added.

interrogation is silence, partly because "reasoning" with Nazis is a fool's game, but also because he seems to understand these circular, mimetic dynamics of judgment. Franz is asked twice, by different Nazi interrogators, "do you judge me?" Franz responds, "I can't look into another man's heart. I judge no one"; and at another time, "I don't judge you and say, 'he is wicked, I am right.' I don't know everything." This is spoken not from the position of a "moderate" bystander, uttered in tepid agnosticism that refrains from being divisive. Rather, his "not knowing everything" is an assertive apophatic *intolerance*, the dangerous exertion of refusing fascism. His courageous, pacific love, his refusal to join the othering, even his refusal to judge, makes him manifest to his persecutors as a critic, a judge, as othering – when he is in fact reversing the othering.

D. THE CROSS: CORONATION IN REVERSE

Freud argued that the experience of a group murder of an alpha male helped catalyze the emergence of monotheism – which was ultimately the return of the repressed mode of alpha-dominance that had structured prehuman species for perhaps millions of years. For the Jews, this return was manifested, first, in the experience of Akhenaten's paternal despotism and its rejection by the people. Then it was echoed in the (speculated) murder of Moses, which Jews repressed through the guilt-fantasy of a returning messiah, resurfaced in Christ's crucifixion. But I noted how Freud, in his speaking more from a position of enlightened anti-mythic anti-ritualism, judged Christianity as a regression into polytheism, in its sacrificial "fantasy of expiation." But one finds much more irony, critique, and reversal in the cross that seems to have evaded Freud. Not only do the gospels suggest something almost anti-expiatory in the cross, as noted above in the representation of an unjust trial. But they also represent an inversion of archaic kingship through ironically portraying the Passion – as I will show – in the very form of a powerful monarch's glorious coronation. Freud did not fully "get the joke," the serious joke, of the gospels. We can affirm Freud's insight, that in Christ there is indeed a resurfacing of a primal human experience of violence and dominance. But, insofar as the Passion captures, inverts, and redirects our sense of praise, glory, and sovereignty – through oddly representing the humiliated through the forms of the exalted – this suggests not a regression into polytheism. Rather, through its analogies to polytheistic kingship, the cross expresses its monotheistic dialectic break with it.

It is a familiar, if mysterious, acclamation that Christ the king is "crowned with glory and honor," much as one would speak, in the ancient world, of a king being crowned in glorious ceremony or a triumphal procession. But one cannot emphasize enough how this "coronation," for the New Testament writers, is revealed precisely through his humiliation.[91] For example, as Joel Marcus notes, Jesus is never called "king" in the book of Mark until his trial and suffering, after which come six such accolades.[92] More intriguingly, Mark superimposes the extravagant Roman ritual of gloriously parading and crowning Caesar onto his rendition of Jesus' execution.[93] The Roman, Caesarian triumph rituals of Mark's day involved several parts: the gathering of the full Praetorian Guard, group acclamation, putting on him a purple robe and crown, giving him Jupiter's scepter, and processing to the Capitoleum ("head hill") with a slave carrying the sacrificial ax along with the bull (or perhaps slaves) to be sacrificed. The final part of the coronation, with authorities to his left and right, was to offer the triumphant one wine – who rejects it – and then slaughter the bull in identification with, or substitution for, Caesar.[94] This is perhaps followed by a natural sign, like a well-timed eclipse, releasing of doves, etc. Mark's Passion adapts the sequence of such political pomp with striking detail – all the way down to the unlikely gathering of the whole company of soldiers; the robe, crown, and scepter; mock acclamation; Golgotha as skull hill; a helper carrying the instrument of torture; the offering and rejection of wine; the co-crucified at Jesus' right and left; and divine wonders of darkened sky and torn curtain.[95]

We may be inclined to see Mark as derivative while Caesar's ritual is the "original," much as crimes are often punished in parody to their offense. For example, when the criminal Carabas was executed for insurrection, his torture parodied kingship: "young men carrying rods on their shoulders as spearmen stood on either side of him in imitation of a bodyguard."[96] Dio Chrysostom also spoke of this kind of crime-

---

[91] E.g., Heb 2:9; Col 2:15; 2 Cor 2:14.
[92] Joel Marcus, "Crucifixion As Parodic Exaltation," 73–4. While the other gospels don't precisely follow the same form, Marcus argues they still preserve this basic ethos.
[93] Thomas Schmidt, "Jesus' Triumphal March to Crucifixion," 30; N. T. Wright, "Upstaging the Emperor."
[94] Such coronation-sacrifices are, per Girard, arguably rooted in the immolation of the king himself, later replaced with an animal (VS 106).
[95] Douglas R. A. Hare, Matthew, 320; cf. Mk 10:35–40.
[96] Philo, Flacc., 38; Marcus, "Parodic Exaltation," 75.

punishment parody, wherein prisoners were, for a short time, sat upon the king's throne, donned with royal clothing, allowed to dictate "orders" and royally luxuriate. But after that they were stripped naked, beaten, and hanged.[97] Insurrectionists, in parody of their rivalry with the king, were often "exalted" on impalement poles or seated on a "throne."[98] Such meanings evidently emanated from crosses (and their little seat-"thrones") in Jesus' day.[99]

But Mark's account is not merely about a punishment parodying its crime. Jesus is indeed seated on a throne, presumably in parody of his perceived danger to the stability of Pilate and Herod's joint thrones, ultimately Caesar's throne. But with Mark we have a parodying of parody. Surely the historical Jesus did not undergo this exact ritual sequence of Caesarian coronation. What is striking is that Mark would superimpose an apparent mob-fueled abortion of justice onto the most respected, powerful ritual of monarchy in the world, while the mob is revealed as "not knowing what they are doing," in a spiral of cowardice and antagonism toward the innocent one. Caesar's ritual may have come first in the order of cultural production, but concerning the primal forces behind political power in human evolution, namely, mimetic ridicule and scapegoating, Mark's Passion evokes the original. Seen in this light, ridicule of the scapegoat came first, while Caesar's coronation is derivative. Political glory is a mere by-product of ridicule. In human evolution, mimetic mocking precedes and gives birth to worship.[100] We naturally worship falsely; the entire political realm knows not what it does.

Mark's literary Christ may be "imitating" the Caesarian ritual; but anthropologically, the Caesarian ritual and the mirage of glory is nothing more than an unwitting imitation of the scapegoating process. This is why Girard can say Christ's revelation holds up a mirror-like reversal and that "violence now imitates the love of Christ."[101] This is the anthropological rationale to the theological rhetoric about Christ "turning sacrifice on its head." If there is a paradox in the cross, it is not from a misty-eyed contrarianism about the weak somehow being strong; for there is

---

[97] Marcus, "Parodic Exaltation," 85.

[98] Ibid., 73; John Granger Cook, *Crucifixion in the Mediterranean World*; D. W. Chapman, *Ancient Jewish and Christian Perspectives of Crucifixion*.

[99] Marcus, "Parodic Exaltation," 84.

[100] In terms of the "order of discovery," James Alison points to Christ's gratuitous self-giving as logically but not *chronologically* prior to mimesis embedded in the scapegoat mechanism (Alison, *The Joy of Being Wrong*, 44, 61, 102, 174, 203, 300).

[101] *TOB* 43f.

"nothing here that is contrary to reason," as Girard writes. Instead, "the paradox of the Cross is that it reproduces the archaic structure of sacrifice in order to stand it on its head. But this inversion is a matter of putting right side up what had been wrong side up since the beginning of the world."[102]

This account of the Cross reveals that what we take as rational, natural, and original – monarchy, authority, political power, coronation, or even civilization itself – are in fact "wrong side up," misperceived and derivative. What we regard as self-evident and valid power is in fact a by-product of the sacrificial mechanism. This is why when Christians applied proto-Isaiah's oracles to the crucified Christ, which proclaimed the glorious dominion of a Davidic heir and his coronation,[103] they were not being merely resentful of the powerful. They were penetrating the illusion of power. For even underneath the glorious Davidic coronation and throne lie the misapprehended mimetic mechanism – which becomes apprehended through clearly representing it. In Samuel, we will recall how Israel's tribes riotously pushed to install a monarch. The biblical author saw this mob misapprehension as the same thing as rejecting God as their king (1 Sam 8:7, 12:12). Crying out "we must have a king reigning over us" is of the same spirit as the lynch mob crying out, "we have no king but Caesar!" (Jn 19:15). Idolatrous rejection of God's reign through the coronation of a monarch is homologous with the lynching of Christ.

The claim "the rulers of this world lord it over, but not so for my kingdom" is not simply a dialectic protest against the world, an ethical denunciation. It is an ontological claim on the nature of politics, desire, and human organization. It shows that what we call "normal" should really be called "average"; we must divide what "is" from what ought to be, denaturalizing the given powers. This is "rethinking sovereignty." Unlike the ancient pseudo-separation of religion and politics – with the sovereign as powerful but unclean and the priest as weak but clean – the cross makes for a striking collision. Christ crucified is the weak sovereign and unclean priest. He is the first among the despised, "the garbage of the world"; in so choosing, the weak and foolish shame the strong and powerful, God chose the "the things that are not to nullify the things that

---

[102] Ibid., 63.
[103] Isaiah 7–9 and 11 all contain oracles traceable to the coronation or the anniversary of the installation of a Davidic king of Judah, possibly Hezekiah (Richard Clifford, "The Major Prophets, Baruch, and Lamentations," 286).

are" (1 Cor 1:27; 4:13). This is, as historian Burton Mack writes, a radical violation of the ways that ancient temple-states separated purity and power and represented sovereignty.[104]

In light of this revelatory payload, the Mosaic distinction between true and false religion is not irrational. There is rationality in Christianity's apparent rhetorical excess – when it denounces the "falsehood" of not just other gods but of the entire civilized order and every power and authority.[105] For the cross, in this sense, supplies the Mosaic distinction with specific criteria of what exactly is "false": a world founded on scapegoating, knowing not what it does, not even knowing what it is doing when it is praising and glorifying its Caesar. But what is essential to the cross as such a revelatory "truth" is not that it speaks as the new rivalry, to scapegoat the scapegoaters, nor does it speak as one who has escaped claims of exclusivity through universality, who is foreign to violence. Rather this voice of truth speaks through a particular excluded one, the mouth of the forgiving scapegoat. He is not seeking vengeance, with blood calling out from the ground as Abel's did; his blood calls out from the ground "a better word" (Heb 12:24), speaking "fear not" and forgiving those who denied him. It is only in this context of a merciful revelation of scapegoating "from within," wherein a divine grace that transcends scapegoating is *also* revealed, that Christianity can refrain from an antagonistic reception of the Mosaic distinction. Per Girard, the Passion is a revelation of the false sacred that constructs the mirage of kingship. Such an antagonistic energy, in time, became forgetfully morphed into monarchic legitimacy, power, and authority, which Mark identifies in Caesar's pomp. But Marcus suggests early Christians would have clearly understood the Passion as a "reversal of reversal," a "negation of negation" – turning penal mockery on its head – thereby revealing "true royalty" in contrast with reigning royalty.[106]

In the passion's "exaltation" of a glorious Lord, we don't have a cosmotheism of divinity appeased in expiation or a polity founded on a justified exclusion. Nor, crucially, do Pilate, Herod, or Judas, as parties to the violence, become anti-types for retribution or cultic immolation, like

[104] Mack, *The Christian Myth*, 143.
[105] E.g., Christ, unlike those blinded by the god of this age (2 Cor 4:4), brought light into the world (Lk 1:78f), drove out the prince of this world, destroying evil spirits (Jn 12:31–3; Heb 2:14), disarmed and triumphed over the powers and authorities and will ultimately destroy them (Col 2:15; 1 Cor 15:24), is the name above every name (Phil 2), and unveiled what has been hidden since the foundation of the world (Mt 13:35).
[106] Marcus, "Parodic Exaltation," 87.

Egypt's Seth. (Although to the extent that Christians have anti-Semitically singled out Jews as uniquely guilty of deicide, this serves to reiterate the cosmotheistic Seth cycle.) Rather, we have an unsettling penetration of the mechanics of how rivalrous, unthinking derision is the operation, not the corruption, of the political. In the Passion we have again a similar-yet-discontinuous play between the archaic and the revelatory, the old and new: "mockery is reversed and the derided victim demands to be taken seriously."[107] In the *ecce homo* of the scapegoat king, the humiliated is exalted, inviting us down into humanity's repressed crypt, the foundation of human culture and consciousness itself.

E. RESURRECTION: SOVEREIGNTY IN REVERSE

Many historical-critical analyses of Christianity, at least since James Frazer's *Golden Bough* (1890), have long emphasized how Christ's resurrection is continuous with paganism, dismissing its claims to uniqueness through demonstrating its numerous mythic parallels. And, once we come to grips with these analogues, we will come to regard belief in Christ to be as arbitrary, banal, and superstitious as we now regard belief in Osiris, Dionysius, or Adonis. Christian apologists – taking these as terms of rivalry – have tended to defensively respond by emphasizing the resurrection's unequivocal discontinuity, isolating the resurrection as sui generis, unlike any other dying and rising gods. This defense can often involve arguing that his resurrection and appearances could not have been a hoax, myth, or delusion but instead an utterly unique "miracle which justifies belief."[108] Interestingly, however, New Testament scholar Richard Miller argues that early Christian theologians never seem to have bothered to conceal how Jesus' resurrection resembled other rising and translated gods in that day.[109] Rather, the similarity of Christ's resurrection was evidently granted while *also* emphasizing its difference.[110] The

---

[107] Ibid., 87; James C. Scott, "A Saturnalia of Power," 202–27.

[108] See, e.g., N. T. Wright, *The Resurrection of the Son of God*; Robinette, *Grammars of Resurrection*, 18.

[109] Miller argues Justin Martyr, Origen, Celsus, Tertullian, Theophilus, and Arnobius all "classed the postmortem accounts of Jesus under the larger 'translation fable' rubric" (Miller, *Resurrection and Reception*, 5, 10, 179, 196 n87).

[110] Ibid., 8, 158, 181. E.g., Athenagoras' *De resurrectione mortuorum* and Tertullian's *De resurrectione carnis* do not attempt historical proof. See also Edward Schillebeeckx, *Jesus*, 354.

meaning of that difference amidst similarity is precisely what is of interest here.

In something of a continuation of the Church fathers, Girard's method clarifies the meaning of this difference. This meaning concerns the mimetic misapprehension of victimage and the unconditionality of a divine love that forgives and transforms it. Girard comes to this view not only by embracing the resurrection's similarities with the archaic sacred but in Christ's achieving a revelatory difference *through* them. Again, Girard sees not a total negation of myth but again a simultaneous "discontinuity and continuity between the Passion and archaic religion. Christ's divinity, which precedes the Crucifixion, introduces a radical rupture with the archaic, but Christ's resurrection is in complete continuity with all forms of religion that preceded it."[111] But, in asserting this continuity, Girard in fact did not elaborate much on how Christ's resurrection referenced the political theology of antiquity. If we briefly consider the resurrection in this context, it shows how that the resurrection's resemblance to archaic political symbols supplied the medium for a critical rethinking of them. As such, it birthed a unique form of life that Miller calls "transcendent rivalry."

Kings and heroes of the ancient Mediterranean were often exalted, upon death, to the divine realm in what are referred to as a "translation" or an "apotheosis." These legends often served to mythologically sediment a dynasty and ensure that a king's reign would continue after his lifetime. Plutarch, for example, noted how it was only natural, reasonable, and just that the "virtues and souls" of great men not be merely sent to a mortal's heaven but be "translated" from "being men to being heroes, and from being heroes to being demigods, and ... having escaped mortality, from being demigods to being gods."[112] Such heavenly translations were not necessarily to be taken literally, as Cicero insisted;[113] but they were certainly taken very *seriously*, as honorific, structuring the very common sense and mental framework of society. In cases where a tomb was empty, it could serve as a monument to the dead king and validate the successors' claims to the throne.[114] We can thus understand why Alexander the Great planned for the disappearance of his body after

---

[111] *BTE* xv, 126.

[112] Miller, *Resurrection and Reception*, 110; Plutarch, *Vita Romuli*, 28.8; Cicero, *De natura deorum*, 2.24.

[113] Miller, *Resurrection and Reception*, 111.

[114] Ibid., 38.

death (to sustain his legacy as a son of Ammon-Zeus), or why Heraclides Ponticus conspired to have his tomb emptied (as a sign of his transcendent glory), or that an empty coffin was politically honorific in King Numa's mythology, or that the myth of Heracles' missing bones were the analogue for the missing remains of a sovereign.[115]

Classical scholarship supplies dozens of other examples of apotheosis, translation, or a resurrected divine hero, revealing the kind of semiotic atmosphere the gospels lived in and potentially accessed. I will point out only a dozen from Miller's work (though we could just as well apply my hermeneutic to other studies). It is not necessary for us here to show the gospels as directly dependent upon these texts, much less that the gospels share their meaning. Rather, Christianity's similarities with the translation/apotheosis mythos mediates its difference from them – namely, an inverted reconfiguration of symbols of sovereignty and glory, redirected toward the humiliated, forgiving scapegoat:

(1) Plutarch and Livy's disappearance and translation myths of Romulus and Remus (the killed and/or disappeared founders of Rome), served as the basis of the funerary consecration of the *principes Romani* and annual rituals of fleeing in fear from his disappeared body.[116] The gospels (and Acts) share similar structures with the Romulus mythos in themes ranging from a missing body, darkness over the land, divine sonship, ascension in a cloud, meeting on the road, a heavenly body, dubious alternate accounts, people fleeing, deification, bright/shining appearances.[117]

(2) Herodotus wrote of a hero-poet, Aristeas, who was translated into heaven after his death, only to return much later, bidding the people to erect an honorary statue of him next to the altar of Apollo – and vanish. He encounters a man traveling along a road, but disappears, leaving the man to report the encounter.[118]

---

[115] Ibid., 41, 54, 56, 165; Plutarch, *Num*, 22.1–5; Arrian, *Anab.*, 7.27.3; Chariton, *Chaereas and Callirhoe*, 3.3.1–7; Diogenes Laërtius, 5.89–91.

[116] Miller, *Resurrection and Reception*, 14, 16; Plutarch, *Vita Romuli*, 27.3–28.6.

[117] Miller, *Resurrection and Reception*, 174. Arnobius of Sicca's *Adversus nationes* (c.300 CE) views the postmortem ascension of Romulus "as analogical, indeed, by precedence, archetypical to the tradition." A vanished body in the Heraclean tradition and the fleeing suggest archetypal relation to the annual, imperial festival of Romulus (July 7) and the reenactment of flight *Poplifugia* (July 5). Miller, *Resurrection and Reception*, 169 n67; Dionysius of Halicarnassus, *Ant rom.*, 2.56.5; Plutarch, *Rom*, 27.7.

[118] Miller, *Resurrection and Reception*, 31.

Between this (and the Romulean structure), one finds resemblances in Paul's Damascus road conversion and the road to Emmaus.[119]

(3) Matthew's birth narrative appears to adapt the mythological signs surrounding the birth of Alexander the Great – a myth that also served as basis for the Suetonian divinization of Augustus.[120]

(4) Mark's temple incident resembles the climactic cleansing of the House of Odysseus at Ithaca.

(5) Brutus' betrayal of Caesar is echoed in the gospels' "men armed with swords and clubs."[121]

(6) Jesus' mockery as king invoked "the ascetic themes of Heracles's labors and tragic death, the archetypal king," and the ascetic certitude of the misunderstood Socrates.[122]

(7) The provision of asylum to foreigners was a hallmark of the Roman emperor, echoed in Matthew's "many will come from the East and West."[123]

(8) Roman representations of power often invoked the vogue orientalism in the first century, reaching east for symbols. Does the Christian resurrection, in its own exaltation of its sovereign, draw upon the Persian theme of resurrection of the dead?[124]

(9) "The jeering reception of the incognito king of Gospel portrayal mimetically drew upon the most famous of all ancient tales, that of the returning king of Ithaca, Odysseus, once having been divinely transformed into a doddering vagrant."[125]

(10) Matthew's Great Commission resembles Julius Proculus' great commission.[126]

(11) Thomas salutes his monarch ("My Lord, my God," Jn 20:28) with the formulaic address reserved for Domitian himself.[127]

(12) Ancient divine heroes like Heracles, Empedocles, Asclepius, and Apollonius all "famously exhibited the power to raise the dead."[128]

---

[119] Ibid., 173–5.
[120] Ibid., 125–7; Plutarch, *Alexander*, 2.1–4, 3.3; Mt 1.1–25.
[121] Miller, *Resurrection and Reception*, 133, 135.
[122] Ibid., 136. For John's Gospel as *imitatio Socratis* (ibid., 162).
[123] Ibid., 153.
[124] Ibid., 155.
[125] Ibid., 163, 168.
[126] Ibid., 170
[127] Ibid.,167; Suetonius, *Dom*, 13.2.
[128] Miller, *Resurrection and Reception*, 159.

+++

The more similar Christ appears to these divinized emperors or heroes, however, the more his difference from them is pronounced. The difference is not just by species but by *genus*. Christ is not here in competitive antagonism with Rome's throne of glory – as if attempting to replace Caesar in a coup. And yet insofar as the risen Christ is exalted within the imperial cultural-linguistic grid, the more he is entirely outside it: for around this time the inducting of a god into the imperial pantheon was not an open affair but a restricted, legal prerogative of the Senate.[129] And while the gospels evidently award Jesus "the highest possible rank, even the rank of the glorified king and founder of the empire, divine Romulus," the gospels' resurrection is entirely distinguished from the spirit of, say, the translated Nero, who returns from the dead to destroy the corrupt Roman aristocracy (written around the time of the gospels).[130] Christ is not a harmonious, continuous fulfillment of the empire, its founders, emperors, or heroes, as Eusebius alleged; and even to simply attack or replace them would still mean a fundamental compatibility between them. Instead, the symbols are again critically redeployed in a reversal or inversion. The shock of the Gospels, then, is not that they contain noticeable parallels with imperial, honorific symbols of that time but that they apply them to a ridiculed, humiliated scapegoat. They are distinguished precisely inasmuch as they apply "such supreme cultural exaltation to an indigent Jewish peasant, an individual otherwise marginal and obscure on the grand stage of classical antiquity."[131] If Christianity resembled the imperial myths less than they do, they could not differ from them as much as they do.

We cannot overemphasize Christianity's Jewish roots; Christ's death and resurrection offer us little meaning if not interpreted in the light of and "in accordance with the Scriptures" (1 Cor 15:3–4). The gospels doubtlessly accessed the Jewish semiotic registry when it came to the resurrection – like Hosea 6 (God raising up the community on the third day) or Isaiah 53's Suffering Servant (picked up by Peter 2:22–4). And the Maccabean torture accounts (especially 2 Maccabees 7:14) suggest further Jewish context for his suffering.[132] But many of the apologetic

---

[129] Émilie Tardivel-Schick, "Why Is Christian Citizenship a Paradox?"
[130] Miller, *Resurrection and Reception*, 176.
[131] Ibid., 180.
[132] E.g., Schillebeeckx sees the appearances of Jesus as largely accessing models in Jewish conversion stories (Schillebeeckx, *Jesus*, 329, 527) and the empty tomb is accessing no

defenses of the resurrection – in the interest of emphasizing biblical uniqueness – avoid or downplay any "pagan" parallels, lest they diminish the Mosaic distinction. Instead of such defensiveness, one must admit that even Judaism's roots, by Jesus' day, were also comingled in the Hellenic cultural matrix. Those similarities, too, help us understand what difference Christ evokes, what it means that followers eventually "worshipped" him, especially with respect to the political question that started this chapter. For, as Miller points out, "no form of resurrection in early Jewish tradition called for worship or *cultus* toward the one raised. Translation [apotheosis] alone called for the worship of the one who had been mortal, then made immortal."[133] It is not only the Jewish roots and symbols that clarify the resurrection of Christ's distinguishing qualities but also the cosmotheistic, Hellenic myths. Interpreting Christ only through the Scriptures, with a mind to differentiating him from the Mediterranean's symbolic world, ironically robs us of how his critical difference from that world was mediated through his similarity with it.

To the extent that the myths of Roman origins were referenced in the gospels, Miller writes, they supplied "the scaffolding for the empire's new *transcendent* rival, Christianity."[134] This is a "transcendent" rivalry in that its sovereign reigns from a cross, and he judges from his silent incompatibility with worldly judgment. This subversion is not frontal attack, nor transcendent escapism, nor dialectic rivalry, nor depoliticization. This Christ is a "transcendent king, not a mundane opponent of the political structures of the day."[135] And yet he is not a non-opponent. There is still some mode of rivalry here, if transcendent. It is subversion without sedition. Approaching the resurrection in this way does not so much *abolish* identity, belonging, and allegiance, which would again only create a new rivalrous identity and allegiance. It rather inverts it in an "ascetic critique of mundane civilization which transvalues

---

semiotic registry beyond Jerusalem (336). His thin treatment of Romulus, Chariton, and Philostratus (or the idea of resurrection as solemn enthronement, 531) is a brief but lost opportunity to consider other extra-Jewish models (341–2, 704, 705 n56.). He at least notes how Plutarch's Romulus resembles the Emmaus story, though this seems to him little more than just Luke's way of "dressing it up" (Schillebeeckx, *Jesus*, 342). I concur, however, here: "with the help of models already generally familiar Luke is *contrasting* Jesus, already acknowledged elsewhere as the actual presence of salvation, with the emperor" (Schillebeeckx, *Jesus*, 343, italics added).

[133] Miller *Resurrection and Reception*, 167.

[134] Ibid., 152. On "novel reconfiguration," see Mack, *The Christian Myth*, 108, 115.

[135] Miller, *Resurrection and Reception*, 135; 137 nn88, 90.

the codes and structures of antiquity, turning them on their head."[136] It walks a fine line, soon lost in the Constantinization of Christianity.

This is to say that whatever the resurrection's "historical" experience was, it was inevitably, unobjectionably made linguistically intelligible through the lexical symbols of glory, sovereignty, apotheosis, and divinization. These, when applied to Caesar's throne, commanded no greater allegiance and devotion. This is the "analogy" with the archaic sacred. But the "dialectic" turn comes when these intense symbols of praise, fear, and glory are redeployed in a total inversion: from the exalted to the humbled, from the sovereign to the scapegoat. To the extent that analogy and dialectic here are combined and interpenetrating, we find that theological methods focused only on proving the resurrection's historicity, so as to prove its status beyond any interpretation, in fact *dampen* the scope of its revelatory meaning, leaving its meaning too misty and depoliticized. Such approaches will tend to emphasize the sheer discontinuity of the resurrection, as a sui generis miracle that founds belief. But this does not safeguard its revelatory value. As Brian Robinette argues, defenses of an *only discontinuous* faith become reduced to a mere proposed belief for cognitive assent.[137] They lend themselves to becoming yet another static, competing identity like the former ones. When faith is reduced to this sheer discontinuity, Burton Mack adds, euphemisms like "Easter," Christ's "appearances," and "spirit" are mystically evoked so as to make some final, indisputable claim on the Absolute, miraculously inaccessible to reason. We might call such assertions, with Mouffe, failures to embrace agonism. As Mack observes, such claims do not so much to enlighten as they "mark the point beyond which reasoned argument must cease. They serve as ciphers to hold the space for the unimaginable miracle that must have happened prior to any and all interpretation."[138] In claiming to be beyond interpretation – we should even say "beyond hegemony," unassailable to any reasoned argumentation – these are rhetorical shortcuts toward *asserting* Christian supremacy without demonstrating it. Instead of treating Christian faith with such discontinuity, Girard's approach instead helps "explain" the context, reason, and anthropological valence of the resurrection. He explores and explains *why* one

---

[136] Ibid., 137.
[137] Robinette, *Grammars of Resurrection*, 54. Such methods are evident in N. T. Wright, Wolfhart Pannenberg, and Gerald O'Collins *inter alia*. Stephen Davis, Daniel Kendall S.J., and Gerald O'Collins, eds., *The Resurrection*.
[138] Burton Mack, *Mark and Christian Origins*, 7.

might consider Christ as Truth, with respect to the transcendence of the victim, without "explaining it away." At the same time, this approach resists resorting to a mere fideistic assertion, to having obtained monopoly on the truth.

The resurrection, in being mediated through symbols of the archaic sacred, operates upon humanity at a level deeper than its cognition, penetrating to the level of "scapegoating" – the *desiring* layer of human behavior, where we "know not what we do." Historical, propositional approaches to the resurrection fail to penetrate to this level in their presumption that reason and language operate at the level of absolute knowledge – when in fact they operate as signs. The resurrection of the scapegoat concerns, in Robinette's gloss on Girard, not just a historical proposition for assent but a self-involving experience that prophesies to a blindness in our desires and perception, *anterior* to our cognition.[139] For the scapegoat concerns how our reason, desires, and perception are themselves radically "dimmed by the false transfigurations of mimetic idolatry."[140] Faith in the resurrection thus means not mere assent to a historical proposition so much as being exposed to a new self-involving way to perceive, a new grammar of reality.[141] Robinette thus suggests "resurrection" is a delimited signifier for an event greater than the word and all its cultural analogues can supply. But this "greater" does not imply a vague fideism that depoliticizes and empties the resurrection of meaning and value. Rather, the more the resurrection of the scapegoat is mediated through the most glorious symbols available, the more it doubly reveals divine gratuity and human blindness. For the resurrection locates Christ's identity not in a defined, monolithic singularity of the divine despot but disseminates it, uncomfortably, infinitely into the persecuted (again, evoked in the parable of sheep and goats). This is a revelation of hiddenness. Thus, Saul is struck with blinding light, that he is persecuting the resurrected Christ in his many hidden guises without knowing it: "why do you persecute me?"[142]

I see harmony here in Assmann's reading of the ban on images: the "intolerance" expressed in this prohibition is not a "'religious arrogation of political power,' but quite the opposite, a blocking of such

---

[139] Robinette, *Grammars of Resurrection*, 291, 296.
[140] Robinette, *Grammars of Resurrection*, 291; Girard, *A Theatre of Envy*, 342.
[141] Robinette, *Grammars of Resurrection*, 56.
[142] Lk 24:36, 47; Jn 20:21–3, 26; Acts 9:4.

arrogation."[143] The resurrection and exaltation of the forgiving scapegoat is not about the arrogation of power but it undermines "every pretense to authority and possessiveness …. It prevents a single image, such would be idolatry."[144] In the scapegoated-and-resurrected sovereign we see not the establishment of a new Roman imperial legend but the undermining of every hold on the Absolute. What does it mean when the Pantocrator is recessive and weak, hidden in our scapegoats? It is sovereignty in reverse. As I will note in Chapter 8, we see here not an imperial monotheism but an apophatic negation that wisely prepares us for the challenges of pluralism.

F. THE LAND AS THE BODY OF A VICTIM: PAGANISM IN REVERSE

We have thus briefly explored how Christ's trial, crucifixion, and resurrection entail a similarity and a separation, both analogy and dialectic with ancient symbols of sovereignty. A final crucial symbol for this chapter is that of land. In Egypt, we explored land in archaic political theology as the slain body of the God. We showed how numerous archaic states and tribes have represented their society, their land, and the cosmos itself as composed in the body of a victim. Much like cosmogonic myths, where the cosmos is made through the body of a victim, Christianity too proclaimed that all things had been created through Christ (Jn 1:3; Col 1:16). But, consonant with our hermeneutic thus far, Christianity is not a repetition of the victimage symbol of land but its reconfiguration.

No theologian so explicitly connects the New Testament's concept of land and victimage as Gerhard Lohfink. His connecting land and Christ's victimage confirms, in one sense, the theme we saw in Egypt – the land as the slain body of Osiris – but with considerable discontinuity as well. The discontinuity is, partly, in the world being "made through Christ," prior to and independent of his crucifixion: his innocence proceeds his lynching, and the world is not an outcome of his killing, unlike the array of cosmogonic myths. Furthermore, as Lohfink shows, the New Testament co-identifies Christ with "the land" in such a way that departs from such myths, even seemingly departing from Judaism. On many points, Christianity differs little in content from its Jewish parent: love of

---

[143] *PM* 131; Albertz, "Monotheism and Violence," 386.
[144] Robinette, *Grammars of Resurrection*, 92, 110.

neighbor, love of enemy, forgiveness, atonement, discipleship, grace-alone salvation, Gentile-inclusion, mercy overcoming wrath, opposition to ritualism, or the individual over false-collectivism: these were all themes available to the Judaism of Jesus' time.[145] Lohfink argues it is only on the issue of *land* that Christianity really offers anything new compared with the "Old" Testament. Whereas Moses did not bring his people into the Promised Land, the New Testament depicts Jesus as indeed doing so. And yet he brings his people into *a redefined* Promised Land, his Body.

The official arrangement of the books of the Tanakh end not in the minor prophets but the books of Chronicles. Its last words follow Cyrus' decree: "The Lord, the God of heaven, has given me all the kingdoms of the earth, and he has charged me to build him a house at Jerusalem, which is in Judah. Whoever is among you of all his people, may the Lord his God be with him! Let him go up."[146] In ending with these words "go up," the Tanakh is clearly referencing an image evoking return and entry into the Promised Land, a symbol of Israel's suspended hope amidst its devastations and exiles. The Torah similarly ended with the death of Moses, who was not permitted to enter the Land but was left in the wilderness. Thus, in both the Torah and Tanakh's conclusions, "the people stand on the threshold of the land of promise, but they are not yet in the Land itself. Everything remains open. The threshold has not yet been crossed. *And the New Testament takes up this very situation. Here the threshold is crossed.*"[147]

John the Baptist, eating locusts and honey out in the desert, is drawn up intentionally to pick up where the Torah and Tanakh left off. At the river Jordan, just as it had been with Joshua, John is at Israel's "threshold situation before its entry into the Land." And yet the Baptist does not cross into the land; he had the people of Israel coming out to him in the wilderness. By contrast, after Jesus' forty days in the Jordan wilderness, coinciding with the exodus wandering of forty years, he did not stay out in the desert but returned into the "the Land," the settlements of Galilee. In contrast with John, Jesus "comes to them in the context of their normal life."[148] That is, instead of ending up where the first Moses did, at the threshold between the wilderness and the land, this second Moses enters.

---

[145] Lohfink, *Does God Need the Church?*, 121f, 124.
[146] 2 Chr 36:23.
[147] Lohfink, *Does God Need the Church?*, 125.
[148] Ibid., 128f.

Lohfink sees this as clearly evoking the inauguration of the Kingdom of God, per Isaiah 52, wherein "God gathers Israel, scattered in exile, and leads it home to the Land ... the eschatological gathering of the people of God is beginning; Israel is being definitively given its land."[149] Seen only through cosmotheistic eyes, we can see why Jesus' gathering of twelve disciples might have appeared to some as an attempted restoration of the political kingdom to Israel, rooted in twelve tribes, to seize back the land from its imperial usurpers.

But the gospels reconceive of this land just as Jewish monotheism reconceived covenant. "Land" here differs radically from any concept of the state; it is no longer compacted with state and soil, even while it is associated with the blood and body of a victim. Osiris' killed and dismembered body (just like Tiamat et al.), was the land; it was the "body of Osiris"; he was reconstituted, post-murder, through the national, ritual procession of Egypt's various states, which numbered the parts of his body. The New Testament's reconfigured "land," too, is a slain victim, constituted in the body of Christ. This is evident, first, in John's baptism of Christ, held at the threshold between exodus and land, where we hear from heaven, "here is my servant," a clear reference to Isaiah's Suffering Servant.[150] This serves, first, to associate Jesus' "entry into the land" with his entrance into suffering.

Secondly, however, entering the promised land of Christ meant not a Joshuanic land grab or a Maccabean revolt. Neither apolitical nor political, entry into this land for his followers coincided with incorporation into the "body of Christ," the Church. This is intriguingly evident in Barnabas selling off his land near Jerusalem to join this body.[151] Having lived abroad, Barnabas likely owned land near Jerusalem, like many Jews then, in the hopes that he might take part in an expectant messianic age to be celebrated in the land. And yet, in a reconceptualizing of this hope, he *sold* his land for the sake of benefiting the community in Jerusalem. His sale enacts Jesus' promise, that those who give up homes, fields, and family to follow him gain a hundredfold. If it is in giving that we receive, we find "the houses and fields that Jesus' disciples will leave are their share in the 'Land.'"[152] That is, those who give of themselves for

---

[149] Ibid., 129f.
[150] Isa 42:1–4.
[151] Acts 4:36–7.
[152] Lohfink, *Does God Need the Church?*, 132f; Mk 10:29f.

the community do not lose but in fact enter and gain their share in the Land – which is the messianic community, the Body of Christ.

If we consider what it would have meant for an Israeli settler then (or now), to sell off land around Jerusalem, this is not a merely "transcendent" or spiritual gesture. It had then, and would have today, a solid, immanent character that, at the same time, does not fit into the rivalrous script of either subordinating to the Romans' occupation or violently resisting it. Sale of land for the sake of joining and building up the Body of Christ is not Gnostic, depoliticized escape; Barnabas' land sale helped constitute a real, visible Body, while being neither zealot nor collaborationist. This takes the cosmotheistic notion of land as the body of a victim and reconfigures it. This body and land, though that of a victim, does not coincide with soil, state, or Temple, but in "Spirit and Truth." It is a "temple" that is made up of the living stones of humans in a community of mutual aid (1 Pet 2:5). It is not a new founding murder to organize an earthly city. Rather, insofar as it is a founding murder of a "heavenly" city, it is incompatible with all earthly cities in giving itself away, selling its goods to share with its new family.[153]

---

[153] The book of Hebrews also decenters notions of political land in speaking of Christ being murdered "outside the city gate," followed by an invitation to join him, in going *outside* the city together, and to "bear the disgrace he bore." The destination of this exodus is underdetermined with respect to land, in that "we do not have a permanent city, but one that is to come" (Heb 13:13).

We may mitigate some potential supersessionism here by considering, per David Carr, the parallel the New Testament draws up between the land, Jesus' death, and Moses' death. We are accustomed to seeing the former as killed and Moses dying of old age or for no known reason – whereas Freud invited us to consider some darker parallels. Carr adds that not only was Moses' burial place unknown, in similarity to the earliest resurrection accounts; but Moses and Jesus both die "on account of the peoples' sins," and they do so *outside* the promised land – that is, *outside* Jerusalem (per Heb 13:12) – so that their followers can carry forward into it (Deut 34:5–6; 1:37; Carr, *Holy Resilience*, 168f).

For Carr, the gospels suggest that we interpret Jesus' death in light of Moses' death, on the threshold of the promised land. Situated at this transition point, their deaths were not a sign of their failure, but their deaths are "vindicated by the ongoing life of their community," in that their people enter the land and live on as Israel. Thus, the Church proclaims that Jesus, like Moses, "bore our sins so that we could live. His death did not hold us back but allowed us to go forward like the wilderness Israelites into new life in the promised land" (Carr, *Holy Resilience*, 170). But, while Carr's reading may mitigate a certain supersessionism, to the extent that one entertains Freud and Sellin's hypothesis, this reiterates a *difference* between the Jewish and Christian symbols of the land: whereas Moses' murder may be the repressed reason as to why he did not enter the land, Christ's murder is represented with explicit clarity.

There are considerable reasons to simply prophesy *against* the imperialistic imaginary of land by invoking perpetual sojourning, much as Schwartz did in *The Curse of Cain*. There she critiqued monotheism's ostensibly unique sense of entitlement and lust to dominate land and women. Indeed, the conquest of Canaan seems one of the more obscene symbols suggesting monotheistic violence.[154] The Christian interpretation of monotheism I offer here, with respect to land, partly concurs, seeking not to underwrite any politicized justification of hubris or make one feel "at home" in any land or governmental apparatus. We identified this in Chapter 6: a great counterweight to land-grabbing hubris emerged through the exodus covenant's anti-monarchic potentialities. This gave way to an emphasis on the exodus' desert, the fidelity of those who, in exile, have not yet let milk and honey cloud their memory. This speaks well to the Jewish spirit of a "life lived in deferment," a tension that is never fully released.

But a pure deemphasis on land must not *depoliticize* through the total evacuation of co-identification, the construction of a collective body. While agreeing that land and body are the most dangerous and fundamental symbols of the political realm, my argument from Mouffe onward has suggested a need for not evacuating but reconfiguring them. The New Testament's noted vivid representation of victimage, body, and land offers a practical symbol as an antidote to depoliticization. So long as we live in a world of hubris and victimization, we cannot abrogate the representation of solid images of land, victims, and collective identification. So long as human association involves constitutive divisions, we must conceive of our associations and identities in a way that seeks to deactivate the *libido dominandi* without repeating it. The valorization of sojourning, alone, may too easily parallel Mouffe's noted depoliticized avoidance of conflict and boundaries, expressed through the mere

---

[154] CC 39ff. Schwartz recognizes how the biblical representation of land-grabbing practices were common to the ancient near east (42) and that biblical monolatry is partly derived from political vassal treaties (26). But she does not theorize how these can be reconfigured; rather, it seems they are simply to be abolished in a boundless inclusivity.

But her brief critiques of landedness, the biblical idealization of the wilderness, and linking "humanity" to the land (and not the nation [43f]) are promising and resonant with this study. One hears parallels with Mouffe in Schwartz's claim: "whatever communities are, they are not a body, and imagining corporate identity as corporeal – as defined by blood and by seed – has served racial, ethnic, and religious hatred all too well throughout history" (97). And yet Mouffe also insists upon the *inescapability* of us/them constructs and the liberating (and dangerous) construction of collective identifications.

"valorization of multiplicity" and an evasion of constructing a "we." Speaking of only sojourning but not the land may fail to constitute a social body of liberation.

To clarify, consider the monotheistic interpretation of land in the Jewish philosopher, Hermann Cohen. Akin to my aims here, Cohen sought not to abolish monotheistic intolerance but to distill the nonviolence within it. With regard to the violence surrounding land, Cohen urged that the cost of Jewish identity rooted in monotheism, in Erlewine's gloss, involves "the agony of statelessness, with the persecutions and endless sufferings that accompany it." Living in such a state of landless suspension is "a necessary condition for Israel to play a universal role in world history." Thus, for Cohen, the *meaning* and application of monotheistic intolerance is precisely in the refusal to grasp for landed power, gaining a monopoly on society. Monotheism's intolerance, rather, is ascetic; it requires "that the Jews forsake certain worldly advantages such as a homeland of their own and the security that affords …. By distinguishing themselves as suffering servants the Jews embrace the agonism in the heart of the monotheistic worldview in a non-violent manner."[155] In this sense, the notion of "special election," yet another infamous sign of intolerance, is not to be done away with. Election need not imply a static, anti-pluralistic identity. Rather, for Cohen, it is to be accepted as a demanding, "perpetual task of infinite responsibility for the Other."[156] Inhabiting monotheistic intolerance, then, meant precisely the opposite of the political grasp for landed power but precisely its apophatic negation: hubris in reverse. This refusal may possibly entail suffering; and yet it is not the Alexanders but the meek who shall inherit the earth.

+++

In conclusion, we have here introduced a rubric for interpreting symbols of power and sovereign authority in Christ's trial, crucifixion, resurrection, and land. Seen in contrast with the notion that monotheism is simply the antagonistic grasp toward a monolithic monopoly on violence, I think a subtle alternative for interpretation is opened up. The method honed here could be extended toward other symbols. For example, applied to the Eucharist, Girard saw this ritual as not merely a kindly meal of

---

[155] Erlewine, *Monotheism and Tolerance*, 166, 172.
[156] Ibid., 175.

friendship that overcomes differences but "cannibalism in reverse." It dramatically resembles humanity's violent crypt, wherein the cannibalistic mob imitates one another, animated by wanting to be the victim they kill. The Eucharist does not escape such victimage; its conflict is *central*. And yet the victim here offers himself as food to those who "know not what they do," inviting victimizers to be transformed into the model of forgiveness. As such, the Eucharist digests us. "Primitive cannibalism is religion, and the Eucharist recapitulates this history from alpha to omega."[157] The Eucharist indeed involves a community "united in othering," in exclusion. But it is a paradoxical revelation of *our* having othered an innocent victim, an exclusion in reverse. In the Eucharist, we see the deeper unity between primary and secondary religion: all religions worship victims, even if primary ones were unaware of it.[158] Applying this hermeneutic in greater detail to any of various theological symbols is a task for other studies. I have merely introduced a method that avoids the dialectic, rivalrous break with archaic religion while avoiding the banal, translatable continuity. One might call it mythospeculative. Such an approach of analogy-amidst-opposition may be explored as resonant with the Catholic model of the *analogia entis*, or what is elsewhere called *dialectic analogy*, or "overaccepting" the archaic sacred.[159]

G. THE MOSAIC DISTINCTION AND CHRISTIAN INTOLERANCE

Monotheism's "intolerance" of cosmotheism ought not to be abolished, as it crucial to the separation of God from the political sphere. At the same time, this incompatibility offers no clean escape from the fundamental elements of the political. One must still *engage* the realities of exclusion, sacrifice, and violence without reproducing them. The exploration above sees in Christ both of these elements, retained in an unresolved tension, a dialectic analogy of critique without antagonism. This model suggests that any attempt to abolish the intolerance of the Mosaic distinction – so as to construct a unity beyond division – does not actually

---

[157] *EC* 217.
[158] Ibid., 211.
[159] Scott Cowdell, *The Nonviolent God*, ch 7. For "dialectical analogy," see John Betz, "Mere Metaphysics." With respect to the *analogia entis* and Przywara here, one would need to reframe my use of the word analogy – which bears the cosmotheistic tone of theo-political compaction – whereas "analogy" can bear the positive connotation of similarity-amidst-difference: participation-in-the-divine-yet-infinite-distance.

escape the constraints of the political. In fact, taking Mouffe's opening theory as a guide, any claims to such transcendence are liable to become caught in rivalrous oppositions, forgetful of their own exclusions. The path to transcending antagonism is not conflict-free consensus but engaged agonism.

Mouffe's agonism concerns the unresolved space between two incompatible realities: democracy's exclusions and liberalism's "intolerance" – its potentially despotic agitation toward creating a worldwide community beyond all differences. While Christ's agonism is less about navigating the worldly city of governance, his bears important resemblances: it lives in the irresolution between two incompatibilities: a humanity evolved through the sacrificial containment of violence and a weak God who is unconditional love, who resists not evildoers. It is still a "kingdom" but entirely unlike those that contain violence. It does not escape or go beyond hegemony – or intolerance, or sacrifice, or myth; it is more like "hegemony in reverse." The orienting principle of this group is not judgment but the one who is judged. It is still a group bound together, even fascinated, by the "glory" of its king; yet the results of worshipping this ridiculed and stripped monarch is perhaps akin to the parable of the emperor having no clothes: Christ's stripping paradoxically renders royalty naked of its prestige. It still constructs a collective identification, a body, a "we"; but it clings to this body the way it clings to land – through mutual aid, ecclesial distribution, and sacrificial giving. In this internal subversion of sovereignty and land, we see divinity separated from the political in a way that does not reassert rivalry through escape into transcendent, pacific, inclusive universalism. Rather, it retains an ever-open crypt, as it were, in the scapegoat-foundation illuminated and remembered. This crypt is in fact the engine and medium of its revelation. In this, Christianity bears fundamental continuity with all the primary religions that, in its own unique way, it surpasses.

And so the seemingly inclusive formula, "in Christ, there is neither Jew nor Greek," does not abolish the Mosaic distinction. Claims to tolerant inclusion, per se, are not particularly unique to Christianity.[160] For example, we learned how imperial monotheism, inclusive amidst its violence, was strategically tolerant and benevolent. The bigger they become the more forgetful they become of the violent forces that found and

---

[160] Plutarch: "nor do we regard the gods as different among different nations nor as barbarian and Greek and as southern and northern" (*ME* 53; Plutarch, *De Iside et Osiride*, ch 67).

structure them. But Paul's inclusivity is not vaguely universal; it is particular, "in Christ," in Christ crucified. Paul speaks of a norm of inclusion only in the frightening context of an exceptional exclusion: the unwitting murder of Jesus Christ. This is not merely an accusation of the accusers but voiced from knowledge of his own blind persecution of Christ's followers. Paul's inclusivity does not attack, replace, or spiritually transcend exclusion. Rather, it animates an upside-down politics, a form of life marked by an unsettling paradox: awareness of one's unawareness of having excluded and crucified the divine Other. The Mosaic distinction abides here – that one cannot find salvation outside this truth. But James Alison clarified how the seeming hubris of this exclusivity ought not to be abrogated but clarified: "There is no grace available to human beings that does not involve a turning toward the victim, that is, a certain form of conversion."[161] Or James Cone: "humanity's salvation is available *only* through our solidarity with the crucified people in our midst."[162]

As I began this chapter, I noted how the Constantinian "separation" of religion and politics masks a deeper, if schizophrenic compatibility, where the state claims the body and the church the "soul." Scholar of early Christian history, Burton Mack, sees this partnership as inherited from Roman imperial forms and animating Christendom's history. He sees a "monocratic" will to power as ultimately characterizing Christianity's version of monotheism. This involves, by Mack's reading, a myopic intolerance, not merely in asserting there is only one god but that there is only one way to obey and please this divine sovereign. Christendom's ossification of God has located all non-Christians on the "disobedient" side of a duality marked by right vs. wrong, us vs. them, and good vs. bad. This monomaniac, monocratic myth, he urges, cannot deal with the real world of plurality.[163] It exudes a fictive cosmic imperialism of Christ, the divine monarch, along with a hubristic, obnoxious, universalist, monolinear, singular, hierarchical aura of exceptionality and uniqueness.[164] Unlike other cultures who have found ways of managing differences without demanding uniformity, he insists, the militant Christian myth "obstructs critical thinking about contemporary social and cultural issues." It has "canceled out the importance, often the memory, of the

---

[161] Alison, *The Joy of Being Wrong*, 93.
[162] James Cone, *The Cross and the Lynching Tree*, 160.
[163] Burton Mack, *The Rise and Fall of the Christian Myth*, 80.
[164] Burton Mack, *Who Wrote the New Testament?*, 306.

indigenous histories of all other peoples converted to Christianity."[165] Echoing commentary on what we have called the Mosaic distinction, Mack argues monotheism in Christianity means nothing but a damnation of its opposite, the idolater, the lost soul, the pagan, the outsider. It has failed to appreciate difference, accept critique, celebrate plurality, negotiate compromise.[166]

But, while one must concede to Mack some accuracy with respect to the historic disposition of Christendom, my study has suggested that, in such an opposition to oppositionalism, there is a failure to see the paradox of intolerance. I have instead tried to conceptualize a deeper, if historically underutilized, operation of monotheism in its apophasis, its intolerance of absolutism. In its apophatic intolerance, we find the patience of eschatological deferral and the reconceiving of symbols of sovereignty and praise. By contrast, when Mack considers the eschatological idea that the Kingdom of God is "never actualized by the kingdoms of this world," he takes this to only mean something violent; monotheism only agitates an itch that perpetually beckons violent scratching: the Christ-king must battle to the end against idolaters. In such a view, Mack sees an allergy to pluralism, a mindset ready to accept "opposition, conflict, and violence in the interest of protecting a monocratic ideal." For, at its root, it involves a "deferral of resolution to the dialectic of Christ as lord and savior." This deferral bestows a "great desire for cleansing and release," a destruction of any who are opposed so as to enthrone the "victor as absolute."[167] Instead of Christianity annexing every culture and story in the world (starting with the Jewish one), and appropriating them into its totalizing myth, Mack instead urges that no single story should be traced through all of western history to the end of the world.[168]

But we should notice what Mack proposes in place of this monocratic mythology. He invokes a non-fictive and non-mythic mode of belonging, promoting instead a disposition in defense of victims that is plural, open, inclusive, and without the exclusive, totalizing imagery.[169] Not only does

---

[165] Mack, *The Christian Myth*, 154.

[166] Ibid., 173–4.

[167] Ibid., 167–9.

[168] Ibid., 168.

[169] Ibid., 106, 173–4, *passim*. He refers to the "Greek notion of … participating in a 'kingdom that was, in effect, an order of things prior to, displaced from, and in contrast to the kingdoms of this world … a theocratic model to counter the tyrannies of the Roman imperium" (138, 164).

this supposed solution to monocratic Christianity fall into to the traps noted in our axial section, but it ironically and tacitly affirms the Mosaic distinction as an absolute. His refusal of a singular story is not a mere transcending of intolerance but an apophatic expression of it. His ostensible exodus from the oppressive Mosaic distinction is his covert affirmation of it. He does not countenance that his concern for victims, his hope for a unity beyond exclusion, may not be the final enlightened embrace of a universal, neutral truth, but a particular form of intolerance, what Girard calls "the secular mask of Christian love."[170]

The Mosaic distinction need not be understood as simply the antithesis of openness, as was discussed in reference to Schwartz's *Curse of Cain.* For example, Schwartz exegeted Deutero-Isaiah as first delivering a vision of a God of "plentitude," but the prophet regressed into intolerance and divine threat once he started condemning false gods. Isaiah must have "feared that his assertions of divine plentitude were not compelling enough and that he had to add, just for good measure, warnings to coerce singular devotion rather than simply invite assent to his ideal of boundless giving."[171] Instead of such coerced, exclusive zeal, Schwartz wants to reject forms of identity that are competitive or based on a sense of "monotheistic scarcity" – the sense that, "once you start loving, either you lose your identity or else the loved one does: someone loses." Instead, she invokes a plentitude that "proliferates identities without violence."[172] She is against "forging identity agonistically" but rather imagining divinity which "gives and goes on giving endlessly without being used up."[173]

While this conviction is laudable – and should be retained – this chapter suggests it fails to think the exception of human violence with a passion. It lacks a full sobriety about the political – that even inclusion contains exclusion. I see a certain realism about the political embedded in the Christian iteration of the Mosaic distinction: in this world, one can only speak of an endlessly giving God – who boundlessly gives, who is "only yes," unconditional love, pure light in whom there is no darkness – while also speaking of our killing this God. This God eternally abides as a "slain lamb," while being, in time, hidden in our scapegoats and "the least of these." Schwartz's vision of rivalry-lessness is indeed beatific, in imagining a world founded without an originary exclusion. But *how* we

---

[170] *ISS* 165.
[171] CC 37; Isa 41:17–9; 44:3–4.
[172] CC 117.
[173] Ibid., 146; 118.

do retain that hope? In a *political* sense, Girard has suggested a view more attentive to the exception: to truly reject or oppose sacrifice in this world means that one accepts it, at least potentially, upon one's self. It means resisting the impulse to exonerate the innocent self and immolate the guilty other. We must instead reconfigure that scapegoating habit into self-examination – taking out the log in one's own eye. We can thus see why Gandhi treated self-purification as the fundamental starting point of political engagement; for the starting gesture of true worship is repentance. "Repentance," as Girard defined it, involves confessing that we may be persecutors without knowing it.[174] The opposite of scapegoating is not depoliticized inclusion; rather, repentance is scapegoating in reverse.

Even the heavenly city is not an exclusion-free utopia; it is not a politics without a scapegoat. The heavenly city is indeed like the earthly cities, in its being founded upon a victim, but in reverse. The Body of Christ is not the collective identity of those piously allied with the innocent One who judges the world; they are a fellowship of those who together admit they would have killed Christ and all the prophets since the foundation of the world. Our relation to the Other has been tragically misguided. It is in light of this penetration of mimetic mechanics that we can interpret what Agamben saw in Paul's messianism, that Christ crucified "divides the division" between Jews and Gentiles: Christ divides the "divisions of law, rendering them inoperative, without ever reaching a final ground."[175] Yes, monotheism invokes an "Othering," in its distinguishing the true from the false. But the Other turns out to be God on the cross, while the hammer and noose are in our hands. Monotheism, in light of Christ crucified, is "us vs them" in reverse. The Body of Christ crucified is the representation of the intolerance of exclusion.

If the Mosaic distinction means the intolerant distinction between true and false religion, the question for continual reflection is what is truth? In Girard, Christianity's answer is partly apophatic and "weak." He concedes that "there is no privileged stance from which absolute truth can be discovered" and adds a crucial utterance: "the Word that states itself to be absolutely true never speaks except from the position of a victim in the process of being expelled."[176] This weighty assertion aligns well with

---

[174] *EC* 198.

[175] Here Agamben's reading of Paul's messianism is suggestive: *The Time That Remains*, 53; 51.

[176] *TH* 435. This paradox is what Burton Mack fails to see in the Christ myth. For him Christianity is ultimately about "an exclusive claim to ultimate justification into an absolute and universal principle of judgment about the rest of humankind ... the only

Mouffe's awareness that a mature pluralism involves no monopolization on the Absolute, no grasping to claim the foundation of society. If there is no privileged stance from which the Absolute can be discovered except in the mouth of the receding victim, our politics are indeed presented with a never-closed crisis. This is both the curse and the truth of Christ's good news.

Christianity supplies explicit content to the Mosaic distinction between true and false religion. It indeed intolerantly states, "there is salvation in no one else" (Acts 4:12); but what exactly is the nature of this intolerance? What does it divide, why, and how? What I have explored here implies not that God is on "our" side and everyone else is on the wrong side. To see this, rather, through a lens of dialectic-analogy, the line of Mosaic "exclusion" is drawn, as it were, upon the body of God. As Girard's theory poignantly argues, the divisions of law stem from the sacred, the originary distinction drawn upon the God, upon the victim as founding exclusion. We can utilize one of Barth's more paradoxical images to make sense of Christ's separation from and unity with archaic divinity: the Mosaic-inflected duality of a God who saves the elect and damns the reprobate is inflicted and divided upon God's very self on the cross. In Christ the seeming incompatibilities of total divine communion and abandonment collide.[177] This helps us interpret a core symbol for Israel that Christ tragically fulfills: in Abraham's cutting a self-maledictory blood covenant with God, the violence of sacrificial compact is oddly reversed: the threat of violence against the party who fails to keep the covenant is placed not at all on Abraham but entirely on *God*.[178] Reconfiguring the sacrificial ritual, this divinity suggests a totally "open" unconditionality, devoid of reciprocity and vengeance; the great *Other* bears no mimetic rivalry. But, given the inescapability of the political, the abandonment of sacrificial violence for the sake of love incurs the potential suffering of it.

---

representatives of a superior and uncompromising social vision" (Mack, *The Christian Myth*, 158).

[177] Barth, *Church Dogmatics*, §II.2. Although language fails me here, this divine image strikes me as an odd mirror reversal of anthropocentric projections onto divinity: per the usual partisan spirit, the god is on our side, against all others – projected onto a metaphysical scale. If repentance and self-critique is the anthropological mode of biblical "truth" for Girard, its metaphysical "projection" is also inverted, and God too repents: "God through his Son could be seen as asking for forgiveness from humans for having revealed the mechanisms of their violence so late" (*BTE* x).

[178] Gen 15:9f; Heb 6:13–20; CC 32.

Put differently, if Mount Sinai means a sort of divisive "hate," Mount Golgotha is Sinai's interpretive key. Yes, Sinai drew up a distinction that evokes "hate"; but in the crucified one, we find hatred and violence are but our own projections of divinity, and "the true God" is entirely love. As an example, recall how in Chapter 1 King's "Letter from a Birmingham Jail" fielded accusations from white moderates, that the civil rights movement was divisive, hateful, and it provoked violence and hatred. King admitted that their program of nonviolent resistance "seeks to create a crisis," to foster a creative tension so as to evoke a resolution unavailable under the deceptively serene conditions of "law and order." But he added that "we who engage in nonviolent direct action are not the creators of tension. We merely bring to the surface the hidden tension that is already alive."[179] Panning out to the widest frame of human evolution itself, our having evolved through scapegoat mechanism is – if Girard's notion of original sin is correct – the original murderous distinction, the genuine engine of hidden tension, fear, and hatred. Sinai and Mosaic intolerance, wrongly seen as the source of hate, instead seek to create a crisis in the sacred that contains violence. This is dangerous, in that it destabilizes society. But the God revealed in this crisis is not the perpetrator but the victim of the scapegoat mechanism. In this sense, if our interests are a deeper nonviolence and love, the intolerant Mosaic distinction ought not to be abolished but fervently maintained. We should interpret the "murderous distinction" through Christ crucified. Golgotha completes Sinai by showing us hatred in reverse: the absorption and transformation of hatred. Golgotha is not the redeployment of hate against the idolater – but the revelation of hate through its forgiveness: in our crucifying Christ, *we* are the hateful idolater prone to scapegoat the one who is *homoousios* with God.

If Akhenaten offers us a violent iconoclasm, which destroys all images except those that worship himself, the Christian iteration of Mosaic anti-idolatry is iconoclasm in reverse: we can now make images of God, so long as they represent the destroyed image of God, Christ crucified. For, at this second Sinai the critique of idolatry hits its most primordial target, the violence that coheres false unity – the lying, collective body of the god. In the jeers of the lynch mob Jeremiah's anti-idolatry is ironically inverted and substantiated: "where are your gods that you made for yourself? Let them come if they can save you, in your time of trouble" (Jer 2:28; Mk

---

[179] Martin Luther King Jr., "Letter from a Birmingham Jail."

15:29f; Mt 27:40f; Lk 23:36f). For the font of idolatrous delusion is not merely the misapprehension of surrogate ritual sacrifices, much less in the fabricated statuary that has lost touch with its violent origins. The heart of idolatry is in the collective murder itself.

When monotheism is treated in this dialectic-analogy manner, it does not necessarily reject the "non-dual thought" of, say, Seng-T'san (d. 609 BCE), who wrote: "If you want the truth to stand clear before you, never be for or against. The struggle between 'for' and 'against' is the mind's worst disease."[180] In light of Christ crucified, such a maxim does not abrogate the Mosaic distinction. Rather, the very identification of the for/against disease, the us/them antagonism, is precisely a penetrating observation of the originary division that Girard calls the scapegoat mechanism. Seng-T'san's deconstruction of antagonism coincides with his affirmation of truth. We must manage this truth in concert with the penetrating truth of Elie Wiesel, that if we really want to move the world beyond division, then paradoxically *"we must take sides."* He, like Mouffe, King, and Girard, understands the political – the inaccessibility of a truly neutral position foreign to violence. For Wiesel saw how "neutrality helps the oppressor, never the victim . . .. Sometimes we must interfere." To be truly non-dual, to refuse to mimetically take sides, means placing the persecuted victim at the "center of the universe."[181]

On this matter of the victim, this is an intolerance that Christianity should not relinquish – no more than liberalism should give up human rights. Intolerance about victimization is a stumbling block that has become our world's cornerstone, in the ubiquitous concern for marginalized persons. That it can turn dangerous, a new cover for neoliberal hegemony, or into a new rallying cry to persecute the persecutors, is not reason enough to abolish it. Nor could we. Instead, we must consider how inclusion and unity are only "true" when exposed to the penetrating light of the victim. Given that any and every human association may be blind to its victims, any theory of inclusivity will need to remain infinitely open to critique, ever under construction, lest it become a new regime of tolerance. Thus, the scapegoat "king" rightly remains uninstantiatable, un-enthroned in history, incompatible with every worldly judgment – even while represented in Christian theology as "the center of the universe."

---

[180] Edward Conze, et al., *Buddhist Texts through the Ages*, 296.
[181] Elie Wiesel, "Acceptance Speech."

Such an eschatological approach to "dominion" is not only evident in the New Jerusalem's temple as the slain lamb – the body of the divine-human-victim (Rev 21:22) – but also in the aforenoted parable of the sheep and goats. This parable prophesies that *no one within history* understands or can lay final claim to their relationship to the victim, who thereby haunts us, world without end. True revelation unveils our opacity. This is a parable ultimately not of othering or constructing an identity against the heathen who lack knowledge of the truth; rather, everyone lacks knowledge of their relation to the Othered. Again, even the good sheep do not grasp their relation to the Other.[182] Given this uncertainty, any inclusion that fails to somehow represent the victim will be in danger of hiding something, in a unity forgetful of its violent foundations.

Judaism's monotheistic intolerance did not abolish but uniquely reconfigured zealous political loyalty. The religion of Christ crucified, in accord with these transformations, reconfigured sovereignty to expose humanity's forgotten foundation: the excluded, scapegoated other. This does not cleanly move us "beyond exclusion," beyond intolerance, beyond myth – into absolute knowledge, reason, and inclusion. It did not erase the us/them antagonisms of violence and oppression. This would have only created a new us/them. Rather, its representation of a founding murder – of one homologous with divinity – ushers us to observe and critique the

---

[182] Hermann Cohen, per Erlewine's reading, critiqued Christianity as mythically mislead with its anthropomorphic deity and "infinitely important 'person'" of Jesus Christ. Cohen instead saw in Judaism "an entirely new and *direct* relationship to emerge between human beings," in which God withdraws "in order to purify the 'relation between human being and human being.' This withdrawal makes the concern for the other person more 'urgent.'" Christianity regresses, for Cohen, on this point: when encountering the suffering Other, Christianity resorts to theodicy abstractions (Erlewine, *Monotheism and Tolerance*, 161). While I do not contest that historic, institutional Christianity has generally failed on this account, I would overaccept Cohen's claim, in the sense of conceding a claim only to modify and reuse it: The New Testament locates God as not only withdrawn but unwittingly murdered. This renders concern for the persecuted more urgent in its emphasis on the unpredictable divine intersection with the other ("Saul why do you persecute me") and the victim cries "they know not what they do" (Acts 9:4; Lk 23:34; Heb 6:6). Nahme draws from Cohen some conclusions resonant with these (Paul Nahme, "God Is the Reason," 138).

To the objection that, "by making God the primary agent in human atonement, Christianity undermines the process by which one becomes an ethical Self" (Erlewine, *Monotheism and Tolerance*, 165), we might consider the ineffable experience of God-as-the-human-victim, whom we fail to see in our blind spot. In concord with Alison and Cone from earlier in this chapter, I agree that one cannot grow the ethical self, "be saved," without attending to that blind spot, as known in the lynched savior.

false powers that generated the human order so as render them inoperative. Such a monotheism reconfigures the us/them duality into a vigilant
apophatic intolerance, an awareness that God may be the hidden victim
and we the persecutor. This intolerance agonistically engages the powers
while it just as emphatically abrogates any hold on the Absolute, a
monopoly on the foundation of society. For its foundation and true
identity is under-determined, "hidden with Christ in God" (Col 3:3).

8

Conclusion

How to Be Intolerant

Exclusive monotheism has its roots mingled in a monolatrous and henotheistic god of primary religions, in sometimes absolutist and imperialistic expressions of forced-unity. But mature monotheism ultimately repurposes this absolutism, in both cataphatic and apophatic intolerance. Its cataphatic intolerance worships the particular, liberating god, a god intolerant of the enslaving and idolatrous gods; this is not a universal but specific revelation. But this praise and allegiance is counterposed with apophatic negation, refusing to represent God through any mediation, pledging a loyalty that cannot be represented through the political sphere. Such monotheistic intolerance opens a space from which all powers stand subject to prophetic critique – all denaturalized, all secularized. This apophatic intolerance refuses any claims to a monopoly on this foundation of society: for the victim is both a symbol of the foundation of society and "the Absolute." This God is not so much "above" the political order as *under* it, as the ever-elusive victim whom we may persecute without knowing it.

In other words, monotheism is not simply about Oneness and unity. It is in fact a division. It divides God from the cosmos and the political sphere, birthing a new *kind* of religion, hiving off from the ancient primary religious compact with the political. It means living in paradoxical incompatibility between the "kingdom of God" and every earthly kingdom. This paradox is dramatized in the scapegoat king who reconfigures the identity, affection, and allegiance of the earthly city. He has no place to lay his head in this world even while desperately seeking to heal it. He is, as Girard writes, "the one that is the most outside yet also the most inside common humanity. He is the most divine and the most human ... God is now on the side of the scapegoat victim."[1] Far from monotheism being a mere galvanization of chauvinism, we can find in it a radical deconstruction. Scholar of religion Atalia Omer is correct to emphasize how "religion" is not merely a source of absolutizing identities but "*de*constructing and reimagining identities."[2]

The monotheistic deconstruction of the sacred becomes more comprehensible in light of Mouffe's account of liberalism and pluralism. Her logic affirms how liberalism involves continual, intolerant agitation toward the observance of human rights, even while this may provoke divisions, conflict, and agonism. Liberalism attempts to speak from a transcendent, universal perspective, somehow standing outside the political – incompatible with the inescapable exclusions of democracy. But it must patiently, agonistically keep up its struggle. It keeps this agonism alive through apophatically negating any hold on absolute knowledge or monopoly on the foundation of society. Neither my account of monotheism nor Mouffe's account of pluralism suggests a depoliticized transcendence that leaves us without values, orientation, or identity. Instead of pluralism meaning a mere "relativization," my account of identity remains ever oriented by the victims and originary exclusions at the foundation of every human association. This orientation is marked by an awareness that any attempt to politically attend to "the victim" will nonetheless contain exclusions – it will be imperfect, hegemonic, and contestable, world without end. Nothing is more crucial than seeing reality from the perspective of victims, yet nothing is more dangerous than claiming a monopoly on that perspective.

With an orientation that refuses unitary political representation, both monotheism and pluralism involve patient engagement in the presence of conflicting plural values. Or, in theological terms, as Edward Schillebeeckx argued, the "eschatological proviso" (that the earthly city simply cannot immanentize the divine reign) does not only relativize the political sphere by exposing its contingent nature. Such a relativization alone would only "throttle back the humanitarian impulse." Rather, to divide the Absolute from the political, as I have put it, means precisely *invigorating* the humanitarian impulse while "orienting" it.[3] This orientation, in my account, is directed toward the "exceptions" of any and every order – its boundaries, its exclusions, its victims. As Walter

---

[1] *BTE* 50; Giorgio Agamben, *The Time That Remains*, 105.
[2] Atalia Omer, "Can a Critic Be a Caretaker?," 472.
[3] Edward Schillebeeckx, *Christ*, 777–8.

Benjamin stated, "the tradition of the oppressed teaches us that the 'state of exception' in which we live is not the exception but the rule ... it is our task to bring about a real state of exception, and this will improve our position in the struggle against fascism."[4] The image that comes to mind, in orienting toward this exception, is the representation of a crucifix, which hangs perpetually before our eyes, silently uttering to all our hidden and unacknowledged persecutions today: "Why do you persecute me?" But this word is eschatological in that its orientation toward the victim can be responded to, but it cannot be definitively resolved within history.

What this means in terms of identity and a sense of belonging is, at least, resisting the compulsion to establish a final and complete identity. It means refusing to fully constitute one's self in total identification with any political form. I hesitate to call this "mystical," but it is indeed a refusal to fill the absence within, refusing to resolve our mimetic instability. It means that the structuring of a political identity – a "we" – may be unavoidable, even necessary in the struggle for justice, but it is always contestable. In other words, we must always ask at whose cost our "unity" is achieved – even while provisional unities, identities, political associations, and policies are an inescapable dimension of life. For Mouffe, this meant giving up notions of "belonging" that conceive the self as part of a complete societal "body."[5] As we saw in cosmotheistic political theology, the state, the land, and the body of a slain victim together represent its "originary exclusion" and its unification; Egypt would reconstitute itself as a total body, composed of Osiris' many parts. For Mouffe, the "body" as a political metaphor is simply too absolutist, complete, and arrived to be true. It immanentizes singularity so as to paper over divisions. The political "body" symbol effaces important conflicts and, as I have put it, flattens out the above eschatological leaven. It overburdens the political realm with more unity than what we can expect of it. Its absorption of alterity into oneness too easily forgets how all unities are founded on an exclusion.

But Mouffe also insists that, given the inescapability of the political, we cannot and must not evade the provisional constructions of a "we."[6] Identity formation, however provisional, must be oriented toward clarifying and transforming conflicts. I take this as an opening by which to offer a twist on her notion of a "body," shifting from political to ecclesial

---

[4] Walter Benjamin, "Theses on the Philosophy of History," thesis 8.
[5] DP 103.
[6] Ibid., 20.

idioms. In my chapter on Jesus Christ (Chapter 7), I affirmed how the body is indeed a key site where politics is symbolized. But instead of treating Christ's nonviolence as the evacuation of the political, the body is reconceived as a site for engaged, active practice (with Barnabas' land-sale in joining the body of Christ as just a small sample). I conceived this as transcending the rivalries of the political realm while not escaping them. The heavenly polis is similar to cosmotheism in that it unites around a victim; and it indeed involves visible practice in conduct, bodily association, and cult. The pilgrim Church is indeed, in one sense, the body of a victim. But it is *unlike* cosmotheistic unity in that the image of a victimized body as the foundation of the social order is transposed into a new register. It is no longer the symbol and foundation for a government, for the containment of violence. The body of Christ as founding victim is more the continued, transcendent, non-instantiable pressure of critique against every earthly city. He is always speaking from the blood in the soil. If his "reign" is ever "immanentized" it arrives not through law, glory, some Christianized America, or any nation. It rather arrives weak and recessive, in fugitive moments as small as yeast and mustard, in tiny sacraments of forgiveness and gathering bodily around the broken body and shed blood of its odd sovereign. And just as one can persecute the Son of Man without knowing it, I imagine every creature, without knowing it, participates in this redemption – this beloved unity that does not destroy difference – if only, for most of us, in fleeting sparks.

In Girard's terms, the instability of mimesis is crucial to interpreting the dilemma of this book: our evolutionary feedback loop has created massive reservoirs of desire and intelligence that grew through the pronounced growth of our mimetic psyche. The chief cost of such gains is our always mimetically feeling a "lack of being" and the compulsion to stabilize this lack by polarizing upon a victim and establishing order and unity. Agonistic pluralism in a Girardian key means embracing our lack of being, consenting to our interdividuality, and taking responsibility for our complicity in the inescapable social web of mimesis. It means learning to not join the mob, even while mimesis and group association are inescapable. We cannot so much "oppose exclusion" as reposition it in tension with every hegemony – including the hegemony we may participate in or vote for. Just as Mouffe's pluralism refuses any central unifying foundation, monotheism robs us of any divinization of the political order. It robs us of an eternal cosmic enemy, a "Seth," a unifying pole who is feared, respected, and expelled as the divine enemy – for enemies are secularized in monotheism. It even robs of an "Osiris," of immanent identification with the body of a founding victim around whom we can unite a political order. Christianity's expression of this monotheism means not an escape from symbols of the divine victim but mystically identifies with the victim at an eschatological distance. This is not an immanent antagonism but a "transcendent rivalry" with the powers of our world. Christianity's monotheism, as a photographic negative of henotheistic completion, problematizes all unities of power by exposing and continually representing the founding murder of the political. As such, Girard is right to see how Christ "brings war not peace, disorder not order, because all order is suspect in a way: it always hides the one whose blood was shed in order to reconcile us."[7] This is how monotheism is an intolerant refusal to divinize victims. But, given the inescapability of the political, to see this is not to "arrive" but to remain continually haunted by the possibility we are victimizers without knowing it.

Given the way I have narrated monotheism, it would be mistaken to confess monotheism as an imaginative exercise for the credulous – trying to believe and live "as if" such a mythic One God lives on high. I'm not suggesting this sort of fideism, even if I have emphasized a certain inescapability of myth. Rather, apophatic intolerance here means something closer to what Agamben saw as the *"as not"* in Paul's messianism: the negation or hollowing out of every mythic Unity and supposedly naturalized power. So too the Christian monotheism I've outlined does not mean believing or pretending "as if" there is a big One God (and that we are, of course, on "his side"). It is about living as though all of the Unitive Powers and fictive gods that animate society's scapegoat mechanism are "as *not*."[8] This is an apophatic intolerance, that unity is always contestable, always potentially hiding injustices. This requires *not* tolerating any final closure of the political, whether in liberal, Marxist, socialist, or any political strategies. This "as not" does not pretend to have transcended "us versus them" association, which would, again, only construct a new one. A Christian account of monotheism means not a universalist escape from exclusion but co-identifying in Christ with the exclusion of God. Or rather – of having excluded God. In other words, if one of our problems of intolerance today is "identity forged negatively against the other," the

---

[7] BTE 141.

[8] Agamben, *The Time That Remains*, 2, *passim*; 1 Cor 7:29f. "the time is short. From now on those who have wives should live as if they do not; those who mourn, as if they did not; those who are happy, as if they were not; those who buy something, as if it were not theirs to keep; those who use the things of the world, as if not engrossed in them. For this world in its present form is passing away."

paradox of Christian "identity" is striking: "I have been crucified with Christ, and I no longer live, but he lives within me," (Gal 2:20). This was said by a man who knew he would have crucified Christ, and his identity was entirely displaced by this disorienting revelation.

This decenters one's identity precisely upon this negatively expelled Other. Far from this being a monotheism that negates or annexes the Other – like Habermas' caution against a monotheism that immunizes "against dissonant experiences" – this is precisely a self that is decentered by a haunting sense that one has never really understood the Other.[9] Put differently, we must of course appreciate the critique of monotheism that it constructs an antagonism with the Other, which sees the Other as not quite yet a person who fails to align with the will of the true God. This is of course vicious. But my account attempts not to abolish this but turn it entirely inside out: living in "Christ crucified" means the self is not yet established, as it has repudiated any claim to have grasped the elusive Other. Such a self is haunted by this Other's promise that he is to be found in our blind spot, our scapegoat, in the hungry, poor, and imprisoned. Here, one's citizenship is in heaven; one indeed lives a life lived in deferment. This (non-) identity begins in "repentance." This identity is indeed "forged negatively against the Other," but *in reverse*.

Even with a disavowal of the Absolute's representation in the political sphere, there remains the inescapability of the political. It is thus incumbent to imagine how such an unconditioned vision, whether in God's universality or liberalism's inclusivity, can navigate a world of the conditioned, in decisions and exclusions. The aversion to any order founded on exclusion operates in an unresolvable tension with the political, the boundaries of democracy. We must paradoxically live between the impossible unconditional and the conditioned – innocent as doves and shrewd as snakes.

If the Mosaic distinction and Liberal distinction divide true and false, it is crucial to not deride or abolish this intolerance but to inquire of its content and criteria. The monotheism I have advanced here paradoxically locates that criterion at the cutting decision upon the "the victim," the founding exclusion. "True religion" unearths that foundation, the one on whom the political line of exception is drawn, and lays it bare in painful perpetuity. Christ crucified, as the "king" and victim-foundation of a heavenly city, means for our earthly city nothing less than thinking the exception with a passion.

---

[9] Jürgen Habermas, *Theory of Communicative Action*, vol. 2, 133; Robert Erlewine, *Monotheism and Tolerance*, 38.

Bibliography

Adams, Rebecca. "Violence, Difference, Sacrifice: A Conversation with René Girard," *Religion and Literature* 25.2 (1993): 9–33.

Agamben, Giorgio. *Homo Sacer: Sovereign Power and Bare Life* (Stanford, CA: 1998).

The Time That Remains: A Commentary on the Letter to the Romans (Stanford, CA: 2005).

The Kingdom and the Glory: For a Theological Genealogy of Economy and Government (Stanford, CA: 2011).

Pilate and Jesus (Stanford, CA: 2015).

Albertz, Rainer. "Monotheism and Violence," *The Land of Israel in Bible, History, and Theology* (2009): 373–88.

Alison, James. *The Joy of Being Wrong: Original Sin through Easter Eyes* (New York: 1998).

Jesus the Forgiving Victim: Listening for the Unheard Voice, Book 2: God Not One of the Gods (Glenview, IL: 2013).

Anderson, Benedict. *Imagined Communities: Reflections on the Origin and Spread of Nationalism* (New York: 1983).

Antonello, Pierpaolo. "Maladaptation, Counterintuitiveness, and Symbolism: The Challenge of Mimetic Theory to Evolutionary Thinking." In *How We Became Human: Mimetic Theory and the Science of Evolutionary Origins*, edited by Pierpalo Antonello and Paul Gifford (East Lansing, MI: 2015), 47–78.

Antonello, Pierpaolo, and Paul Gifford, eds. *Can We Survive Our Origins?* (East Lansing, MI: 2015).

Antonello, Pierpaolo, and Paul Gifford. *How We Became Human: Mimetic Theory and the Science of Evolutionary Origins* (East Lansing, MI: 2015).

Appadurai, Arjun. "Dead Certainty: Ethnic Violence in the Era of Globalization," *Public Culture* 10.2 (1998): 225–47.

Aquinas, Thomas. *Summa contra gentiles*, vol. 3. Translated by English Dominican Fathers (London, UK: 1928).

Summa theologiae, vol. 44. Translated by Thomas Gilby (New York: 1972).

Aran, Gideon, and Ron E. Hassner. "Overview of Religion and Violence in Jewish Tradition." In *Oxford Handbook of Religion and Violence*, edited by Michael Jerryson, Mark Juergensmeyer, and Mark Kitts (Cambridge, MA: 2013).

Arenas, Pedreo Augustín Díaz. *Relaciones Internacionales de Dominacíon* (Bogotá, Colombia: 1998).

Armit, Ian. "Violence and Society in the Deep Human Past," *British Journal of Criminology* 51.3 (2011): 499–517.

Asad, Talal. *Formations of the Secular: Christianity, Islam, and Modernity* (Stanford, CA: 2003).

Assmann, Jan. *Moses the Egyptian* (Cambridge, MA: 1997).

Herrschaft und Heil: Politische Theologie in Altägypten, Israel und Europa (Munich: 2000).

"Theology, Theodicy, Philosophy: Introduction." In *Religions of the Ancient World: A Guide*, edited by Sarah Iles Johnston (Cambridge, MA: 2004), 531–46.

"Axial 'Breakthroughs' and Semantic 'Relocations' in Ancient Egypt and Israel." In *Axial Civilizations and World History* (Leiden, NL: 2005), 133–56.

"Monotheism and Its Political Consequences." In *Religion and Politics: Cultural Perspectives* (Leiden, NL: 2005), 141–59.

"The Advance in Intellectuality." In *New Perspectives on Freud's Moses and Monotheism*, edited by Ruth Ginsburg and Illana Pardes (Halle, Germany: 2006), 7–18.

Of God and Gods: Egypt, Israel, and the Rise of Monotheism (Madison, WI: 2008).

"Myth As 'historia divina' and 'historia sacra'." In *Scriptural Exegesis. The Shapes of Culture and the Religious Imagination: Essays in Honor of Michael Fishbane*, edited by D. A. Green and L. S. Lieber (New York: 2009), 13–24.

The Price of Monotheism. Translated by Robert Savage (Stanford, CA: 2010).

"Religion and the (Un)translatability of Cultures," lecture, University of Oxford (June 2011), www.youtube.com/watch?v=FR7DUt6pAUU&t=18s, accessed May 10, 2018.

"Cultural Memory and the Myth of the Axial Age." In *The Axial Age and Its Consequences*, edited by Robert N. Bellah and Hans Joas (Cambridge, MA: 2012).

Cultural Memory in Early Civilization: Writing, Remembrance, and Political Imagination (Cambridge, UK: 2012).

"Jan Assmann, Ramesside Theology and Its Place in the History of Religion," Lecture at Academia delle Scienze di Torino, May 15, 2015, www.youtube.com/watch?v=A6aFPQtK8XM&t=774s, accessed December 18, 2020.

From Akhenaten to Moses: Ancient Egypt and Religious Change (Cairo, Egypt: 2016).

"Freud, Sellin, and the Murder of Moses." In *Freud and Monotheism: Moses and the Violent Origins of Religion*, edited by Gilad Sharvit and Karen S. Feldman (New York: 2018).

The Invention of Religion: Faith and Covenant in the Book of Exodus (Princeton, NJ: 2018).

Aubral, François. "Discussion avec René Girard," *Esprit* 429 (1973): 559.

Avalos, Hector. *Fighting Words* (New York: 2005).

Bailie, Gil. *Violence Unveiled: Humanity at the Crossroads* (New York: 1996).

Barker, Margaret. *The Great High Priest: The Temple Roots of Christian Liturgy* (London, UK: 2003).

Becking, Bob, ed. *Orthodoxy, Liberalism, and Adaptation: Essays on Ways of Worldmaking in Times of Change from Biblical, Historical and Systematic Perspectives* (Leiden, NL: 2011).

Becking, Bob, Karel Van der Toorn, and Pieter W. Van der Horst, eds. *Dictionary of Deities and Divinities in the Bible* (Leiden, NL: 1995).

Bellah, Robert. "Religious Evolution," *American Sociological Review* 29 (1964): 358–74.

"What Is Axial about the Axial Age?," *European Journal of Sociology* 46.1 (2005): 69–89.

"Heritage of the Axial Age: Resource or Burden." In *The Axial Age and Its Consequences*, edited by Robert N. Bellah and Hans Joas (Cambridge, MA: 2012), 447–68.

Benjamin, Walter. "Theses on the Philosophy of History." In *Illuminations*, edited by Hannah Arendt (New York: 1968).

Reflections: Essays, Aphorisms, Autobiographical Writings. Translated by Edmund Jephcott (New York: 1986).

Bernstein, Richard J. "Jan Assmann: The Mosaic Distinction and Religious Violence," *Graduate Faculty Philosophy Journal* 32.1 (2011): 1–32.

Boehm, Christopher. "Retaliatory Violence in Human Prehistory," *The British Journal of Criminology* 51.3 (2011): 518–34.

Boulding, Kenneth. "Twelve Friendly Quarrels with Johan Galtung," *Journal of Peace Research* 14.1 (1977): 75–86.

Boyarin, Daniel. "Martyrdom and the Making of Christianity and Judaism," *Journal of Early Christian Studies* 6 (1998): 577–627.

"The Christian Invention of Religion: The Theodosian Empire and the Rabbinic Refusal of Religion," *Representations* 85.1 (2004): 21–57.

Breasted, James. *Development of Religion and Thought in Ancient Egypt* (New York: 1959).

Dawn of Conscience (New York: 1961).

Bright, J. *A History of Israel*, 2nd ed. (Philadelphia: 1972).

Brown, Raymond. *Introduction to the New Testament* (New Haven, CT: 1997).

Burkert, Walter. "Glaube und Verhalten: Zeichengehalt und Wirkungsmacht von Opferritualen." In *Le sacrifice dans l'antiquité*, Entretiens sur l'antiquité classique 27, edited by J Rudhardt and O. Reverdin. (Vandoeuvres, Genéve: 1981), 91–125.

Homo Necans: The Anthropology of Ancient Greek Sacrificial Ritual and Myth. Translated by Peter Bing (Berkeley, CA: 1983).

The Orientalizing Revolution (Cambridge, MA: 1998).

Canetti, Elias. *Crowds and Power.* Translated by C. (Harmondsworth: 1973).

Carr, David. *Holy Resilience: The Bible's Traumatic Origins* (New Haven, CT: 2014)

Carrasco, David. *City of Sacrifice: The Aztec Empire and the Role of Violence in Civilization* (Boston, MA: 1999).

Carter, Stephen S. "Must Liberalism Be Violent?: A Reflection on the Work of Stanley Hauerwas," *Law and Contemporary Problems* 75.4 (2012): 201–18.

Cataldo, Jeremiah. *Breaking Monotheism: Yehud and the Material Formation of Monotheistic Identity*, Library of Hebrew Bible/Old Testament Studies 565 (New York: Bloomsbury, 2014).

Cavanaugh, William. "Killing for the Telephone Company: Why the Nation State Is Not the Keeper of the Common Good," *Modern Theology* 20.2 (2004): 243–74.

The Myth of Religious Violence (Oxford, UK: 2012).

Chait, Jonathan. "The 'Shut It Down' Left and the War on the Liberal Mind," *New York Magazine*, April 26, 2017.

Chandler, Daniel, and Rod Munday. "Symbolic Violence." *Dictionary of Media and Communication* (Oxford, UK: 2011), www.oxfordreference.com/view/10.1093/oi/authority.20110803100546777, accessed May 11, 2018.

Chapman, D. W. *Ancient Jewish and Christian Perspectives of Crucifixion*, WUNT 2.444 (Tübingen, Germany: 2008).

Chilton, Bruce. *The Temple of Jesus: His Sacrificial Program within a Cultural History of Sacrifice* (University Park, PA: 1992).

Jesus and His Context: Temple, Purity, and Restoration (Leiden, NL: 1997).

Clifford, Richard. "The Major Prophets, Baruch, and Lamentations." In *The Catholic Study Bible* (New York: 2006), 280–335.

Cliteur, Paul. *The Monotheist Dilemma or the Theology of Terrorism* (Amsterdam/Antwerp: 2010).

The Secular Outlook: In Defense of Moral and Political Secularism (Hoboken, NJ: 2010).

Coakley, Sarah. *Sacrifice Regained: Reconsidering the Rationality of Religious Belief* (Cambridge, UK: 2012).

Collins, Brian. *The Head Beneath the Altar: Hindu Mythology and the Critique of Sacrifice* (East Lansing, MI: 2014).

Cone, James H. *The Cross and the Lynching Tree* (Maryknoll, NY: 2011).

Connolly, N. D. B. "Charlottesville Showed that Liberalism Can't Defeat White Supremacy. Only Direct Action Can," *The Washington Post* (August 15, 2017).

Connelly, William E. *Why I Am Not a Secularist* (Minneapolis, MN: 2000).

Pluralism (Durham, NC: 2005).

Conze, Edward I. B. Horner, David Snellgrove, and Arthur Waley, eds. and trans. *Buddhist Texts through the Ages* (New York: 1954).

Cook, John Granger. *Crucifixion in the Mediterranean World* (Tübingen, Germany: 2014).

Cook, Stephen. *The Social Roots of Biblical Yahwism* (Atlanta, GA: 2004).

Corrigan, John, and Lynn S. Neal, eds. *Religious Intolerance in America: A Documentary History* (Chapel Hill, NC: 2010).

Counet, Patrick C. "The Divine Messiah: Early Jewish Monotheism and the New Testament." In *The Boundaries of Monotheism: Interdisciplinary Explorations into the Foundations of Western Monotheism*, edited by Anne-Marie Korte and Maaike de Haardt (Leiden, NL: 2009), 28–52.

Cowdell, Scott. *René Girard and Secular Modernity* (Notre Dame, IN: 2013).

Cowdell, Scott, Chris Fleming, and Joel Hodge, eds. *Violence, Desire, and the Sacred*, vol. 1 (New York: 2014).

Cross, F. M. *From Epic to Canon: History and Literature in Ancient Israel* (Baltimore, MD: 1998).

Day, Dorothy. "Why Do the Members of Christ Tear One Another," *The Catholic Worker* (February 1942).

Davis, Stephen, Daniel Kendall S. J., and Gerald O'Collins, eds. *The Resurrection: An Interdisciplinary Symposium on the Resurrection of Jesus* (New York: 1999).

Decreus, Thomas, and Matthias Lievens. "Hegemony and the Radicalization of Democracy: An Interview with Chantal Mouffe," *Tijdschrift voor Filosofie* 73 (2011): 677–99.

Deneen, Patrick. *Why Liberalism Failed* (New Haven, CT: 2018).

Derrida, Jacques. *Archive Fever: A Freudian Impression*. Translated by Eric Prenowitz (Chicago, IL: 1998).

Deutscher, Isaac. *The Non-Jewish Jew and Other Essays* (New York: 1968).

Dever, William. "How Was Ancient Israel Different?" In *The Breakout: The Origins of Civilization*, edited by Martha Lamberg-Karlovsky (Cambridge, MA: 2000).

Dias, Brian G., and Kerry J. Ressler. "Parental Olfactory Experiences Influences Behavior and Neural Structure in Subsequent Generations," *Nature Neuroscience* (2013): 1–9.

Dillon, Michael, and Julian Reid. *The Liberal Way of War: Killing to Make Life Live* (London, UK: 2009).

Deloria, Vine, Jr. *God Is Red: A Native View of Religion* (New York: 2003).

De Lubac, Henri. *The Discovery of God* (Grand Rapids, MI: 1996).

Doran, Robert. "Apocalyptic Thinking after 9/11: An Interview with René Girard," *SubStance* 115.37.1 (2008): 20–32.

Drake, H. A. "Monotheism and Violence," *Journal of Late Antiquity* 6.2 (2013): 251–63.

Dumouchel, Paul. *Violence and Truth: On the Work of René Girard* (Palo Alto, CA: 1988).

  The Barren Sacrifice: An Essay on Political Violence (East Lansing, MI: 2015).

  "A Covenant among Beasts: Human and Chimpanzee Violence in Evolutionary Perspective." In *Can We Survive Our Origins?*, edited by Pierpaolo Antonello and Paul Gifford (East Lansing, MI: 2015).

Dupuy, Jean-Pierre. *The Mark of the Sacred*. Translated by M. B. DeBevoise (Redwood City, CA: 2013).

Ellens, J. Harold, ed. *The Destructive Power of Religion: Violence in Judaism, Christianity, and Islam* (Westport, CT: 2007).

Eller, Jack David. *Cruel Creeds, Virtuous Violence: Religious Violence across Culture and History* (Amherst, NY: 2010).

Eibl-Eibesfeldt, Irenäus. *Love and Hate: The Natural History of Behavior Patterns*. Translated by Geoffrey Strachan (New York: 1996).

Eisenstadt, Samuel. "The Axial Conundrum between Transcendental Visions and Vicissitudes of Their Institutionalizations: Constructive and Destructive

Possibilities." In *The Axial Age and Its Consequences*, edited by Robert N. Bellah and Hans Joas (Cumberland, MD: 2012), 277–93.

Eliade, Mircea. *A History of Religious Ideas*, vol. 1. Translated by W. R. Trask (Chicago, IL: 1979).

Erlewine, Robert. *Monotheism and Tolerance: Recovering a Religion of Reason* (Bloomington, IN: 2010).

Eusebius Pamphilius. *Church History, Life of Constantine, Oration in Praise of Constantine*. Translated by Philip Schaff (New York: 1890).

Evans, Brad. *Liberal Terror* (Cambridge, UK: 2013).

"Liberal Violence: From the Benjaminian Divine to the Angels of History," *Theology and Event* 19.1 (2016): 607272.

Evans, Brad, and Julian Reid. *Resilient Life: The Art of Living Dangerously* (Cambridge, UK: 2014).

Firth, Raymond. *Tikopia Ritual and Belief* (Boston, MA: 1968).

Fleming, Chris. *René Girard: Violence and Mimesis* (Cambridge, UK: 2004).

Foucault, Michel. *Discipline and Punish: The Birth of the Prison*. Translated by Alan Sheridan (New York: 1977).

Freeman, Kathleen. *Ancilla to the Pre-Socratic Philosophers: A Complete Translations of the Fragments in Diels*, Fragmente der Vorsokratiker (Cambridge, MA: 1962).

Freud, Sigmund. *The Future of an Illusion* (New York: 1961).

Beyond the Pleasure Principle. Translated by James Strachey. (London, UK: 1961).

Moses and Monotheism (New York: Vintage Books, 1967).

"Civilization and Its Discontents." In *The Freud Reader*. Translated by James Strachey, edited by Peter Gay (New York: 1989), 722–71.

The Standard Edition of the Complete Works of Sigmund Freud. Translated by James Strachey (London, UK: 1994).

Frost, Kathryn M. "Freud, *Moses and Monotheism*, and the Conversation between Mimetic Theory and Psychoanalysis." In *The Palgrave Handbook of Mimetic Theory and Religion*, edited by James Alison and Wolfgang Palaver (New York, 2017).

Frymer-Kensky, Tikva. "The Atrahasis Epic and Its Significance for Our Understanding of Genesis 1–9," *The Biblical Archaeologist* 40.4 (1977): 147–55.

Galtung, Johan. "Violence, Peace, and Peace Research," *Journal of Peace Research* 6.3 (1969): 167–91.

Gans, Eric. "René et moi." In *For René Girard*, ed. Sandoor Goodhart et al. (East Lansing, MI: 2009), 19–25.

Garnsey, Peter. "Religious Toleration in Classical Antiquity," *Studies in Church History* 21 (1984): 1–27.

Garrels, Scott, ed. *Mimesis and Science: Empirical Research on Imitation and the Mimetic Theory of Culture and Religion* (East Lansing, MI: 2011).

Gay, Peter. *A Godless Jew: Freud, Atheism, and the Making of Psychoanalysis* (New Haven, London, UK: 1987)

Gay, Peter. ed. *The Freud Reader* (New York: 1989)

Gibbon, Edward. *The History of the Decline and Fall of the Roman Empire*. Edited by J. Bury (London, UK: 1909–14).

Girard, René. *Deceit, Desire, and the Novel: Self and Other in Literary Structure.* Translated by Yvonne Freccero (Baltimore, MD: 1965).

"Dionysus versus the Crucified," *Modern Language Notes* 99. 4 (1984): 816–35.

"Generative Scapegoating." In *Violent Origins: Ritual Killing and Cultural Formation,* edited by Walter Burkert, René Girard, and Jonathan Z. Smith (Redwood City, CA: 1987), 149–90.

Job: The Victim of His People. Translated by Yvonne Freccero (Redwood City, CA: 1987).

Things Hidden Since the Foundation of the World. Translated by Stephen Bann and Michael Metteer (Redwood City, CA: 1987)

"The Logic of the Undecidable: An Interview with Thomas F. Bertonneau," *Paroles Gelées* 5 (1987): 1–24.

The Scapegoat. Translated by Yvonne Freccero (Baltimore, MD: 1989).

"Origins: A View from Literature." In *Understanding Origins,* edited by Francisco J. Varela and Jean-Pierre Dupuy (Dordrecht, NL: 1991).

A Theatre of Envy: William Shakespeare (New York: 1991).

Girard Reader. Edited by James G. Williams (New York: 1996).

"Interview with René Girard: Comments on Christianity, Scapegoating, and Sacrifice," *Religion* 27.3 (1997) 249–54.

"Victims, Violence, and Christianity," *The Month* 259.1564 (1998): 129–35.

"Violence in Biblical Narrative," *Philosophy and Literature* 23.2 (1999): 387–92.

"The Bloody Skin of the Victim." In *The New Visibility of Religion: Studies in Religion and Cultural Hermeneutics,* edited by Graham Ward and Michael Hoetzel (London, UK: 2008), 59–67.

Battling to the End: Conversations with Benoît Chantre. Translated by Mary Baker (East Lansing, MI: 2010).

Sacrifice. Translated by Matthew Pattillo and David Dawson (East Lansing, MI: 2011).

The One by Whom Scandal Comes (East Lansing, MI: 2014).

"Interview with David Cayley, The Scapegoat, pt 4," Canadian Broadcast Company, March 11, 2016, www.cbc.ca/radio/ideas/the-scapegoat-the-ideas-of-ren%C3%A9-girard-part-4-1.3483817, accessed April 27, 2020.

Glick, Peter. "When Neighbors Blame Neighbors: Scapegoating and the Breakdown of Ethnic Relations." In *Explaining the Breakdown of Ethnic Relations: Why Neighbors Kill,* edited by Victoria M. Esses and Richard A Vernon (Hoboken, NJ: 2008), 123–46.

Gnuse, Robert. *No Other Gods: Emergent Monotheism in Israel* (Sheffield, UK: 1997).

"Intellectual Breakthrough or Tyranny?: Monotheism's Contested Implications," *Horizons* 34 (2007): 78–95.

No Tolerance for Tyrants: The Biblical Assault on Kings and Kingship (Collegeville, MN: 2011).

Goldhagen, Daniel Jonah. *Hitler's Willing Executioners: Ordinary Germans and the Holocaust* (New York: 1996).

Goodhart, Sandoor. *The Prophetic Law* (East Lansing, MI: 2014).

Goodman, Martin. "Trajan and the Origins of Roman Hostility to the Jews," *Past and Present* 182 (2004): 11–2.

Gopin, Marc. *Between Eden and Armageddon: The Future of World Religions: Violence and Peacemaking* (Oxford, UK: 2002).

Gordon, Robert. "Introduction to Israel's God." In *The God of Israel*, Oriental *Publications* 64, edited by Robert Gordon (Cambridge, UK: 2008).

Green, Clifford, ed. *Karl Barth: Theologian of Freedom* (Minneapolis, MN: 1991).

Griffiths, John Gwyn. *The Origins of Osiris and His Cult* (Leiden, NL: 1980).

   The Divine Verdict: A Study of Divine Judgment in the Ancient Religions (Leiden, NL: 1991).

Gruenwald, Ithamar. "Intolerance and Martyrdom: From Socrates to Rabbi 'Aqiva." In *Tolerance and Intolerance in Early Judaism and Christianity*, edited by Graham Stanton and Guy Stroumsa (Cambridge, UK: 1998).

Gutmann, Amy, ed. *Human Rights As Politics and Idolatry* (Princeton, NJ: 2001).

Habermas, Jürgen. *Theory of Communicative Action*, vol. 2: *Lifeworld and System: A Critique of Functionalist Reason*. Translated by Thomas McCarthy (Boston, MA: 1989).

Halbertal, Moshe, and Avishai Margalit. *Idolatry*. Translated by Naomi Goldblum (Cambridge, MA: 1992).

Hall, Douglas John. "Against Religion: The Case for Faith." *The Christian Century* 128.1 (2011): 30–3.

Hamerton-Kelly, Robert. *Sacred Violence: Paul's Hermeneutic of the Cross* (Minneapolis, MN: 1991).

Hardin, Michael. *Reading the Bible with René Girard* (Lancaster, PA: 2015).

Hare, Douglas R. A. *Matthew: Interpretation* (Louisville, KY: 1993).

Haring, James W. "'The Lord Your God Is God of Gods and Lord of Lords': Is Monotheism a Political Problem in the Hebrew Bible?," *Political Theology*, January 12, 2017, www.tandfonline.com/doi/full/10.1080/1462317X.2016 .1263028.

Hauerwas, Stanley. *War and the American Difference: Theological Reflections on Violence and National Identity* (Ada, MI: 2011).

   "Rights Language and the Justice of God," *ABC Religion and Ethics*, November 2, 2012, www.abc.net.au/religion/articles/2012/11/02/3624140 .htm, accessed January 8, 2017.

Hauerwas, Stanley, and William Willimon. *Resident Aliens: Life in the Christian Colony* (Nashville, TN: 1989).

Haw, Chris. "Human Evolution and the Single Victim Mechanism: Locating Girard's Hominization Hypothesis through Literature Survey," *Contagion* (2017): 191–216.

Hayden, Tom. "Christian Extremists in Iraq," June 22, 2005, www .huffingtonpost.com/tom-hayden/christian-extremists-in-i_b_3039.html, accessed March 2, 2017.

Hendel, Ron. "Israelite Religion." In *Encyclopedia of Religion*, vol. 2., edited by L. Jones (New York: 2004), 4742–50.

   "The Exodus As Cultural Memory: Egyptian Bondage and the Song of the Sea." In *Israel's Exodus in Transdisciplinary Perspective: Text, Archaeology,*

Culture, and Geoscience, edited by Thomas E. Levy (New York: 2014), 65–77.

Herbener, Jens-André P. "On the Term 'Monotheism'," *Numen* 60 (2013): 616–48.

Heschel, Abraham. *The Prophets* (New York: 2001).

Hessler, Peter. "Akhenaten," *National Geographic* 231.5 (2017): 121–43.

Heyman, George. *The Power of Sacrifice: Roman and Christian Discourses in Conflict* (Washington, DC: 2007).

Himes, Kenneth. "Peacebuilding and Catholic Social Teaching." In *Peacebuilding: Catholic Theology, Ethics, and Praxis*, edited by Scott Appleby, Robert Schreiter, and Gerard Powers (Maryknoll, NY: 2010), 265–99.

Hitchens, Christopher. *God Is Not Great: How Religion Poisons Everything* (New York: 2007).

Hobbes, Thomas. *The Elements of Law Natural and Politic* (Oxford, UK: 1994).

Hodder, Ian, ed. *Religion in the Emergence of Civilization: Çatalhöyük As a Case Study* (New York: 2010).

Hodder, Ian. *Violence and the Sacred in the Ancient Near East: Girardian Conversations at Çatalhöyük* (Cambridge, UK: 2019).

Hodge, Joel. "Terrorism's Answer to Modernity's Cultural Crisis: Re-Sacralizing Violence in the Name of Jihadist Totalitarianism," *Modern Theology* 32.2 (2016): 231–58.

Hoffmeier, James. *Akhenaten and the Origins of Monotheism* (Oxford, UK: 2015).

Horsley, Richard. *Jesus and Empire: The Kingdom of God and the New World Disorder* (Minneapolis, MN: 2003).

Huntington, Samuel P. *Clash of Civilizations and the Remaking of World Order* (New York: 1996).

Ignatief, Michael. *The Warrior's Honor: Ethnic War and the Modern Conscience* (New York: 1997).

Jantzen, Grace. "New Creations: Eros, Beauty, and the Passion for Transformation." In *Toward a Theology of Eros: Transfiguring Passions at the Limits of Discipline*, edited by Virginia Burrus and Catherine Keller (New York: 2007), 271–90.

Jaspers, Karl. *The Origin and Goal of History* (London, UK: 1953).

Joas, Hans, and Wolfgang Knöbl. *War in Social Thought: Hobbes to the Present* (Princeton, NJ: 2013).

Johnson, Keith. *Karl Barth and the Analogia Entis* (London, UK: 2011).

Juergensmeyer, Mark. *Terror in the Mind of God: The Global Rise of Religious Violence* (Berkeley, CA: 2001).

Terror in the Mind of God, 3rd ed (Berkeley, CA: 2003).

"Religion the Problem?" *The Hedgehog Review* 6.1 (2004): 21–33.

Kant, Immanuel. *Metaphysics of Morals*. Translated by Mary J. Gregor (Cambridge, UK: 1996).

Critique of the Power of Judgment. Translated by Paul Guyer and Eric Matthews (Cambridge, UK: 2000).

King, Martin Luther, Jr. "Letter from a Birmingham Jail." In *I Have a Dream: Writings and Speeches That Changed the World*, edited by James M. Washington (San Francisco, CA: 1992), 83–100.

Kirsch, Jonathan. *God against the Gods: The History of War between Monotheism and Polytheism* (New York: 2005).

Kirwan, Michael. *Girard and Theology* (New York: 2009).

Knoppers, Gary N. "Ancient Near Eastern Royal Grants and the Davidic Covenant: A Parallel?" *Journal of the American Oriental Society* 116.4 (1996): 670–97.

Kokenniemi, Martti. *The Gentle Civilizer of Nations: The Rise and Fall of International Law 1870–1960* (Cambridge, UK: 2002).

Konner, Melvin. "A Bold New Theory Proposes That Humans Tamed Themselves," *The Atlantic*, March 2019.

Kynes, Will, "Satan." In *The Oxford Encyclopedia of the Bible and Theology*, edited by Samuel Balentine (Oxford, UK: 2015), 264–7.

Laclau, Ernesto, and Chantal Mouffe. *Hegemony and Socialist Strategy: Towards a Radical Democratic Politics* (New York: 1985).

Lacoue-Labarthe, Philippe. "Mimesis and Truth," *Diacritics* 8.1 (1978), 10–23.

Lang, Bernhard. *Monotheism and the Prophetic Minority* (Atlanta, GA: 1983).

Launderville, Dale. "Ezekiel's Throne-Chariot Vision: Spiritualizing the Model of Divine Royal Rule," *Catholic Biblical Quarterly* 66 (2004): 361–77.

Lefebure, Leo. *Revelation, the Religions, and Violence* (Maryknoll, NY: 2000).

Levine, Baruch. "Assyrian Ideology and Biblical Monotheism," *Iraq* 67 (2005): 411–27.

Levinson, Bernard M. "The Reconceptualization of Kingship in Deuteronomy and the Deuteronomistic History's Transformation of Torah," *Vetus Testamentum* 51 (2001): 511–34.

Lewis, C. S. *The Allegory of Love: A Study of Medieval Tradition* (New York: 1958).

Lichtheim, Miriam. *Ancient Egyptian Literature. Vol II: The New Kingdom* (Berkeley, CA: 1976).

Locke, John. *Two Treatises of Government and A Letter Concerning Toleration.* Edited by Ian Shapiro (New Haven, CT: 2003).

Lohfink, Gerhard. *Does God Need the Church?: Toward a Theology of the Church* (Emeryville, CA: 1999).

Ludwig, Theodore M. "Monotheism," *Encyclopedia of Religion*, 2nd ed., edited by L. Jones (Detroit, MI: 2005).

Lukianoff, Greg, and Jonathan Haidt. "Better Watch What You Say: The Coddling of the American Mind," *The Atlantic*, September 2015.

Luther, Martin. "Temporal Authority." In *Selected Writings of Martin Luther*, vol. 2, edited by Theodore G. Tappert (Minneapolis, MN: 2007), 265–320.

MacDougall, Scott. "Scapegoating the Secular: The Irony of Mimetic Violence in the Social Theology of John Milbank." In *Violence, Transformation, and the Sacred*, edited by Margaret Pfeil and Tobias Winwright (Maryknoll, NY: 2011), 85–98.

Machinist, Peter. "How Gods Die, Biblically and Otherwise: A Problem of Cosmic Restructuring," In *Reconsidering the Concept of Revolutionary Monotheism*, edited by Beate Pongrantz-Leisten (Winona Lake, IN: 2011), 189–240.

MacIntyre, Alasdair. *After Virtue: A Study in Moral Theory* (South Bend, IN: 1981).

Mack, Burton. *Mark and Christian Origins: A Myth of Innocence* (Philadelphia, PA: 1988).

    Who Wrote the New Testament?: The Making of Christian Myth (San Francisco, CA: 1995).

    The Christian Myth: Origins, Logic, and Legacy (New York: 2003).

    The Rise and Fall of the Christian Myth (New Haven, CT: 2017).

Marcus, Joel. "Crucifixion as Parodic Exaltation," *Journal of Biblical Literature* 125.1 (2006): 73–87.

Markschies, Christoph. "The Price of Monotheism." In *One God: Pagan Monotheism in the Roman Empire*, edited by Stephen Mitchell and Peter Van Nuffeln (Cambridge, UK: 2010), 100–11.

Martin, David. "Axial Religions and the Problem of Violence." In *The Axial Age and Its Consequences*, edited by Bellah, Robert N. and Joas, Hans (Cambridge, MA: 2012), 294–316.

Martin, James. *Chantal Mouffe: Hegemony, Radical Democracy, and the Political* (Milton Park, UK: 2013).

Martin, S. Angus. "The Origins of Agriculture: A Biological Perspective and a New Hypothesis," *Australian Biologist* 6 (June 1993): 96–105.

Martínez, Desiderio Parrilla. "Mimesis, Ritual Sacrifice, and Ceremony of Proskynesis," *Contagion* 24 (2017): 57–72.

Marvin, Carolyn, and David Engle. "Blood Sacrifice and the Nation: Revisiting Civil Religion," *Journal of the American Academy of Religion* 64.4 (767–80).

Marx, Karl. "Contribution to the Critique of Hegel's Philosophy of Right. Introduction." In *Karl Marx: Early Writings*. Translated and edited by T. B. Bottomore (New York: 1964), 55–9.

McCarraher, Eugene. *The Enchantments of Mammon: How Capitalism Became the Religion of Modernity* (Cambridge, MA: 2019).

Mendenhall, George. "The Monarchy," *Interpretation* 29 (1975): 155–70.

Metz, Johann Baptist. *The Word in History*. Edited by T. Patrick Burke (New York: 1966).

Michel, Casey. "How Liberal Portland Became America's Most Violent City," *Politico*, June 30, 2017, www.politico.com/magazine/story/2017/06/30/how-liberal-portland-became-americas-most-politically-violent-city-215322, accessed December 18, 2020.

Michels, Scott. "How Evangelicals Gained Political Power," *The New York Times*, The Retro Report, www.nytimes.com/video/us/100000006182547/evangelicals-political-power.html, accessed May 25, 2020.

Miller, Richard Brian. *Terror, Religion, and Liberal Thought* (New York: 2010).

Miller, Richard C. *Resurrection and Reception in Early Christianity* (New York: 2015).

Moberly, R. W. L. "Is Monotheism Bad for You? Some Reflections on God, the Bible, and Life in the Light of Regina Schwartz's The Curse of Cain." In *The God of Israel*, University of Cambridge Oriental Publications 64, edited by Robert P. Gordon (Cambridge, UK: 2007), 94–112.

Morris, Ellen. "The Pharaoh and Pharaonic Office." In *A Companion to Ancient Egypt*, edited by A. B. Lloyd (Oxford, UK: 2010), 201–17.

Mouffe, Chantal. *Hegemony and Socialist Strategy* (New York: 1985).

The Democratic Paradox (New York: 2005).

"Religion, Liberal Democracy, and Citizenship." In *Political Theologies: Public Religions in a Post-Secular World*, edited by Hent de Vries and Lawrence E. Sullivan (New York: 2006), 318–26.

Agonistics: Thinking the World Politically (New York: 2013).

For a Left Populism (New York: 2018).

Murphy, R. F. "Intergroup Hostility and Social Cohesion," *American Anthropologist* 59 (1957): 1018–35.

Nahme, Paul E. "God Is the Reason: Herman Cohen's Monotheism and the Liberal Theologico-Political Predicament," *Modern Theology* 33.1 (2017): 116–39.

Nelson, Eric. *The Hebrew Republic: Jewish Sources and the Transformation of European Political Thought* (Cambridge, UK: 2011).

Nichols, Stephen G. "Doomed Discourse: Debating Monotheisms Pre- and Post-Modern," *Modern Language Notes* 126.4 (2011): S12–31.

Niebuhr, H. Richard. *Radical Monotheism and Western Culture* (New York: 1943).

Nietzsche, Friedrich. *The Gay Science*. Translated by Walter Kaufmann (New York: 1974).

The Antichrist (New York: 2010).

The Will to Power. Translated by Michael A. Scarpitti and R. Kevin Hill (New York: 2019).

Omer, Atalia. "Can a Critic Be a Caretaker?: Religion, Conflict, and Conflict Transformation," *Journal of the American Academy of Religion* 79.2 (2011): 459–96.

"Modernists Despite Themselves: The Phenomenology of the Secular and the Limits of Critique as an Instrument of Change," *Journal of the American Academy of Religion* 83.1 (2015): 27–71.

"Religious Peacebuilding: The Exotic, the Good, the Theatrical." In *The Oxford Handbook of Religion, Conflict, and Peacebuilding*, edited by Atalia Omer, R. Scott Appleby, and David Little (Oxford, UK: 2015), 1–31.

Oughourlian, Jean-Michel. *The Mimetic Brain*. Translated by Trevor Merrill (East Lansing, MI: 2016).

Pakkala, Juha. *Intolerant Monolatry in the Deuteronomistic History* (Göttingen, Germany: 1999).

Palaver, Wolfgang. *Politik und Religion bei Thomas Hobbes: Eine Kritik aus der Sicht der Theorie René Girards* (Innsbruck, Austria: 1991).

"A Girardian Reading of Schmitt's Political Theology," *Telos* 93 (1992): 43–88.

"Hobbes and the Katéchon: The Secularization of Sacrificial Christianity," *Contagion* 2 (1995): 57–74.

"Carl Schmitt's 'Apocalyptic' Resistance against Global Civil War." In *Politics and Apocalypse*, edited by Robert Hamerton-Kelly (East Lansing, MI: 2007).

"The Ambiguous Cachet of Victimhood." In *The New Visibility of Religion: Studies in Religion and Cultural Hermeneutics*, edited by Graham Ward and Michael Hoetzel (London, UK: 2008), 68–87.

René Girard's Mimetic Theory (East Lansing, MI: 2013).

"Europe and Enmity." In *Violence Desire, and the Sacred*, vol. 1, edited by Scott Cowdell, Chris Fleming, and Joel Hodge (New York: 2014), 171–81.

Panikkar, Raimundo. "Is the Notion of Human Rights a Western Concept?" *Diogenes* 120 (1982): 75–102.

Parpola, Simo. "Assyria's Expansion in the 8th and 7th Centuries BCE and Its Long-Term Repercussions in the West." In *Symbiosis, Symbolism, and the Power of the Past: Canaan, Ancient Israel and Their Neighbours from the Late Bronze Age through Roman Palestine*, edited by W. G. Dever and S. Gitin (Winona Lake, IL: 2003), 99–112.

Pearce, Matt. "A Guide to Some of the Far-Right Symbols Seen in Charlottesville," *The Los Angeles Times*, August 14, 2017.

Peterson, Erik. "Monotheism as a Political Problem" in *Theological Tractates*, edited and translated by Michael J. Hollenbach (Redwood City, CA: 2011).

Pinker, Steven. *The Better Angels of Our Nature: Why Violence Has Declined* (New York: 2011).

Pritchard, James B., ed. *Ancient Near Eastern Texts Relating to the Old Testament* (Princeton, NJ: 1969).

Propp, William. "Monotheism and 'Moses': The Problem of Early Israelite Religion," *Ugarit-Forshungen* 31 (1999): 539.

Przywara, Eric. *Analogia Entis: Metaphysics – Original Structure and Universal Rhythm*. Translated by John Betz and David Bentley-Hart (Grand Rapids, MI: 2014).

Queiruga, Andrés Torres. "Monotheism and Universal Brother-/Sisterhood." In *Monotheism: Divinity and Unity Reconsidered*, edited by Erik Borgman, Maria Clara Bingemer, and Andrés Torres Queirga (London, UK: 2009). Reprinted in *Concilium* 2009.4: 67–78.

Ranieri, John. "What Voegelin Missed in the Gospel," *Contagion* 7 (2000): 125–59.

   Disturbing Revelation: Leo Strauss, Eric Voegelin, and the Bible (Columbia, MO: 2009).

Rappaport, Roy. *Ritual and Religion in the Making of Humanity* (Cambridge, UK: 1999).

Rashkover, Randi, and Martin Kavka, eds. *Judaism, Liberalism, and Political Theology* (Bloomington, IN: 2013).

Ratzinger, Joseph. *Truth and Tolerance: Christian Belief and World Religion*. Translated by Henry Taylor (San Francisco, CA: 2004).

Rawls, John. *A Theory of Justice* (Cambridge, MA: 1971).

Redekop, Vern Neufeld, and Thomas Ryba, eds. *René Girard and Creative Reconciliation* (Lanham, MD: 2014).

Redford, Donald. *Egypt, Canaan, and Israel in Ancient Times* (Princeton, NJ: 1992).

   "The Monotheism of Akhenaten." In *Aspects of Monotheism*, edited by Donald B. Redford, Hershel Shanks, and Jack Meinhardt (Washington, DC: 1997), 11–26.

Rempel, Marcus Peter. *Life at the End of Us versus Them: Cross Culture Stories* (Victoria, BC: 2017).

Reynolds, Thomas E. "Beyond Violence in Monotheism: Interfaith Possibilities in René Girard's Theory of Mimetic Rivalry," *Studies in Interreligious Dialogue* 19.1 (2009): 81–101.

Richmond, Oliver. "A Post-Liberal Peace: Eirenism and the Everyday," *Review of International Studies* 35 (2009), 557–80.

Robinette, Brian. *Grammars of Resurrection: A Christian Theology of Presence and Absence* (New York: 2009).

Rojtman, Betty. "The Double Death of Moses." In *New Perspectives on Freud's Moses and Monotheism*, edited by Ruth Ginsburg and Illana Pardes (Halle, Germany: 2006), 93–116.

Rose, Phil. "Divinizing Technology and Violence: Technopoly, the Warfare State, and the Revolution in Military Affairs," *Journal of Contemporary Religion* 27.3 (2012): 365–81.

Rousseau, Jean-Jacques. *Rousseau: The Social Contract and Other Later Political Writings*. Edited by Victor Gourevitch (Cambridge, UK: 1997).

Sahlins, Marshall. *Stone Age Economics* (New York: 1972).

Said, Edward, Christopher Bollas, and Jacqueline Rose. *Freud and the Non-European* (New York: 2004).

Sauls, Scott, and Gabe Lyons. *Jesus Outside the Lines: A Way Forward for Those Who Are Tired of Taking Sides* (Carol Stream, IL: 2015).

Sawyer, John F. A. "Biblical Alternatives to Monotheism," *Theology* 87 (1984), 172–80.

Schäfer, Peter. "The Triumph of Pure Spirituality." In *New Perspectives on Freud's Moses and Monotheism*, edited by Ruth Ginsburg and Illana Pardes (Halle, Germany: 2006), 19–43.

Schillebeeckx, Edward. *Jesus: An Experiment in Christology* (New York: 1981). *Christ: The Experience of Jesus As Lord* (New York: 1983).
"Culture, Religion, and Violence: Theology as a Component of Culture." In *The Collected Works of Edward Schillebeeckx*, vol. XI (New York: 2014).

Schmidt, Thomas. "Jesus' Triumphal March to Crucifixion: The Sacred Way As Roman Procession," *Bible Review*, February (1997): 30–7.

Schmitt, Carl. *The Concept of the Political*, Expanded ed. (Chicago, IL: 2007). *Political Theology: Four Chapters on the Concept of Sovereignty*. Translated by G. Schwab (Chicago, IL: 2005)

Schreiter, Robert J. "The Catholic Social Imaginary and Peacebuilding." In *Peacebuilding: Catholic Theology, Ethics, and Praxis*. Edited by Scott Appleby, Robert Schreiter, and Gerard Powers (Maryknoll, NY: 2010), 221–39.

Schwager, Raymund. *Must There Be Scapegoats?* (New York: 2000).

Schwartz, Regina. *The Curse of Cain: The Violent Legacy of Monotheism* (Chicago, IL: 1998).

Scott, David, and Charles Hirschkind, eds. *Powers of the Secular Modern: Talal Asad and His Interlocutors* (Redwood City, CA: 2006).

Scott, James C. "A Saturnalia of Power: The First Public Declaration of the Hidden Transcript." In *Domination and the Arts of Resistance: Hidden Transcripts* (New Haven, CT: 1990).

Seidlmayer, Stephan. "The First Intermediate Period (c. 2160–2055)." In *The Oxford History of Ancient Egypt*, edited by Ian Shaw (Oxford, UK: 2000), 108–36.

Selengut, Charles. *Sacred Fury: Understanding Religious Violence* (Lanham, MD: 2003).

Sellin, Ernst. *Mose und seine Bedeutung für die israelitisch-jüdische Religionsgeschichte* (Leipzig, Germany: 1922).

Shahid, Waleed. "America in Populist Times: An Interview with Chantal Mouffe," *The Nation*, December 15, 2016. www.thenation.com/article/america-in-popu list-times-an-interview-with-chantal-mouffe/, accessed May 11, 2018.

Simonse, Simon. "Tragedy, Ritual and Power in Nilotic Regicide: The Regicidal Dramas of the Eastern Nilotes of Sudan in Comparative Perspective." In *The Character of Kingship*, edited by Declan Quigley (New York: 2005), 67–100.

"Kings and Gods as Ecological Agents: Reciprocity and Unilateralism in the Management of Nature," *Contagion* 12–13 (2006): 31–46.

Kings of Disaster: Dualism, Centrism, and the Scapegoat King in Southeastern Sudan (East Lansing, MI: 2018).

Sloterdijk, Peter. *God's Zeal: The Battle of the Three Monotheisms* (Cambridge, UK: 2009).

Smelik, K. A. D., and E. A. Hemelrijk. "Who Knows Not What Monsters Demented Egypt Worships?" In *Aufstieg und Niedergang der römischen Welt Geschichte und Kultur Roms im Spiegel der neuere Forschung* II 17.4 (New York: 1984), 1852–2001.

Smith, Jonathan Z. "The Domestication of Sacrifice." In *Violent Origins: Ritual Killing and Cultural Formation*, edited by Walter Burkert, René Girard, Jonathan Z. Smith, and Robert Hamerton-Kelly (Redwood City, CA: 1987), 191–238.

"Dying and Rising Gods." In *The Encyclopedia of Religion*, vol. 4, edited by Mircea Eliade and Charles J. Adams (Oxford, UK: 1987), 2535–40.

Smith, Mark S. "The Death of 'Dying and Rising Gods' in the Biblical World: An Update, with Special Reference to Baal in the Baal Cycle," *Scandinavia Journal of the Old Testament* 12.2 (1998): 257–313.

The Early History of God: Yahweh and Other Deities in Ancient Israel, 2nd ed. (Grand Rapids, MI: 2002).

The Origins of Biblical Monotheism: Israel's Polytheistic Background and the Ugaritic Texts (Cambridge, UK: 2003).

God in Translation: Deities in Cross-Cultural Discourse in the Biblical World (Tübingen, Germany: 2008).

Smith, Morton. "The Common Theology of the Ancient Near East," *Journal of Biblical Literature* 71 (1952): 135–47.

Smith, W. R. *The Religion of the Semites*, 3rd ed. (New York: 1927).

Smith, Richard. "Freud and Evolutionary Anthropology's First Just-So Story," *Evolutionary Anthropology* 25 (2016): 50–3.

Soggin, J. A. "The Davidic-Solomonic Kingdom." In *Israelite and Judaen History*, edited by J. H. Hayes and J. M Miller, OTL (London, UK: 1977).

Souillac, Geneviève. "Violence, Mimesis, and War," *Peace Review* 26.3 (2014): 342–50.

Sparling, Robert Alan. *Johann Georg Hamann and the Enlightenment Project* (Toronto, Canada: 2011).

Springs, Jason. "On Giving Religious Intolerance Its Due: Prospects for Transforming Conflict in a Post-Secular Society," *Journal of the American Academy of Religion* 28.3 (2012): 1–30.

    Healthy Conflict in Contemporary American Society: From Enemy to Adversary (Cambridge, UK: 2018).

Sproul, Barbara. *Primal Myths: Creation Myths Around the World* (New York: 1979).

Stark, Rodney. *One True God: Historical Consequences of Monotheism* (Princeton, NJ: 2001).

    For the Glory of God: How Monotheism Led to Reformations, Science, Witch-Hunts, and the End of Slavery (Princeton, NJ: 2004).

    Discovering God: The Origins of the Great Religions and the Evolution of Belief (New York: 2007).

Steinmetz-Jenkins, Daniel. "Jan Assmann and the Theologization of the Political," *Political Theology* 12.4 (2011): 511–30.

Stout, Jeffrey. *Democracy and Tradition* (Princeton, NJ: 2005).

Stroumsa, Guy. "Myth into Novel." In *New Perspectives on Freud's Moses and Monotheism*, edited by Ruth Ginsburg and Illana Pardes (Halle, Germany: 2006), 203–16.

    The End of Sacrifice: Religious Transformations in Late Antiquity (Chicago, IL: 2009).

Taggar-Cohen, Ada. "Political Loyalty in the Biblical Account of 1 Samuel xx–xxii in the Light of Hittite Texts," *Vetus Testamentum* 55 (2005): 251–68.

Tardivel-Schick, Émilie. "Why Is Christian Citizenship a Paradox?" *Church Life Journal*, November 13, 2018. https://churchlifejournal.nd.edu/articles/why-is-christian-citizenship-a-paradox/, accessed April 29, 2020.

Taylor, Charles. "Notes on the Sources of Violence: Perennial and Modern." In *Beyond Violence: Religious Sources for Social Transformation in Judaism, Christianity and Islam*, edited by James L. Heft (New York: 2004), 15–42.

    A Secular Age (Cambridge, MA: 2007).

Teeter, Emily. *Religion and Ritual in Ancient Egypt* (Cambridge, UK: 2011).

Thaler, Mathias. "The Illusion of Purity: Chantal Mouffe's Realist Critique of Cosmopolitanism," *Philosophy and Social Criticism* 36.7 (2010): 785–800.

Themnér, Lotta, and Peter Wallensteen. "Armed Conflicts, 1946–2012," *Journal of Peace Research* 50.4 (2013), 509–21.

Thomas, Scott M. "Culture, Religion and Violence: René Girard's Mimetic Theory," *Millennium: Journal of International Studies* 43.1 (2014): 308–27.

Timmer, Daniel. "Is Monotheism Particularly Prone to Violence?: A Historical Critique," *Journal of Religion and Society* 15 (2013): 1–15.

Ulucci, Daniel. *The Christian Rejection of Animal Sacrifice* (Oxford, UK: 2011).

Valentino, Benjamin. *Final Solutions* (Ithaca, NY: 2005).

VanRiesen, Renée. "A Violent God?: Philosophical Reflections on Monotheism and Genesis 22." In *The Law of God*, edited by Pieter Vos and Onno Ziiljstra (Leiden, NL: 2014), 173–93.

Vattimo, Gianni, and René Girard. *Christianity, Truth, and Weakening Faith: A Dialogue.* Edited by Pierpaolo Antonello and translated by William McCuaig (New York: 2010).

Victus, Solomon. "Monotheism, Monarchy, Monoculture: Ecological Concerns and Nature Worship," *Asia Journal of Theology* 24.2 (2010): 179–96.

Voegelin, Eric. *Science, Politics, and Gnosticism* (Washington, DC: 1986).

  The New Science of Politics: An Introduction (Chicago, IL: 1987).

  Order and History, vol. 1: Israel and Revelation (Columbia, MO: 2001).

von Balthasar, Hans Urs. *Theo-Drama: Theological Dramatic Theory,* vol. 4. Translated by Graham Harrison (San Francisco, CA: 1994).

Wallace, Mark. *Fragments of the Spirit: Nature, Violence, and the Renewal of Creation* (New York: 1996).

Waller, James E. "The Ordinariness of Extraordinary Evil: The Making of Perpetrators of Genocide and Mass Killing." In *Ordinary People as Mass Murderers,* edited by Olaf Jensen and C. C. W. Szejnmann (London, UK: 2008), 164–83.

Ward, Graham, and Michael Hoetzel, eds. *The New Visibility of Religion: Studies in Religion and Cultural Hermeneutics* (London, UK: 2008).

Waters, Tony, and Dagmar Waters, eds. *Weber's Rationalism and Modern Society* (New York: 2015).

Watts, Joseph, Oliver Sheehan, Quentin Atkinson, Joseph Bulbulia, and Russell D. Gray. "Ritual Human Sacrifice Promoted and Sustained the Evolution of Stratified Societies," *Nature* 532.228 (2016): 228–31.

Weaver, J. Denny. *The Nonviolent Atonement* (Grand Rapids, MI: 2001).

Weber, Max. *Ancient Judaism* (New York: 1967).

Weil, Eric. "What Is a Breakthrough in History?" *Daedalus* Spring (1975): 21–36.

Weil, Simone. *Intimations of Christianity among the Ancient Greeks* (London, UK: 2003).

  Letter to a Priest (New York: 2003).

Weinfeld, Moshe. *Deuteronomy and the Deuteronomic School* (University Park, PA: 1992).

  The Place of the Law in the Religion of Ancient Israel (Leiden, NL: 2004).

Weiss, Bari. "When the Left Turns on Its Own," *The New York Times,* June 1, 2017.

Wiesel, Elie. "Acceptance Speech," Nobel Peace Prize, Oslo, December 10, 1986. www.nobelprize.org/prizes/peace/1986/wiesel/26054-elie-wiesel-acceptance-speech-1986/, accessed March 28, 2020.

Williams, James G. *The Bible, Violence, and the Sacred: Liberation from the Myth of Sanctioned Violence* (San Francisco, CA: 1991).

Williams, Rowan. *Christ on Trial: How the Gospel Unsettles Judgment* (Grand Rapids, MI: 2003).

Wills, Lawrence M. "The Death of a Hero." In *Religion and Violence: The Biblical Heritage,* edited by David A. Bernat and Jonathan Klawans (Sheffield UK: 2007).

Wilson, John. *The Culture of Ancient Egypt* (Chicago, IL: 1951).

Wink, Walter. *Engaging the Powers: Discernment and Resistance in a World of Domination* (Minneapolis, MN: 1992).

Wiseman, T. P. *Remus: A Roman Myth* (Cambridge, UK: 1995).

Wistrich, Robert. "Sigmund Freud's Last Testament." In *New Perspectives on Freud's Moses and Monotheism*, edited by Ruth Ginsburg and Illana Pardes (Halle, Germany: 2006), 45–64.

Wrangham, Richard. *The Goodness Paradox: The Strange Relationship between Virtue and Violence in Human Evolution* (New York: 2019).

Wright, N. T. *The New Testament and the People of God* (Philadelphia, PA: 1992).

"Upstaging the Emperor," *Bible Review* 14.1 (1998): 17.

The Resurrection of the Son of God (Minneapolis, MN: 2003).

Yasukata, Toshimasa. *Lessing's Philosophy of Religion and German Enlightenment* (Oxford, UK: 2002).

Yerushalmi, Yosef Hayim. *Freud's Moses: Terminable and Interminable* (New Haven, CT: 1991).

Yusa, Michiko. "Henotheism." In *The Encyclopedia of Religion*, 2nd ed., edited by L. Jones (Detroit, MI: 2005), 3913–4.

Žižek, Slavoj. "Against Human Rights," *New Left Review* July/August 34 (2005): 115–31.

"The Violence of the Liberal Utopia," *Distinktion* 9.2 (2008): 9–25.

Index

For EU product safety concerns, contact us at Calle de José Abascal, 56–1°, 28003 Madrid, Spain or eugpsr@cambridge.org.

www.ingramcontent.com/pod-product-compliance
Ingram Content Group UK Ltd.
Pitfield, Milton Keynes, MK11 3LW, UK
UKHW010250140625
459647UK00013BA/1762